A Whole Empire Walking

A WHOLE EMPIRE WALKING

REFUGEES IN RUSSIA DURING WORLD WAR I

PETER GATRELL

INDIANA UNIVERSITY PRESS

Bloomington and Indianapolis

This book is a publication of
Indiana University Press
601 North Morton Street
Bloomington, Indiana 47404-3797 USA

www.indiana.edu/~iupress

Telephone orders 800-842-6796
Fax orders 812-855-7931
Orders by e-mail iuporder@indiana.edu

The paper used in this publication meets the minimum
requirements of American National Standard for Information
Sciences—Permanence of Paper for Printed Library
Materials, ANSI Z39.48-1984.
Manufactured in the United States of America

Library of Congress Cataloging-in-Publication Data

Gatrell, Peter.
A whole empire walking : refugees in Russia during World War I / Peter Gatrell.
p.   cm. — (Indiana-Michigan series in Russian and East European studies)
Includes bibliographical references and index.
ISBN 0-253-33644-9 (cloth : alk. paper).
1. World War, 1914–1918—Refugees. 2. World War, 1914–1918—Russia.
3. Refugees—Russia. I. Title. II. Series.
D638.R9G38   1999
940.3'086'91—dc21   99-34159

1 2 3 4 5 04 03 02 01 00 99

I dedicate this book to
Jane, David, and Lizzy Gatrell,
and to my parents-in-law
Kate and David Shoenberg,
not forgetting its kindly godparents
Edward Acton and Bill Rosenberg

See that little stream—we could walk to it in two minutes. It took the British a month to walk to it—a whole empire walking very slowly, dying in front and pushing forward behind. And another empire walked very slowly backward a few inches a day, leaving the dead like a million bloody rugs. No Europeans will ever do that again in this generation.

—F. SCOTT FITZGERALD, *TENDER IS THE NIGHT*

We know that you are victims of the entire affair, that you were the first to sustain the blows of our enemies. We shall not forget this. . . . Trust in our sympathy; believe that, after the war, we shall come to you and endeavor to restore everything that you have lost.

—A. I. SHINGAREV, *IZVESTIIA VSG*, 19, NOVEMBER 1915

I emphatically urge that those who concern themselves with the collection of information about refugees should hold on to everything that comes into their possession, rejecting nothing, retaining every little scrap of information, every personal opinion, without reservation and without stricture, storing everything away for the future scholar.

—SERGEI PLATONOV, *IZVESTIIA VSEROSSIISKOGO KOMITETA DLIA OKAZANIIA POMOSHCHI OSTRADAVSHIM OT VOENNYKH BEDSTVII*, 15 MAY 1917

CONTENTS

ACKNOWLEDGMENTS

The story of how this book came to be written is one of friendship, scholarly cooperation, and generous institutional support. John Breuilly, Bob Davies, Yoram Gorlizki, Edmund Herzig, John Klier, Billie Melman, Boris Mironov, Hilary Pilkington, Alfred Rieber, Teodor Shanin, Charles Timberlake, and David Turton all offered encouragement and advice at an early stage of the project. I recall helpful conversations with two of my colleagues, Patrick Joyce and James Vernon, both of whom also provided thought-provoking written comments on a brief draft of my first thoughts. Edward Acton and Bill Rosenberg invited me to contribute a chapter on refugees to the *Critical Companion to the Russian Revolution* (Indiana University Press and Edward Arnold, 1997), which gave me an opportunity to prepare some preliminary thoughts for publication. Steve Smith sent a characteristically incisive and encouraging letter, just when I needed it most. Jimmy White not only offered detailed observations about the Latvian and Lithuanian dimension of refugeedom, but also kindly translated extracts from Lithuanian sources for my benefit.

Other scholars were no less helpful. John Barber posed some pertinent questions when I delivered a paper at the annual conference of the British Association of Slavonic and East European Studies in spring 1997. Alessandro Stanziani, Andrea Graziosi, and Jutta Scherrer did the same at a conference organized by the Feltrinelli and Gramsci foundations in Cortona in the autumn of 1997. Michael Bravo urged me to try out some of my ideas to a group of social anthropologists in Manchester. My colleague Rosemary Morris put me in touch with Professor Gilbert Dagron of the Collège de France, who alerted me to the importance of Thomas Whittemore and to the whereabouts of his papers—which, alas, I was unable to consult. I had a brief yet illuminating conversation with Elizabeth Koutaissoff, who reminisced about her life in Volynia before the First World War; my thanks to Michael Kaser for introducing me to her. Susan Causey and Alexander Margolis helped to smooth my path on a highly productive research trip to St. Petersburg. Roger Bartlett and Edmund Herzig put me in touch with Latvian and Armenian historians respectively, for which I am most grateful. My good friend Richard Davies made me welcome at the Leeds University Russian Archive. Eric Lohr generously allowed me to read his work in progress on the deportation of German settlers and also pointed out references that I had missed. Vera Tolz made helpful comments on national identity in imperial Russia. New friends in Russia, such as

Vladimir Zakharov of the History Department, Kursk Pedagogical University, offered help in tracking down material in Kursk, Voronezh, and elsewhere that I
would otherwise have missed. I also value greatly the advice and assistance of
Vadim Zuev at the State Hermitage museum in St. Petersburg. Viktor Kel'ner placed
his encyclopedic knowledge at my disposal and helped me find my way around the
riches of the National Library in St. Petersburg. Academician Boris Anan"ich offered assistance, friendship, and support. In Moscow my access to archives was
facilitated by Oleg Airapetov and Oleg Khlevniuk. I hope all these friends and colleagues are not disappointed with the final outcome.

I would have been unable to write with any confidence about Latvian refugees
were it not for the helpful advice and dedicated research assistance of Dr Aija
Priedite at the Department of Philosophy, Latvian Academy of Sciences. Dr Priedite
discovered a great deal of new material and kept me supplied with translations
from Latvian. Her ability to understand my needs and to respond to my questions made my work much easier. I look forward to seeing the results of her own
studies on the development of modern Latvian culture. Similarly, the research assistance provided by Dr Shoushanik Khachikian, senior research worker at the
Matenadaran in Erevan, Armenia, enabled me to understand better the position of
Armenian refugees in the Caucasus. She provided me with transcripts of articles
from leading Armenian newspapers and with some archival material. I am extremely grateful to both these scholars for taking time from their own projects to
assist me with mine.

Nor do I forget the assistance provided by the staff of many archives and libraries. The staff of the British Library, the Bodleian Library, and Cambridge University
Library helped me to locate some of the less obscure material; so too did the staff
of the Inter-Library Loans department of the John Rylands Library, University of
Manchester. I am also grateful to Peter Liddle for letting me examine the small
collection of Thurstan papers at the University of Leeds Brotherton Library. Particular thanks are due to the ever-helpful librarians in the Slavic section of Helsinki
University Library, which maintains outstanding facilities for research in the field
of imperial Russian history. The Center for Russian and East European Studies at
the University of Illinois supported me for a fortnight at its summer research workshop. There I received excellent help from the staff of the superb Slavic Reference
Library, notably Helen Sullivan and Julia Gauchman. The maps in this book were
drawn by Nick Scarle at the Cartographic Unit, University of Manchester, and I am
grateful to him for the care he has shown.

Much of the detailed research for this book was carried out in Russia. In St.
Petersburg I received indispensable help from the staff at the Russian State Historical Archive (RGIA), particularly Agnesa Valentinovna Muktan and (in the RGIA
library) Natalia Evgen'evna Kashchenko. Also in St. Petersburg, the hard-pressed

staff of the Russian National Library (including those at the newspaper repository on the Fontanka) kept me supplied with the material I needed. In Moscow I found the staff at the Russian Military History Archive, particularly Tat'iana Iur'evna Burmistrova, extremely helpful. No less responsive was the head of the reading room at the State Archive of the Russian Federation (GARF), Nina Ivanovna Abdulaeva, as well as Aleksandr Vladimirovich Kostenetskii and his assistants in the archive repository. The chief archivist (Viacheslav Nikolaevich Kozliakov) and his assistants at the State Archive of Iaroslavl' oblast were superb in understanding my needs immediately and allowing me to make full use of my limited time there (my thanks to Bob Lewis for arranging the visit that made this possible). I also received efficient help from Ms. Gunta Minde during a short visit to the Latvian State Historical Archive in Riga.

Edward Acton, Bob Millward, Bill Rosenberg, Harry Shukman, and Steve Smith wrote statements to funding agencies in support of the research; their support meant a great deal to me. Financial support was forthcoming from the Arts Research and Graduate School, University of Manchester. Generous assistance was also given by the University's Research Support Fund, which allowed me to employ researchers in Russia and the FSU and to travel to distant libraries and archives; I am grateful to Nigel Vincent for his initial advocacy on my behalf. Special thanks are also due to the Kennan Institute for Advanced Russian Studies for material support at an early stage that enabled me to work in the Library of Congress. Most of all, I owe an enormous debt of gratitude to the British Academy for awarding me a two-year Research Readership (1995–97), without which it would have been impossible to make rapid progress on this book. Ken Emond was my main contact in the British Academy, and I want to thank him for his unfailing help.

Countless conversations with friends and colleagues revealed different perspectives and possible lines of research. I am especially grateful to Yoram Gorlizki, David Hoffmann, and Jay Winter, who commented encouragingly on a first draft of the manuscript. They offered much helpful advice, which I have tried to follow. Hilary Pilkington deserves special thanks for sharing with me her important study of forced migrants in post-communist Russia, prior to publication. She also prompted me to think more carefully about some of the issues raised in my own work, not least by acting as discussant at a seminar paper I gave at the Centre for Russian and East European Studies, University of Birmingham. Toward the end of my research, I was fortunate to establish contact with Peter Holquist, whose perceptive comments and fertile suggestions were much appreciated. These kind scholars should not be blamed for any of the shortcomings of this book.

At Indiana University Press, I wish to express my appreciation to Janet Rabinowitch and her colleagues, above all to Jane Lyle, whose interest in my manuscript and eagerness to find ways to improve it meant a lot to me.

I have also incurred debts of a more personal kind. In St. Petersburg I received a warm welcome from the Mutushev household: Zinaida Samuilovna, the late Gavriil Akhmedovich, Iiulia Gavriilovna, and family. They made my stay pleasant and comfortable. I spent a happy month in Moscow in the delightful company of Maya Akhmedovna Smirnov-Mutusheva, whose own grandparents and mother were forced out of Dvinsk (Daugavpils) in 1915, before they found sanctuary in Khar'-kov. She is a remarkable person.

My parents and my brother were a constant source of encouragement. So too were Liz Shoenberg and Peter Shoenberg. Kate and David Shoenberg have always offered a warm welcome in Cambridge. For many years Betty Croston has done her best with a student of limited abilities in her Iyengar Yoga class; I owe her a great deal. Longer ago still, Alice Teichova helped me to establish myself in academic life, for which I shall always remain grateful. Many other friends and colleagues, none more so than David Denison, have followed my progress on this book with the kind of interest that made me think it was worthwhile to persevere.

I could not have written this book without the support of the British Academy. Edward Acton and Bill Rosenberg backed my successful application for funding and watched the project take shape. I am happy that they should share in the dedication of this book.

Jane Gatrell shared my enthusiasm for the topic, tolerated my preoccupation with it, and took time from her own busy schedule to talk with me about the issues it raises. She knows how much this project has meant to me. David and Lizzy Gatrell have helped me to maintain a sense of perspective. Their company enriches my life in ways I cannot begin to describe. This book is also for all of them, with all my love.

A WHOLE EMPIRE WALKING

Kingdom of Poland

Suwalki
Plotsk
Lomza
Kalisz
Warsaw
Piotrkow
Siedlce
Radom
Kielce
Lublin
Chelm

Baltic Sea

Estland
St. Petersburg
Novgorod
Livland
Kurland
Pskov
Kovno
Vitebsk
Vilna
Smolensk
POLAND (see inset)
Grodno
Minsk
Mogilev
Kaluga
Volynia
Chernigov
Orel
Podolia
Kiev
Poltava
Kursk
Bessarabia
Kherson
Ekaterinoslav
Taurida

Arkhangel'sk

Olonets
Vologda
Perm
Iaroslavl'
Kostroma
Viatka
Tver'
Vladimir
Nizhnii-Novgorod
Kazan'
Ufa
Moscow
Orenburg
Riazan
Simbirsk
Tula
Penza
Samara
Tambov
Saratov
Voronezh
Khar'kov
Don
Astrakhan

Black Sea

CAUCASUS (see map 3)

Caspian Sea

Pale of Jewish settlement

International frontier

0   500 km

The Russian Empire in 1914

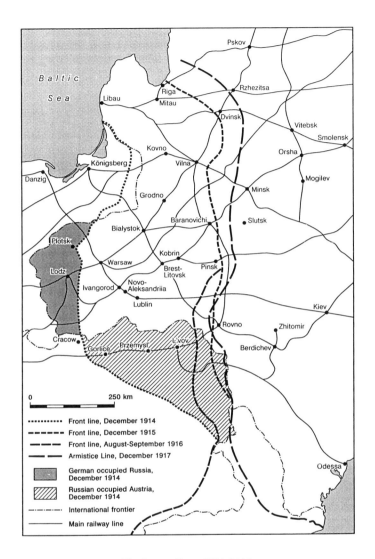

The Eastern Front, 1914–1918

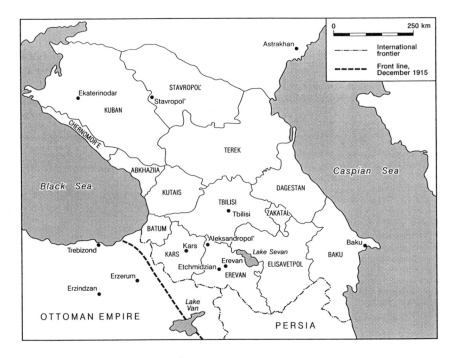

The Caucasus, 1914–1918

The Caucasus, 1914–1918

INTRODUCTION

HUMANITY UPROOTED

Most informed observers expected the war that began in Europe in July 1914 to be over in a matter of weeks. The prevailing expectation of a short war was closely tied to conceptions of a war of movement, of brief and decisive military maneuvers that would bring one army to a speedy victory over another. Throughout Europe, the initial mobilization of soldiers evoked a wave of popular enthusiasm that drew upon unconcealed optimism about the war's brief duration. Crowds of volunteers at recruiting offices conveyed an image of mass movement, underlying which "undiscovered reservoirs of hatred" could be drawn upon to sustain the anticipated conflict.[1] After the first bloody encounters, however, troops became entrenched in fixed positions; "repeated efforts to outflank the foe merely prolonged the line of trenches until it became continuous."[2] The war dragged on interminably, with a military resolution to the conflict increasingly remote. Images of movement soon gave way to more disturbing visions. Soldiers confided in letters home that the military stalemate had given rise to a profound sense of weariness, an "inexhaustible docility."[3] Particularly on the western front, where the combined length of trenches on both sides amounted to 25,000 miles, the continental armies struggled to gain more than a few yards of territory during the battles of 1915 and 1916. Given the slow rate of progress, some British officers sarcastically calculated in 1917 that it would take 180 years to arrive at the Rhine.[4] "I don't know what's to be done," lamented Lord Kitchener; "this isn't war."[5] The eastern front manifested greater maneuverability, partly because the Russian high command was able to impose little effective control over the different armies in the field, which often acted independently of one another. Even so, stalemate duly set in on the eastern front as well, since it was difficult to assemble sufficient quantities of men and munitions in conditions of secrecy that might allow for a surprise breakthrough.[6]

Whereas fighting men frequently encountered immobility and deadlock, large

Note: Dates are given according to the Julian calendar, which was observed in pre-revolutionary Russia; in the twentieth century it was thirteen days behind the Gregorian calendar.

numbers of non-combatants experienced war in terms of spatial displacement. Civilians rather than armies were much more likely to be uprooted and forced to
traverse huge swaths of territory. The refugee, rather than the common infantry-
man, enjoyed the dubious privilege of physical mobility. During the war, and in its
aftermath, contemporaries spoke of "columns" or "waves" of refugees. These images
had long since been abandoned in descriptions of the contending armies, but they
captured reality for millions of civilians. On the eastern front, many civilians covered far more miles in the course of the war than did men in uniform. Like foot
soldiers, refugees were compelled to move with whatever belongings they could
carry on their backs. But soldiers could (at least if things went according to plan)
count on back-up support. Letters and parcels kept them in touch with home;
immobilized officers and soldiers consumed books and newspapers voraciously. By
contrast, charity was the best that refugees could expect until they found somewhere new to settle. Their homes had been abandoned and, in some cases, occupied by enemy intruders. Lines of communication were severed. Until refugees obtained some kind of safe haven, they lacked an opportunity to read or write. Nor
do the differences end there. Soldiers had a chance to become heroes; but no refugee was lionized.[7] Even in death, military and civilian casualties were accorded
different treatment. There are no war graves for the thousands of refugees who died
en route to a "place of safety." The literature of war scarcely paid them any attention.
No Owen or Remarque dwelt on their plight; no "passing-bells" tolled for the refugees who moved—and sometimes died—like cattle. This contrast deserves to be
included in the ironies of the First World War.[8]

The experiences of Russian civilians during the First World War have yet to
attract systematic attention. In large measure this reflects historians' understandable
preoccupation with the organization and behavior of workers and peasants during
the tumultuous months of 1917. Even studies of popular attitudes and activity
during the Russian revolution have tended to neglect groups that are not easily
subsumed within the conventional categories of historical inquiry. The social history of the revolution has concentrated on organized social forces, whose representatives and spokesmen left behind compelling accounts of political struggle and
whose actions impinged directly on the existing forms of state power. Historians
have scarcely begun to step outside the world of elite politics and the revolutionary movement, or to look beyond the dynamics of labor protest and organization.
The huge body of Soviet scholarship on 1917 tended to emphasize the role of the
Bolshevik Party in subverting established political forms. The dominant narrative
found little room for any social activity that could not easily be accommodated
within the framework of conventional political organizations or linked to the revolutionary teleology that legitimized the Bolshevik triumph.

One neglected aspect of Russia's wartime experience concerns the impact of enormous waves of population movement, much of it involuntary, on urban and rural society. Three sources of displacement spring to mind: first, the mobilization of soldiers for the tsarist army, and the subsequent repatriation of those who were sent home as invalids; second, the resettlement on Russian territory of prisoners of war from the German and Austro-Hungarian armies; and, third, the mass movement of civilians from the front lines to the Russian interior, particularly during the summer and autumn of 1915.[9] This study focuses on civilian displacement in the Russian empire. According to official statistics, refugees numbered at least 3.3 million at the end of 1915.[10] By April 1916, a further 500,000 refugees were recorded on Russian territory, not including the Caucasus. These figures certainly underestimate the size of the refugee population. One careful calculation, taking account of under-registration, put the total number at just over 6 million by the beginning of 1917, including 367,000 refugees in the Caucasus.[11] As a result, refugees probably accounted for something like 5 percent of the total population. To put these numbers into perspective, the size of the industrial working class (excluding artisans) on the eve of the October revolution amounted to just over 3.5 million men and women. In 1917, "refugees" (*bezhentsy*) outnumbered the industrial proletariat.[12]

Unlike prisoners of war, who were often confined to camps in remote parts of the empire, refugees came to be concentrated disproportionately in existing urban settlements. Towns and cities were transformed as a result. By the middle of 1916, more than one in ten inhabitants in some of Russia's largest towns were refugees. They made up 15 percent of the population in Nizhnii Novgorod, and around 25 percent in Ekaterinoslav and Pskov. Almost 30 percent of the inhabitants of Samara were refugees.[13] Population displacement on this scale and at this intensity was unprecedented in Russia's recent history, and would be exceeded only by the Nazi invasion of 1941, which displaced around 10 million people. In Eugene Kulischer's words, "In two short years the movement of refugees and evacuees was as considerable as it had been during the migration to Siberia over a 25-year period, 1885–1909."[14] Displacement represented a distinctive feature of Russia's wartime history and had profound implications, both for refugees themselves and for those with whom they came into contact.

My purpose in this book is in part to consider the causes, dimensions, and spatial patterns of this tortuous refugee trail in the Russian empire during the First World War, to examine the political repercussions the refugees provoked, and to discover the kind of humanitarian responses they prompted. But I wish to go further than this: I seek to grasp the impact of war on the construction of a new social category, which cannot—and not just for the most obvious reason—readily be placed within the conventional typologies of social stratification in tsarist Russia. On one level, the large displaced population made nonsense of official attempts to maintain the fiction of social stability in wartime. On another level, established taxonomies of social description—whether ascribed "estate" (*soslovie*) or class— were subverted and redefined.[15] I hope to show that this process must in part be situated within the broad framework of political struggle in the twilight years of the old regime. The constitution of what I shall call "refugeedom" helped not only to undermine established notions of social status and social control, but also to give shape to an emerging public sphere in Russia, whose spokesmen challenged established political, social, and cultural practices. In this way, I seek to come to a clearer understanding of the ways in which involuntary population displacement came to be problematized in wartime.

At the same time, I am interested as much in refugees' own sense of self as I am in the creation of a category that served to underpin professional self-esteem and to legitimize civic activism. Did refugees regard themselves as marginal? What kind of control did they seek to secure over the resources deployed in their "relief"? To the extent that their world had been dismantled, what capacity did they have to reassemble it, and upon what foundations?[16] I shall argue later on that refugees became aware of their predicament and began to become conscious of an entitlement to assistance and dignity. Nor should one overlook refugees' sense of attachment to a "homeland." Unlike the archetypal exile, the internally displaced *bezhentsy* normally expected to return; politicians such as the liberal parliamentarian Andrei Shingarev (see the epigraph page) promised that their homes would be restored to them. But what did "going home" mean to the refugee? Certainly it entailed attempts to reconstitute the household and to restore the family economy; it often involved issues of compensation. More radical projects may also have been broached. The experience of living for months or years as refugees changed the outlook, ambitions, and expectations of those who had been displaced. The sense of sharing stories of dispossession and adventure, of having participated in a "national" calamity, of having asserted one's rights—all these experiences, achievements, and memories were elements in refugee life.

The exploration of refugees' self-perception also requires consideration of the relations they enjoyed with host communities in the Russian interior: with peasants as well as professional relief workers, with urban residents as well as officialdom. I attempt to define the cultural norms that underlay the efforts made by those who came to the assistance of refugees. I am inspired by the apposite questions posed in a different context by Joan Scott: "How are those who cross the thresholds received? If they belong to a group different from one already 'inside,' what are the terms of their incorporation? How do the new arrivals understand their relationship to the place they have entered?"[17] These questions invite us to attend to the meaning, resilience, and viability of the threshold itself, particularly in regard to ethnic markers. How easily, for example, did Russia's Jews leave the infamous Pale of Settlement and establish themselves in a new place? How might Latvians be "incorporated" in unfamiliar surroundings? Did Russian refugees cross the threshold with less difficulty and with a greater prospect, hope, or intention of being "absorbed"? My findings will, I hope, contribute to the ongoing debate about the constitution of social identities in early-twentieth-century Russia, by making these in part the outcome of interaction between the settled and the displaced populations of war-torn Russia.[18]

My pursuit of refugees has a wider resonance. Refugees were perceived as being different. As one astute and sympathetic contemporary put it, "We have created something akin to a new Pale of Settlement, jealously guarded by the relevant authorities. Society has renounced the refugees, as if they were a vile disease that can be mentioned only in private and in hushed tones."[19] Their difference reflected above all the drastic immediacy of expulsion, their enforced mobility and relocation in the Russian interior. Non-refugees were normally members of settled communities or, if migrants, knew where they were headed, and why. To be a refugee, however, was to have been deprived of the chance to decide whether to stay or to leave. No one consulted refugees; they sometimes had only a few hours to pack their possessions. They had no itinerary, no scouts or predecessors, no maps, and normally no precise destination. Unlike Russian peasant migrants or workers who had contributed to unprecedented spatial mobility in the generation before the outbreak of the war, refugees were bereft of contacts to exploit and lacked the opportunity to confer with those who had traveled the road in advance. Whereas the motives for prewar migration were clear, displacement seemed like a meaningless momentum.[20]

The non-Russianness of many refugees compounded the sense of difference. In peacetime, relatively few non-Russian minorities engaged in widespread migration within the boundaries of the Russian empire.[21] Jews, Latvians, Lithuanians, and Poles had in the past responded to political or religious oppression by emigrating. But emigration, unlike internal migration, entailed quite different choices and implications. Exit meant an irrevocable departure from the tsarist state, rendering the emigrant invisible and immune from domestic attention. War brought about an abrupt transformation in the status and visibility of Russia's ethnic minorities, concentrated as they were in the empire's borderlands, which were quickly ruptured. This vulnerability prompted many hundreds of thousands of them to flee into the Russian interior, where they became immediately visible. Hastily created communities provided an opportunity to draw attention to the losses they had incurred. Before long, members of the patriotic intelligentsia, previously deprived of much scope to proselytize among their compatriots, began to contrive claims to the "national interest" embodied in the suffering refugee population.

Yet it cannot be assumed that refugees shared or accepted the agenda drawn up by national elites. By what means did the daily routines or aspirations of refugees come to express "national" ambition, as distinct from other projects? To what degree did the mass of refugees make sense of their experiences in terms of national identity? We should not close our eyes to the possibility of other kinds of identity, as demonstrated by the anthropologist Liisa Malkki in her powerful study of Hutu refugees in Tanzania during the mid-1980s. Drawing a distinction between the culture of the Mishamo refugee camp and that of the settlement at Kigoma township, she writes, "The camp refugees perpetuated and reified that very categorical order in terms of which they were displaced, while the town refugees' lives seemed to have the effect of challenging and dissolving totalizing, essentializing categories." That is, the incarceration of Hutu refugees in an isolated camp environment helped to produce a specific kind of composite "Hutuness" which embodied notions of purity, integrity, and collective worth. By contrast, township refugees discovered the possibility of escaping "refugeeness" through the anonymity conferred by the urban milieu.[22]

The relationship between refugees and the settled population was asymmetrical. Asymmetry expressed itself in the conduct, attitudes, and assumptions manifested by those who exercised power over refugees. (Only rarely did refugees exercise power over one another.) In order to underline this point, it is important to relate refugeedom to other social groups that have been marked in cultural, ideological, and political terms. As Iris Young has argued, "while the privileged group is defined as active human subject, inferiorized social groups are objectified, substantialized, reduced to a nature or essence. . . . By virtue of the characteristics the dominated group is alleged to have by nature, the dominant ideologies allege that those group members have specific dispositions that suit them for some activities and not others. Using its own values, experience, and culture as standards, the dominant group measures the Others and finds them essentially lacking, as excluded from and/or complementary to themselves." But, she goes on to say, "the essence of the more highly valued or 'pure' side of a dichotomy usually must be defined by reference to the very category to which it is opposed." In other words, social differences are invariably given a substantive and essentialist content by those who claim cultural or political superiority, whereas such differences should more properly be exposed as relational.[23]

To be sure, categories of difference can be contested by members of the "other," that is, by the objects of domination themselves. In the rewarding formulation of Denise Riley, "The members of an exhorted mass—whether of a race, a class, a nation, a bodily state, a sexual persuasion—are always apt to break out of its corrals to re-align themselves elsewhere." What matters, it seems to me, is to identify the moments and uncover the causes of such an escape from categorization.[24] In the present context, I am interested not only in the creation of a specific refugee category, and the realignments it implied, but also in the possibility of breaking out from refugee status to achieve a different status, and the option of "returning" to the refugee fold if circumstances permitted or the gains appeared to make the transition worthwhile. Put differently, under what conditions did refugees break free of the designation they were assigned (or espoused)? In what ways did they seek to transcend refugeedom?[25] How, if at all, did refugees find it possible to combat the "disease of thinking in essences"?[26]

Ultimately, the study of refugeedom poses a challenge to the grand narratives of class that underpin much of the literature on revolutionary Russia that has been written over the past generation. There is much here that historians of early-twentieth-century Russia can learn from those who work from within a postmodern perspective or who are sympathetic toward this position. Consider the words of Homi Bhabha, who is otherwise at pains to distance himself from a postmodernist approach: "The great connective narratives of capitalism and class drive the engines of social reproduction, but do not, in themselves, provide a foundational frame for those modes of cultural identification and political affect that form around issues of sexuality, race, feminism, the lifeworld of refugees or migrants, or the deathly social destiny of AIDS."[27] In the late twentieth century, we have become familiar with the coexistence of the myriad forms of identity that spring up in a world of extreme spatial mobility and transience. I wish to argue that these uncertainties were also at play in wartime Russia, and that population displacement and disruption of established categories of social status offered evidence of the confusing multiplicity of identity.

To pursue this argument, it is worth drawing attention to recent work in cultural studies emphasizing not only the prevalence of spatial mobility in the contemporary world, but also "the impossibility of completing the journey." In one formulation, the apparently marginal are regarded less as victims of modernity than as makers of the modern world. The implications for historical research on migration, social identity, and war are profound.[28] In terms that draw upon the writings of Michel Foucault, Iain Chambers writes of the capacity of language to challenge and transform the status of marginalized groups in the present day: "We move from the politics of margins to the politics of difference: a movement that overthrows the previous power/knowledge axis that once positioned and presumed to fully explain the margins, the periphery, the 'others.'"[29] If this kind of approach can yield insights (as I think it does) into the "position" of previously subaltern groups, why should it not pay dividends by helping us to rethink the status of "marginalized" groups in imperial Russia? Why not begin to reflect more fully about the "new languages for construing, understanding and evaluating the subject" in tsarist Russian society?[30]

The attentiveness inspired by modern cultural theory to the descriptive terms of social investigation, to the acquisition and presentation of knowledge as a way of ordering the social world, and to the construction of "humanitarian narratives" has begun to emerge in some recent work on Russian history.[31] Joan Neuberger focuses on contested identities in late imperial Russia, and the way in which these were expressed in cultural forms. Specifically, she argues that "hooliganism" was in part a construct that embodied deep-seated discontent in Russian society. Inter alia, she draws attention to the "myriad other groups of the population" that are hidden from histories of the revolution.[32] Neuberger's remarks on the transformation and the defilement of public space are obviously pertinent to a study of population displacement. In an analogous project, Cathy Frierson seeks to show how educated society came to understand and "conquer" the unknown peasantry through "textual construction," which generated not a single image but a range of meanings, or—as she puts it—an iconostasis. Outside observers projected onto the peasantry their own misgivings about the future course of Russian society and, ultimately, a sense that they alone were guardians of humanity and civilization.[33] These issues also figure prominently in this book, which considers refugees as a group whose "condition" was created not just by objective circumstance—their enforced relocation—but also by the gaze of politicians or professionals who sought in various ways to order refugee life.

This process of definition must be related quite precisely to the circumstances of displacement. As suggested above, the "rootlessness" of refugees embodied a particular challenge for those with whom they came into contact. Having been driven into the Russian interior, refugees were at the same time propelled into official, public, and private consciousness. These levels of awareness must be reconstructed carefully and with proper attention to the nuances of public discourse and private sensibility. We must concede the understandable wish to "do something" in order to prevent further suffering. But we should also acknowledge that intervention was designed not only to mitigate the ordeal of refugees, but also to sustain and protect those who ministered to them. We ought not, for example, to overlook the prevailing fear of pollution associated with refugeedom.[34] In a different context, historians have attended to the fears posed by "wandering and rootless people confined by no boundaries, subject to no restraint of custom or kin, without visible means of support or a settled place in society." These insights have an obvious resonance for the historian of refugeedom; refugees, like dirt, constitute "matter out of place . . . that which must not be included if a pattern is to be maintained."[35] Furthermore, the ethnicity of many refugees not only conferred a relatively lower status upon them than upon the Russians, but also created conditions in which such societal fears might become particularly powerful. Serious misgivings were most evident with respect to Jewish refugees: "Such people present the danger that by asserting their real power they may subvert a social structure which is founded on the premise of their impotence."[36] Without doubt, keen humanitarian motives were manifested in charitable relief efforts. But we should not neglect the other impulses that were at work in the individual psyche and in society at large.

The term "refugee" is deeply loaded with questions of "political choice and ethical judgement."[37] In common parlance, refugees are all those who have left their homes involuntarily as a result of war, famine, or some such calamity. Current international law imparts a much narrower definition, with an emphasis on the liability of an individual to persecution. Thus, the 1967 United Nations statute, echoing the 1951 UN Convention relating to the status of refugees, speaks of "any person who is outside the country of his nationality . . . because he [sic] has or had well-founded fear of persecution by reason of his race, religion, nationality, membership of a particular social group or political opinion and is unable or, because of such fear, is unwilling to avail himself of the protection of the government of the country of his nationality."[38] It is evident that many people, including dependents of those individuals referred to in the UN statute, may be excluded from the legal formulation. Certainly, many who are forced by a search for work or food to cross international borders fall outside the provisions of international law and do not qualify as statutory refugees, even though they may feel that their situation is the result of a failure by government to afford them basic "protection."[39] It is also crucial to add that the UN convention on refugees does not include those who have been displaced but who have not actually left their country of origin. They are often at much greater risk than those who have crossed a frontier, and it is more difficult to assist them, particularly if their displacement is brought about by war. They may be reluctant to identify themselves, for fear of increasing exposure to their opponents.

At one level, the condition of being a refugee is impossible to conceive without the prior existence of the modern, sovereign nation-state. There were no "refugees" in a modern sense during the Thirty Years' War; those who fled the bitter fighting in central Europe sought the protection of an alternative authority, but they neither lost nor acquired "rights" as understood in the modern world. They became homeless, but not "stateless." The emergence of sovereign nation-states offering their citizens protection and, later, access to civil rights was a necessary condition for the invention of a refugee population.[40] So, too, was the recognition by other states that they could and would offer assistance to those suffering persecution. Such assistance was necessarily selective; to become a refugee required the promise of being accepted by (if not necessarily in) another country. Thus, as Aristide Zolberg has emphasized, the emergence of "the classic type of refugee" must be related to the "broader universe . . . [of] interacting political entities." These interacting political entities are national governments, whose decisions over whom to admit or to deny entry constitute one of the hallmarks of national sovereignty.[41]

The experience of twentieth-century Europe confirms the importance of politi-

cal dynamics. As the establishment of successor states in Europe after the First
World War demonstrates, new "nation-states" often defined themselves by excluding minority national groups from membership. In an influential discussion,
Hannah Arendt focused on the corruption of a traditional doctrine of human rights
and the substitution of nationally guaranteed rights, available to those of the politically dominant nationality. Where rights were denied, many members of minority
communities fled or were compulsorily relocated, as happened in the exchange of
Turkish and Greek minorities in the early 1920s. Those who were forcibly displaced, and who found themselves under the jurisdiction of a foreign authority,
forfeited entitlements that they obtained hitherto as citizens of another state. Refugees were rendered both homeless and stateless, "welcomed nowhere and . . . assimilated nowhere."[42] Both Arendt and Zolberg argue that the first great wave of
refugees in the twentieth century was created by the establishment of states that
were unable or unwilling to integrate minorities. The difficulty with this approach,
which focuses on the causal connection between nation-state formation and refugee
displacement, is that it overlooks the possibility that refugeedom—in the specific
form of ethnically targeted and displaced victim groups—might also contribute to
the creation of new states. What begins as internal displacement in imperial polities
may end in a constellation of forces driving the project of nation-state formation.

Political circumstances cannot be obliterated from any attempt to write the history of refugeedom. Political considerations are also deeply embedded in measures
to deal with its consequences. Over time, "there has been a secular evolution from
particularistic practices, reflecting the willingness of specific states to grant asylum
to individuals and groups of special concern, to a more universalistic definition
of refugees and a concomitant institutionalized apparatus for dealing with them,
founded on the acknowledgment by a duly constituted international political community of a special obligation toward the categories of persons specified in that
definition." Part of the process of extending the definition of refugee status has been
the decision since the 1960s to include people who have been displaced as a result
of violence "that is not necessarily directed at them as individuals but makes life
in their own country impossible." However, individual states interpret their obligations toward refugees in different ways, and the elaboration of a group designation
rather than an individual condition has not prevented states from seeking to discriminate between different categories of forced migrants.[43]

Few images evoke greater pity than those created by the plight of refugees in
modern societies. According to the United Nations High Commission for Refugees,
in 1995 the global refugee population amounted to 23 million people, with a further 26 million who are classified as internally displaced, an estimated increase of
53 percent during a single decade.[44] In one general account of "the unwanted" in
Europe, refugees are portrayed as miserable and powerless, uprooted from familiar

comforts, impoverished and bereft of citizenship rights and status; they are suspended "outside the framework of the civilized community," where they exemplify "a new variety of collective alienation."[45] A sea of refugees generates waves of sympathy and may prompt acts of collective good intention. Michael Marrus has drawn attention to the role of non-governmental organizations in helping to sustain hundreds of thousands of refugees in the immediate aftermath of the First World War. The historical record also yields evidence of impressive individual kindness.[46] At the same time, the evident impotence of refugees is paralleled by our own sense of powerlessness, induced by the size of the refugee population and the magnitude of the international effort required to address both the symptoms and the underlying causes of the "problem."[47]

Recent events in Europe and in other parts of the globe reinforce the prevailing emphasis on dispossession, alienation, and human tragedy. In the collapsing Soviet Union, a multinational state whose development had been associated with considerable population dispersal, hundreds of thousands of citizens were forced to leave their homes in the wake of social and ethnic unrest. Citizens of the former Soviet state settled in whichever republics—subsequently, states—corresponded to their particular national affiliation. By the spring of 1990, Armenia was home to more than 230,000 Armenian refugees who were forced to leave Azerbaijan, while 210,000 Azeris settled in Azerbaijan. More than 150,000 Russians fled their homes in central Asia or the Baltic states to settle within the territory of the RSFSR, although many more Russians continue to live in what has become known as the "near abroad."[48] Official agencies did not respond favorably to this exodus; at one extreme, the authorities in Moscow refused to provide housing or food to refugees. Private agencies tried to fill the gap, but with very limited resources. Other republics established immigration quotas. As during the First World War, population displacement had a sharp ethnic edge, stretched slender resources, and heightened the sense of moral panic and civic crisis.

Following the line of argument advanced above, it might be thought that refugees were and are by definition dispossessed, marginalized, and defeated. We need, however, to be on our guard against an understandable tendency to treat refugees entirely as helpless casualties of war. To be involuntarily displaced is by definition to fall victim to forces beyond one's control and to be thrown on the mercy of unfamiliar institutions, staffed perhaps by unsympathetic personnel with no sense of obligation to the strangers in their midst.[49] More recently, however, some anthropologists have urged that the refugee is as much a constructed category as a social or humanitarian "problem." Refugees should not be regarded as passive victims, waiting only to be reinstated in their earlier domicile. Repatriation is less important than the creation of a "healed community," in the absence of which refugees are condemned to be perceived (and to perceive themselves?) as "outsiders."[50] This fruitful approach implicitly invites us to attend to the realm of politics: not, it should be emphasized, by focusing exclusively on the high-level politics of global relief projects, but also by considering closely the local forces that may secure or else conspire against the restoration of community, security, and dignity. In a rather different formulation, it has been argued that in some circumstances revolution rather than the restoration of a status quo may be desirable. Not only might the emergence of refugee movements be a consequence of social change; revolutions and wars of liberation may entail improvements for many refugees by promoting a "humane form of adjustment."[51]

In thinking more broadly about the definition and status of refugees, we ought to remember that some states have enacted close controls over entire sections of the population, denying them modern citizenship rights in the process. From this perspective, enforced flight from one country to another might be regarded as an opportunity rather than a dead end, as an assertion of independence rather than a desperate gamble. By the same token, an escape by members of an oppressed minority to another location within the boundaries of the existing state may allow them space to seek the security and protection afforded by co-religionists or members of a common ethnic group. More generally, such shifts of entire population groups may also undermine existing systems of domestic control and subordination, generating the momentum for a transformation of state power. This is in no way to minimize the significance of those refugee movements that were a response to genocidal intent and which resulted in colossal human degradation, suffering, and killing. But a focus on spatial mobility does serve to emphasize just how crucial an element in the preparation of genocide is the process of physical confinement. The twentieth-century evidence shows that isolation and containment are necessary preconditions for mass murder.[52] In other circumstances, refugees may discover strength in solidarity and even attain a kind of liberation in place of collective bondage. Historians should be alert to the potential that may exist for refugees to establish their own "healed communities." They should also take account of the potential for refugees to subvert the status quo.[53]

In wartime Russia, displaced people were and remained subjects of the tsar. They did not cross an internationally recognized border, but the tsarist state admitted no doubt about their status as refugees, because they had been forced to leave their homes by the threat of violence. The official parlance of tsarist Russia acknowledged the role of domestic agents of force in a formal decree, issued in 1915, which stated that "refugees [*bezhentsy*] are those persons who have abandoned localities threatened or already occupied by the enemy, or who have been evacuated by order of the military or civil authority from the zone of military operations" (termed *vyselentsy*). This official statement added another dimension to refugeedom, stipulating that refugees included "also emigrants [*vykhodtsy*] from states hostile to Russia." In legal terms, the tsarist state therefore allowed for the inclusion of Ruthenians from Austrian-ruled Galicia, as well as of Armenian subjects of the Ottoman empire, toward whom Russia might be expected to have particular obligations.[54] The tsarist lexicon had hastily been extended, with conceptual and administrative difficulties that had yet to impinge fully on official consciousness.

In the modern era, a distinction is often drawn between approaches that, on the one hand, treat refugees as victims of emergencies requiring an urgent humanitarian response and, on the other, deal with refugees as a foreign policy or security issue. Recent discussions have also focused on the human rights dimensions of involuntary population displacement. I hope to be able to demonstrate that all these concerns were present to a greater or lesser extent during the First World War. The old regime responded with a series of administrative measures. Members of the imperial family lent their names to new agencies for emergency relief. The "refugee problem" also allowed civic leaders to challenge traditional procedures, and to argue that bureaucratic regulations and devices were no longer relevant to the needs of Russian society. At the same time, notions of what constituted "society" were being questioned by refugees themselves.

I make no claim that refugees brought about the Russian revolution. But the explosive growth in the numbers of displaced persons had a profoundly "unsettling" effect on the state as well as on Russian society. Through their own actions, as well as the license given to humanitarian impulse and organization, refugees "sharpened distaste for the status quo and defined its new allegiances."[55] Opponents of the old regime asserted their claim to deal sympathetically and effectively with the refugee question. Refugeedom generated new antagonisms in tsarist Russia, created additional grounds for political opposition, contributed to the destabilization of the economic foundations of the state, and helped unravel the empire's territorial configuration. Refugees forced themselves into the political spotlight for several critical months, until attention switched to the even more basic questions of food supply and economic collapse.[56] Even then, refugeedom lost none of its potential to reinforce ideological alignments, to disclose political intentions, and to reveal cultural perceptions.

My conceptualization of refugeedom invites us to extend our focus without losing sight of broader issues of social and political transformation—in Steve Smith's words, "to reveal how the apparently marginal, when set in relation to other phenomena, can lay bare the unacknowledged workings of larger systems of power."[57] Refugeedom was bound up with debates about the Russian polity and Russia's postwar territorial frontiers. But still more was at stake. To be a refugee was to betray uncertainty about one's place in the existing social framework. Meanwhile, the condition of being a refugee challenged other social groups to begin to situate refugees in an unraveling polity, and in the process to constitute their own sense of purpose. Thus refugeedom not only entailed displacement and "re-placement" in territorial terms; it also served as a metaphor of a broader and profoundly disturbing quest for identity.

1.

∽

War and the Origins of Involuntary Displacement

Behold, the Lord . . . will surely violently turn and toss thee like a ball into a large country.

—Isaiah 22:18

Different pieces of ground told different stories to different people. We also knew that for years now there had been no country here but the war.

—Michael Herr, Despatches

The forced migration (vyselenie) of refugees has acquired a spontaneous and chaotic character.

—General Gulevich, 16 August 1915

Events on Russia's western front gave rise to acute anxieties almost immediately, as it became clear early in the war that Russia had been forced to yield territory to the enemy.[1] Defeat on the battlefield did not spare civilians, who were confronted with a stark choice: whether to remain behind under enemy occupation or to flee eastward. Certain civilians had no choice at all. In 1914, tens of thousands of Poles followed in the wake of the retreating Russian forces. During the great retreat in 1915, their number swelled still more. "As soon as our troops withdraw, the entire population becomes confused and runs away."[2] Sometimes they fled, lest they lose contact with relatives on Russian territory, including fathers and sons who were serving at the time in the tsarist army.[3] True, this did not always imply a move to distant locations; in the initial phase of retreat, refugees would often stay close by Russian troops, in the hope or expectation that the army would quickly recapture land from the enemy.[4] But many peasants despaired of continuing to farm when horses and livestock had been badly depleted by requisitioning. They expressed a wish to seek a better life "in the depths of Russia."[5] Other motives also came to the surface. Sometimes civilians were warned that "voluntary" departure was the only alternative to almost certain conscription by the enemy.[6] Civilians were prompted to leave their homes by the fear of being terrorized by enemy troops. Nor were these fears misplaced: "Rumors are rife that the Germans have behaved abominably toward the local population."[7] These verdicts generally supported the view that population displacement was the product of mass panic by civilians who nevertheless exercised a degree of choice.

Yet displacement was by no means dictated solely by a fearful civilian response to punitive action by the enemy. The Russian general staff disposed of sweeping powers to enforce the resettlement of civilians, where this was deemed appropriate. Army regulations permitted the military authorities to assume absolute control over all affairs in the theater of operations. The commander-in-chief (until August 1915, Grand Duke Nicholas, cousin to the tsar) was empowered to instruct all public officials to carry out his orders. Initially this gave the army jurisdiction over Finland, Poland, the Baltic provinces, and a large part of Petrograd, including the city itself. As the Russian army retreated, its rule extended to other parts of European Russia. This prompted strong opposition from cabinet ministers and parliamentary deputies from the western borderlands, but to no avail.[8] Although they had failed to capture land belonging to Germany, the generals could thus at least claim to have taken control of a broad swath of Russian territory.[9]

This jealously guarded license provided one of the main impulses behind population displacement. Within the extensive theater of operations, the Russian high command was accused of pursuing a scorched earth policy and driving civilians from their homes.[10] Archival evidence supports this view. General Ianushkevich, chief of staff of the Russian army, ordered the destruction of crops in Galicia; livestock, farm equipment, and church bells were removed to the safety of the rear. Reports reached Stavka that entire villages had been destroyed.[11] Civilians were inevitably vulnerable to this treatment, and the army sometimes removed them indiscriminately from districts close to the front.[12] Sometimes they were hurriedly conscripted, in order to deny the enemy the use of their labor power. "We didn't want to move, we were chased away. . . . We were forced to burn our homes and crops, we weren't allowed to take our cattle with us, we weren't even allowed to return to our homes to get some money," in the words of one group of refugees.[13]

But in truth the army went out of its way more to target vulnerable minorities, in an attempt to find scapegoats for military failure. Jews suffered most acutely. The negative association between Jews and frontier security had been deeply ingrained in military consciousness ever since Nicholas I had decreed that they could not live within 50 kilometers of the western frontier.[14] Russian generals confidently asserted that "the complete hostility of the entire Jewish population toward the Russian army is well established."[15] At all levels in the chain of command, there was a widespread willingness to single out Jews for immediate deportation. German colonists in the southwest ("although they are Russian subjects, they are not Orthodox") also found themselves the target of military wrath. They were forced to move hundreds of miles from the vicinity of the front.[16]

In this manner the flow of refugees and other displaced persons from Russia's imperial borderlands assumed unprecedented and unexpected dimensions, contributing to public perceptions of the war as a national catastrophe.

THE FIRST PHASE OF WAR

The pattern of defeat was established early in the war. Between August and December 1914, the German army repelled the Russian onslaught in east Prussia, advanced steadily along the Baltic coastal region, and made preparations to march on Warsaw. By the end of the year, the Russian army had lost control of the major industrial town of Lodz, leaving the German army a mere 50 miles from the Polish capital, which had now become home to an estimated 100,000 Jewish and Polish refugees.[17] To the north, the enemy advanced deep into the region of Kaunas (Kovno), capturing the Latvian port city of Liepaja (in German, Libau). German soldiers destroyed farmsteads in Lithuania, forcing the owners to seek shelter in Vilna.[18] The retreat from Poland had devastating consequences for civilians: "Well-to-do people have become poverty-stricken refugees; those with large families have lost their children en route, and have been forced to leave behind their sick relatives, whom it was not possible to save."[19]

Defeat also prompted harsh action on the part of the Russian high command against the large Jewish population scattered throughout the western borderlands. Local army commanders accused Jews of spying for the enemy, for example by using the information about military maneuvers and troop numbers that they had garnered from their role as government contractors. Russian troops, including Cossack soldiers far from home who were encountering Polish Jews for the first time, easily mistook Yiddish for German, and this ignorance only reinforced the message from their superiors that Jews were not to be trusted. Expressions of patriotism by Jewish politicians were to no avail.[20] Even well-meaning outside observers betrayed a deep-seated prejudice, suggesting that Jews were so destitute that they would stop at nothing, even treachery, to obtain additional cash.[21] The war provided their neighbors with an opportunity to denounce Jews, for reasons of personal animosity and in the hope of some reward for turning "spies" over to the authorities.[22] Such distorted preconceptions underpinned widespread attacks on individual Jews and their property by military commanders and their subordinates. As early as September 1914, a local army commander expelled the entire Jewish population from the small Polish fortress town of Pulawy (Novo-Aleksandrovsk), giving them just twenty-four hours' notice. This was by no means an isolated instance. Jews were frequently taken hostage, supposedly in order to deter their neighbors from helping the enemy.[23] Using the likelihood of espionage as a pretext,

General Ruzskii, commander of the northern front, ordered the entire Jewish population to leave Plotsk province in January 1915.[24] By one estimate, more than 600,000 Russian Jews were displaced even before the mass deportations began in the summer of 1915.[25]

Farther south, the tsarist army enjoyed greater success in its first campaign against Austria-Hungary. Russian troops attacked through Galicia, capturing L'vov only a month after the outbreak of war. But military success, no less than military failure, also bred civilian misfortune. Ukrainian activists who, with little hindrance from the Austrian authorities, had campaigned for a "free Ukraine" were forced to flee to the relative safety of Vienna and thence to Berlin.[26] Nor was the Russian army alone in dedicating itself to the deportation of civilians. The newly installed governor Count Georgii Bobrinskii, a devoted and determined russophile, regarded Galicia as an inherent part of Russia that needed to be "cleansed" and integrated with the tsarist empire. With the support of a dedicated group of officials from Russia's southwestern provinces (Kiev, Volynia, and Podol'ia), Bobrinskii embarked on his purification program. Several dozen Ukrainian Uniate church leaders and other local notables—including the famous Ukrainian historian Michael Hrushevsky, as well as the metropolitan of the Uniate church—were deported to Siberia. In Galicia itself, priority was given to Russian as the sole official language; schools were instructed to abandon instruction in other languages.[27] A particularly harsh fate befell the Jewish population of Galicia. Many fled westward, trying to escape the campaign of terror unleashed by Russian troops.[28] Eminent Galician Jews who stayed behind were held hostage, in a crass attempt to safeguard the lives of Russian subjects of the tsar who had fallen into German or Austrian hands.[29] Others were subsequently expelled from Galicia on the orders of Ianushkevich, who cited the need to "protect" the non-Jewish population from the consequences of collaborationist intrigue by Galician Jews.[30] Nor did Ianushkevich spare German peasants who had lived in Galicia for several generations. They were unceremoniously told to pack their bags and move eastward. Galicia thereby became the first major site of mass civilian displacement during the war.[31]

To cap four months in which military disasters outnumbered Russian successes, the Transcaucasus also became a theater of war, following the Ottoman bombardment of Russia's Black Sea ports in October 1914. Although the Turkish army ground to a halt during the harsh winter of 1914, the attack threatened to resume after a brief lull. With the support of a recently created Armenian National Bureau, 10,000 Armenians voluntarily enlisted in the Imperial Russian Army, where they joined around 100,000 Armenian regulars in hope of liberating historic Armenia from Ottoman rule. In addition, four volunteer units were formed for action across the Turkish border, "notwithstanding the muzzles of Turkish guns that were pointed at their backs." Prominent Ottoman Armenians made their way from eastern Anatolia to Tbilisi, Baku, or Erevan.[32] The mobilization of Armenians in the Russian empire, the organization of volunteer units to operate on Turkish soil, and the indications of pro-Russian sympathies among some of the sultan's Armenian subjects enraged Turkish politicians and military leaders and provided an ominous indication of the terrible events to come.[33] Before the year was out, the governor of Tbilisi had begun to draw attention to the influx of refugees from Ottoman Armenia, Syria, and Iran.[34] The Armenian Committee for the Relief of War Victims appealed to Armenian communities in Petrograd, Moscow, Odessa, Ekaterinodar, and elsewhere to assist as many as 100,000 refugees. The committee noted that "this is fast becoming a national question."[35] Other minorities in the region expressed anxieties about the volatile situation created by this displacement. The Georgian population of the Caucasus expected that they would be economically "enslaved" by the Armenian newcomers. Some members of the local Muslim community also feared that Armenians would blame them for the actions of the Ottoman regime.[36]

Summarizing the impact of the first campaigns, an intelligent and well-informed public figure commented that "the enemy has destroyed everything, leaving nothing intact. Villages have been devastated, houses burned; where before the war there was plenty [*blagopoluchie*], now there is ruin and the inhabitants have been deprived of all that mattered to them."[37] Russia's civilian population paid a heavy price for the lack of a speedy resolution to the armed conflict.

DEFEAT, DISARRAY, AND DISPLACEMENT

Worse was to come in the spring and summer of 1915, as the German army moved northeast to occupy all of Poland, Lithuania, and large parts of Belorussia. In April, General Mackensen launched a fierce offensive against the Russian Third Army, stationed between Cracow and Gorlice. During the next five months, the Russian army suffered losses of around one million war dead and wounded, while a further one million were taken prisoner.[38] Each month gave rise to fresh military catastrophes. Warsaw—"historic Polish capital, the greatest Jewish centre in Europe, the third city of the Russian empire"—fell on 22 July.[39] The fortresses of Ivangorod (Deblin; located in Kozenitskii uezd, Radom province) and Brest-Litovsk succumbed as well. By the middle of August, no Russian troops remained on Polish territory.[40] Farther north, the German army consolidated the gains made during the previous year's offensive. Riga itself—the fourth-largest city of the Russian empire, with a population of 530,000 in 1914, two-thirds of whom were Latvian—was threatened by troops who dug in no more than 25 miles from the city's outskirts; the city had already become filled with refugees from the western region of

Latvia.[41] In Lithuania, the town of Kaunas—with 88,000 inhabitants, half of them Jewish—fell on 4 August. Vilna—more than twice as large, with a mixed Jewish, Polish, and Lithuanian population of 204,000 in 1914—was occupied early in September. Even Petrograd could not be regarded as immune from a German onslaught; plans were made in August for the removal of state archives, art treasures, and gold reserves to Vologda.[42] Austrian troops reconquered Galicia, capturing Przemysl on 20 May and L'vov on 9 June, allowing them to join up with the Germans in Russia's southwest. The enemy entered the province of Volynia on 13 August. General N. I. Ivanov, commander-in-chief of the southwestern front, instructed his subordinates to prepare for the evacuation of Kiev, a proposal that sent government ministers into paroxysms of fury. Nor was Odessa immune from the panic induced by the succession of defeats suffered by the imperial army.[43]

These military misfortunes presaged an enormous wave of civilian displacement. Against the background of defeat and retreat (the Russian army had been pushed 300 miles east of the line they held in August 1914), Polish, Jewish, Latvian, Ukrainian, Lithuanian, and Russian civilians left their homes and fled eastward. On 22 June, General Danilov, chief quartermaster of the Northwestern Front, informed the Union of Towns about the mass influx of refugees from the Polish provinces into Belorussia. The union's executive acknowledged the urgent need for canteens and sanitary facilities to alleviate civilian suffering.[44] The month of July brought no respite. General Alekseev recognized the scale of the problem: "Refugees have no idea where to go; no one gives them any instructions or regulates their movement in the event of further retreat." He urged Danilov to "take immediate and decisive measures to deal with this serious and threatening phenomenon."[45]

Not all civilians in the front zone became refugees. Many were prevented from fleeing by the rapidity of the German and Austro-Hungarian advance.[46] Others were determined to resist displacement: "I was born in this cottage [*khata*]; here I was born and here I thought I'd die," in the words of one elderly refugee.[47] In many cases, however, fear of the unpredictable behavior of German and Austrian troops was again sufficient to induce the immediate abandonment of homes and farmsteads. Galician peasants and townspeople anticipated reprisals for the sympathetic reception they gave (or would be suspected of having given) to the Russian army. Their abrupt departure often had tragic consequences.[48]

The tactics of the Russian high command once more contributed, in some cases decisively, to the displacement of civilians.[49] Army officers in the northwest instructed the local population to flee, without seeking to discriminate between those who might be of service to an enemy occupation force and those who could not be. In vain did Latvian political leaders and relief workers protest that it made no sense to deport civilians of all ages from the province of Kurland: "Old men, youths under the age of 15, women with young children—none of these groups serve any military purpose, and they cannot render any assistance to the enemy."[50] In other instances the army enlisted able-bodied males for the purpose of engineering work, only to find that their relatives understandably accompanied them during the great retreat.[51]

Belorussia suffered heavily from the influx of refugees. "Waves of refugees" (one contemporary estimate put their number at 250,000) packed the road out of Brest-Litovsk leading toward Slutsk and Minsk.[52] The small town of Kobrin was described as overflowing with civilians from Chelm (Kholm) province, who turned the surrounding area into "a densely packed bivouac."[53] A further 200,000 refugees passed through the province of Vitebsk; around 25,000 of them settled in the town, whose population two years earlier had stood at 108,000.[54] Provincial towns and villages were transformed overnight into feeding stations. Roslavl', a modest town in Smolensk province with around 28,000 inhabitants before the war, found itself home to 80,000 refugees by the late summer of 1915, most of them encamped close to the railway station. They refused to move unless guaranteed a proper berth.[55] Entire provinces adjacent to the theater of war—Pskov, Smolensk, Vitebsk, Minsk, and Mogilev—were "crowded to the limit."[56]

Farther south, the "diabolical sadist" Ianushkevich was again hard at work, ordering Jews and Germans to leave the province of Volynia, lest they seize the opportunity to collaborate with the advancing enemy. Other minorities were similarly targeted. Thus the tsarist army retreated in the reluctant company of hundreds of Ukrainian, Jewish, Polish, and German hostages, who were thought to harbor "criminal intentions."[57] By the end of 1915, around 400,000 refugees, most of them Ukrainians from Galicia, had passed through the province of Volynia on their way east to cities such as Kiev and Odessa, and beyond to the provinces of Poltava and Ekaterinoslav and the Don oblast. Towns such as Berdichev (with an estimated population in 1914 of 77,000, four-fifths of whom were Jewish) and Zhitomir (the administrative capital of the province, with a population of 93,000, half of them Jewish) received thousands of refugees; the local authorities attempted to disgorge them as soon as possible.[58]

There was a constant turnover of refugees as a result of military intervention; on the southwestern front, the ambitious General Ivanov unilaterally ordered the expulsion of refugees from Chernigov and Poltava in late September, enraging government officials and politicians alike.[59] Acting on the army's instructions, the governor of Mogilev ordered refugees to leave the town within twenty-four hours.[60] Nor did this arbitrary action cease in the autumn of 1915. In March 1916, the army gave 15,000 refugees crowded into Dvinsk (Daugavpils) only a few days in which to leave the town by one of three designated routes.[61]

To the extent that civilians were forced by Russian commanders to leave their homes, it was disingenuous of the minister of the interior, Prince Shcherbatov, to tell colleagues at the inaugural meeting of the special council for refugees that the flight of civilians was "a purely spontaneous phenomenon [*stikhiinoe iavlenie*]," caused by the advance of German troops.[62] Shcherbatov returned to this theme when the Duma deputy L. K. Dymsha complained about the hostile and insulting treatment that the civilian population had received at the hands of tsarist troops; the minister retorted that military behavior had no bearing on refugeedom [*sic*], which in his opinion was "caused by a desire for self-preservation."[63] Other commentators, particularly in the liberal press, took a less coy line, openly acknowledging the routine use of compulsion, particularly as applied to Jews and Poles. Indeed, so widespread were the army's tactics that a leading tsarist dignitary observed that "refugees" constituted a minority of the displaced population, compared to the hundreds of thousands of those who had been forcibly displaced (*vyselentsy*).[64]

TARGETING MINORITIES

Russia's minorities continued to suffer the consequences of military paranoia throughout 1915. At the beginning of May, all Jews in Kaunas (Kovno) and Kurland provinces, living west of the Kaunas–Ponevezh–Posvol–Bauske line, were ordered to leave their homes and move east. These ferocious instructions were frequently implemented with great callousness.[65] Around 200,000 Baltic Jews were affected by the "reprisal" for the supposed betrayal of Russian troops by their co-religionists in Kaunas. The sources speak menacingly of population "cleansing" (*ochishchenie*).[66] At army headquarters, Ianushkevich took the lead in singling out Jews for special treatment, encouraging what the minister of the interior described as "a pogrom mood" in the army. Many instances were reported of attacks on Jews in the province of Vilna, and of the panic they induced among Jewish refugees.[67] According to one scholar, "Only the speed of the enemy advance and the disintegration of much of the organization of the rear during the chaos of the retreat saved tens of thousands more Jews from forced resettlement deep in the interior of Russia."[68] Whether the rapidity of the Russian retreat prevented the army from attempting to perpetrate systematic atrocities on Jews is difficult to judge. Certainly, Jews continued to be deported during the summer and autumn of 1915, notwithstanding Danilov's attempt to restrict the deportations.[69] In September and October, for example, Russian troops forced the Jewish population to leave thirty-six towns in Minsk province and ordered all Jews out of Pskov.[70] Nor did improvements in the army's fortunes soften this hard line: Russian generals refused to listen to heartfelt appeals—"in the name of our children, our weak women, our feeble old folk"—for Jews to be allowed to return to their homes when the front line stabilized.[71]

The crude and desperate measures employed by the Russian army were not confined to the Jewish and Polish population of the Russian empire. Gypsies were deported from the vicinity of the front in July and August 1915.[72] German subjects of the tsar were, like Jews, an object of military distrust, although they too proclaimed their loyalty to Russia and served in the Russian army.[73] The tsar banned the use of the German language at the outbreak of the war, forbade public gatherings of those of German extraction, and closed down their newspapers. Many members of the Baltic German nobility and civil servants were summarily dismissed from public office.[74] More ominous still, the Russian high command and the Ministry of the Interior drew up plans as early as August 1914 for the deportation of German settlers from several districts in the western borderlands. One leading government official expressed a widely held view: "The colonists . . . live so detached an existence from the native Russian population that, all in all, they constitute a ready base for a German attack through our southern provinces."[75] By the end of the year, after a vitriolic press campaign, steps were taken to drive them all out of Russian Poland.[76] Around 200,000 individuals were affected by this action, their journeys to Siberia supervised by armed military or police detachments. The right-wing leader of the Astrakhan' People's Monarchist Party favored their deportation to uninhabited islands or unoccupied parts of the Caspian shoreline.[77] There was no respite in 1915. Ivanov suggested that Russia's German settlers be treated like the Jews and made to deliver up hostages; under his draconian proposals, failure to supply bread for the army would render the hostages liable to the death penalty.[78] Throughout the summer months, German settlers were driven from their farms in Volynia, Kiev, and Podol'ia to designated destinations, despite the reservations expressed in some military and civilian quarters.[79] Nor did the deportations cease in the following year; General Brusilov forced a further 13,000 settlers out of Volynia during the offensive in June 1916 and dispatched them to Penza, Riazan', and Tambov. Many of the Germans who had settled in Riga were also deported in 1916.[80] Protestations of collective loyalty were to no avail, and were likely to be met with the claim that they were being deported for their own protection.[81]

More complex were the issues raised by measures taken against the property of these settlers. The combined landholdings of German farmers probably exceeded three million hectares, although in terms of the area sown to crops, their farms accounted for a tiny fraction of the total arable acreage.[82] The tsarist government embarked on a series of legislative measures in February 1915 to expropriate those German colonists (as well as Austrian and Hungarian farmers) who lived in the frontier zone. Exceptions were made for those of Orthodox faith or Slavic nationality, as well as those who could demonstrate that their family members or ancestors had volunteered to fight in the Russian army.[83] Delays in implementing the new law (there was supposed to be a ten-month period of grace) prompted the military to take more direct action. In excess of 200,000 German settlers in the province of Volynia were forced to leave their homes during 1915, making way for 40,000 refugee settlers, who received land on the understanding that they would hand over part of the harvest to the state.[84] In the districts of Zhitomir and Novogradvolynia, Ukrainian refugees from Galicia appropriated the farms hurriedly vacated by the beleaguered German farmers.[85] In the area around Liublin, an additional 50,000 settlers were either conscripted or deported.[86] Those who refused to make way for refugees put the lives of hostages in great danger or might themselves be liable to summary field court-martial.[87] Further measures followed in December 1915, which extended the coverage of the February law to twenty-nine provinces of European Russia, as well as to Finland, the Caucasus, and the Amur region. Whereas the earlier law exempted lands that had been granted to colonists at the time of their initial settlement, the December law subjected these lands as well to expropriation. Families of German descent who had lived for generations in Volynia, Kiev, and Podol'ia, as well as in the Volga region, were unceremoniously shipped to Siberia or central Asia, in a brutal foretaste of the horrors inflicted upon the next generation under the Stalin regime. We shall see later how they fared in their new location.

These actions need to be placed in the context of broader cultural anxieties. The Russian government did not hesitate to exploit popular hostility to what was conceived as German economic domination, which served as justification for attacks on German-owned factories, estates, shops, and banks. In his annual report for 1914, the governor of Tula province described how "the people have formed the view that Germans, even those who are Russian subjects, are enemies of the fatherland, that there is no place for them on Russian soil and that the land that belongs to them here should be given to Russian peasants."[88] German shops and warehouses in Moscow were subject to frenzied looting and arson over several days at the end of May 1915. These attacks took place against the background of further government legislation, directed particularly at German smallholdings. Anti-German sentiment could also be mobilized to attack a different target: some Russians, arguing that the process of expropriation did not go far or fast enough, blamed this lack of vigor on the supposed pro-German sympathies of the imperial court. Patriots and populists evidently had more illustrious figures in their sights than the humble German farmer.[89]

Ianushkevich regarded the expropriation of the property of German settlers as a golden opportunity to reward Russian soldiers who had distinguished themselves in battle, and to provide an incentive for those who might be tempted to surrender because they were not "materially interested in resisting the enemy."[90] This prompted the minister of agriculture, A. V. Krivoshein, to explode with rage at a meeting of government ministers ("I may not shout at the crossroads and in the street"). Krivoshein's colleagues shared his view that the chief of staff had gone too far.[91] Some local officials sought to preempt action by military leaders toward the Volynia and Volga Germans, in contrast to their acquiescence in the operations launched against Russian Jews. Nonetheless, expropriation took place on a wide scale.[92] Paul Miliukov and other parliamentarians criticized military behavior and government legislation alike, arguing that it set a poor example for Russian peasants, among whom expectations had now been aroused of more radical measures to expropriate property owners.[93]

Farther north, the enemy advance prompted a mass evacuation of Latvian farmers and agricultural workers from the Kurzeme Heights, south of Riga. These refugees jammed the roads leading to Riga and Dvinsk.[94] Local Latvian leaders blamed tsarist officials for the panic induced by the German advance. Nabokov, the governor of Kurzeme, abandoned his post at the earliest opportunity, leaving behind no arrangements for the care of the local population. Two-thirds of the population of northwestern Latvia crossed the Dvina River and either settled on the Vidzeme plateau or moved farther east. According to one account, 500,000 Latvians became refugees.[95] The threat to some of Russia's main industrial centers in the northwest prompted tsarist officials to take swift action. In Riga, the governor-general, General P. G. Kurlov, ordered the evacuation of workers on 17 July 1915. Following consultations with the local war industry committee, Kurlov drew up a schedule for the removal of highly skilled workers along with their factories, to be followed by workers whose departure was to be approved by the local labor exchange, after conferral with employers in European Russia. A third category comprised workers who left voluntarily. In practice, most workers evacuated themselves more or less spontaneously, clambering onto goods wagons and making their way to the Russian interior as best they could. All kinds of people, not just workers, joined the desperate scramble to find a safe haven.[96] The consequences for a major imperial city such as Riga were devastating; at the start of the war it numbered 480,000 inhabitants, but by early 1917 only 240,000 remained. By the beginning of November 1915, around 75,000 factory workers had fled east, accompanied by 145,000 dependents, perhaps as much as three-quarters of the workforce.[97] Many of those who remained behind were Latvian, Lithuanian, Polish, and Russian refugees as well as the plethora of staff in the various agencies for refugee relief.[98] A secret deal was struck between the Russian Twelfth Army and the Latvian committee for the relief of war victims, whereby the committee would supply the army's engineers with able-bodied men, in exchange for a fee that could be used for the program of refugee assistance.[99]

The Caucasian front presented an equally disturbed picture. The Russian army crossed the border in early May 1915. Held up by a Turkish counteroffensive, Russian commanders ordered troops to withdraw from the region around Van. In chaotic circumstances, some of the local Armenian population managed to flee to the relative safety of the Caucasus; others were left behind in the hasty retreat.[100] Worse still, youthful Turkish radicals blamed Armenians for the defeats already suffered by the Ottoman army in the winter of 1914 and early 1915, and charged them with having instigated an uprising in the town of Van against Turkish rule.[101] Those who remained behind after July suffered a terrible fate. Using as a pretext the events at Van, and in accordance with emergency legislation ordering the deportation of communities suspected of espionage or treason (or whose presence was not conducive to military effectiveness), the Turkish authorities turned on the entire community. Hundreds of thousands of Ottoman Armenians were butchered, or were driven from their homes and forced to endure long and humiliating marches to the south, from which many never recovered. In its intent and enactment, this policy amounted to a clear case of unremitting genocide, a "Bartholomew's Day massacre" on a national scale.[102] German officers stationed in Turkey were instructed to maintain strict silence on "the Armenian issue," and German newspapers, acting on government orders, made no mention of the massacres. Turkish scholars, like the Ottoman government at the time, insist in public that no genocide took place.[103] Historians continue to debate its magnitude.[104]

Only a minority of victims managed to escape to safety, either in Syria or in the Transcaucasus. According to one account, a quarter of a million Armenians managed to flee across the Russian border during August 1915. Perhaps as many as one-fifth of them died en route.[105] By the beginning of 1916, at least 105,000 ex–Ottoman Armenians had sought refuge in Erevan alone, which became even more of an "overgrown village" during the course of the war (its population in 1914 barely reached 30,000). The total number of Armenian refugees tripled during the following twelve months.[106] In further retaliation against the Ottoman Armenians, their abandoned farms were rapidly assigned to 750,000 Turkish refugees from western Thrace. Ironically, the beneficiaries were casualties of the Balkan War of 1912, in which Armenians had fought alongside Turkish army units.[107]

INITIAL REACTIONS

The actions of Russian military commanders provoked outrage among cabinet ministers and parliamentarians, who feared the social and economic consequences of displacement. They agreed that civilians should normally be allowed to decide for themselves whether or not to leave their homes. Force should be used "very carefully," and only in exceptional circumstances.[108] Senator A. B. Neidgardt spoke in favor of restricting migration from the war zone and attacked the vigorous efforts of the Russian front commanders to empty whole villages of their population. Not only did refugees hinder the war effort, by disrupting troop movement and military supplies, but their relocation prevented them from playing a proper part in hampering the German foe: "Mass refugee movement is harmful to the state. . . . The enemy does not then face the threat of partisan activity; there are not millions of hostile eyes that need to be watched and from which the enemy needs to hide his military secrets." Neidgardt concluded that to leave the native population *in situ* would also place on the German authorities the burden of feeding them, and would expose the enemy rather than the Russian people to the danger of epidemic disease from hungry and ill-clothed victims.[109] The Polish Duma deputy Henryk Swencicki (1852–1916) supported his opinion, on the grounds that otherwise the vacated territory would be settled by German colonists, while D. I. Zasiadko pointed out that Russian troops could not then count on material assistance from "loyal subjects" of the tsar when they came to recapture the occupied territory.[110] This echoed the views expressed by the minister of the interior, who argued that any further outflow of refugees must be stemmed: "The men are followed by their women, their children, their belongings, and their cattle. Additional millions will invade the Russian interior, to empty it [i.e., of food] and to starve. If the Ianushkevich tragedy continues, it would be more appropriate to leave the population to the enemy; better that they die under the boot of the Germans than that they finally ruin the whole country, which is already groaning under the avalanche of refugees."[111] Developing this idea, Zasiadko feared that the mass displacement threatened to "ruin hordes of comfortably off and wealthy people and to turn them into proletarians."[112]

Alexander Lednicki, the Polish political leader, provided another perspective. He supported, albeit from a different standpoint, Neidgardt's view that civilians should remain in their homes. Lednicki believed this was their "patriotic duty"; in contrast to Neidgardt, however, his sense of national obligation reflected a belief that the Polish "homeland" deserved better of Russia. It ill behooved Russian troops to force Polish civilians to abandon their homes.[113] The opposite view was articulated by G. G. Zamyslovskii, who maintained that those who stayed behind were likely to be conscripted by the enemy to dig trenches, repair railway track, and supply foodstuffs. Whether willingly or not, these civilians would certainly be helping the German and Austrian war effort. Not for him the possibility of partisan bands! Better that they "suffer on the altar of the fatherland and fulfill their heavy duty"; better that they be compelled to leave their homes in order to work for the greater good of Russia, in return for which they would be entitled to relief by the tsarist state.[114]

In phrases that were to be repeated many times, refugees were described as a "human wave" and as a "hungry and angry flock of locusts" that passed through the Russian interior, devouring everything in their path. In Odessa, "indescribable scenes of stupidity" were recorded, as civilians struggled to flee in the wake of Russian troops. "Soon only Siberia will be left for the habitation of those Russians who are not in uniform," complained Krivoshein on 24 August.[115] Other reports of refugee movements painted a depressing picture of military incompetence and brutality, compounded by the lack of a responsible and clear-headed civilian counterweight to the army command. The French ambassador, Maurice Paléologue, confided in his diary: "Everywhere the departure was marked by scenes of violence and looting, beneath the obliging eye of the authorities."[116] Meanwhile, the tsarist government issued regulations designed to curb the "spontaneous" flow of refugees from the western borderlands to the Russian interior. Refugees were warned not to listen to rumors, but instead to trust official announcements. "Too precipitous a flight may sometimes undermine and deprive one of the assistance that is made available to refugees. Whoever flees danger, where there is none, cannot expect to count on the support of others. Whether there is an actual threat posed by the enemy and whether inhabitants should flee are matters that will be announced in good time by army headquarters or the local military authorities."[117] Few refugees heeded this warning, let alone found it remotely reassuring.

Population displacement on this scale and intensity placed an intolerable burden on the overstretched Russian railway network. Troops, military equipment, and industrial plants were being evacuated from the front more or less simultaneously. Many railway personnel had been conscripted. Refugees added to the problems faced by the railway administration, as the minister of transport despairingly admitted in September 1915. Government officials attempted to "plan" the shipment of refugees, but were frustrated by the competing demands of other agencies for scarce rolling stock.[118] Nonetheless, tens of thousands of refugees slowly made their way eastward by train. The head of the Rovno railway district, which contained some of the most severely stretched lines, reported that the transport of refugees during September and October 1915 entailed the use of around 35,000 wagons. A further 42,000 wagons had been used on the line between Riga and Orel, via Vitebsk and Briansk, in order to ship tens of thousands of refugees and their meager possessions.[119] Similar reports were received from the officials in charge of the Moscow–Iaroslavl'–Rybinsk line, the Aleksandrovsk line between Moscow and Brest-Litovsk, and the Moscow–Kazan' line. In all, some 115,000 wagons—equivalent to one-fifth of the total stock in 1915—were involved in the evacuation of refugees (and industrial equipment) from the western borders in just two months.[120]

Lines were frequently subject to traffic jams, which became a familiar sight during the autumn of 1915.[121] Trains halted for long periods at small stations where there were few facilities or supplies, but often passed quickly through mainline stations. Conditions on board the refugee trains were squalid and demoralizing. Refugees sometimes spent days in the company of decomposing corpses, the victims of cholera, dysentery, or pneumonia.[122] Trainloads of Jewish refugees were sometimes pelted with stones by hostile onlookers encouraged by local army commanders to despise these vulnerable *vyselentsy*.[123] Trains arrived and departed unsystematically. Cars were coupled and uncoupled without any advance warning to passengers.[124] As a result, many families were separated.[125] There were other hazards as well. Refugees sometimes installed boilers in unheated railway freight cars, creating a fire hazard. When the authorities warned of the dangers, refugees replied, "It's all the same to us, whether we die of frostbite or from fire."[126]

Not all refugees traveled by rail.[127] Those who traveled on foot or by oxcart faced other kinds of difficulty. The quality of roads in European Russia and in Poland left much to be desired, and during the autumn rains many of them turned into quagmires, trapping the wheels of carts, which were often abandoned. Roads jammed with retreating troops made it impossible for refugees to move at anything other than a snail's pace. While refugees who climbed aboard railway freight cars were liable to be shunted from place to place, at least they were normally offered some protection from the elements.[128] Those who went east by road had to find or make what shelter they could. The only advantage they enjoyed over rail passengers was that they found it slightly easier to determine their own route.[129]

By no means all refugees retreated meekly and quietly to the Russian interior. Throughout the late summer of 1915, generals and ministers alike expressed concern about the disruption and public disturbances that characterized refugees' movement eastward, particularly when they traveled on foot. Disorder took several forms. Refugees were accused of stealing fuel and food from the indigenous population. During their departure from Russian Poland, refugees reportedly ripped apart entire woodlands in a desperate search for fuel; "this gives rise to extremely quarrelsome relations between local people and refugees; peace and stability will be possible only if compensation is offered to those who have suffered losses at the hands of refugees."[130] The governor of Mogilev anticipated that there would soon be bloodshed if refugees did not show greater respect for property. He called for Cossacks to be deployed, lest public order collapse completely.[131] In a similar vein, the governor of Volynia reported that many refugees, particularly those who left Galicia in the summer of 1915, were "incensed and indignant at having been forced to move; they panicked during the retreat, attacking and destroying property, and inflicting many losses on the local population." Local police and village authorities, he continued, were powerless to prevent refugees from roaming the countryside and looting at will. Charged with trespassing on Russian farms, refugees countered that they had lost everything.[132] Ministers anticipated many more such encounters when refugees eventually settled in the Russian interior.

The unwillingness of refugees to keep to the routes that were supposedly ear-marked for them represented another form of disorderly behavior. In vain did the government's leading official in the southwest issue leaflets instructing refugees about the means of travel and prescribing a route, as part of a scheme for the "rational" distribution of the displaced population.[133]

This brings us to the question of what belongings refugees could take with them. Some refugees drove horses ahead of them and were thus able to save some of their most valuable assets, but these were the lucky ones. Horses had to be grazed and fed, and an unknown number of draft animals perished en route.[134] Other refugees were forced to sell horses at a fraction of their prewar market value (Jews were forbidden to buy from refugees and from deported German settlers).[135] Thou-sands of horses were simply abandoned. In the course of one and a half months, around 50,000 horses were placed at the disposal of the regional refugee commis-sioner. He offered them to provincial zemstvos in European Russia, but the authori-ties would agree to accept them only on condition that they could inspect each ani-mal, something that the commissioner regarded as a ludicrous waste of resources. Cattle herds were also decimated.[136] One optimist suggested that farmers could buy replacements in Russia at a reasonable price. But optimism was in short supply among refugees.[137]

We can only surmise what proportion of their movable assets peasant refugees were able to salvage (the total value of farm buildings, houses, and agricultural equipment might amount to more than 1,300 rubles for the wealthiest peasant households in the western borderlands).[138] Obviously, the heaviest farm equipment had to be left behind, along with the basic immovable element of the peasant house-hold—the stove. But smaller items—work tools, clothing and bedding, utensils, perhaps spinning wheels and small looms—might be salvaged. If we assume, some-what heroically, that the peasant economy of Starobel'sk uezd in Khar'kov province was typical of the farms abandoned by the peasantry of the western borderlands, then refugees were on average probably deprived of around two-fifths of their assets. If they were unable to rescue or retain any of their livestock—a fair assumption—this figure would rise to three-quarters. Assuming that 500,000 peasant house-holds were caught up in the process of displacement, the value of assets that were lost during the war amounted—at a conservative estimate—to at least 500 million rubles. This was equivalent to around 5 percent of all peasant property (other than land) in 1914.[139]

Some contemporary observers affected bemusement at the belongings that refu-gees managed to bring with them. One old man was found staggering along with pieces of a double bed; another carried a large box containing a few chickens; a peasant family arrived in Petrograd with eight large sacks of rye. In each case the newspaper reporter made patronizing remarks about the "usefulness" of these items.[140] Other commentators were more sympathetic and less inclined to poke fun. Bishop Serafim of Ekaterinburg expressed admiration for an individual who not only had avoided becoming separated from his five small children, but also had brought with him a sewing machine and five canaries; the bishop was promised a young bird if the owner succeeded in getting them to breed in their new home.[141] By and large, however, journalists acknowledged that refugees preferred to have with them a tangible reminder of the life they had left behind, even when this upset the sense of order that relief agencies intended to promote. In Petrograd, for example, the Central Registration Office initially refused to allow refugees to hold on to livestock and pets, "but such was their attachment and so moving their devotion that the authorities relented."[142]

CONCLUSION

By the autumn of 1915, Russia's enemies had seized fourteen provinces with a combined population before the war of more than 35 million. The existing population of Chelm, Lublin, Radom, Suwalki, Grodno, Kovno, Kurland, Vitebsk, Minsk, Livland, and Estland had been badly depleted. Of those who had left during the terrible summer months, several hundred thousand refugees had temporarily found shelter, but three-quarters of a million remained in transit as of mid-September.[143]

Population displacement was ultimately caused by the advance of German and Austrian troops into Russian territory. But this explains little of the intensity and character of displacement. Although those who found an explanation in terms of "spontaneity" deliberately or unwittingly camouflaged the active intervention of Russia's own armed forces, the part played by the Russian army in this dramatic upheaval was evident to any objective observer. Jews and Germans left involuntarily by order of Russian military commanders, who were acting out of a warped belief in the political unreliability of these ethnic minorities and, in the case of Ianushkevich, in the hope of rewarding outstanding Russian soldiers. "The deported German colonists are not refugees," insisted General Danilov, and he might equally have excluded Jewish deportees from this category.[144] Leading members of the Polish and Ukrainian middle class were likewise taken hostage and compelled to move east.[145] Some critics of the army's behavior reckoned that no more than one-fifth of displaced civilians had chosen to leave their homes in 1915; the rest were forced migrants.[146]

For a while, contemporaries retained the distinction between *vyselenie* and refugeedom. "Refugeedom is something spontaneous; but forced resettlement is arbitrary behavior [*proizvol*]," wrote a Russian doctor in April 1916, criticizing the actions of the tsarist army; "and when *vyselenie* ceases, we shall find it easier to combat refugeedom."[147] But during 1916 one can detect an elision in contemporary doctrine between forced displacement and voluntary migration. The growing preference in official and semi-official circles for the term "refugee" (*bezhenets*) shows a willingness to draw a veil over the tactics of the Russian army (and, perhaps, a readiness to consign the despised German settlers to oblivion).[148] Instead, the emphasis fell instead upon the harsh measures inflicted by the enemy: "On the borders of our Russian homeland is a ruthless scourge; the blood is flowing in Poland, Galicia, Lithuania, the Caucasus. The enemy does not spare the land it has seized; whatever cannot be taken is destroyed. The population flees in a great horde from wretched native towns and villages."[149] The Russian public quickly became accustomed to talk of an "unparalleled, spontaneous, indescribable horror" that afflicted hundreds of thousands of civilians close to Russia's borders. One observer summed up the mass movement as the "great exodus," affecting Russian and non-Russian alike.[150] The flight of Russian Jews, in particular, was invested with dire expectations. But attempts to determine the direction of Jewish resettlement served only to highlight the degree to which other refugees were now beginning to populate— perhaps even to "overwhelm"—Russian space. If their migration was depicted as "spontaneous," what certainty was there that refugees would be any more orderly and disciplined when they reached their final destination? All these anxieties underlay broader questions about the source of political authority and administrative responsibility in wartime Russia. It is to the political dimensions of displacement that we now turn.

2.

◦~◦

THE POLITICS OF REFUGEEDOM

*And what about the refugee question? I simply choose at random one
question out of a whole series which cannot but cause us, the
representatives of the people, as much anxiety as it causes all Russian
people* [sic]. *Is this refugee question and the complete inability of the
government to manage it . . . can this be a normal situation?*
—V. M. PURISHKEVICH, 12 FEBRUARY 1916

*This spontaneous process, unheard of and unprecedented in the history
of mankind, taking the form of a people's pilgrimage, will have untold
consequences.*
—*EKATERINOSLAVSKAIA ZEMSKAIA GAZETA*, 6 NOVEMBER 1915

The events of summer 1915 demonstrated to critics of the old regime that Russia's
rulers exercised no control over the Russian high command. The truth of the matter
was that the government tried and failed to curb the arbitrary behavior of the
generals. At private meetings and in the corridors of power, furious exchanges bore
witness to the fraught relationship between Russia's military and civilian authorities. Few ministers supported the brutal actions ordered by the notorious chief of
staff, Ianushkevich. Parliamentarians and public activists accused the army's general headquarters (Stavka) of incompetence, cruelty, and lack of foresight. But their
criticisms extended also to government ministers, provincial governors, and other
servants of the state. Even those less inclined to pass political judgment maintained
that the hectic and chaotic movement of refugees underlined the incompetence of
tsarist ministers and officials. Anxieties about the consequences of refugeedom for
public health and public order spoke additionally of antagonism and conflict between educated society and the tsarist state. Public activists claimed the right to
become involved and to criticize the absence of a clear and coherent social policy.
Liberal figures in local government, together with elected parliamentary representatives, professional associates, and technical experts, all used the plight of the refugees for their own purposes: to claim additional resources from central government,
to assert professional competence and integrity, and, more generally, to demonstrate
that social welfare and individual freedom could be delivered only by a reformed
polity. To this extent, refugees became the pawns in a tortuous game of political
intrigue.

The key players in this struggle were, on the one hand, the Ministry of the Interior and, on the other, the newly formed "public organizations" (*obshchestvennye organizatsii*)—the unions of towns and zemstvos. Friends in high places, particularly foreign correspondents such as Bernard Pares and Isaac Don Levine, regarded these unions ("social Russia") as the prime agents of Russia's salvation. These enthusiasts gave a glowing account of public activity and minimized the part played on the home front by the unions' political opponents.[1] The public organizations sought to redefine the relationship of state and educated society, and to entrust greater responsibilities to the representatives of educated society. These ambitions extended as much to matters of civilian welfare as they did to questions of military production and procurement. It was idle to expect that Russia's emerging public sphere would be indifferent to the numbers, condition, and treatment of refugees.[2]

THE EMERGENCE OF A "REFUGEE QUESTION"

Dramatic and disturbing news of mass population displacement erupted in the summer months of 1915. Public disquiet about the impact on civilians of military action found an outlet in the corridors and chamber of the State Duma, whose summer session opened on 19 July 1915, the first anniversary of the outbreak of war. Not surprisingly, given that the Duma had not met since the end of January, the political atmosphere was highly charged. Talks between the leaders of the Cadets, Octobrists, Progressists, and liberal Nationalists led to a rapprochement that culminated in the creation of the Progressive Bloc, whose demands included a government that would enjoy public confidence.[3] Leaders of the main party fractions in the Duma adopted a cautious approach to the refugee question, perhaps fearing that their bid to persuade the government to make political concessions would be compromised by too obvious an attempt to jump on the bandwagon of the public organizations. Among rank-and-file deputies, however, feelings ran high; if anything, jealousy of the ambitions of the unions of towns and zemstvos spurred them on to attack both the army leadership and tsarist officials. A meeting of senior parliamentarians in late July heard devastating reports from two Polish deputies about the plight of Polish refugees. The arch-conservative Germanophobe Vladimir Purishkevich supported them to the hilt. On the left of the political spectrum, the Georgian Menshevik N. S. Chkheidze spoke of the appalling situation in Armenia. Other deputies urged the Duma to consider the likely consequences of population displacement for living conditions in the Russian interior.[4] On the same day, a group of elected representatives from the northwest and southwest regions proposed a parliamentary commission on refugees.[5] There was thus a dual edge to the knife of parliamentary criticism, aimed at officialdom as well as the Russian high command.

Further momentum was achieved on 22 July, when a group of predominantly nationalist deputies met privately at the offices of the Ministry of the Interior (MVD), whose incumbent, Prince N. B. Shcherbatov, had recently taken up his post.[6] The veteran parliamentarian Jan Garusevich pointedly asked if the removal of thousands of local inhabitants from the vicinity of the front was absolutely necessary. The right-wing nationalist Vladimir A. Bobrinskii described conditions in Volynia, where 30,000 refugees from Austrian-ruled Galicia had sought temporary shelter in a forest; the local police had refused to issue them work permits, on the grounds that they were enemy nationals.[7] Pursuing a different tack, N. I. Antonov urged the government to make use of the experience of the Siberian resettlement administration in what he termed "mass transfers of people," an indication that some parliamentarians were prepared to envisage an expanded role for the Ministry of the Interior. No one had a kind word to say about the provincial governors, who were answerable to the MVD and who appeared only too willing to acquiesce in the decisions made by the army.[8] Shcherbatov leapt to their defense, arguing that they had to follow the orders of the military authorities, and concluded by informing his audience of his decision to establish a department to oversee refugee affairs.[9] But an internal reorganization hardly appeared likely to satisfy critics of government inactivity and gubernatorial negligence. Nor would such a move silence the gathering chorus of voices that charged the tsarist army, and specifically Stavka, with a heavy-handed approach to the civilian population.

Privately, the government expressed grave misgivings about Russia's military leadership. Given the circumstances of the retreat, a direct challenge was now posed to civilian administration in the remaining parts of European Russia.[10] Ministers gathered in August 1915 to contemplate the magnitude of the movement of refugees. Much of their time was taken up with the impact of the army's actions on the Jewish population, although they set their discussion of the disorderly movement of refugees in the context of widespread concern about the consequences of military administration on the western front, where army commanders uprooted people in order to depopulate territory prior to its complete abandonment to the enemy. "Stavka does not seem inclined to give up its Kutuzov-like enticement, in the hope of defeating the German offensive by laying waste the territory they have occupied."[11] The discussion continued with a graphic summary of the consequences of military behavior:

People are torn from their birthplaces, given only a few hours to collect their things, and driven toward an unknown destination. Before their eyes, their remaining possessions, and frequently their very houses, are set afire. It is easy to understand the psychology of these forced refugees. They are hardly likely to have accumulated a fund of goodwill toward an authority which permits actions that are incomprehensible, and not only to simple people. And this bewildered, irritated, exhausted crowd spreads like a continuous flood along all the roads, obstructing military transport, and bringing complete chaos into the life of the rear. . . . This human mass is pouring over Russia in a broad wave, everywhere increasing the burdens of wartime, creating supply crises, increasing the cost of living, and exciting already frayed tempers. Only very recently, after this malevolent force had become elemental, has Stavka begun to understand that this situation cannot be allowed to continue, and it has tried to cooperate with the government's demands that civilian authorities be involved in the regulation of the refugee movement.[12]

At the ministers' meeting on 4 August, Minister of Agriculture A. V. Krivoshein drew liberally upon the rhetoric of apocalypse. Population displacement had the terrible consequence that "curses, sickness, misery, and poverty are spreading all over Russia." Warming to his theme, Krivoshein continued in biblical terms, pointing out that "the naked and the hungry spread panic everywhere, dampening the last remnants of the enthusiasm which existed in the first months of the war. They come in a solid phalanx, trampling down the crops, ruining the meadows, the forests. . . . The second great migration of peoples arranged by Headquarters is dragging Russia into the abyss, into revolution, and into destruction."[13] By the middle of August, other ministers had come to share this vision. Shcherbatov spoke "of Jews chased on by whips—in the midst of this tired, hungry, abused mob, some kind of mad bacchanalia is taking place. Drunkenness, robbery, debauchery are flowering. The reports that come to me state bluntly that Cossacks and soldiers are deliberately dragging families of refugees behind them, in order to have women during the march to whom they can give looted property."[14] The French ambassador Maurice Paléologue, having spoken with government ministers, wrote in a similar vein: "Hundreds of thousands of wretched people . . . were herded like cattle by Cossack troops, abandoned at railway stations, and left exposed to the elements on the edge of towns, dying of hunger, exhaustion, and cold. And along the way, to raise their spirits, these pitiful multitudes encountered the same hatred and contempt. . . . Throughout their sorrowful history, the Jews have not known a more tragic exodus."[15]

Members of the State Duma lambasted army commanders, in particular Ianushkevich, for their harsh and uncompromising behavior. The Polish parliamentarian Swencicki accused Stavka of seeking to turn the front into a desert, so that troops could fire at will across an empty terrain. He protested that the Russian army burned down entire villages, forcing people to seek sanctuary in neighboring settlements before those, too, were torched in turn. German troops would be delighted, he thought, by the tactics of the Russian army, because the land "clearances" made it easier for German immigrants to colonize the vacant territory.[16] The liberal lawyer and state senator A. F. Koni censured Russian commanders for using force against the civilian population; in this he was supported by the leading Jewish lawyer G. B. Sliozberg and by the Latvian religious figure and politician I. O. Sanders.[17] The emerging consensus was that the army's actions would likely prove self-defeating, but that little could be done, given the freedom of maneuver that the army claimed across much of the western borderlands of the Russian empire and the resolutely intransigent stance adopted by Ianushkevich. In any case, Ianushkevich enjoyed the protection of the commander-in-chief, Grand Duke Nicholas, for whom many liberal politicians had great (if misplaced) respect.[18] There is no doubt also that some of his subordinates personally endorsed Ianushkevich's directives and implemented them with enthusiasm.[19]

THE MOBILIZATION OF "EDUCATED SOCIETY"

Russia's military leaders were not without their allies, particularly among some sections of the resurgent public organizations. To account for this apparent paradox, we need briefly to retrace our steps. At the outbreak of war, the tsarist government had approved the formation of two umbrella organizations, the All-Russian Union of Zemstvos (VZS) and an equivalent Union of Towns (VSG).[20] Their task was "exclusively [sic] to aid the war wounded and sick for the duration of the present conflict," and to this end the two agencies were placed "under the flag" of the Russian Red Cross.[21] Patriotic, purposeful, and proud of their "practical" intent, they had forged close contacts with military chiefs over the course of several months' hectic activity, particularly on the northwestern and southwestern fronts.[22] The war revived claims on the part of the unions' leaders to assume greater executive responsibilities, particularly in view of the evident deficiencies of existing bureaucratic methods of the administration of defense production and procurement, which had brought Russia to the brink of catastrophe.[23]

The government, not surprisingly, made plans to curb the activities of the public organizations, arguing that they were a flag of convenience for the Cadet Party. But this tactic was thwarted by the support they received from the army leadership.[24] Confident that they already had the government on the run for its failure to improve supplies to the armed forces, the unions of towns and zemstvos sought to focus on the issue of civilian welfare. They charged civil servants with neglect, citing evidence that officials in the western provinces not only had been idle but had been among the first to desert their posts, exposing the indigenous population to the threat of enemy advance and to the often brutal and inept behavior of undisciplined civilian sentries who were charged with the maintenance of order on the ground.[25] Both the army and the public organizations encouraged local civilians to form "citizens' committees" (*obyvatel'skie komitety*) to fill the administrative vacuum. This kind of interference did not endear either of them to central government.[26]

Purportedly non-political, the public organizations could thus hardly escape political involvement. Serious and effective action meant coordination, and this in turn implied some engagement with existing agencies of the state, including the army. By the middle of 1915, the leaders of both unions were actively engaged in the welfare of large numbers of refugees, many of whom remained in areas under military jurisdiction. Army commanders regarded the unions as an irreplaceable means of providing emergency food and medicine to local people who had been displaced and become homeless; they were also expected to encourage refugees to keep out of the way of retreating troops. On the northwestern front, for example, General Iu. Danilov asked the VZS and VSG at the end of June to assist the large number of refugees arriving daily in Smolensk and Mogilev.[27] The unions promptly sent this and subsequent messages to the minister of war, pointing out that the public organizations needed one million rubles: "We stand empty-handed before the avalanche of refugees."[28] In the meantime they dispatched various plenipotentiaries to provincial towns where refugees had already begun to gather.[29] As a result of the information they accumulated, the leaders of the VSG began to formulate a program of action. Three zones were to be created: that closest to the front line would detain and feed the refugees, then release them to the second zone, where they would be counted and examined for infectious diseases before being "filtered" carefully to the third safety zone, where they were to be registered and evacuated to designated parts of the Russian interior, in accordance with their qualifications and the demand for their labor.[30]

Certainly, VZS and VSG officials in the field censured army commanders who engaged in the forced removal of local people from their homes. Some union leaders took the view that the army was in danger of undermining its own tactics, insofar as refugee displacement impeded military transport. A special conference in Petrograd under the aegis of the regional committee of the Union of Towns heard one speaker from the front paint a graphic picture of the measures directed at the Jewish population in Riga, Vilna, Mitau, and Dvinsk, who had been given only two hours to pack their belongings.[31] However, most union activists set aside their misgivings in order to deal with the consequences of refugeedom; inevitably, this entailed practical collaboration with the army. The public organizations met with army commanders in Brest-Litovsk and drew up plans for the organized evacuation of refugees. Arrangements were made to "filter" refugees, in order to minimize the risks of a serious outbreak of infectious disease.[32] This kind of close cooperation became much easier after August, when Nicholas II publicly announced the dismissal of Ianushkevich—not to placate the public organizations, but to prepare the way for the tsar's assumption of the post of supreme commander. The VZS and VSG breathed a huge sigh of relief at the prospect of a new broom at Stavka.[33]

Most army commanders themselves had nothing but praise for the public organizations. Without the Union of Zemstvos, for example, the army would have been overwhelmed by the problems of providing baths and laundry facilities, and of evacuating sick and wounded soldiers. But the army chiefs reserved their greatest approbation for the way in which the unions dealt with the welfare of refugees. Responding to an inquiry from Stavka, the commander of the Fourth Army commented (with some verbosity) that "all their manifold and highly productive activity, informed by a lively commitment and lack of formality on the part of the unions' personnel, can be described only with feelings of profound gratitude."[34] Other generals were somewhat more critical of the Union of Towns, but the high command concurred that the Russian army enjoyed indispensable assistance from the public organizations.[35] Stavka reinforced this point by contrasting the unions' professionalism and organization with the inexperience and inefficiency of other civilian agencies at the front, including those dedicated to the relief of refugees.[36]

Closer still were the ties between leading members of the public organizations (notably the VZS) and the Russian high command under its new chief of staff, M. V. Alekseev.[37] A telling indication of their common outlook was the readiness with which the leaders of the Union of Zemstvos transferred Jewish employees from the front to duties in the rear, in order to placate those generals who maintained that Jewish members of the "third element" were poisoning the minds of the Russian soldier.[38] Thanks to concessions such as these, as well as the range of welfare activities they sponsored, the Union of Zemstvos enjoyed a good measure of autonomy at the front, to the evident anger of government officials.[39]

The situation in the Russian interior was a different matter, and was complicated by the challenge mounted by the public organizations to the civilian government. From the point of view of central government, the involvement of the unions of zemstvos and towns at the front was worrying enough. In a bold move, the leaders of the public organizations proposed to centralize decision-making rather than allow individual municipalities and zemstvos to determine their own policies and programs of action.[40] That coordinated action by municipal and zemstvo agencies should be extended to the rear, in order to facilitate the resettlement and relief of refugees, proved anathema to most government ministers; yet this was precisely what the public organizations had in mind.[41] Not only did the zemstvo union leadership draw attention to the broad scope of refugee relief—"the distribution of allowances, the care of children, medical attention, the provision of work relief, the question of accommodation etc."—it also asserted, more radically, that the needs of refugees could not be distinguished from those of the settled population with whom they increasingly came into contact.[42] The representatives of state authority should, it was argued, be brought to heel before they could do any more damage. The chaos that had previously characterized the dispersion of refugees could not be tolerated further; too much was at stake, both for refugees themselves and for the local population. Only the public organizations could organize the supply and distribution of the means to inspect and disinfect the refugee population; only the unions of zemstvos and towns could adequately implement a coordinated and "rational" plan for refugee resettlement. A national calamity would be prevented only if coordinated action were taken by the public organizations.[43]

Zemstvo and municipal activists drew a contrast between the broadly positive relationship they enjoyed with the military authorities at the front and the sour attitude of central government, which sought to curb attempts by the public organizations to assume overall responsibility for refugee relief. Political issues were never far from the surface. The displacement of civilians did not just raise questions of public health, legal rights, and economic reconstruction, wrote one young critic of the status quo; "this is a political question, in that refugees have become an object of politics in the hands of the government—or, more accurately, not politics but political intrigue [*politikanstvo*]."[44]

The attempt to seize the political initiative culminated on 22 August with the creation of the Joint Section for Refugee Welfare.[45] The section was administered by a bureau (christened Sobezh) consisting of M. M. Shchepkin, A. N. Sysin, and S. V. Bakhrushin from the VSG, together with N. V. Iakushkin, A. K. Vrangel', and F. V. Tatarinov from the VZS. Sobezh created subdivisions to deal with employment, refugees' property, and child welfare, and to collect statistics, giving notice of its intention to establish supremacy in the sphere of refugee relief.[46] Many of its staff were young, radical professionals, with a background in medicine, law, and the humanities, who were motivated by a firm sense of public duty toward the displaced and by a strong aversion to bureaucratic practice.[47] They had little patience with officials in the Ministry of the Interior or with provincial governors who wrestled with the care and relocation of refugees.[48]

THE TATIANA COMMITTEE

The politics of refugee relief in the Russian rear were further complicated by the active involvement of another agency, which was neither a creature of central government nor part of the "public" sphere. The Tatiana Committee for the Relief of War Victims (Komitet Ee Imperatorskogo Vysochestva Velikoi Kniazhny Tatiany Nikolaevny) came into existence on 14 September 1914. Taking its name from the tsar's second daughter, who served as its patron, it was originally established to care for war widows and soldiers' offspring.[49] Those invited to attend its deliberations read like a roll call of leading figures in the court and the State Council: Princess Elena Saksen-Altenburgskaia, Elizaveta Aleksandrovna Naryshkina (a mistress of the court), Count G. A. Bobrinskii (the governor of Galicia), Archbishop Evlogii of Volynia, and other dignitaries including A. N. Kulomzin, S. P. Glezmer, and N. P. Muratov.[50] In the summer of 1915, the Tatiana Committee added the care of refugees (including the provision of orphanages and schools for refugee children) to its earlier responsibilities. Its chairman, state senator Aleksei Neidgardt, emphasized that the committee would also aid civilians who had not fled, but who suffered nevertheless from the effects of war.[51] Funds came from a government grant, as well as from donations and fundraising activities. Tatiana committees also sprang up in many provinces and towns, where they alone commanded sufficient resources to initiate emergency welfare programs. Their staff worked independently of other agencies, but also cooperated with local authorities, public organizations, diocesan committees, national committees, and provincial governors, who frequently served as chairmen. According to one account, where local agencies subordinated themselves to the Tatiana Committee, the relief of refugees proceeded with much greater success.[52] The Perm' branch, for example, took charge of 25,000 refugees, as well as arranging food and medical treatment.[53] From Novgorod it was reported that the Tatiana Committee had "mobilized the strongest elements in the province," including the governor and municipal councilors, as well as members of the nobility, zemstvos, and local judiciary.[54]

As we shall see, the Tatiana Committee played a vital role in refugee relief, but its broader political significance is what concerns us here. During the autumn of 1915 it became a pawn in the game of confrontation between public organizations and central government. This was inevitable; Neidgardt's list of the committee's responsibilities bore a close resemblance to that of the VZS and the VSG, except that Neidgardt intended to work with tsarist ministers and officials, rather than to supplant them.[55] The Union of Towns attacked the Tatiana Committee for its bureaucratic procedures and arbitrary practices.[56] But the Ministry of the Interior insisted that the committee had a clear purpose: "to rush to provide help to refugees where it is needed, to go where the alarm is sounded."[57]

A key element in the battle with the public organizations was the unions' assertion of their right to establish the size of the refugee population.[58] The public organizations regarded the gathering of such data as a necessary precondition of refugee relief, and one that required the maximum possible coordination of local authorities—precisely the kind of cooperation for which the unions were ideally placed. But this vital task raised more profound issues of particular concern to government. Ministers dreaded the possibility that the unions' personnel—the "third element"—could take advantage of this license, not only to count the number of sick and needy refugees, but also to spread revolutionary propaganda with impunity. Their suspect political attitudes had long stuck in the throats of government bureaucrats; fears of this "enemy within" never left the more conservative elements in the tsarist state.[59] By the beginning of 1916, the "third element" numbered close to 334,000 personnel at the front alone. In the rear, each zemstvo provincial and district board increasingly co-opted doctors, agronomists, and engineers to assist with the new tasks assumed by the two unions, as well as by the joint organization for the supply of the army (Zemgor), established in July 1915.[60]

For this reason, the issue of data collection gave rise to a protracted dispute in the winter of 1915 between the public organizations and the tsarist government. Writing to the Special Council for Refugees on behalf of the unions of towns and zemstvos, Prince G. E. L'vov protested that the government had effectively deprived them of responsibility for gathering data on the number, status, and residence of refugees, by transferring this task to the Tatiana Committee.[61] He pointed out that the unions had already begun to gather a great deal of information about refugees and were best placed to conduct a national census. In his view, the Tatiana Committee should restrict itself to data concerning orphans and broken families.[62] Although L'vov acknowledged the need to avoid unnecessary duplication of effort, he argued that the decision to entrust the registration of refugees to another agency was bound to create the impression locally that the central government did not trust the public organizations. There was more than an element of truth in this complaint: the cabinet took the line that the registration of refugees was a political matter, which it deemed inappropriate for the unions to address. L'vov was sent packing, his only recourse to this snub being to leave letters from the Tatiana Committee unanswered.[63] No degree of objection to the defeat of statistical science by "administrative artifice" could prevent the failure of the public organizations to obtain control of sensitive information at a national level. The abortive struggle for statistical supremacy typified their marginalization.[64] In a bitter polemic written after the battle had been lost, Shchepkin denounced the "systematic struggle against the unions" and the official machinations that were designed to silence the public organizations.[65]

MINISTERIAL ATTACK: THE FORMATION OF THE SPECIAL COUNCIL FOR REFUGEES

Population displacement thus had all the makings of a major political crisis. Ministers could not wait for the Duma or the public organizations to set the pace.[66] A bureaucratic reaction was not long in coming. In the first place, Shcherbatov appointed two plenipotentiaries to organize refugee relief on the southwest and northwest fronts. These men, Prince N. P. Urusov and Sergei Ivanovich Zubchaninov, both members of the State Council, took up their posts at the end of July.[67] They were given responsibility for "arranging the removal [*vyselenie*], direction, and methods of transportation of refugees"; for the provision of refugees with food and medical and veterinary help; and for "organizing refugees in their current place of residence until they come under the care of local authorities."[68] Zubchaninov, in particular, appears to have lost no time in setting up a rival organization to the Union of Zemstvos, drawing upon the authority vested in him by the MVD. He christened it Severopomoshch' ("Northern Aid"). Urusov's organization, to which he gave the name Iugobezhenets ("Southern Refugee"), never matched its northern counterpart in terms of creating subordinate agencies.[69] Urusov worked instead alongside existing institutions of refugee relief, with whom he sometimes enjoyed a frosty relationship.[70] The creation of these bureaucratic agencies was a clear attempt to put the public organizations in their place.[71]

Secondly, Shcherbatov introduced a bill on 5 August 1915 "to provide for the needs of refugees." This term, he made clear, extended to all those who had been forced to leave their homes, whether "voluntarily" or by order of the military authorities. His purpose was to subject all displaced people to systematic government supervision.[72] But Shcherbatov also sought to seize the initiative from the Duma. Parliament had already recommended that the four special councils for defense, food supply, transport, and fuel supply be supplemented by a special body for refugee affairs. Government ministers decided to support the move, "in order to remove sole responsibility for the horrors in the life of the refugees from the government and to share it with the Duma." The minister of the interior ostensibly wanted to ensure that there would be no complaints about the uses to which appropriations for refugee relief were being put by government agencies.[73] As with the other special councils, however, the government managed to meet the demands of parliamentary critics without yielding its overall authority for affairs of state. The proposal was briefly delayed by wrangling over the composition of the new body, but at the end of the month—following the emergence of the Progressive Bloc in the Duma and the subsequent adjournment of parliament—the tsar approved the formation of the Special Council for Refugees (Osoboe soveshchanie po ustroistvu bezhentsev). The new body was to disburse funds for refugee relief (25 million rubles were set aside initially), oversee the registration and relocation of refugees, and "return them to the place of their permanent settlement and restore their affairs, as well as making arrangements for their future." It also arranged loans for refugees, and ascertained the value of property that refugees had been forced to abandon, as well as compensating refugees for losses incurred as a result of military action and for property that had been requisitioned. Finally, the council was to attend to the spiritual and educational needs of refugees, and to act as a liaison between refugees and the relatives they had left behind.[74] Following an intervention by the leading Armenian Cadet politician Mikhail Papadzhanov, the government agreed that the council would also look after the needs of persons displaced from foreign states, this being designed to assist Ukrainians ("Ruthenians") and Armenians fleeing, respectively, Austrian and Turkish persecution. They were entitled to refugee status if they left their homes and placed themselves under the protection of the tsar.[75]

This constituted a huge agenda, and as with the other special councils, the government cast its net widely in order to find a suitable mixture of bureaucratic and voluntary expertise. The new council was chaired by the minister of the interior.[76] Seven other ministries were represented: Foreign Affairs, War, Finance, Education, Transport, Trade and Industry, and Agriculture. The Tatiana Committee and the Russian Red Cross (headed by the tsar's cousin, Prince Aleksandr Ol'denburg) were each given a seat on the council. So, too, was the head of the army's sanitary-evacuation section. Seven seats apiece were reserved for members of the Duma and the State Council.[77] One representative was allowed from each of the various national organizations that had recently been formed. The new body also included a "special commissioner for refugees," who attended ex officio. This followed a lively discussion among the members of the Special Council at its first session on 10 September, some of whom felt that the proposed official would encroach on the prerogatives of provincial governors, others that he would interfere in the activities of local public organizations. He acted as the executive arm of the Ministry of the Interior, and had overall responsibility for the resettlement and organization (*ustroistvo*) of refugee affairs in the Russian interior. He was also required to serve as a liaison with agencies, including the Union of Towns, that were already engaged in relief work. But he was answerable only to the minister of the interior.[78]

In line with its aversion to the public organizations, the government envisaged only a minor role at the national level for the unions of towns and zemstvos, even though their spokesmen hoped for a change of heart that would give them greater responsibility for refugee relief. The unions were each allotted one miserly seat on the council, their modest representation amounting to a contemptuous dismissal of the role envisaged for the public organizations.[79] The appointment of special regional commissioners for refugee relief was a further nail in their coffin. Government ministers had little difficulty in curbing their ambitions, given the treasury's control of financial resources. Neither the VZS nor the VSG was in a position to satisfy the demands made on them by individual towns and zemstvos, which were funded directly by the Special Council.[80]

In protest at its treatment of the Union of Zemstvos, Prince L'vov resigned from the Special Council at the end of 1915. (Out of pique he refused to commit the union to intervene in central Asia during an outbreak of epidemic disease among refugees in 1916.)[81] Instead, individual zemstvos and municipalities were required to continue with the practical tasks of refugee scrutiny, resettlement, and relief, drawing upon their own limited resources or those supplied by the central government. Where there were no zemstvos, the provincial governor was empowered by the decree of 30 August to call upon "all local voluntary forces" to take part in refugee relief, including (as the Duma had insisted) religious leaders "irrespective of faith and nationality."[82] In practice, much of the responsibility for the administration of refugee relief rested with the provincial governors or the new regional commissioners, who were, of course, accountable only to the MVD, and who frequently by-passed the Special Council altogether.[83]

Bureaucratic initiatives of the kind described above did not deter the public organizations from continuing their attack on official procedures. "Everything is done haphazardly, without any sense of consequences or perspective," wrote Sergei Bakhrushin, an active member of the Union of Towns, adding that the unions of towns and zemstvos were being kept in the dark.[84] Bakhrushin also spoke for many critics of the old regime when he lamented the impact of population displacement on the empire's national minorities: "Entire national cultures are threatened, and it is the duty of Russian society to save them from complete annihilation."[85] Further criticism of central government came at a meeting of the two unions held in Moscow between 7 and 9 September 1915. Delegates attacked the government for its failure to control a refugee movement that "threatened the welfare of the state." Only the active and "comradely" cooperation of the public organizations could create order out of chaos.[86] More radical proposals were made by a commission that met under the auspices of the Moscow provincial zemstvo, which called for a national body for refugee relief, whose members should include representatives from the unions of towns and zemstvos, central cooperative unions, and trade unions.[87] Similar claims were advanced by a regional congress in Khar'kov at the end of November, whose delegates bemoaned the lack of any nationwide coordination of refugee relief and any system of accountability. The familiar cry went up that "just as the war is a matter of state and its conduct assigned to the organs of state power, so the resettlement and relief of refugees should be entrusted to the forces of educated society and the people."[88]

Such proposals may have seemed more like a futile last gasp than a rallying call to action.[89] Nevertheless, the attempt to couple refugee relief to political reform took shape in other parts of the empire. Long-standing demands for the introduction of a volost zemstvo were revived by liberal doctors at an extraordinary congress of the Pirogov Society in spring 1916.[90] Other public activists took the campaign in a different direction, arguing that the refugee problem required an extension of local representative institutions to areas of the empire where they had previously been absent. A retrospective analysis of the situation faced by refugees who moved to

Siberia made the point that they had been treated with far greater consideration and sensitivity in the "zemstvo provinces" than they were elsewhere (including, of course, Siberia), where tsarist officials treated refugees with high-handed contempt. In addition, relief workers found a disturbing lack of charitable activity and public health facilities, which for so long had been the pride of zemstvos in European Russia.[91] From Irkutsk came a demand that zemstvo institutions and municipal self-government be introduced at once, with equal rights for all sections of the population to participate in local government and to organize themselves freely.[92] The self-appointed leaders of the Latvian community complained that the evacuation of people and property from Riga was hampered by the absence of zemstvo institutions that could otherwise have introduced a degree of order into what was a chaotic process.[93] As if to reinforce the close connection between the war effort and domestic politics, the VZS also claimed that the lack of self-government in Russian Poland made its work at the front indispensable.[94]

However, the public organizations discovered to their chagrin that they could not count on the Duma to come to their aid. Growing timidity on the part of the Progressive Bloc deprived parliament of much of its residual prestige as a forum for debate (it did not help that the Duma met infrequently during the second half of 1915 and throughout 1916).[95] The unions of towns and zemstvos were left stranded. It was typical of this marginalization that a newspaper dedicated to advertising the role of public organizations was forced to close in December 1915, after just ten issues, in which it had promised to "monitor the activity of all agencies . . . and to explain the direction of public endeavors with respect to refugee relief."[96] In April 1916 the tsar ordered the unions to hold no further public congresses and conferences. Although the government later relented, it was a sign of the times that congresses of the two unions scheduled for December 1916 were banned.[97] More humiliation was heaped upon Sobezh, the coordinating office for refugee relief, which was forced to close all but one of its divisions by the end of 1916, leaving it in charge of a network of children's homes and orphanages. This did not amount to a very impressive record.[98]

As if government intransigence and parliamentary stalemate were not enough of a handicap, the public organizations also suffered from internal divisions. These arose from a lack of homogeneity in their social composition and political outlook. As William Gleason has shown, the leaders of the provincial zemstvos—most of them members of the landed gentry—found themselves at odds with their professional employees. Statisticians, agronomists, nurses, and doctors regarded the war as an opportunity to introduce more democratic procedures into the affairs of the zemstvos, in the first instance by organizing themselves as a more coherent "third element," in order to circumvent the nobility's attempts to marginalize them. By 1916, zemstvo employees had begun to draft their own agenda; for example, those in Minsk and Mogilev withdrew their labor in protest of the class-based character of the provincial unions. The collapse of the old regime in February 1917 allowed the third element to give full vent to this sense of alienation, as well as their frustration that the public organizations had not made a greater impact.[99]

According to Gleason, the noble elite manipulated the content of the Union of Zemstvos' journal—with its emphasis on "the latest sanitation device, therapeutic cure, or hospital design"—in order to prevent the discussion of political issues.[100] But even these apparently mundane technical questions demonstrated not only expert knowledge but also the further crystallization of a vigorous public sphere. Liberal doctors used their professional forum to assert the belief that "the relief of refugees is a question for the entire people and should accordingly be handed over to them."[101] They devised elaborate plans for the medical examination, assessment, and treatment of refugees. Lawyers, psychiatrists, and teachers envisaged a similarly prominent role for themselves. Russia's refugees formed a part of the discourse of professional self-promotion. The assertion of professional autonomy also symbolized the rift between old and new styles of public duty.[102]

CONCLUSION

In this manner, the sudden, sweeping, and often brutal displacement of several million subjects of the tsarist empire became in August 1915 a matter of "state importance," engaging the attention of generals, ministers, civil servants, courtiers, and Russia's educated public. The underlying responsibility for having caused this displacement remained a matter for conjecture: the degree to which refugees were provoked by the Russian army or had "chosen" to leave their homes continued to be a matter for animated discussion in the corridors of power and in the congresses of the public organizations.[103] Wherever responsibility lay, however, it was clear that civilian agencies, rather than the army, would have to deal with the resettlement and welfare of several million refugees.

The public portrayal of a "refugee crisis" during the second half of 1915 bore a close resemblance to the "shell shortage" that erupted in the winter of 1914. Mitrofan Shchepkin made the analogy explicit: "This [refugeedom] is the war brought to our very doorstep, to our peaceful surroundings. There are no trenches here, but we find ourselves without shell, and yet we must fight."[104] In both instances the emergency occurred without warning, causing widespread public anxiety and accusations of official mismanagement. The difficulty of formulating an adequate response was compounded by a dearth of information and a lack of clearly defined responsibilities.

Public organizations lost no time in challenging the competence of existing bureaucratic agencies. Although they were outmaneuvered by the Ministry of the Interior, nevertheless the unions of towns and zemstvos sought to rally Russia's "public forces" behind an alternative vision of the "national interest." Central government agreed to make funds available to individual municipalities and zemstvos (as well as to the Tatiana Committee), allowing them the necessary scope to provide assistance to refugees, but ministers refused to concede that the public organizations should take over primary responsibility for the administration of refugee relief at the national level. Thus the ambitions of the public organizations were rudely and quickly shattered. The creation of the Special Council was a tacit acknowledgment not only that the initiatives promoted by the unions of towns and zemstvos were insufficient to cope with the influx of refugees, but that they should ultimately yield to the overarching control of the state.[105]

It remained possible for local liberal leaders and their professional staff to assert a civic impulse. Even if, as one commentator noted, "the business of refugee relief is a state matter [*gosudarstvennoe delo*] . . . nevertheless its realization and implementation must be entrusted to public forces."[106] Events were to bear this out. Yet, as the immediate crisis abated, it became apparent that the public organizations were left with duties but no power. This unresolved tension and disappointment made for an unstable political framework for handling the refugee crisis and would lead to a settling of scores when the old regime collapsed in February 1917.

~

3

RESETTLEMENT AND
RELIEF OF REFUGEES

The elements have risen. Where they will stop, how they will settle down, what events will accompany them—all this is an equation with many unknowns. Neither governmental, public, nor charitable organizations have the forces to bring the elements into their proper course.

—A. N. IAKHONTOV, 4 AUGUST 1915

The road itself is a passing of stories, with its listeners in the grass on either side.

—JOHN BERGER, *A SEVENTH MAN*

By the autumn of 1915, the magnitude of the refugee movement could be neither doubted nor disguised. In Petrograd, the center of the country's political life, the public had become accustomed to the presence of countless refugees. Government ministers, officials, and public activists had begun to consider the likely consequences of refugeedom and to formulate an appropriate response. But only a minority of refugees entered the Russian capital. What would provincial society make of this phenomenon, over which it seemed impossible to exercise any control? In order to answer this question, we must draw a distinction between territory that came under the jurisdiction of the Russian high command and the rest of the tsarist empire, where civilian administration remained intact. In the former, much of the responsibility for refugee relief fell upon the bodies created by Zubchaninov (Severopomoshch') and Urusov (Iugobezhenets), as well as upon the public organizations at the front.[1] In the rear of European Russia, the public organizations had to come to terms with the authority vested in provincial governors and local government boards. Besides these contending political forces, a plethora of charitable, religious, and semi-official agencies devoted considerable energy to the relief of refugees, without sharing the political vision and sense of civic activism espoused by the public organizations.[2]

Whether in the exposed western borderlands or in the Russian interior, the peregrinations of refugees were invested with dire consequences. One leading spokesman for the Union of Towns spoke for many when he pointed to the "threat of the spread of infectious diseases, serious social complications arising from the encounters between newcomers and the settled population, and the prospect of a collapse in the economic foundations of the entire country."[3] To what extent could control be exercised over the settlement of hundreds of thousands of desperate refugees? Should they be encouraged to settle in towns or in the countryside? What provision could be made for refugees in the short and the medium term, and by whom? It is with such questions of administrative practice and charitable provision that the present chapter is largely concerned.

CRUCIBLES OF DESPERATION:
THE WESTERN BORDERLANDS AND CAUCASUS

In the first instance, thousands of refugees were displaced from the immediate vicinity of the front to an adjacent area. This applied to provinces such as Minsk, Livland (in Latvian, Vidzeme), and Podol'ia. Many more refugees congregated in the neighboring provinces of Mogilev, Vitebsk, and Kiev.[4] Whether or not they had crossed provincial boundaries, these refugees—like the settled population of the western borderlands—came under the overall authority of the Russian high command. Those closest to the front were inevitably vulnerable to German or Austrian attack. An official attached to the northern front experienced mixed emotions as he watched farmers stubbornly and assiduously continuing to sow their fields under periodic enemy fire.[5] Tens of thousands of refugees crowded into the small Belorussian towns east of Brest, such as Kobrin, hoping soon to be allowed to return to their homes. In the middle of July 1915 they found themselves under attack by German planes; the enemy advance then drove them slowly east toward Smolensk. One eyewitness described them as "in terrible condition, without shelter, without bread, without hope, feeble and apathetic."[6] Direct responsibility for their welfare rested with either Zubchaninov or Urusov, the two special commissioners for refugees appointed in July 1915. Faced with criticism from the public organizations, and hampered by conflicts between central government and the unions of towns and zemstvos, Zubchaninov struggled to deal with what he termed a "catastrophic situation."[7]

Zubchaninov and his subordinates often found it difficult to persuade refugees to leave their temporary abode and move to the interior of Russia, even when it became apparent that they were threatened by a renewed German advance and their numbers daily swelled by a fresh influx of refugees. The displaced population had already come to depend on the hot meals that they received once a day and feared that they would starve en route to a new destination.[8] Without fodder, refugees who had managed to hold on to their horses were simply unable to move any farther. Other considerations also played a part. The railways could not be relied upon to transport refugees in sufficient numbers, which caused huge congestion at provincial stations at least until the end of November 1915. Zubchaninov offered refugees sufficient provisions to subsist upon while they journeyed to the interior, as well as to make fodder available for their draft animals, although he complained that the Union of Zemstvos opposed these tactics.[9] At the same time, Zubchaninov protested that he had to devise an administrative network to cope with the passage of refugees, in the absence of local officials, most of whom had been evacuated to places such as Mogilev or Kaluga. For these reasons, many refugees were loath to move far from their homes. "We've already come far enough"; "It can't get any worse than this"; "Where is there for an old woman to go?"; "We want to go home"; "Let me die here—I shan't leave"; "As long as no one is shooting at us, we're not going anywhere." Others linked their fate to that of the public organizations, indicating that they would leave only if and when the Union of Zemstvos moved its operations farther east: "If you shift, we'll move on as well."[10] Still others, especially if they were Jews and German settlers, had little choice but to obey military instructions to move and to join the "huge general stream of refugeedom."[11]

A unique account of refugees' experience as they moved through Pinsk and across the Pripet marshes reveals a bleak picture of vulnerability, desperation, and improvisation. The entire contingent of refugees suffered from exhaustion brought about by the slow rate of progress and the need to set off before dawn.[12] Roads became clogged with troops and military equipment, and carts became stuck. From time to time, refugees came under aerial bombardment by German planes; mothers covered the heads of their children in a futile gesture of protection. Refugees scavenged food from retreating troops, aware that some of it had been looted from private stores. Without flasks or other containers, they were unable to carry fresh water.[13] The soldiers had already emptied the wells of clean drinking water before the refugees reached them. Those who drank from the deceptively clear water of the marshes around Pinsk risked serious stomach upset and death from the poisonous microorganisms it contained. "The children cried, shrieked, demanded something to drink, dragged themselves to the ditches, and often drank this dreadful water." Mothers who were close to death despaired of finding someone to look after their young children and on occasion drowned them in the swamp. Those who dropped dead were discarded by the roadside or thrown into the marsh. Families became separated and spent anxious weeks uncertain about the fate of their loved ones.[14]

Newspapers also carried graphic reports of the desperate plight of refugees on the move. Belorussian refugees were unable to give their dead a decent Christian burial: "Eyewitnesses report that children are thrown into a common pit, like potatoes."[15] Thousands of Polish refugees arrived in Chernigov province during September, October, and November 1915, after an exhausting journey via Gomel' or

Kiev. Mealtimes and prayers in the makeshift encampments were interrupted by loud wailing when they "remembered their birthplaces, the people dear to them whom they had left behind, and the graves on the roadside that were the final resting place of their relatives who had not survived the journey."[16] In the Caucasus, too, Armenian refugees made their way toward the relative safety of Aleksandropol', leaving the roads strewn with corpses.[17]

Memoirs written long after the event convey the same sense of public chaos, human calamity, and bodily degradation. The young Konstantin Paustovsky, working in Russian Poland and Belorussia as a medical orderly, recalled

> sand dunes, shell-pocked roads, panic-stricken villagers. Crawling towards us, up to the wheel-hubs in sand, were carts loaded with refugees. . . . The sultry evening was full of turmoil. Dozens of fires burned in the village square. Around them, Polish peasants who had fled from their villages sat or lay on the ground near their covered wagons. Babies howled, turning blue in the arms of their exhausted and dishevelled mothers. . . . Old Jewesses in red wigs came out of their hovels dragging the accumulated junk of a lifetime—ancient quilts, crockery, sewing machines, copper basins green with age. They tied them up in shawls and sheets, but I could not see a single wagon to haul them away.

Paustovsky went on to recount pitiful stories of half-starved refugees, of children trampled to death in the stampede for food, of women forced to give birth in the woods, and of old men and women left for dead at the roadside.[18]

Military witnesses also demonstrated a capacity to sympathize with the plight of refugees. One Russian general reported from Chelm province that "they bear their misfortune with stoic fortitude, putting their trust in the help of God, the tsar, and ordinary folk; their hatred for the Germans knows no bounds."[19] General Alfred Knox, British military attaché with the Russian army, described the miserable predicament of Polish refugees, albeit with the kind of fatuous disregard for their sensibilities evident in someone who could always find a safe billet: "Whole families with all their little worldly belongings piled onto carts, two carts tied together and drawn by a single miserable horse, one family driving a cow, a poor old man and his wife each with a huge bundle of rubbish tied up in a sheet and slung on the back. I took a photograph of three Jews, who thought their last hour had come when told to stop. . . . I passed twenty continuous miles of such fugitives. If asked where they were going, they replied that they did not know. . . . The whole of the Polish peasantry seemed to migrate from the districts east of the Vistula."[20]

Following the dreadful and concerted Ottoman policies of deportation and extermination, thousands of Armenians fled from Turkish Armenia to the relative safety of the Russian Transcaucasus. According to various estimates, between 200,000 and 300,000 Ottoman Armenians had hastened across the border by the end of 1915, many of them in the space of a few weeks.[21] With great difficulty, given the condition of local roads and the absence of railway lines, they made their way from the region around Lake Van to established communities in already overcrowded villages and towns in the two uezds of Erevan and Elizavetpol'. In Aleksandropol' (modern-day Leninakan), relief workers found hundreds of refugees sheltering in railway wagons. Most suffered from dysentery or typhus, and had to share limited space with the corpses of those who had died en route.[22] The fortress town of Kars also offered apparent security, although this was later exposed as a cruelly thin veneer. Large numbers of refugees made for the Etchmidzian monastery at Igdir, a renowned place of learning and the seat of the Armenian Catholicos.[23] So many refugees were sick and malnourished (food had to be transported laboriously from Tbilisi and Erevan, and desperate refugees scavenged among the rubbish heaps) that mortality reached 50 percent in some locations. Poor drinking water encouraged the rapid spread of cholera. Proper medical facilities were put in place only in September.[24] The Armenian painter Martiros Saroian wrote to his friends, "Having spent nearly a month in this hell I have had to go back to Tbilisi."[25] In Tbilisi itself, "our children fell down and died from hunger on the main streets," wrote one eyewitness. The governor responded with an order banning any more refugees from settling in the city and forcing them to move to Erevan, where conditions were even worse.[26] The surrounding countryside scarcely offered better protection; most refugees found shelter in cattle pens, and only the seriously ill secured a place on the earth floor of the village school. In the Caucasus there seemed no end to the ordeal of refugees.[27]

PANIC IN THE PROVINCES

In the Russian interior, tsarist officials complained that they had little accurate information about the numbers, condition, and destination of refugees. Refugees did not move according to a predetermined timetable or a definite schedule of resettlement, and this reinforced the sense of impending chaos and confusion.[28] When information about refugee movement did filter through, it rang alarm bells in each governor's office and on each provincial zemstvo board. Each zemstvo board was bombarded with telegrams on a daily basis, detailing the number of refugees expected imminently to arrive in the province. The authorities in Kostroma pointed out that they could not accept anything like the 45,000 refugees who were apparently destined for the province in late September and October (one report spoke of 100,000 refugees); their consternation was all the more acute in view of the likelihood that the refugees would be unable to move farther east, because of the poor rail service beyond Kostroma and the imminent closure of the Volga River to traffic.[29] One uezd zemstvo official in Kursk province wrote in September 1915 to the executive committee of the VZS, requesting funds to assist 30,000 refugees in transit; within two weeks, this figure had quadrupled.[30] City authorities in their turn were also thrown into turmoil by the "disturbing apparition" of refugees.[31] The governor and mayor of Petrograd made no secret of their wish that refugees would be dispatched to other, more remote parts of the country at the earliest opportunity.[32] Some governors or their subordinates unilaterally switched the destination of refugee trains, sending them (for instance) to Turkestan rather than Siberia, and justifying their action on the grounds that their province was already over-crowded.[33] Keeping track of refugees who had traveled by road rather than by rail was virtually impossible.[34]

It was not just the number of refugees that caused a rising tide of panic, but their physical condition. Municipal leaders from Minsk province listened to reports of cold, hungry, and desperately ill refugees who arrived daily at railway stations (again, those who arrived by road were in even worse condition).[35] Twenty thousand reached Pinsk by 10 September. All of them were exhausted by the voyage. The town councilors were particularly concerned to prevent severely infected refugees from entering the town; they planned to build a new hospital on the outskirts for victims of cholera.[36] These measures oftentimes came too late to prevent the spread of epidemic disease. Cholera and typhus raged throughout southern Lithuania, Belorussia, and the provinces of Russia's southwest, prompting refugees to move or to be pushed farther east.[37]

Refugees who had survived the journey from the vicinity of the front faced all manner of immediate difficulties, particularly if they had traveled with only a handful of belongings. Food, housing, sanitary needs, and fresh clothing had to be found. Zemstvos provided underwear, shoes, and other items for refugees. Those suffering from infectious diseases required immediate attention. Once basic needs had been assessed, answers had to be found to the questions that refugees were asking. Children anxiously sought to establish whether their parents were alive or dead; adults yearned to be reunited with offspring with whom they had lost contact. Adult refugees badly needed legal advice about their status and entitlements to relief and financial compensation for the losses they had suffered. Children needed to be found somewhere to continue their education. Many able-bodied refugees longed to find work.[38]

Refugees were scattered far and wide, "from the remote Siberian taiga to scorching Turkestan."[39] It was not unusual for refugees to cross ten provincial frontiers. Many ended up in the southern province of Ekaterinoslav, in the central black earth province of Tambov, in the mid-Volga provinces of Saratov and Samara, and still farther afield. By the end of May 1916, there were 242,000 registered refugees in Ekaterinoslav (representing 7 percent of the provincial population), 166,000 in

Samara (4.4 percent), 127,000 in Tambov (3.6 percent), 114,000 in Khar'kov (3.3 percent), 113,000 in Saratov (4 percent), and 40,000 in Kazan' province. Some displaced persons, as we saw earlier, remained close to the front; an estimated 140,000 refugees remained in the southwestern province of Volynia in February 1916; in June 1916 there were 121,000 in Livland (7 percent of the province's total) and 115,000 in Minsk province (4 percent of the total).[40]

Refugees also found their way to the Urals, western Siberia, and even the Far East. The provincial governor of Ufa in the southern Urals reported that 228,000 refugees had entered his province during 1915, of whom 70,000 had settled there.[41] Arriving in Tomsk oblast, one of the centers of the prewar migration to Siberia, refugees hoped to obtain plots of land. To begin with, the local authorities made no distinction between refugees and the settlers, and undertook to explore the possibilities of setting aside farmland in Barnaul and Biisk uezds for up to 250 refugees in the first instance, with the assistance of the government's resettlement agency.[42] This is one of the relatively rare instances of refugees' readiness to put down permanent roots in the Russian interior. But the practice was regarded with some misgivings by government officials, who bemoaned the intense pressure that refugee settlement would place on the stock of Siberian farmland.[43] In the Far East, the Priamurskii krai had become home to some 4,000 refugees by the beginning of 1916. Several hundred crossed to the island of Sakhalin, where they lived quite comfortably.[44]

Some provinces, in central Russia as well as farther afield, virtually escaped the influx of refugees. The reasons for the uneven distribution of refugees still need to be unraveled.[45] A determined governor might arbitrarily refuse to accept refugees and insist on their immediate deportation. The governor of Simbirsk pointed out that the province was "already overflowing with refugees."[46] The Red Cross noted that officials in Kiev and Podol'ia adopted the same approach.[47] In the north Caucasus, too, the governor of Kuban closed the province to refugees in November 1915, although small numbers continued to settle there.[48] This kind of behavior probably became more widespread during 1916, when the Special Council stipulated that refugees should be prevented from moving from the province in which they had settled, unless they received official permission to do so.[49]

However, we should not be led by such regulations to think of the movement of refugees as a single journey from one destination to another. For many refugees the experience was one of continuous movement (although not for the *vyselentsy*, who were prevented from leaving). They were always vulnerable to abrupt decisions by the authorities to move them on. This happened to refugees on the northern front at the end of July and the beginning of August.[50] In September 1915, the chief of the Kiev Military District ordered refugees to leave the overcrowded city, pointing to the need to give priority to Russian troops.[51] Several thousand traveled from the western borderlands to Tashkent, where around 250,000 displaced people were registered by October 1915, 100,000 of whom were refugees. But by the middle of 1916 they were on the move again, arriving in the Volga towns of Samara and Bogorodsk, as well as in the Urals, where the climate was less oppressive and where pressures on accommodation, construction materials, and foodstuffs eased some-what.[52] This followed heart-rending accounts of refugee mortality in Turkestan, where refugee children, in particular, suffered from epidemics of smallpox and typhus, and where the hot summer threatened to bring an outbreak of malaria if preventive measures were not taken.[53] In a similar vein, a party of several thousand refugees was transferred from the remote Amur oblast to more congenial conditions in Perm'.[54] Faced with urban overcrowding in European Russia and a shortage of agricultural labor, some refugees were evacuated yet again, this time from cities such as Petrograd to villages in the depths of Russia, where peasant households received an allowance for their maintenance.[55]

Not all journeys involved long distances. The authorities in Moscow, home to some of Russia's worst tenements and flophouses (condemned in 1914 but now temporarily in use once more), built a new "model village" two miles outside the city for 5,000 refugees and dispatched them forthwith.[56] The main point, how-ever, is that many refugees were constantly on the move; the condition of refugee-dom remained synonymous with spatial mobility and uncertainty. Refugees who refused to leave towns and cities when asked to do so by municipal governors found themselves deprived of benefit payments. Several local councilors protested this crude attempt to deprive vulnerable refugees of subsistence; others colluded with the authorities. Determined refugees who insisted on remaining in what they deemed a relatively secure environment were often obliged to forfeit their welfare entitlements.[57]

EMERGENCY ASSISTANCE TO REFUGEES

The first priority was to ensure that the refugees were reasonably well fed. To what extent did refugees go hungry, and, if they did so, was their predicament more severe than that of their neighbors in Russia's densely populated and expanding urban centers? It is difficult to establish the quantity and quality of food consumed by people on the move. Obviously the refugee population lacked the resources at the disposal of the Russian army, which ensured that soldiers enjoyed a higher standard of nutrition than they had in peacetime. Nor could refugees initially draw upon the relatively abundant resources that were available to the settled population during 1915.[58] Much depended upon the resourcefulness of local officials, such as those employed on behalf of Severopomoshch', who devised a number of strategies to cajole merchants, army commanders, and municipal bureaucrats into releasing stocks of food. Refugees in Roslavl'—most of them Polish—received a daily portion of soup (one liter), one and a half pounds of bread (approximately 615 grams), half a pound of fresh meat (205 grams), 32 grams of fat, a quarter of a pound of groats (102 grams), 32 grams of sugar, 4 grams of tea, and such fresh vegetables as were available. The beneficiaries reportedly expressed their satisfaction with these rations, perhaps not surprisingly in view of the desperate straits in which they had found themselves en route to a place of safety.[59] It is unlikely that many others enjoyed a similar standard of nutrition. The staple diet provided by the mobile canteens set up by relief agencies tended to be basic, bland, and monotonous, consisting of tea, soup, bread, and kasha. Better food, or better-prepared food, would have reduced the incidence of serious stomach ailments.[60]

Questions concerning nutrition do not exhaust the issues that link food availability and population displacement. More was at stake than the apportionment of a sufficient number of calories. As has been well said, "Food is rich in codes of communication, memory and emotion. A forcible alteration of food habits goes to the very heart of tradition, expectations and identity."[61] How did refugees feel about having to forgo the domestic rituals of food preparation and consumption and to forage as best they could for food? How did they adjust to their dependence on charitable food parcels or leftovers? What were the psychological consequences of having to consume such food in public? Refugees often had to make do with food that turned their stomachs. From Iaroslavl' it was reported that Ukrainian peasants (*khokhly*) were being housed in a monastery where they received "Lenten food [*pishcha postnaia*], although they cannot live without meat and lard. For dinner they are given either fish soup or mushroom soup. But they don't eat smelt. . . . They can only recall these soups with disgust."[62]

There was also an urgent need for housing, which prompted similar initiatives and forced refugees to make similar adjustments. Emergency accommodation was found in railway stations, schools, empty factories, breweries, hotels, bathhouses, army barracks, monasteries, synagogues, theaters, cinemas, cafes, and even prisons.[63] From Tomsk came a report that local residents were offering accommodation in their own homes to refugees. Other Siberian towns placed resettlement shelters (that is, barracks and hostels used by settlers before 1914) at the temporary disposal of refugees, although it was agreed that in the long term they should be housed in apartments.[64] In Rostov the administration of the Vladikavkaz railway offered its warehouses to the municipal refugee committee and set aside wagons for bathing, cooking, and medical care for up to three thousand refugees.[65] The Tatiana Committee built a hostel for refugee children in Petrograd, which comprised "several pavilions, extremely original in design and construction."[66] Not all initiatives met with equal success. In Novocherkassk, the local refugee committee intended to

use the building owned by the right-wing Union of Russian People to house orphaned refugees, but the estimated costs of adapting the building proved too high,
and the committee was compelled to look elsewhere for appropriate accommodation.[67]

If the numbers and material needs of refugees seemed "overwhelming," their
physical condition was no less precarious. Many displaced persons fell victim to
cholera, typhus, dysentery, and smallpox en route to a place of safety. Children were
vulnerable to measles, scarlet fever, and diphtheria.[68] Intestinal illness was rife.[69]
Cholera and measles reached Voronezh, Ekaterinoslav, and other provincial towns
in September 1915. Tuberculosis became quite widespread.[70] The incidence of infectious disease placed a severe strain on medical personnel, whose resources had
already been stretched by twelve months of war. It appears that in some instances
refugees were poorly looked after, by virtue of a shortage of trained staff. In central
Asia, fewer than one hundred doctors and feldshers (health-care auxiliaries) cared
for 80,000 refugees, far too few in view of the condition of the refugees and the
spread of typhus and smallpox.[71] In Voronezh, the local relief committee agreed that
all refugees should be subject to "vigilant medical inspection," and those at risk
were to be hospitalized with all speed. By October, it was reported that the town
of Saratov—"solid and well built to the point of dullness," in Paustovsky's view—
badly needed a new hospital, particularly to attend to the needs of refugee children.[72] Not all local authorities were quite so willing to accommodate sick refugees.
In Poltava, the town council complained to the provincial governor that the province's main hospital—administered by the zemstvo—had refused to admit refugee
children who were suffering from scarlet fever. The municipal and zemstvo hospital
in Simbirsk declined to admit the chronically ill, and the town council was obliged
to ask the local Tatiana Committee to accept responsibility for their care.[73] As winter approached, typhus replaced cholera as the main threat to public health. Conditions were particularly atrocious in the Caucasus, where in an oblast containing
35,000 refugees, around 400 deaths were reported daily: "Local agencies are powerless to help." In Turkestan, infant and child mortality reached emergency proportions. Not since the great cholera epidemic of 1848 had Russia faced such a health
crisis.[74]

PUBLIC PROVISION, PRIVATE RESPONSES

Early accounts of the attention bestowed on refugees emphasize a broad and
speedy response (at least after some initial trepidation), in which charitable impulses were combined with expediency. Just as the outbreak of war had prompted

national unity, so the initial influx of refugees reportedly generated widespread sympathy and a generous reaction to appeals for help. Many kinds of support involved face-to-face assistance. The "exhausted and terrified" refugees who arrived in Kostroma in July received a warm welcome.[75] Here, as elsewhere, arrangements began to be made for the distribution of food parcels and medical assistance.[76] Emergency canteens were created, including special provision for the dietary needs of Jewish refugees. Hospital administrators set aside wards for those who required immediate medical attention. Collections of money, food, shoes, and clothing became commonplace. Church services became an occasion to show one's generosity to "war sufferers." Banks and firms donated funds. Inevitably, most of the burden of relief fell upon Russia's towns and cities, where voluntary charities to assist the poor had begun to emerge after the turn of the century.[77] Individuals who responded to appeals to relieve the suffering of Armenian refugees enclosed messages of support along with their donations: "I hope that my donation will at least help a family of poor refugees, and I shall send five rubles each month until the end of the war"; "My sympathy is much greater than the widow's mite that I am sending; may God comfort the Armenians."[78] Those who campaigned to improve the lot of refugees comforted themselves with the knowledge that the Russian public had an "instinctive" desire to help the less fortunate.[79]

Committees created at the outbreak of war for the purpose of assisting soldiers' dependents turned their minds to the relief of refugees.[80] Most towns, including those hundreds of miles from the front, hurriedly formed new committees to deal with the relief of refugees. As early as 4 August 1915, the municipal authorities in Perm'—a modestly sized provincial town in the Urals, more than 1500 kilometers from the front line—established a special committee to assist refugees, with five subcommittees that looked after refugees' need for housing, medical attention, food and clothing, and employment. Another subcommittee processed the refugee population, and dealt with refugees who had been separated from members of their families. The authorities turned their attention to the minutiae of refugee relief, agreeing to set aside funds for the purchase of bread and milk, and to acquire 500 sets of bed linens, 1,000 straw mattresses, 3,000 teacups, plates, and wooden spoons. Similar arrangements were reported from Ekaterinburg.[81] In Simbirsk, the diocesan council and the Tatiana Committee drew up a similar list of items, petty in themselves but vital to the comfort of refugees: soap, sugar, tea, clean linens, mattresses, pencils, mugs, and cutlery.[82] In Taganrog, "feelings of Christian charity toward their suffering brothers welled up among the local population, conscious also of their duty before the motherland," as a result of which the town organized the distribution of Christmas trees and sweets to refugee children. Youngsters were shown films that were thought likely to be interesting and instructive.[83] The local inhabitants of Tomsk—initially accused of being "unwelcoming" to refugees—developed a particular attachment to the children's home, which they supported assiduously.[84]

Subsequent reports elaborated this image of uninterrupted benevolence. The Tatiana Committee drew attention to dozens of its provincial branches that brought together local officials, priests, landlords, teachers, lawyers, and peasant officers.[85] Urusov's organization relied upon the same kind of local elite—in other words, those who enjoyed "a certain authority."[86] In the aftermath of the first big wave of refugee movement, the Ministry of the Interior asked provincial governors what role local officials had played in arranging for the emergency care and relocation of refugees in rural Russia. The answers painted a bright picture of humane and selfless intervention by hundreds of land captains who organized relief with the assistance—not partnership—of a range of local bodies, and who had begun to inculcate in the local population "the sense of one's moral obligation to come to the aid of the victims of war."[87] Even where provinces had been "overwhelmed" by the scale of the refugee influx, as in Tula, governors reported that emergency facilities were in place to feed refugees.[88] Children who had been abandoned in Baranovichi were taken to Petrograd, where "traditional Russian kindliness in the face of adversity will ensure that these poor nameless children will be adopted."[89] The Tatiana Committee reported proudly that the speedy establishment of orphanages and refuges in Russia's major towns meant that "the issue of children who have been thrown upon the mercy of fate has lost its original intensity."[90]

A particularly important role was played by the Orthodox church. Bishops had already begun to serve as chairmen of provincial Tatiana committees. The diocesan committees devoted part of their energies to the welfare of priests and nuns, making arrangements for the evacuation of church property and reestablishing seminaries and monasteries in the Russian interior.[91] But they appropriated a much broader range of functions than this and did not confine their activities to members of the clergy who had been displaced. During the summer of 1915, the synod issued instructions for diocesan committees to engage in refugee relief. It was the duty of priests to visit refugees on a regular basis, to remind them of their religious obligations, to ensure that they were supplied with an icon and psalter, and to arrange religious readings and instruction. Their moral as well as spiritual requirements should be heeded. Priests were enjoined to promote useful and honest toil among refugees, to encourage the proper use of leisure time, and to check that refugees looked after their bodies, washed their clothes, and kept their surroundings clean. Refugees needed also to be reminded of any government decrees and regulations that they should abide by.[92] In Vladimir, the diocesan committee arranged emergency shelter for refugees prior to their resettlement in local villages. Its counterpart in Ekaterinoslav met refugees at railway stations, arranged emergency accommodation (the committee prided itself on the iron bedsteads and stuffed mattresses), and delivered food from the canteen owned by the Union of Russian People. In Ekaterinburg, clergy were urged to attend in particular to the needs of poor refugees of the Orthodox faith. Spiritual and material needs justified this kind of intervention.[93]

In his annual report for 1915, the municipal governor of Nikolaev spoke of the relief measures taken by the city council to set aside apartments and provide food and medical care; similar support had been provided by the local committee of the Union of Towns.[94] The provincial governors of Ufa and Kursk were also eager to emphasize the degree of cooperation to be found among all relief agencies; so, too, was Count Tolstoi, the mayor of Petrograd.[95] Provincial newspapers endorsed these sanguine assessments. Local committees for the relief of the sick and wounded quickly adapted to take on additional responsibility for the care of refugees In Iaroslavl', buildings, beds, and blankets were set aside for refugees.[96] Local dignitaries sponsored fireworks displays, concerts, and popular festivals (*gulian'e*) to welcome the strangers and to raise funds. In Khar'kov, the Union of Towns arranged theatrical performances for newly arrived refugees in the local workers' rest home "as a first practical step" to alleviate suffering. The Tatiana Committee in Tver' raised money from the sale of flowers and postcards featuring a portrait of the tsar's daughter.[97] Workers at the Tula Cartridge Works decided, with the approval of the provincial governor, to establish their own committee for the relief of refugees, although its relationship with the existing municipal organization was an uncomfortable one.[98] A sour note was introduced by a newspaper report on the plight of refugees in Samara, where the Union of Towns, the Union of Zemstvos, and the local Tatiana Committee squabbled over their respective responsibilities for the care of refugees in the city.[99]

New kinds of associative activity also began to be harnessed to the task of refugee relief. In Ekaterinoslav, the governor drew attention to the role of local cooperatives; in Orel, several credit unions were engaged on emergency refugee projects. In September 1915, a congress of cooperatives resolved to create guardianships with—unusually—the participation of refugees themselves, and to urge cooperatives to cater to their needs, for example by sewing warm clothes. Voluntary organizations flourished as local citizens became aware of the scale of the refugee movement. From Petrograd came reports of an organization called "Fraternal Response" (Bratskii otklik) whose members planned to accompany refugees en route from the front to a place of safety. In Moscow, a group calling itself "Rapid Aid to Refugees" operated canteens and hostels at some of the city's main railway stations.[100]

Before long, however, the strain on local finances—and thus on reserves of municipal goodwill—began to show. Few local authorities had anticipated a constant wave of refugees, as occurred in the late summer of 1915. Impoverished by years

of fiscal neglect and overwhelmed by pressing social and economic problems, it is
not surprising that many local authorities felt overwhelmed by this new responsibility. Subventions from municipal budgets, supplemented by organized lotteries to
raise extra cash, were sufficient for only the most basic purposes.[101] When the
public organizations met in Brest-Litovsk at the end of July 1915 to debate the lack
of central control over refugee settlement, their main aim was to keep refugees out
of urban Russia, to which end they advocated the creation of transit points at Pskov,
Dvinsk, Minsk, Gomel', and Kiev. To do nothing was to invite those authorities who
had arranged their affairs more promptly to unload refugees on towns that were
unprepared. In this manner, expediency helped as much as charitable impulse to
condition local responses to the emergency.[102]

Many local government officials expressed serious misgivings about the burden
they were expected to shoulder. Several cities and towns were, by their own admis-
sion, bursting at the seams. In Moscow and Kazan', for instance, the university
medical schools now provided care and rehabilitation for thousands of disabled,
sick, and wounded soldiers. Moscow was described as a "giant hospital." Refugees,
who would only add to the stock of human misery, needed to be moved on at the
earliest opportunity.[103] Other towns likewise proclaimed their inability to do more
than provide for the short-term needs of refugees before sending them on their
way, lest they "engulf" the urban space any further. The small provincial town of
Rybinsk reported in September that it was "full," and that the 3,000 refugees already settled there threatened the welfare of the town. The population of Pskov
almost doubled during the second half of 1915, from 50,000 to 90,000, prompting
similar complaints.[104] In Ekaterinoslav, the city authorities pointed out that prewar
in-migration had put the housing stock and health services under enormous strain,
and had contributed to soaring prices for basic goods. In the circumstances, it was
imperative to deter refugees from attempting to settle in the city.[105] The authorities
in Tomsk complained that refugees continued to pour into the town throughout August and early September, and urged that the tide be stemmed before thousands of
displaced people became trapped by the onset of winter weather. Municipal cemeteries could no longer cope with the demand for burial space. In Roslavl', for example, where more than 75,000 refugees were in transit camps in the middle of
September, a local landowner refused to set aside land for the extension of the
town's cemetery; as a result, the town council sought permission to requisition his
land.[106]

Notwithstanding the unease of municipal authorities about the influx of refugees, urban settlements acted as a particular magnet for the displaced. Around
84,000 refugees had settled in Petrograd by December 1915; three months later,
the refugee population of Russia's capital had reportedly jumped to 100,000.[107] Ten
thousand refugees in Nizhnii Novgorod had turned the famous market district into

a "living town"; refugees constituted one-quarter of the total urban population.[108] The population of Ekaterinoslav was swelled by the influx of 30,000 refugees, who accounted for almost a quarter of the total by the summer of 1916.[109] In Khar'kov (whose population, including the suburbs, stood at 244,170 on 1 January 1914), refugees numbered 45,000; by early 1916 they made up one-fifth of the city's rapidly expanding population. In the city of Samara, the refugee population amounted to 41,000 in June 1916, equivalent to an astonishing three-tenths of the total. Briansk, a small town of 35,000 before the war, underwent a massive transformation: by early 1916 its population had jumped to 85,000, including 18,000 refugees.[110] Closer to the front, refugees in Vitebsk (18,000 in June 1916) constituted 17 percent of the total; in Minsk (also home to 18,000 refugees) the proportion was the same. The small town of Pskov contained 8,000 refugees by June 1916, nearly a quarter of its total population.[111]

What of the responses of established urban communities to the appearance of refugees? Some early appeals for help made much of the expectation that refugees "will not be staying long in our midst. The enemy will leave the frontiers of Russia, and the refugees will once more return to their own homes."[112] Other observers spoke condescendingly of "our transient guests."[113] But few people probably believed this kind of gung-ho patriotism, which was in any event quickly supplanted by the realization that refugees would be around for some time to come. As the journal of the Union of Zemstvos acknowledged in the autumn of 1915, "We must not lose sight of the fact that the refugees are our guests, and not for a brief period, either." Some of them would wish to stay permanently.[114] Refugees who remained for any length of time quickly exhausted the resources and patience of the urban population. By September 1915, at least one local newspaper complained that some local citizens spent too much time in the cinema and paid insufficient attention to the needs of the indigent newcomers.[115] Tikhon Polner suggests that initial sympathy and hospitality rapidly evaporated as their neighbors realized that refugees had no money to pay for accommodation or food. In some places, "there were fears of disorders and riots."[116] Refugees were given a warm welcome in Orenburg, although their relations with the local population cooled somewhat once the latter realized the extent of their commitment. This pattern was repeated elsewhere, giving rise to expectations that the state should play a much larger role in refugee welfare.[117]

At a more mundane level, complaints were made that refugees did not appreciate the generosity of local people: "One good turn deserves another," in the words of an author writing in the Samara diocesan bulletin, a year after refugees had first settled in the town.[118] Although refugees were entitled to charitable assistance, they "should not be taught to become parasites and spongers."[119] There are plenty of examples of prejudice and jealousy on the part of people who felt that refugees were unwilling to work in order to support themselves, and that they would in general place an intolerable burden on their hosts. "They will probably want coffee with cream and not with milk," cried the residents of Ekaterinburg, evidently shocked by such extravagance. Uncorroborated reports appeared of refugees who took posts as domestic servants, only to decamp in the middle of the night with the belongings of the employers whose trust they had betrayed.[120]

These tensions were compounded by the realization that the financial support offered to many refugees was more generous than the allowances paid to families of conscripted men. In Khar'kov, for example, refugees were entitled to six rubles per month for food, and six rubles for housing. Following protests that soldiers' dependents received only four rubles twenty kopecks for food and five rubles for housing, the allowances paid to refugees were promptly reduced.[121] A further cause for complaint, as we shall see, was that refugees of different nationalities received differing levels of welfare benefit. Few issues could be guaranteed to provoke greater indignation and resentment.

Opportunism, greed, and—at times—class enmity colored the response of local people toward refugees. In Iaroslavl', "intellectual and well-to-do refugees have been forced to suffer many tribulations, because many local householders for some reason do not want to lease their apartments, or else stipulate draconian conditions, asking for three months' rent in advance."[122] In Smolensk, the municipal authorities declared war on inflated rents. In Tver', a blistering attack was launched on those "dishonest, greedy and callous people who are prepared to live at the expense of those of our unfortunate brothers, devastated by the war"; the councilors promised a "relentless" struggle against such exploitation.[123] In Russia's capital city, the police launched their own campaign by checking furnished apartments and hotels to gain a more precise picture of the availability of housing.[124]

Plenty of other opportunities presented themselves to people who wished to exploit the vulnerability of refugees. The *izvoshchiki* (cab drivers) in Petrograd charged extortionate fares to the distressed passengers who arrived at the Warsaw railway station.[125] Nor was the Orthodox church immune from accusations of heartlessness. The Special Council for Refugees heard that clergymen were demanding large amounts of money in order to conduct religious ceremonies, including burial services, for refugees. Some priests offered refugees accommodation in church buildings, but in penny-pinching fashion did not provide adequate lighting or ventilation.[126]

Yet there were also reports that "relations between local residents and our comrades (i.e., from Riga) are cordial. The ordinary people regard us as victims who have fled the horrors of war. They give us presents, and ask after those who are most needy. Russian workers look upon us differently, as special mates who can throw a shaft of sunlight into their dark barracks. They are very curious about our former living conditions, pay, orderliness, tidiness, and so forth."[127] Moscow workers who belonged to sick clubs reportedly organized a collection for refugees and helped them to find work in the city, notwithstanding opposition from their less "conscious" colleagues.[128] Nor were all local landlords rapacious and opportunistic. A report appeared in a refugee newspaper of a "kindly landlord" who had reduced his rent upon learning that the tenants were to be refugee women and children: "There are people in Petrograd with a soul and a conscience!"[129]

Positive assessments of popular sentiment are also to be found in the reports of provincial governors, as in Kursk, where it was noted that "no one has declined to aid and assist the refugees." Students offered to give lessons to refugee children, and doctors to treat refugee patients without charging for their services.[130] In Irkutsk, teachers enrolled peasant refugees in special schools, funded in part by voluntary deductions from their salaries.[131] Boy Scouts in Petrograd joined in the task of finding accommodation for refugees. According to a leading liberal newspaper in Russia's capital city, "Notwithstanding their abiding reputation for being egotistical, indifferent, and unsympathetic to the fate of others, the population has for the most part responded warmly and compassionately to the hordes of refugees."[132] Nor were the moral consequences of refugeedom overlooked: the appearance of refugees in Siberia had the salutary effect of bringing home the horrific consequences of war to the local population.[133]

REFUGEES IN THE RUSSIAN COUNTRYSIDE

For these reasons—the creation of an organized relief effort, the scope for refugees to establish community solidarity, the access to schools, churches, newspapers, and theaters—refugees were reluctant to sever their links with urban life, notwithstanding the grudging welcome they might receive from hard-pressed urban residents. Unless they were experienced farmers or agricultural laborers, refugees regarded life in the village as distinctly inferior to that in town; and even those who could turn their hand to farming knew that once they began to farm a plot of land in Russia, they might find it difficult to return to their homeland. Other refugees never even entertained the prospect of a rural existence. To leave the relative security of the town for the dubious comfort of the village was a prospect that they regarded with alarm, "and not without reason."[134]

Many refugees nonetheless chose or were forced to settle in the countryside. Reports reached Vladimir that the government had plans to settle some refugees in deserted peasant dwellings and to encourage peasants to adopt others as farm workers. There was even talk, "in extreme cases," of forcing refugees to move to villages, where they would form "a kind of military colony." But the tsarist state—

perhaps because of fears of peasant protest, perhaps remembering previous experiments with military settlements—never worked out a systematic plan of settlement, leaving this instead to the discretion of provincial governors and local authorities.[135]

What was the reaction of the Russian peasantry to these strangers in their midst? Most peasants lived out their lives within the framework of a village community, a thriving forum that regulated the behavior of, allocated resources among, and gave meaning to the lives of its peasant members. One did not earn membership and thus entitlement to the protection and benefits of the community; one belonged by virtue of birth. Given this sense of communal belonging and kinship ties, the war was bound to be a disturbing process. The exposure of rural communities to the arriving refugees formed but one aspect of a profoundly unsettling experience for Russian villagers. The peasant community had simultaneously to come to terms with the hasty departure of its adult men, frequently heads of households who had overall responsibility for the allocation of tasks within the household or *dvor*, as well as for decision-making in the community as a whole. Other familiar faces came and went: teachers, priests, agronomists, veterinary specialists, and land surveyors left to take up positions elsewhere, while disabled soldiers and prisoners—in addition to refugees—arrived in the village. In other words, the notion of community was being redefined: strengthened perhaps by the departure of outsiders who represented officialdom and by the collapse of commitments of labor and cash to the local landlord economy, but challenged by the arrival of new strangers. But issues of membership, departure, and exclusion constitute an agenda for future research: much more work needs to be done before reliable conclusions can be drawn. Certainly peasants displayed widespread aversion to fellow villagers who had once belonged to the commune but were now deemed to have made themselves "outsiders" by having taken advantage of the Stolypin legislation to privatize their plots. But these victims of peasant communal anger and violence had, so to speak, offended the community from within. Refugees "belonged" to a different category, at least from the perspective adopted by influential government advisers, who expressed doubts about the desirability of placing refugees with peasant communities. According to a group of lawyers in October 1915, "The rural volost assemblies are entitled to arrange for the guardianship [*opeka*] only of those people who are members of the village or volost society; and in no way can refugees belong to such societies, since they are completely different from the Russian peasant masses by virtue of custom and tradition."[136]

Peasants appear to have been more receptive and tolerant toward outsiders who found themselves staying in the village through no fault of their own. Refugees from Grodno were lodged with Russian peasants in the central industrial region and were "treated as members of the family."[137] The governor of Stavropol' reported in

February 1916 that local peasants "regard the fate of refugees with broad sympathy and compassion," although he did not say on what basis he arrived at this conclusion. In Tver', refugees met with a "good-natured welcome and sympathy," again according to the provincial governor. His colleague in Kiev spoke of the "cheerfulness" with which peasants came to the assistance of refugees. Here, as elsewhere, peasants donated grain to feed the newcomers, in response to local appeals by the Tatiana Committee to contribute to the campaign for "scoops from the 1915 harvest."[138] A correspondent for *Irkutskaia zhizn'* wrote of the cordial reception that refugees had received from Buriat herdsmen in Siberia.[139] In the Caucasus, Armenian farmers extended a warm welcome to refugees, "out of humanity and common national feeling."[140] In Ekaterinoslav, peasant cooperators sought to settle some of the newcomers on vacant state land, and to rent privately owned land on their behalf. More remarkable was the suggestion that peasants and refugees should get to know one another better: "In order to understand and meet the needs of refugees as quickly as possible, we should invite one or two of their number to attend the executive committee of the cooperative."[141]

In the absence of organized poor relief and other formal institutions in the village, the influx of refugees necessarily entailed a good deal of rapid improvisation. Each governor had a story to tell of the charitable activity undertaken by peasant officers, such as the local village scribe, foreman, or elder—in short, "the most respected peasants."[142] The governor of Akmolinsk spoke of the generosity of peasant leaders who "have spared neither effort nor money in constantly touring the locality and in a flurry of paperwork."[143] Provincial governors described the participation of village teachers, priests, doctors, and peace arbitrators in local charitable guardianships, which registered new arrivals and distributed food and cash allowances.[144] But the readiness of the village elite to assist refugees could not disguise the difficulties and the costs incurred by ordinary peasant households.

An anonymous peasant diarist provided a unique insight into the reception that refugees encountered, not from village officials but from ordinary peasants. He drew his readers' attention to the fact that finding refugees somewhere to live was a sensitive issue. Peasants were inevitably put to a great deal of trouble and expense. The village assembly devoted several hours to discussing the arrangements for accommodating refugees and supplying them with fuel. Several peasant families maintained that they had already made a disproportionate contribution to the war effort by sending their menfolk to the army: should they also have to bear the burden of supporting refugees? There was talk of a rotation of duties, whereby refugees would stay for a month with one household and then be taken in by another; to those members of the assembly who thought this an insulting arrangement, others replied that refugees were likely to be indifferent to this kind of disruption. Someone proposed that those who refused outright to take in refugees should pay compensation to their neighbors "for the overcrowding and inconvenience." Many peasants complained that refugees had unrealistic expectations of village life, wanting three hot meals a day and an oven that was never allowed to go cold. Yet the lively debate in the peasant assembly revealed more than a little compassion and insight into the needs of refugees: "They have little to wear, nothing to put on their feet, and there may have been nothing for them to eat." This was coupled with a resolute insistence that, while they could take in 140 refugees, the village had no room for the 330 individuals whom the zemstvo wished to settle there.[145] In a familiar refrain, peasants' readiness to offer hospitality was qualified by the knowledge that they would be expected to shoulder the burden themselves, without any official financial assistance.[146]

Particular tensions were expected to be generated by the appearance of Russian Jews in rural areas from which they had previously been excluded. Government ministers extrapolated from isolated incidents to predict the imminent disintegration of public order as a consequence of the enforced proximity between local people and Jews: "In various localities the atmosphere became more and more dangerous; the Jews were furious with everyone and everything, while the local inhabitants were angry at the uninvited guests who, moreover, were being denounced as traitors and were angered by conditions under which it became impossible to survive."[147] Notwithstanding these comments, which have been repeated by scholars subsequently, it is not clear that there were widespread outbreaks of peasant protest against Jewish refugees.[148] These fears have to be set in the context of past encounters that no doubt lingered on in official memory.[149] Conditions in 1915 and 1916, however, were very different, and this may explain why the "Jewish question" is rarely raised in the reports submitted to the MVD by provincial governors. Peasants enjoyed an upturn in their economic fortunes; many had extra cash in hand, and there was no lack of work. Jewish refugees hardly seemed a significant threat to current prosperity, having in any case little in common with the stereotyped Jewish plutocrat or moneylender. It should be remembered that many of the participants in pogroms during 1881–82 and 1905 were not villagers but deracinated peasants, members of an urban lumpenproletariat who were looking for jobs in towns and ports. They competed for jobs with Jewish workers. Precisely because no constraints could be imposed by the land commune or by members of the peasant household, these groups were particularly prone to participate in pogroms. It should not come as a surprise that peasants reportedly maintained amicable relations with Jews newly arrived in villages in the central black earth region.[150] In Nizhnii Novgorod, Jewish refugees were given a warm welcome by villagers who offered gifts of flour and firewood. Although the atmosphere appears to have deteriorated in later months, this reflected widespread pressures on the peasant economy, conditioning their attitude toward all newcomers, not just Jewish refugees.[151]

RECKONING WITH REFUGEEDOM

Refugeedom implied a reconsideration of the representation of space. To appreciate this point, one has only to recall how repeatedly provincial and municipal authorities argued that the "limits" of towns and provinces had been reached—in other words, that the ratio of population and territory in a particular locality had reached critical proportions. Whether or not an individual province or town could or would admit additional numbers of refugees, their very presence forced local authorities and professional people—statisticians, doctors, engineers, agronomists—to rethink the relationship between people and territory, between "man" and "nature." In the Don oblast and in Kuban', a commission was set up to define the "capacity" (*emkost'*) of the region. Local agencies in Siberia made precise estimates of the number of refugees that the towns could accommodate.[152] However, Urusov took the view that this was too important a matter to be left to local officials, such as volost clerks; special commissioners should undertake the job instead. By November he instructed his staff to calculate how many refugees could be allocated to each province, so that the proportion of refugees would not exceed 5 percent of the provincial total.[153]

There are numerous other instances in which local opinion was mobilized in "defense" of a particular conception of political arithmetic. Petrograd, for example, became the site of acrimonious exchanges about the number of people that the capital city could "contain," an issue regarded in some quarters as embracing "interests of state," in the pursuit of which it became "expedient" to take steps to evacuate thousands of refugees to the surrounding countryside or to less congested parts of the empire.[154] A secret discussion took place in the cabinet, where ministers focused on the deteriorating food supply in the capital. Having ruled out the evacuation of soldiers, the government planned to alleviate pressure on resources by removing "superfluous ballast," including the refugee population, whose chief reason for living in Petrograd was the hope or expectation of receiving a higher allowance or higher wages.[155] The contrary view was expressed in the Special Council by the chairman of the Tatiana Committee, Senator A. B. Neidgardt, who argued that the 35,000 refugees registered in Petrograd (his figures referred to September 1915) could not be regarded as an excessive number, particularly given that "there are not a few towns where such a number would be equivalent to the size of the indigenous population."[156]

The Ministry of the Interior repeated the tactic a few months later, when it ordered that all refugees who were in receipt of government relief were to leave Petrograd no later than 1 September 1916, to relieve overcrowding in the capital.

Once again, Neidgardt protested that the size of the population in the Russian capital had already begun to fall from 100,000 to less than 80,000, at least half of whom did not rely on state welfare. He was supported by the leading lawyer A. F. Koni, who complained that what the MVD proposed was immoral and unworkable. The spokesman for the Lithuanian National Committee pointed out that refugees were vulnerable to the emotional consequences of yet another upheaval in their lives; in any case, some refugees had decided of their own volition to move elsewhere. The general consensus among liberal members of the council was that the economic problems besetting Petrograd should not be laid at the door of the refugee population. But Stürmer retorted that he had already made up his mind and saw no reason to change his decision.[157] In a different vein, the veteran economist P. I. Georgievskii suggested that it would not be difficult to accommodate as many as 3 million refugees in the Russian interior, whose population exceeded 100 million; villages with up to twenty households could easily make room for an extra three refugee households apiece. The main issue was to allocate the refugee population in a "correct" fashion, avoiding their concentration in overcrowded conurbations.[158]

As we saw in the previous chapter, overall responsibility for the relief of refugees was vested in the Special Council for Refugees. In January 1916 the Special Council formally stipulated a range of benefits to which refugees were entitled. These included the right to food (including one hot meal per day), housing (including heating and light), medical attention, clothing, footwear, and linen. Benefit payments for food and lodgings could be revised upward if the refugee was single; and a sliding scale was introduced to reduce per capita allowances for large families. The official regulations also made provision for the availability of legal aid for refugees and education for refugee children. Refugees were to be offered help in looking for work. Financial help was to be provided for the maintenance or repair of any belongings that had an economic purpose. In addition, the council undertook to attend to refugees' religious and cultural needs. Finally, refugees were entitled to free passage on the railway network to a place of settlement (as well as free travel if they subsequently moved to jobs in the agricultural sector). Further work is needed to establish the degree to which these rules were followed or modified by the Council of Ministers. In practice, they appear to have been a statement of good practice, to which local agencies in the voluntary sector as well as provincial refugee commissions were instructed to adhere.[159]

What kind of burden did the care of refugees impose on the Russian treasury? In all, the tsarist government and its successor spent more than 600 million rubles, directly and indirectly, on the relief of the refugee population up to and including October 1917.[160] This amounted to around 1.5 percent of the total war expenditure. To put it into perspective, this sum was equivalent to one-fifth of the transfer payments made to soldiers' families.[161] In part, this disparity was a result of the huge numbers of men who passed through the Russian army's conscription machine. But it also reflected the official view that refugees should contribute to their own maintenance and take advantage of private charitable assistance, whereas soldiers' families were believed to be in serious economic distress as a result of conscription, injury, and death of the male breadwinner. Twelve months after it was formed, the Special Council came under pressure from the Ministry of Finances to curtail spending, on the grounds that the relief of refugees had never been expected to cost so much. Government ministers agreed that the Special Council should seek ways to curb its allocations to relief agencies, particularly as many refugees were thought to be claiming benefits from more than one source. It was in this context that the allowance paid to refugees was cut in 1916 and other measures were taken to reduce the cost of relief.[162]

This account of government and voluntary initiatives would not be complete without mentioning the extensive records that were kept of refugees. The army encouraged the public organizations to maintain proper records, partly to improve the distribution of food, but also as a means of checking that refugees did not harbor deserters.[163] Many municipal authorities required refugees to submit to close questioning and to supply information about their place of origin, family status, and occupation, in exchange for which they were entitled to claim financial support. This entitlement could subsequently be withdrawn if a refugee declined to accept work.[164] The provincial Tatiana committees made equally strenuous attempts to obtain information from refugees. In Khar'kov, for example, the local relief committee demanded proof from each applicant that "he had genuinely arrived from a locality that suffered from the effects of military action"; non-Russian refugees were additionally required to show whether or not they received any support from the relevant national committee.[165] National committees for refugee relief were urged by the government to issue a certificate of nationality to refugees; this was especially important in view of the frequency with which Latvian refugees were mistaken for German settlers.[166] Throughout Europe, the war promoted an orgy of paperwork. Russia was no exception, and refugeedom became the single most important stimulus to the gathering and processing of information about the tsar's subjects.

CONCLUSION

The sudden appearance of several million refugees in the western borderlands and the interior of European Russia posed a challenge to provincial authorities and citizens that was unprecedented in its scale and intensity. The needs of refugees were urgent and profound. Local people drew upon and extended the existing networks of charitable relief, in an impressive demonstration of the scope and vitality of civic activism. Organized relief did not substitute for demonstrations of sincerity and personal kindness.[167] Peasant communities and cooperatives harnessed their established mechanisms of self-help to the task of assisting the newcomers. Municipal activists and villagers alike absorbed themselves in refugee relief, with understandable disquiet about its longer-term implications: they were overstretched long before the refugees made their presence felt. This makes the relief effort all the more impressive in retrospect. At the highest levels of state, too, officials wrestled with the financial consequences of refugee displacement. Some of the worst fears—of urban collapse, of widespread pogroms—were not realized, a mark perhaps of the wilder flights of imagination to which the events of 1915 gave rise, as well as a tribute to the vitality and energy that went into refugee resettlement and relief.

Underlying the humanitarian relief efforts and making them manageable was a composite picture of the deserving, suffering, and vulnerable refugee. It is to the construction of this consolidated image, as well as to contrary imaginings, that the following chapter is devoted.

4.

∾

CONSOLIDATING REFUGEEDOM

There are refugees and "refugees."
　—*MOSKOVSKIE VEDOMOSTI,* 11 OCTOBER 1915

Continue to love the refugee.
　—A. B. NEIDGARDT, QUOTED IN *TRUDOVAIA POMOSHCH',* 9, 1916

*It should not be forgotten that refugees are living people; they have had
the misfortune to be displaced, but they are human beings all the same.*
　—EDITORIAL, *BEZHENETS,* 18 OCTOBER 1915

The tsarist government and the public organizations competed for the right to assume overall administrative responsibility for the fate of refugees, a struggle in
which the bureaucratic forces emerged victorious by virtue of their tight grip on
financial resources. Yet, as we have seen, the familiar state–society antagonism does
not do full justice to the realities of refugee relief. The basic tasks of providing
emergency relief and attempting to resettle refugees were implemented by a range
of bodies in the government, "public," and voluntary sectors. But it was one thing
to provide funds and for various local agencies to make arrangements for emergency
material assistance, by providing food, clothes, shelter, and fuel. How could this
effort be bolstered, once the first charitable impulses had worn out?[1] What assumptions were made about refugees? How and to what extent did ordinary Russians
grow accustomed to certain standards of concern and become conscious of a
broader sense of obligation toward refugees? How important were newspapers and
photographs in helping to shape popular opinion about refugees and to organize
programs of social welfare? What kinds of stories did Russians tell one another in
order to justify the sustained forms of assistance that would lead either to an increased burden on the public purse, or to a more extensive voluntary commitment, or to both? What fears were projected onto refugees? How, finally, did it come
about that the movement of "the most varied elements" acquired the designation of
"refugeedom" (*bezhenstvo*)?[2]

IMAGINING THE REFUGEE: THE RUSSIAN MEDIA

Let us begin with the suggestion that the impulse to relieve suffering was based
on the elaboration of compelling narratives of suffering, misery, and despair—that

is, pain that could be countered only by private charity or organized public relief. Despite the fact that the supply of funds rested with the central government, the day-to-day welfare of refugees ultimately depended on semi-official agencies and voluntary involvement.[3] In this respect, at least initially, their position was not un-like that of Russia's poor, for whom organized public assistance had been virtually nonexistent before 1914. The analogy was made in an ironic editorial in the con-temporary press, by a critic who sought to shame the government into more orga-nized intervention: "The refugee is much like the pauper, who can be 'relieved' with a five-kopeck piece. There's your coin, be thankful. If you're not satisfied with that, then you've just got no manners [*znachit grubiian*]."[4] But official relief, even when it began to take shape, was never regarded as a sufficient panacea, particularly in view of the distinctly modest achievements to its credit before the war. Personal generosity continued to matter, as religious leaders never tired of pointing out: "God has favored us with an abundant harvest from our fields, gardens, meadows, and orchards. Share some of these gifts from God with those who have been deprived of everything by the savage enemy."[5]

Much depended on the images that were generated in the mass media, calculated to appeal either to charitable sentiments or to more selfish considerations. The role of the eyewitness as a privileged observer of refugees' condition and needs was all-important. As a leading general wrote in his memoirs, "Only those who have actually seen the flight of the Russian population can in any way conceive the hor-rors that attended it."[6] The newly established journal *Armianskii vestnik* published regular reports from correspondents who had seen the heart-rending condition of Armenian refugees and wished to share their exclusive knowledge with a wider audience. One relief worker in the small town of Aleksandropol' bore "witness to the death throes of starving people, listening to their last anguished groans or accompanying the carts that took corpses to common graves."[7]

It became necessary to shape the experience of onlookers in a way that could readily be understood by those who had not been present at the moment of the refugees' expulsion, but who were now expected to devote time and material re-sources to the sustained relief of their suffering. Graphic and poignant pictures of refugees reinforced the culture of humanitarianism. In its New Year issue for 1916, the "family journal" *Rodina* published a drawing by I. Gur'ev entitled "Two Flights," in which the plight of the refugee family was juxtaposed with the flight of Mary, Joseph and Baby Jesus to Bethlehem. Accompanying verses urged the refugees not to lose courage.[8] Editors often focused on a single refugee family. Some of the poses were clearly contrived to create a genre photograph of the kind that had become fashionable at the turn of the century; the journal of the Tatiana Committee occa-sionally pictured "refugee types" (*tipy-bezhentsy*).[9] Other images emphasized in-stead the magnitude of the refugee movement; typical of these was a picture of a throng gathered outside a refugee sanctuary in Petrograd. A photograph in the newspaper *Refugees' Life* of a makeshift shelter carried the caption "Gypsy encampment of refugees."[10] More distressing were the snapshots and sketches of the wayside graves that testified to sorrow, suffering, and loss, images that appeared in a variety of sources. During 1916 and early 1917, photographs began to appear of the atrocities committed by Turkish troops in Ottoman Armenia, with a pointed reminder that "they [refugees] are far away, far away from you . . . you cannot see them"—the implication being that the printed image was a necessary substitute.[11] The importance attached to photographs is also suggested by the arrangements made for an exhibition of refugee life, to include a pictorial record of the homes the refugees had abandoned and the lives they now lived.[12]

Sometimes the photographic medium drew attention not to refugees' degradation, but rather to the impact of private benevolence on their mood. In December 1915, for example, *Letopis' voiny* published photographs of two smiling refugee children with the caption "Refugees do not lose heart." Another picture, timed for the Christmas break, portrayed "A refugee child who has lost her parents and who has found shelter with an unfamiliar woman." Other photographs showed refugees eating the remnants of the soldiers' meal, cleverly implying that the Russian soldier was the refugee's friend, not the source of mass suffering and sorrow.[13] In an important new departure, from the late summer of 1916 the bulletin of the Tatiana Committee regularly carried photographs of young refugee children who had lost their parents. Prince Urusov's organization also published poignant photos of orphaned children, in the hope that someone would recognize them: "Isidor, five years; Demian Makhnovskii, two years, mother dead, father in hiding; unknown girl; unknown boy, four years old. . . . " The distressed, frightened, and bewildered faces of these children seem to acknowledge that the prospect of their being reunited with their parents was remote. The photographs were calculated to emphasize that strenuous efforts should nevertheless be made to this end.[14]

Journalists and publicists also played their part in the manufacture of refugeedom. One irate correspondent spoke of meeting a young mother who was carrying a dead child in her arms and who wanted to find a less shocking place to stay: "If the state can demand of people that they give up their lives, health, and strength, why can it not confiscate spare rooms from those people who are indifferent to the fate of refugees?" She ended her letter with a damning indictment of Russian attitudes and responses, observing that Jews had set aside synagogues for Jewish refugees and Catholics had founded new orphanages, but that the Russian authorities in Iaroslavl' dumped refugees in factories and empty theaters: "Can we call ourselves Christians? Is this how to overcome the enemy?"[15] Stories were framed in such a way as to alert local people to the consequences of failing to come to the aid of needy refugees. The well-regarded provincial newspaper in Iaroslavl' urged its readers to collect clean clothes, in order to forestall the spread of infectious disease. The appeal to self-preservation was coupled with an emotional outburst: "Let us assure ourselves that the people of Iaroslavl' have not stopped being sympathetic to the misfortune of others."[16] In Tomsk, the local press reported the story of a young refugee child who had been left to wander off without supervision and who had died after falling into a fire.[17]

Engrossing stories of human despair could exert an equally sensational influence on public opinion, by reminding readers of the consequences of refugeedom. In a common formulation, refugees were depicted as a discrete population whose "daily life vacillated between a dreadful yesterday and an unknown tomorrow."[18] The elaboration of this temporal state required narrative skill and dramatic artifice. Consider the emotional appeal published in one newspaper on behalf of a woman who had lost her child. "On the 23rd of September, the three-year-old son of a Latvian refugee woman, Olga Stengel, came up missing. His name is Karl. . . . He is wearing dark blue clothes. He speaks no Russian. His mother asks all well-meaning people to let her know where her child can be found and to return him to the barracks where she is living, at 2, Balashovsk railway station."[19] We cannot know whether Olga found her son. Was he whisked off to an orphanage or a "children's colony" in the countryside? Was he able to give his name to those who found him? Did he become "Russian"? An even more dramatic tale was told at some length by a desperate and exhausted Russian man:

> In August 1915 my wife Iuliania Romanovna Bychuk, a native of Kovaliuk, a peasant belonging to the Roman Catholic faith and of Russian nationality, born 9 December 1884, and our three children—Anna, eight years old; Marianna, five; and Liudvig, three—were evacuated from the village of Liubichin, Kravoverbsk volost, Vlodavsk uezd, Chelm province, to the interior of Russia. In accordance with my wishes, my wife and children were dispatched on horseback together with her father and brother to meet up with me in the village of Kolpashevo, Tomsk province, Narymskoi krai [this was a distance of approximately 3,500 km]. In the small village of Siniavka, Slutsk uezd, Minsk province, the horse collapsed and died. My wife and children were taken by soldiers on board a military transport. Where they were taken, nobody knows. Her father and brother Mikhail Kovaliuk are presently living in the village of Suslov, Ponomarovsk volost, Birskoi uezd, Ufa province.
>
> Twice I have traveled to Kolpashev village, to the town of Tomsk, and to other places, but my attempts to trace my family have so far been to no avail. It seems that I've been all over Russia, and submitted requests for information to some 100 committees, but nowhere have I been able to find my family.
>
> I am taking the liberty of asking the esteemed staff of this newspaper to take whatever steps they can to help me be reunited with my nearest and dearest. Have pity on this unhappy man and on his little ones. Show us Christ's compassion and help this miserable wretch in his hour of need. Don't ignore my request for help. Send

any news to the following address: Kiev, Sofievsk uezd, Kiev branch of the Tatiana Committee, to the attention of Ivan Grigor'evich Bortnik.[20]

Narratives did not have to be couched in such alarming and tragic terms to produce a dramatic effect. A poignant tale, complete with happy ending, was told of a refugee woman ("from someplace in the northwest region") who occupied a bed in a hospital in Samara. The "harsh fate" of an abrupt departure had led to her being separated from her three-year-old daughter, whose whereabouts were unknown. One night a party of refugee children arrived at the hospital. All of them were found emergency accommodation in hospital wards, but one young girl was left without a bed. The sick refugee woman offered to share her own bed with the girl. When morning broke, the child was revealed—"as if by a miracle"—to be her own long-lost daughter. Mother and daughter had been reunited by an extraordinary stroke of fortune. This tale simultaneously reminded readers of the many thousands of stories with a less happy outcome.[21]

Sometimes the pain of refugeedom was conveyed obliquely by rather labored attempts at humor. A correspondent of *Birzhevye vedomosti* dwelt in a lighthearted way on the tale of an elderly refugee who had arrived in Petrograd and had been picked up at the railway station by a cab driver who proceeded to take him to the shelter on Angliiskii prospekt. Knowing not one word of Russian, the old man panicked, thinking he was being carted off to prison. He arrived in a distraught state at the refuge, where the relief workers gradually managed to piece together his story. The paper's audience was invited to sympathize with the refugee, but also to smile at his predicament and to reflect on how different he was from the comfortable armchair reader.[22]

Other means of dramatizing the plight of refugees included the use of street collections and public appeals in order to raise money, as an alternative to private donations.[23] Concerts and auctions of works of art were also popular means, not only of fundraising but also of advertising charitable activity. The small Armenian community in Kiev arranged a musical evening to raise money for refugees in the Caucasus, while a group of "Armenian ladies" in Moscow organized concerts, plays, and lectures for the same purpose.[24] The Tatiana Committee in Petrograd devised a program of entertainment that included orchestral works by Chopin and Tchaikovsky, as well as a series of tableaux in which the "death of a volunteer" was followed by a portrayal of "the refugee woman."[25] National newspapers carried front-page advertisements for private charities that devoted their efforts to refugee relief in Russia's towns and cities. Diocesan committees also issued their own bulletins and newspapers devoted to refugee welfare. Last but not least, new publications dedicated most or all of their pages to the condition of refugees: these included *Bezhenets* (Moscow), *Severnyi bezhenets* (Novgorod, weekly), *Zhizn' bezhentsev,*

Vestnik Vserossiiskogo obshchestva popecheniia o bezhentsakh, Iugobezhenets, and *Sput-nik bezhentsa* (Moscow). These developments in the Russian media signaled a meta-morphosis, whereby the predicament of the individual refugee was transformed into the condition of refugeedom.[26]

DISORDER, DEMORALIZATION, AND DEFENSELESSNESS

A critical element in the construction of a humanitarian narrative was the em-phasis on the helplessness of the refugee. As we saw earlier, contemporary views were polarized between those who found an explanation for refugeedom in the brutal measures inflicted on the local population by the Russian armed forces and those who attributed displacement to the "spontaneous" movement of ordinary sub-jects who sought to escape the invading enemy, but who lacked control over their own affairs. The latter view tended to prevail in public, for obvious reasons: with a grand rhetorical flourish, the Saratov diocesan journal suggested that refugees "had quit their birthplace in order to give greater scope for our valiant army to spread its eagle wings."[27] Whatever the explanation, the refugee was a defenseless and frightened victim of circumstance. As a consequence, it became possible to articulate a vision of collective public responsibility for the fate of the displaced. As one official put it, "Refugeedom is a calamity, like an earthquake, and it is incum-bent on the entire mass of people from the highest to the lowest to respond."[28] The public reaction to their plight hinged upon the reiteration of refugee impotence. Contrasts were drawn between the steady and controlled movement of Russian peasants to western Siberia before 1914 and the sudden, unchecked "flood" of refugees. In one sense this analogy could be exploited by educated society to un-derline the lack of government preparedness and the need for "public" intervention. At the same time, it emphasized the haphazardness of the refugee journey, the lack of organization, and the risks that refugees posed to settled communities.[29]

It is difficult to tell the extent to which such perceptions corresponded to refu-gees' own experiences. Refugees were surely devastated by the experience of en-forced departure, by the deprivation of comfort it implied, by the destruction of family ties, and by the threat of serious illness. This supposition is based on com-ments from welfare workers, public activists, and journalists, whose sensibilities colored their descriptions of the refugee experience. For the most part they drew attention to passivity and a lack of self-control. A correspondent with the liberal newspaper *Birzhevye vedomosti* wrote of a visit to a group of refugee women and children who "watched intently as I scribbled with my pencil, as if expecting jour-nalists to find the loved ones whom they had lost en route to Petrograd."[30]

One authority speaks of an initial capacity for communal self-preservation, which then yielded not to individualism but to anarchism born of collective desperation:

> At the beginning, the refugees preserved their organization as village communities, and advanced under the leadership of their clergy and elders, who acted as their representatives in all negotiations with local authorities and with the relief organizations. But eventually the character of the movement changed. Those who had horses pushed on ahead; and the mass of people who followed were no longer members of an organized community, but a mere mob, tired, hungry and almost beyond restraint.[31]

This narrative, however, not only exemplifies awareness of the trauma of dislocation, but also betrays a pronounced fear of the social consequences of communal disintegration. These anxieties did not originate with the war. Concern about crime, hooliganism, and moral degradation had surfaced throughout educated society and among the tsarist police before 1914. As Joan Neuberger has demonstrated, prewar Russia witnessed a struggle for control of urban space, where notions of respectability and "culture" were at stake. In this context, hooliganism challenged the right of an emerging middle class to exercise power and authority in the city center, and mocked the attempts by its spokesmen to assert social control in constantly changing urban surroundings. Disorder was associated with the growth of an unsettled population; young peasant in-migrants behaved in an uncouth, uncontrolled, and violent manner, lacking the restraint imposed by domestic discipline or family responsibilities. With the outbreak of war, and the creation of a much more numerous unsettled population, it is not surprising that the alarm should have been raised about the prospect of further outbursts of deviant behavior. Against this background, it is easy to see how contemporaries might magnify the degree of chaos evident in the retreat eastward.[32]

Confrontations did indeed take place between refugees and local inhabitants, but that fact did not necessarily reflect a collapse of social cohesion. Nor is there much evidence that leadership within the refugee community was quickly dissipated. The war provided an opportunity for many refugees to "pull together" and to reconstitute communities in new locations. Relief workers placed great emphasis on the need to keep established communities intact and, wherever possible, to encourage refugees to submit to the leadership of elected village commissioners: "The most important principle is that of mutual assistance among the group, with the strongest helping the less strong." For that reason, it was important that zemstvos and other agencies took account of the solidarity of the group and did not scatter refugees.[33] Polish refugees enjoyed a close relationship with the Catholic priests who accompanied them on the journey eastward. Priests provided spiritual guidance and comfort; they also ensured that refugees responded to official instructions as to their eventual destination.[34] During the spring of 1916, the tsarist government discussed the need to offer financial recompense to the hard-pressed officers of the peasant community (the Russian mir and the Polish *gmina*), whose services were much in demand and greatly appreciated. This hardly implies a collapse of communal organization.[35]

Yet the written accounts continued to place most of the emphasis on disorder, demoralization, and loss of control. Refugees panicked as they struggled to free themselves from the German and Austrian threat; "even to secure a place in a cattle truck they had to use incredible force" to fight their way on.[36] Relief agencies were sensitive to the need to deter "mob" behavior and to forestall "natural panic" among local inhabitants. (Some relief workers deliberately played upon fears of public disorder, suggesting that hungry refugees would be driven to loot stores or steal from private homes if they were not given adequate supplies of food.)[37] Published narratives drew graphic attention to individuals who had taken refuge along river banks or in forests close to their home before they ran out of patience or fell ill, throwing themselves in disorganized fashion on relief organizations.[38] The historian of zemstvo operations noted that village elders, priests, teachers, and university students struggled to serve the needs of the refugees and protect them from speculators en route to a place of safety.[39] Refugees had, understandably, been unable to give deceased relatives and friends a proper burial. Once again, the emphasis was on the need to create order out of chaos and to portray the virtues of local *intelligenty* who displayed care and concern for the dispossessed, diseased, and downtrodden refugees. Such accounts drew attention to the moral and administrative superiority shown by educated society over officials who behaved in an intemperate, thoughtless, and haphazard manner.[40]

"SOME OF THE SADDEST PEOPLE THAT EVER WERE SEEN"

Inevitably, one of the most common images conveyed was that of the sick refugee.[41] Sickness intensified the drama of refugeedom by emphasizing the harmful consequences for both the displaced and the settled population. The routes followed by successive streams of refugees—along the Volga River and the Trans-Siberian Railway—readily became associated in the public mind with infection.[42] The municipal governor of Rostov-on-Don expressed concern at the public health consequences of the "influx of masses of refugees" who, along with Turkish prisoners of war, had spread infectious diseases.[43] In one of the few recorded references to Russia's Gypsy population, *Birzhevye vedomosti* reported the arrival of fifteen Gypsies in the capital, some with symptoms of severe intestinal illness.[44] A zemstvo doctor urged the need to inspect all passengers on incoming refugee trains as closely as possible, because refugees frequently hid the corpses of their relatives without regard for the public health consequences.[45] There was no respite for the refugees, who were firmly fixed in the popular mind as real or potential carriers of disease and thus as obvious candidates for preventive medicine, emergency treatment, or isolation. Refugees had the capacity to wreak havoc on the health of the Russian interior.[46]

Typical of the prevailing emphasis on sickness was a report published by the American archeologist and Byzantinist Thomas Whittemore, who traveled throughout European Russia between November 1915 and January 1916. Whittemore visited a number of provincial towns as well as Moscow, Petrograd, and Kiev, describing his tour as a "display of America's sympathy towards Russia."[47] In Tambov, a modest provincial town with a population of 53,000 on the eve of war, Whittemore noted that refugees had been scattered throughout the town; their dispersion "kept them out of reach of organized control and rendered any kind of general supervision impossible." Many of them lived in the local theater, close to the railway line, in a state of absolute squalor. In Saratov, a young Polish doctor from Radom worked "heroically" in appalling conditions. Typhus was already rampant. Here, as elsewhere, there were a "conscientious but insufficient number of medical personnel and feldshers."[48] Few towns provided refugees with adequate washing facilities. In Samara, a "shockingly overcrowded" town, Whittemore saw a "corpse that lay around for days on end without being removed." Farther east, in Orenburg, Ufa, and Tashkent, conditions were even worse. Summarizing his findings, he pointed out that the crowded, dirty, unhealthy conditions in which refugees were "coiled like serpents" created a perfect breeding ground for infectious diseases, which were spread through the schools, workshops, and other public places frequented by refugees. Whittemore applauded the role played by municipal agencies, as well as the national committees and the local Tatiana Committees, but bemoaned the absence of any central authority that might coordinate their activities. He recommended the construction of dedicated barracks, bathhouses, and laundries; these should be located on the outskirts of towns. Barracks should be capable of accommodating up to two hundred refugees. Whittemore advised that refugees "be taken regularly in squads like soldiers to a bath" in order to check that they washed themselves and disinfected their clothes and bedding; they could also ensure that latrines were properly disinfected. Of the towns he visited, only Penza and Khar'kov had begun to arrange matters to Whittemore's satisfaction. It was not too late for others to follow their example and prevent the widespread dissemination of infectious disease throughout the country: "I do not wish to support the impractical and the impossible. But the problem is a desperate one and unless something is done there will be in the spring an epidemic of unparalleled violence."[49]

No less remarkable was the testimony of the English nurse Violetta Thurstan. Thurstan's narrative of "some of the saddest people that ever were seen" offered a powerful and evocative account of cholera and death. At times the personal element intruded very directly, as in her discussion of sick children: "How I longed to waft some of them straight to England and install them in a certain cottage in Somerset that I wot of, feed them all on cream and let them play out of doors all day long." Thurstan also understood that the desire to maintain family integrity conflicted with public health imperatives. A clear tension emerged where families sought to remain together, but where medical authorities wished to isolate infected individuals. She described the resistance mounted by family members to attempts to segregate the healthy from the diseased.[50] This emphasis on disease helped not only to justify expert medical intervention but to alert the public to the desperate plight of fellow human beings. A correspondent from Erzerum described the scenes of degradation which led to "our unfortunate sisters and widows who have to live off scraps of leftover food or who freeze to death."[51] In Irkutsk, a deputation of refugees pleaded with the Union of Towns to be sent elsewhere in order to receive adequate medical treatment: "There's nothing for it otherwise but to throw ourselves in the river rather than wait in line."[52] Such descriptions easily overrode images of the refugee as a "sober, hard-working," stoic casualty of war, which surfaced only rarely in stories of displacement.[53]

Sickness helped to define the refugee; it also underlined the indispensability of the medical profession. John Hutchinson has shown that the epidemic of 1915 transferred the initiative within the medical staff of the public organizations from field surgery and hospital medicine toward bacteriology, epidemiology, and hygiene, in which men such as L. A. Tarasevich and A. N. Sysin came to prominence, the former as a leading bacteriologist, the latter as the chief epidemiologist within the Union of Towns. Most effective, in their view, were improved sanitation and isolation facilities; vaccination and disinfection programs came too late to have much impact on mortality rates.[54] Zemstvo doctors advocated the isolation and forced removal of sick refugees from the front. Moscow's physicians divided the city into ten districts, each with up to sixty beds for refugees who suffered from infectious disease.[55] More work needs to be done on the specific encounters between refugees and medical personnel, including the possibility that refugee communities contained their own doctors. Here I simply draw attention to the fact that the war contributed to the further medicalization of social issues.[56] The war also increased the status of zemstvo doctors and medical specialists, who articulated a vision of a national authority under the control of health professionals.[57]

The humanitarian project extended also to a preoccupation with the psyche of refugees. In Kiev, the refugee relief committee expressed concern that "the horrors experienced by refugees have produced an epidemic of psychiatric abnormalities." Refugees were traumatized by attacks made upon them by German airplanes, which caused them mental torment (*stradanie dushi*).[58] Powerful stories were told of women who cast their starving children into the graves they had dug for their dead husbands or who drowned their children in the marshes around Pinsk.[59] From the beleaguered Transcaucasus came reports that desperate Armenian mothers in the village of Bagrikal had thrown first their children and then themselves into the river.[60] Violetta Thurstan began her report on refugee conditions in 1916 by emphasizing the potential loss of self-respect induced by "overcrowding, lack of privacy, and the indiscriminate mingling of the decent and the dissolute." She fixed subsequently upon examples of complete mental breakdown, victims of psychological torment who had become "human derelicts in the asylum."[61] She was not alone in reflecting on this aspect of refugeedom: "Who knows," wrote a correspondent in Iaroslavl', "what impression may have been made on the small souls by the dreadful memory of being uprooted from their native villages and forced on to wagons. . . . Who knows? Perhaps the pure hearts of these small creatures, unable to draw strength, are already broken in pieces and crippled for the rest of their lives, just as are the hearts of their morose, exhausted mothers and fathers."[62]

Russian psychiatrists responded to this felt need, albeit with a keen eye for professional self-interest. Doctors in Moscow set aside 100 beds for the treatment of mentally ill refugees. The distinguished psychiatrist V. M. Bekhterev proposed to establish a clinic in Petrograd to treat refugees suffering from nervous and psychiatric disorders. The initiative required financial support from the Tatiana Committee, some of whose members expressed misgivings that Bekhterev intended to set up a general institute for private psychiatric purposes on the pretext of treating refugees. One critic felt that the projected cost of treatment was too high, "taking into account that the sick refugees do not all belong to the same class of the population." Bekhterev eventually got his way.[63]

THE RESTORATION OF THE REFUGEE FAMILY

At the core of the humanitarian initiative was the desire to protect and wherever possible restore family integrity.[64] Sitting in private session, the Special Council for Refugees revealed that the concern to keep families intact distinguished liberal from bureaucratic opinion. Prince Shcherbatov, minister of the interior and chairman of the council, maintained that his primary responsibility was to direct refugees to appropriate destinations, irrespective of the impact of this policy on family structure. By contrast, parliamentary members argued that this policy was likely to wrench families apart.[65] In practice, Shcherbatov's unsentimental approach yielded to more liberal practices by the exponents of refugee relief. One of the most important initiatives was the attempt to track down relatives on behalf of refugees. Again, the telling of stories played a crucial part in the humanitarian project. The leading newspaper of Moscow's Progressist party carried a heart-rending story of an eleven-year-old boy, Sergei Kulikov, who had taken three weeks to reach Moscow on his way to look for his grandmother, who lived in Nizhnii Novgorod. His father was at the front, and his mother had died. Sergei was asked how he felt: "I'm terribly tired, I haven't slept for three weeks, I'm hungry. . . . I'm surviving somehow. I just want to find my granny." The Moscow municipal board gave him a train ticket to his final destination.[66]

The archives of local Tatiana committees and of the public organizations also testify to the enormous effort that was involved in the process of reuniting families.[67] Often these initiatives met with great difficulty. The Union of Towns published long lists of children who had lost contact with their parents, in the hope that an adult would recognize one of the names. But "experience has shown that the surnames given by the children bear little or no relation to the names of their parents. . . . Consequently great care should be exercised when using these lists to compare possible spellings." Sometimes children could give only a first name; sometimes the lists poignantly noted that a child had died ("Anna, one and a half years old—Krivoe selo, died"). The accumulation of personal detail and the creation of a caseload constitute a distinctly modern element and a major departure from past practice.[68]

Underlying such tactics was the long-standing belief among educated Russians that family breakdown was associated with crime.[69] Zemstvo professionals made much of the decline in patriarchal authority associated with population displacement. The historian and public activist Sergei Bakhrushin spoke of refugee children who had been "cast to the mercy of fate," who could not adjust to organized lodgings and who promptly absconded. Other juveniles lived in close proximity to unfamiliar adult men and women, which contributed to their disorientation and "hysteria." Children had been deprived of schooling, work, and friendships. Many of these "homeless waifs" (*besprizorniki*) had grown accustomed to charity, which they now felt entitled to supplement by begging and other stratagems.[70]

These concerns about the moral consequences of family disintegration were shared by members of the Special Council, who lamented the rising numbers of orphaned refugees; this tragic phenomenon reinforced the belief that their care had become a matter of "state significance."[71] In other words, the attempt to restore "broken" families could not be sustained, and a substitute had to be found for the family unit. The Special Council took the view that society had a responsibility to supply the kind of discipline that parents could no longer provide. Many refugee orphans were placed in homes administered by the Tatiana Committee, whose officials favored a rural environment. Children should be evacuated from overcrowded and dangerous cities to the countryside, not only for the good of their physical health, but also because they could be made to appreciate the benefits of hard work and be taught to respect private property.[72] Housed in small village communities ("colonies"), children could be looked after by professionally trained care workers.[73] The focus was not solely upon orphans: some children had been rejected by their parents and "discarded like an unwanted pair of shoes."[74] What mattered was the creation of a regime that provided fresh food, good standards of personal hygiene, and organized games, together with a rigorous timetable for work, rest, and play. Where parents were reluctant to entrust their offspring to these colonies, they needed to be persuaded of the social, physical, and moral advantages of doing so. The growth of children's colonies during and after the First World War suggests a widespread espousal of such dogmatic certainties among Russia's emerging professional social workers.[75]

Diocesan committees, as might be expected, set great store by the promotion of schooling. In Irkutsk, schools afforded an opportunity to teach children the habit of good speech, to encourage them to read improving texts, and to offer religious instruction, as well as to perform simple arithmetic and answer basic historical questions. They also provided a suitable place to monitor the physical condition of children. Peasant children from the western borderlands were taught the importance of taking a hot bath during the winter months. As a result, children who had been taken from a temporary hostel now found a "warm welcome and tenderness" in the seminary school. Clothed and "fed to their heart's content," refugee children "understood well" that they were the object of devoted care. Education had a didactic and moral purpose.[76]

THE SOCIAL AND CIVIC STATUS OF THE REFUGEE

The impact of refugeedom on downward social mobility reinforced the sense of disorder. The British writer Stephen Graham described a visit to the estate of "Madame E.," whose orchard was guarded by "one of the unfortunate refugees from the territory now occupied by the Germans. Two years ago he had been a prosperous farmer with his own land and horses and cows and what not, now he is a miserable half-savage [sic] in sheepskins lying in a rain-soaked straw shelter in the orchard—sans land, sans wife, sans everything."[77] The fate of farmers also became a regular preoccupation of the Latvian Central Refugee Committee, which bemoaned the extent of economic distress among those who had been independent and affluent.[78]

Newspapers reminded their readers that refugees with higher education were unable to trade on their qualifications. As a consequence, these unfortunates lived a humble existence in the Russian interior.[79] In southwest Russia, the "refugee intelligentsia" were in even more desperate straits than ordinary refugees (*prosto-*

narod'ia), who were at least familiar with manual work.[80] The "women of independent means" who arrived in Tomsk found it difficult to come to terms with the
demeaning prospect of working as domestic servants.[81] In Petrograd it was reported
that *intelligenty* had no resources to speak of: "For them to go on to the street to
beg is unthinkable . . . and to live among the poorest elements of society in shelters
and feeding points is beyond endurance."[82] Newspapers regularly carried reports of
the distressing conditions that once-respectable refugees were forced to endure. The
liberal Iaroslavl' newspaper *Golos* published a graphic account of the temporary
housing set aside in a former factory, and concluded that such atrocious conditions
should be reserved for hooligans, not for genteel citizens who had been caught up
in the trauma of war.[83]

Accounts were not unanimous in drawing attention to a perilous decline in social status. A blistering piece of journalistic invective offered a sarcastic commen-
tary on the refugee flâneurs who paraded Moscow's streets. The anonymous author
drew a sharp distinction between the "genuine" refugees—women and children
from the western borderlands—and the undeserving refugees who had left behind
comfortable jobs in government offices or who had been wealthy landlords, merchants, or factory owners. Much of their time was spent "hanging out" in public spaces—theaters, cinemas, restaurants, and streetcars—where they loudly condemned Moscow for its crude manners and its dirty appearance ("so unlike
home"). These men and women ("refugees with means," the *novye zriteli* or "new
spectators") had no claim on popular sympathy.[84] A week later, the paper printed
a polite rebuke from a former clerical officer (*starshii deloproizvoditel'*) in the tsarist
administration who had been displaced no less than three times in the space of a
few months. He pointed out that most such refugees earned only a pittance and
had been forced to leave their belongings behind. Few could afford trips to the
theater, and if it was true that refugees thronged the streets, the simple fact was that
"we've been thrown out of our houses." But he could not resist coupling this re-
joinder with a sideswipe at members of the "free professions" for the way in which
they flaunted their new wealth—"manufacturers, merchants, chemists, doctors,
lawyers, engineers, dentists, craftsmen, most of them Jews—contractors of various
description."[85] Some refugees were perfectly capable of flinging mud at one another,
thereby reinforcing popular prejudice.

In a similar manner, distinctions were sometimes drawn between the "genuine"
refugee, on the one hand, and those who were simply seeking to evade military
service, or who kept on the move in search of better economic conditions: "One is
ashamed of the millions of innocent sufferers," wrote one journalist in 1915. But
there are also "fugitives [*begletsy*], a troublesome crowd, well off and eager to save
their own skin." These people played on the fears of the settled population and
sowed panic and discord wherever they went.[86] Narratives could operate both

ways: stories of refugees who shirked work gained currency (see chapter 6). Significantly, people who evaded the draft by becoming bogus factory workers were dismissed as "refugees" by the Bolshevik journal, *Voprosy strakhovaniia:* "The composition of these refugees is extremely diverse and variegated. There are corn merchants and clerks, owners of draycarts, restaurateurs, former pubkeepers, even landlords." Thus the response of outsiders to the plight of refugees frequently mixed compassion with fear. When fear was compounded by uncertainty about the identity of the "deserving" and undeserving refugee, humanitarianism might evaporate quite rapidly.[87]

At times these complex emotions yielded to the heroization of the refugee. Violetta Thurstan leavened her narrative by drawing attention to the epic dimension of the refugee experience, in a manner that hinted at the equation of refugee and Christian sacrifice: "It must be remembered that their sorrow is no sordid one; it is grand, romantic, tragical, and it is a vicarious one, for they have suffered and died in order that our homes, our country, and our children shall be safe." This device, making connections between the sacrifice of Christ, the suffering of Russian soldiers, and the torment endured by refugees, was compelling. It also implied that the same Christian charity should be shown to refugees as had been offered to soldiers and their families during 1914 and 1915.[88]

Other rhetorical devices were employed in an attempt to characterize refugees as insiders rather than outsiders. One motif portrayed the refugee as the archetypal patriot who transcended the narrow confines of status or class. Refugees demonstrated their loyalty at every turn. They had taken with them what property they could, rather than abandon it to the enemy. Their fathers, brothers, and sons enlisted in the tsarist army; they themselves worked for the war effort.[89] As was pointed out in September 1915, "Refugeedom is an unprecedented phenomenon. It is a new form of civic status. The refugee carries within himself a civic awareness of the fact that he belongs to Russia. He sacrifices his property in the interests of that greater whole which he considers to be his homeland. The refugee is a trustworthy and honored citizen-hero [*zasluzhennyi grazhdanin-geroi*]. And for that reason he has no need of charity."[90] Similar sentiments—emphasizing the rights as well as the "duties" of refugees—were expressed elsewhere.[91] In these circumstances, casual handouts were inappropriate; refugees had a right to be supported by the state, without being considered "superfluous or a burden": after all, wrote A. Sprude, "refugees are just as much citizens of Rus' as are you, dear reader."[92] "I am a citizen of this homeland," proclaimed V. Tkach in October 1916, pointedly indicating that he was originally from "Kholmskaia Rus'," that is, from Chelm province.[93]

This emphasis on citizenship, however, surfaces only rarely in the historical record. Refugees were normally perceived as unfortunate victims of war, not as citizens.[94] Their petitions to relief agencies for financial and material assistance were accompanied by pitiful stories of dispossession and despair, rather than being couched in terms of entitlement. The prevailing tone was struck by Vera Krinitskaia from Warsaw, who asked for warm clothes ("I am ashamed to ask for this help, but I am in great need"), and by Martin Rosenberg, a soldier from Kurland, who hoped "that my humble prayer and cry for help will not go unanswered."[95] Consequently, the refugee remained for the most part an outsider. Marked by a specific kind of misfortune, the refugee was an unlikely candidate for "assimilation," although assimilation might be a by-product of relocation amid a settled population.[96] A report from Stavropol' concluded that, thanks to organized relief, "all refugees are living in virtually the same conditions as the local population."[97] However, this drew attention to similarities in material circumstance, not to any underlying intention to integrate refugees and the settled population. It is unusual to find a different kind of approach, although in Iaroslavl' an attempt was made to treat indigent professional refugees and local *intelligenty* alike. This became apparent when the special commissioner for refugees instructed the municipal refugee committee to close the door of the new canteen to local people. The argument of the local committee—that all members of the intelligentsia, whatever their origin, were suffering material deprivation and needed to be fed—had no effect on the government. For the most part, however, it appears that civic duty and private sympathy dictated that special provision needed to be made for refugees. To that extent, they were condemned to remain outsiders.[98]

Some refugees certainly had a clear grasp of the need to assert their rights in the face of overbearing and inflexible behavior by the authorities. Sometimes refugees found petty rules and regulations irksome, as when the management of the main hostel set aside for them in Petrograd insisted that they adhere to stringent rules on lights-out, reveille, and smoking in dormitories.[99] Missing from contemporary official accounts, however, is the evidence that many refugees succeeded in asserting their right to decent and humane treatment. Sometimes this determination took the form of a refusal to accept the destination that had been stipulated by government or other public agencies for refugee relief. In one prosaic instance, refugees balked at the suggestion that they leave the relative warmth of their railway freight car and expose themselves to the sharp Siberian outdoors.[100] A resolute group of refugees from Vitebsk rejected outright the offer of a transfer from Iaroslavl' to the surrounding countryside. Another party of 134 Polish refugees, originally from Chelm and languishing at the time in Samarkand, demanded to be reunited with their compatriots in European Russia, giving as their reason the acute suffering induced by a monotonous diet of camel meat and poor drinking water. The Ministry of the Interior granted their request.[101]

Refugees also demonstrated a capacity to press for better conditions in their new location. A refugee who had settled in a village in Kostroma province complained in mid-1916 that the monthly sugar ration no longer sufficed and should be raised to the level to which the urban population was entitled. Refugees, he went on, had to buy most of their necessities; they were not in the fortunate position of the peasants. "We miserable refugees are living on a well-trod road where there is nothing at all for us."[102] Two men wrote to the local newspaper in Iaroslavl' to complain that the soup they were served in the canteen contained cockroaches. They pointed out that "each charitable institution must, like any commercial organization, observe the basic conditions of health and hygiene." Peevish and even pompous as it may seem from a distance, their letter can also be read as an assertion of the dignity of the individual and a reminder that refugees were entitled to a decent subsistence.[103]

Individuals also demanded to be treated fairly and with respect. Dr. Elena Krzhizhanovskaia, originally from Grodno, asked the local refugee committee to offer her temporary employment appropriate to her experience and qualifications, a request that was subsequently granted.[104] Local specialists were also reminded of their professional responsibilities toward refugees. A municipal doctor was reported to the Iaroslavl' medical council for failing to treat refugees, including pregnant women.[105] One Jan Lidak, the son of a 74-year-old refugee woman, took his case directly to Zubchaninov when it became apparent that the doctor at one of Riga's hospitals had consigned her to an unheated room despite the fact that she was suffering from dropsy.[106] Individual refugees were not bereft of support when their personal circumstances became difficult or even dangerous. Far from being isolated, they might draw upon local liberal opinion to defend their rights. Provincial liberal newspapers played an important role in this regard. In Iaroslavl', for instance, the highly regarded newspaper *Golos* mounted a vigorous campaign when a local police official was found to have assaulted a refugee. The reporter clearly felt it important to emphasize that the victim of this violent attack was a virtuous and respectable person: "He is an Old-Believer, very devoted to his faith, modest, quiet, and never drinks at all."[107] This liberal newspaper asserted the right of refugees to be protected from overbearing and unaccountable officials, a right that extended to refugees no less than to other groups in society. Victims of crime could even count on national publicity: a railway official was arrested in Minsk after witnesses saw him steal 100 rubles (a large sum) from a refugee priest.[108]

Refugees did not always succeed in this regard, and on occasion local relief committees lost patience with refugees who became too assertive. In March 1916, refugees in Iaroslavl' complained that they were living in huts that had no fuel or water supply. The governor called upon the municipal refugee committee to respond, which it did, pointedly: "The committee considers it unacceptable that refugees should be unwilling even to fetch water, as the majority of local residents are required to do." In this instance, the refugees were reminded that their status did not entitle them to privileged treatment, particularly if it favored them over and above the local population. The committee refused to deliver meals to the barracks until the refugees complied.[109] Some committees displayed rather more understanding of the needs and susceptibilities of refugees. In Saratov, for example, the refugee commission considered how best to deal with overcrowding in the town, but resolved that it had neither the "moral nor the juridical right" to compel refugees to settle outside the urban milieu.[110]

We have talked of narratives and practices that produced an image of the refugee, and of the attempts by refugees to assert a sense of dignity and worth. What of the refugee's legal status? We should remind ourselves of the definition with which the tsarist state worked throughout 1915 and 1916: "Refugees are those persons who have abandoned localities threatened or already occupied by the enemy, or who have been evacuated by order of the military or civil authority from the zone of military operations; also emigrants from states hostile to Russia."[111] This allowed the authorities to claim jurisdiction over refugees from Austria-Hungary as well as over those who fled the genocide in Ottoman Armenia, to whom Russia had a "moral obligation." According to one report, these refugees were to be allowed to become Russian citizens.[112] Although there was no ambiguity about the right of Russian refugees to remain under the protection of the tsarist state (giving them an advantage over Europe's postwar refugees, who "lacked a natural place of permanent asylum"), nevertheless their displacement put them at the mercy of government officials, who themselves lacked clear guidance about the treatment to be accorded displaced people.[113]

Many refugees arrived in the Russian interior without the kind of documentation that the subjects of the tsar were normally expected to possess. Of these, the paper granting right of abode (*vid na zhitel'stvo*) was the most important indication of status. Without these papers, potential employers were loath to offer work to refugees, lest they fall afoul of local police officials.[114] Other considerations also made life difficult for refugees who lacked the proper documents. Some officials suspected them of engaging in espionage; in Tula, for instance, the police reportedly believed that the Germans had sent agents to spy on the local ordnance factory.[115] It is not difficult to imagine how wartime fears of enemy subversion were projected onto refugees. Their uncertain status left them in limbo and created the conditions in which such assumptions could be made.

The assertion by refugees of their right to justice and dignified treatment was directed no less firmly at Russia's liberals than it was at the tsar's officials, whom they encountered at every turn. Can we be certain that issues of self-respect and civic equality were at the center of attention when the liberal professionals in the zemstvos and municipalities, and in Russia's burgeoning charitable agencies, intervened? Did they extend the hand of friendship and speak on equal terms; or did they—in their own way—betray a similar kind of unease and even disregard for the refugees whom they organized and counted, and whose needs they assessed? This question is difficult to answer, but it needs to be confronted. There are, for example, isolated instances in which refugees were invited by local municipal authorities to serve on committees for refugee relief. But this does not appear to have been common practice.[116] Refugees were subject to the intervention of professional relief workers; they were not supposed to participate in the enhancement of their own welfare. Few attempts were made to ask refugees for an opinion about their plight, to consult them about strategies for their relocation, or to involve them in measures designed to assist them in the short and longer term.[117] Some professional activists acknowledged aspects of the problem; one doctor commented in 1916 that "relief assumes a form that demeans human dignity."[118]

Accounts of refugee relief allude to the role of the public organizations in offering legal advice across a range of issues. According to the historian of the Union of Towns, refugees approached its lawyers in a virtual state of "outlawry, their various rights being continually infringed," for instance by officials who arbitrarily seized their property.[119] Local officials sometimes acknowledged that the plight of refugees had been exacerbated by the suddenness with which they had been transported from the war zone to the interior, at which time they were divested of their draft animals, carts, and other belongings.[120] Here, then, was another opportunity to become involved in the affairs of the refugee. By so doing, the liberal stalwarts of the public organizations were able not only to confirm the outrageous behavior of army commanders and civil servants, but also to underline the need to treat the refugee as a deserving supplicant, whose personal dignity was affronted and whose property had been violated. The forced displacement of people was bad enough, but, as one sympathetic observer put it, "the question of the state's obligation to compensate for the damage and loss caused by the war has become, along with the refugee question, a matter of pressing concern which has not yet been resolved from a judicial point of view."[121]

We cannot leave the question of refugeedom without considering the legal and social distinction that was drawn between refugees and the "forced migrants," or *vyselentsy*. In the first instance the distinction drew attention to the fact that many refugees had been forced to leave their homes by the Russian army. In this regard, some observers linked the term specifically to the Jewish population; others pointed to the fate of Poles as well. Thus the chairman of the Tatiana Committee pointed out that refugees left their homes "of their own free will," whereas the *vyselentsy* "have abandoned their homes and deserted their property, not of their own volition but as a result of orders and under pressure from the authorities."[122] But as suggested earlier, this usage was quietly dropped lest it bring to mind painful memories of the arbitrary behavior of Russia's military commanders.[123] Instead the term became reserved for one specific form of population displacement, the evacuation of German settlers from European Russia. It goes without saying that thousands of displaced German colonists did not enjoy much official or public sympathy. An attempt at the beginning of 1915 by the Khar'kov branch of the Tatiana Committee to come to the aid of German settlers seems to have been an isolated instance. In any case, the committee was told to stop this practice, on the grounds that the Germans were "administrative exiles" (*administrativno-vyslannye*).[124] Some of them attempted to settle in Orenburg and the Turgai region, but the hostility of the local inhabitants forced them to move farther east, to established German colonies in Tomsk, Tobol'sk, and Enisei oblast. Toward the end of 1915, a meeting of officials and relief workers in Irkutsk heard an uncompromising report of the dire conditions in which German and Austrian nationals were kept, without access even to the meager relief to which administrative exiles were entitled. Forced to resort to begging, they simply alienated the local population, whose own resources were very limited. The solution was to treat these forced migrants on the same basis as political prisoners and refugees—that is, to offer them at least a rudimentary state allowance.[125] The courageous approach made by the Tatiana Committee met with a frosty response in Petrograd. The Special Council for Refugees quietly (and complacently) observed that these forced migrants did not suffer real hardship, were supported by fellow Germans, and should not be entitled to official relief.[126]

The determined efforts of the government and the police to encourage out-migration from overcrowded urban centers, partly to improve their sanitary status, partly to reduce the financial burden on municipal treasuries, and partly to boost the supply of potential agricultural laborers, galvanized many refugees to protest. They had good reason. Where the threat to withdraw benefits failed to persuade refugees to resettle, more direct action was employed. The tactics were regarded as all too reminiscent of the initial program of forced migration.[127] The police in Pskov and Vitebsk announced their intention to eject refugees from those provinces, unless they had relatives with whom to live or guaranteed sources of income. Well-informed sources complained that the police had taken the opportunity to move against local residents, a sure sign that Jews were being singled out.[128] In Orenburg, refugees protested that the local municipal authorities had forced them out of town after one week, in order to accommodate a fresh influx of displaced persons.[129] Refugees who had settled in Irkutsk (there were 10,000 by October 1915) objected vociferously to plans to disperse them to god-forsaken and isolated villages—"You might as well drown us in the Angara River"; "The Siberians are an evil lot—they kill people off."[130] Ukrainian refugees who had settled in Tashkent had no wish to be evacuated by well-meaning government officials who were concerned about the growing health crisis in central Asia. The refugees had already built schools and workshops, and wished to stay put. Their wishes were eventually respected.[131]

Throughout the various accounts of refugeedom, readers were invited not only to sympathize with the displaced and the dispossessed, but also to celebrate the virtue and selflessness of the voluntary social worker. Many of the vivid descriptions of distressed and apathetic refugees served only to bring into sharp focus the energy and vitality of those who dispensed relief. "It must be rather more agreeable to the unfortunate recipient of charity to be made to feel a welcome guest at the little feast," said Violetta Thurstan, *à propos* of Moscow's British community.[132] From Simbirsk came a paean of praise to the energetic yet modest volunteers who worked on behalf of the diocesan refugee committee: "These people have made a contribution without any fuss or advertisement, responding to the appeal of their pastors. . . . Let us give them heartfelt thanks, on behalf of the refugees and on behalf of the simple Orthodox Russian narod [people]."[133] The Tatiana Committee supposed that its staff would work without being paid for their contribution to relief work; the sole rewards were medals and other decorations, and only for those not already in state service.[134]

Violetta Thurstan was particularly impressed by the activities of Russian students, such as those in Kazan' who organized thousands of refugees and who provided bakeries and abattoirs, as well as the opportunity to learn carpentry, bootmaking, and tailoring: "It was perfectly delightful to see how the students were loved and trusted. To give money to the refugees is one thing; to actually live with them and share their life is quite another."[135] Other observers also drew attention to the importance of the student body. In Nizhnii Novgorod, the Tatiana Committee originated within the "pedagogic sphere," because teachers were able to inculcate in students the need for a sympathetic response toward refugees. Students—"by and large a poor group"—could organize street collections and also prompt their parents to make a contribution to the relief effort.[136] A special newsletter issued on behalf of students in Rostov was filled with poems, prayers, stories, and drawings. The young editor, P. Levitskii, editorialized: "We know that our contribution is modest, but we are certain that one little pebble given sincerely will be the most precious consolation, showing refugees that they are not abandoned and giving them the strength to bear their heavy cross until the very end."[137]

The prevailing assumption held that refugees were passive creatures upon whom relief agencies could practice benevolence and impose discipline. Notwithstanding the oft-repeated comments about refugees' apathy, their passivity became something of a virtue. Refugees were not expected to play a part in determining their own destiny. The perspective adopted by relief organizations fostered the creation of a refugee object who was to be acted upon. In terms that may be borrowed from the

insights of Michel Foucault, those who intervened from a liberal standpoint represented a different kind of regime, one that sought to replace the traditional "police-
administrative" practices formerly pursued in the Russian *Polizeistaat*. They did not
renounce discipline; on the contrary, they affirmed the superiority and virtue of its
liberal incarnation.

RECORDING REFUGEEDOM FOR POSTERITY

Refugees may have been outsiders (the *vyselentsy* most certainly were), but that
does not mean that they were necessarily voiceless or that they lacked a history.
Toward the end of 1916, a distinctive approach toward refugees can be detected in
the offices of the Tatiana Committee. Two moments stand out as being particularly
significant. First, the committee launched an ambitious program to publicize the
history of refugeedom, by means of a special exhibition that was scheduled to take
place in the spring of 1917. Underlying this initiative was the belief that the Russian public needed to be better informed about the living conditions and activities
of refugees, who were not all "beggars, idlers and spongers." The exhibition was to
be funded by private contributions and sponsored by eighty-two refugee organizations.[138] In its preliminary proposal, the Tatiana Committee spoke of four main
themes that needed to be highlighted: conditions in Russia's borderlands before
and during the war (including "the destruction of settlements, property, and artistic monuments"); their "sorrowful journey," including the background to their
displacement, the course of the refugee movement, and the assistance given by
government and public organizations; the living conditions in their new homes
(including "the work undertaken by refugees and their impact on the local population"); and lastly, the restoration of normal life in the regions cleared of enemy
occupation.[139]

Certainly the leaders of most national committees saw the proposal for an exhibition on "Russia and Her Devastated Borderlands" (*Rossiia i razorennye okrainy*) in
a positive light.[140] Not only would it help to challenge prevailing misconceptions
about the "idle refugee"; it would also afford an opportunity to display the talents
and cultural attributes of national minorities in the Russian empire, most of whom
impinged only tangentially on the consciousness of the "Russian foreigner." Accordingly, the Latvian Central Welfare Committee called upon its local affiliates to submit handicrafts and agricultural produce, as well as testimonies of defense work and
photographs of living conditions. According to a subsequent account, several governors took the view that crafts and other items should be submitted without any
national attribution, but rather as products of provincial life. Arguably, however, the
source of particular exhibits was less important to the national committees than the

decision of the organizers to include a record of enemy occupation and despoliation of the imperial borderlands.[141]

In a related initiative, the Tatiana Committee sponsored a remarkable project designed to gather material from refugees at first hand about their experiences before, during, and after displacement. "An extremely important indicator [i.e., of the refugee movement] is the stories of refugees themselves."[142] Refugees were encouraged to describe their experiences in their own words. If they needed help in formulating a coherent narrative, the Tatiana Committee obligingly published a schedule of twenty-four questions that might be asked. (See Appendix 2.) The aim was to secure stories from "simple people," not just from educated refugees. Other kinds of testimony were also sought: photographs, drawings, reports, memoirs, stories, and *belles lettres;* "the material that is collected . . . will be collated and organized systematically and will form part of a projected volume of "Collected Materials on the History of the Refugee Movement during the World War."[143] This doctrine represents a significant shift away from the earlier emphasis on supervision and discipline, which inevitably tended to deny a voice to refugees.[144]

This project, which eventually yielded several published accounts of episodes in the lives of refugees, straddled the final months of the tsarist regime and the short life of the provisional government.[145] Throughout 1917, a subcommittee of dignitaries, officials. and historians continued to encourage the collection of material for the projected history of refugeedom, "recognizing that facts and observations, even if they seem at first to be insignificant and trivial, may prove to be of great interest. . . . The most important thing is for the description to be sincere and truthful."[146]

CONCLUSION

An emphasis on the magnitude of chaos and spontaneity in the displacement of refugees served to justify government intervention, but also allowed the professional intelligentsia to buttress its claims to expert mediation in the project of refugee relief. However, the rhetoric of displacement, disorder, and disease must be deconstructed. Confusion undoubtedly existed, but it was not limited to refugees who had been forced to leave their homes at a moment's notice. Displacement caused no less of a panic in government circles and in provincial society. But the evidence also suggests that community solidarity among refugees had not completely shattered. Organized attempts were made to reconstitute communities, often (as we shall see) reinventing them in a "national" form.

The widespread tendency to consider the plight of refugees from either a victimological or a public order perspective missed important elements of refugeedom. Like other "marginal" social groups, refugees had the potential to organize themselves, to affirm their right to dignified and humane treatment, and also to assert claims to be accorded at least the same rights in the imperial polity as people who had not been displaced. In this regard, the war created some unexpected opportunities. By employing the language of citizenship, as some did, refugees could in principle count upon the support of liberal opponents of tsarism, who had found a new battle to fight. Whether a liberal regime would in turn guarantee full rights to displaced persons in a reformed polity was much less certain.

Refugees were determined not to be overlooked in the chaotic conditions of the time. They refused to be stigmatized by tsarist officials, let alone to be treated with contempt. But this self-assertion also carried with it an important paradox. Their very claim to be heard—and fed, sheltered, and offered medical treatment—contributed to the creation of a refugee category from which escape could prove extremely difficult.[147] To demand attention was also to assume the status of a victim, since this was often the only means of obtaining material support from hard-pressed agencies. Other rights, including the right to be regarded as a member of civil society, were more difficult to acquire. In this respect, the emergence of national committees became an important means of articulating a different kind of identity. Problematic as such claims were to the tsarist regime, they posed no less of a challenge to the emergent liberal opposition.

Cultural attitudes on the part of the settled population also reinforced a sense that refugees could be amalgamated into a distinct category. In the short term it was relatively easy to stimulate prompt relief efforts by telling dramatic tales of suffering and hardship. But refugees could easily become an object of contempt, because they disturbed, threatened, and even shattered the prevailing public space. Furthermore, as diseased bodies ("dying like flies" in the Caucasus), some refugees were liable to be incarcerated in special barracks or hospitals, where they could be isolated from the local population.[148] It is easy to forget the novelty, suddenness, and sheer scale of the influx of unfamiliar faces. "Refugees, as a new social factor breaking into people's lives, arouse a whole range of issues, fears, and questions, which have little to do with altruistic sentiment," wrote the editor of *Bezhenets*. How was this challenge to be met?[149]

In prompting local people to offer charitable assistance to refugees, officials and journalists created an easily recognizable image—reinforced by vivid snapshots—of "ill old men, weak women with a horde of children, barefoot, ravenous, and half-naked."[150] By labeling and merging the newcomers in this way, public organizations, charities, and official agencies drew attention to the peculiarities of the refugee, to the unfortunate combination of degradation and helplessness that he or she embodied. Even the expression of gratitude was shaped by onlookers in such a way as to convey a sense of the pitiful and childlike refugee.[151] As a result, it became possible to create a single category of difference. "The word 'refugees' signifies a numerous body of people, people of any age, sex, and social status"; "Old men, children, women, girls—they are all 'refugees'," wrote one popular storyteller.[152] Thus, in the process of drawing a distinction between refugees and themselves, members of Russian educated society helped to construct an image of an archetypal or "essential" refugee. Nevertheless, as we shall see in the next chapter, contrary tendencies might operate to sustain a more differentiated image.

Drawing "Dva begstva" [Two Flights] by I. Gur'ev. *Rodina: illiustrirovannyi zhurnal dlia semeinogo chteniia* [Motherland: Illustrated Journal for Family Reading], no. 1, January 3, 1916.

"Latvian refugees near Riga." *Sinii zhurnal,* no. 39, September 26, 1915.

Refugees en route from the Baltic region to the Russian interior.

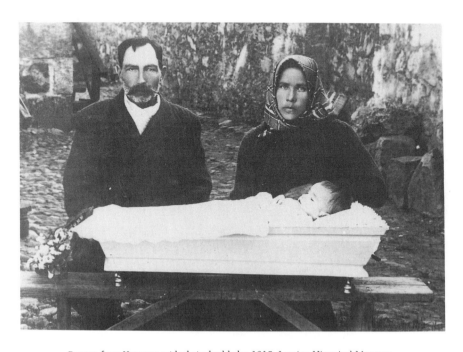

Parents from Kurzeme with their dead baby, 1915. Latvian Historical Museum.

Latvian refugees camped in the forest, 1915. Latvian Historical Museum.

Latvian refugees in Roslavl', 1915.
The Russian soldiers are bystanders. Latvian Historical Museum.

Refugee children and Russian troops. Russian State Photographic Museum.

"Jewish refugees in the forest on the outskirts of Vilna."
Sinii zhurnal, no. 39, September 16, 1915.

"Refugees eating the remnants of the soldiers' meal," with inset,
"Without a father or mother." *Letopis' voiny,* no. 91, May 14, 1916.

"Refugees do not lose heart."
Letopis' voiny, no. 71,
December 24, 1915.

"A refugee child who has lost her parents finds refuge with a stranger."
Letopis' voiny, no. 71, December 24, 1915.

The Severopomoshch' [Northern Aid] canteen in Vidzeme, 1916.
Latvian Historical Museum.

"Refugees on Angliiskii prospekt, Petrograd." *Sinii zhurnal,* no. 33, August 15, 1915.

"Registration of refugee children in Petrograd." *Sinii zhurnal,* no. 53, 1915.

Refugee children in Petrograd engage in a snowball fight.
Komitet Ee Imperatorskogo Vysochestva Velikoi Kniazhny Tatiany Nikolaevny
[Committee of Her Imperial Highness Grand Duchess Tatiana Nikolaevna], vol. 1, 1916.

Children's orphanage run by Khar'kov Ladies' Committee. *Komitet Ee Imperatorskogo Vysochestva Velikoi Kniazhny Tatiany Nikolaevny*, vol. 1, 1916.

Children's home in Minsk province. *Komitet Ee Imperatorskogo Vysochestva Velikoi Kniazhny Tatiany Nikolaevny*, vol. 1, 1916.

Sewing workshop for refugee women. *Komitet Ee Imperatorskogo Vysochestva Velikoi Kniazhny Tatiany Nikolaevny,* vol. 1, 1916.

The Ekaterinoslav Council of National Organizations for Refugee Relief.
Komitet Ee Imperatorskogo Vysochestva Velikoi Kniazhny Tatiany Nikolaevny, vol. 1, 1916.

5.

⌒

REFUGEES AND GENDER

*The old beliefs, the time-honored foundations, the customary forms
are breaking down. They have lost their meaning and force. Thanks
to the triumph of political reaction, new foundations and renovated
forms have not yet emerged, and people have lost their way.*
—DMITRII ZHBANKOV, "SEXUAL BACCHANALIA
AND SEXUAL COMPULSIONS" (1908)

*What is there to cry about, when there is so much of interest before
you?*
—E. SHVEDER, *BEZHENTSY*

*And how do refugees live locally? They starve, run around naked, and
live in appalling conditions and in such destitution that they drive
their wives and daughters on to the street to join the ranks of
prostitutes.*
—E. M. ROZENBLIUM, SPEECH AT THE EXTRAORDINARY
PIROGOV CONGRESS, APRIL 1916

The constitution of refugeedom entailed several implications for notions of gender
in late imperial Russia. Although the fact attracted scarcely any comment, relatively
few refugees were able-bodied men, many of whom had already been conscripted
into the Russian army.[1] By implication, patriarchal forms of authority were called
into question from the very moment of displacement. It fell to the adult women
among their number to attend to the immediate needs of the refugee population,
many of whom were directly dependent upon them.[2] At the same time, the war
presented opportunities for other women. Educated women, who had slowly begun to enter Russia's public sphere, were allowed to claim a particular duty to care
for refugees—men, women, and children—who entered the Russian interior. This
gendered expertise further enhanced their civic profile, which had already been
boosted by the entry of women into the sphere of military nursing.[3] Since feminine
duty was deemed to lie in the care and treatment of wounded soldiers, it was but
a short step to the assertion of feminine obligation toward other victims of war. The
articulation of concern for family integrity also implied the partial feminization of
public discourse.[4] Russian women asserted the right to get involved, precisely because issues of household collapse and reconstitution were at stake. So, too, were

the care and rehabilitation of orphans, for whom special provision had to be made. This suggests the elaboration of a range of claims to specific female responsibilities, some of which had no precedent in imperial Russia.

Other issues were also at stake, in addition to the articulation of feminine responsibility for the health, security, and moral well-being of refugees. The preponderance of women among the refugee population had profound repercussions for the public profile of women—and men, as we shall see shortly. Traditionally, women tended to migrate to towns to a much lesser extent than did men, although this picture was beginning to change around the turn of the century. The war loosened the remaining constraints on women's spatial mobility, driving them from their homes and compelling them not only to assume new kinds of domestic responsibilities, but also to enter public spaces that had previously been closed to them. But the contrast between peacetime migration and wartime displacement needs to be drawn more carefully. As Barbara Engel has demonstrated, peasant women who left the fields for the city before 1914 were released to a degree from the constraints of the patriarchal peasant household.[5] The growth of new employment opportunities in the expanding urban-industrial war economy gave a new impetus to the prewar pattern of migration. However, the implications were quite different for refugee women, who were often obliged to travel with their dependents. From this point of view, refugeedom did not reinforce the sense of liberation associated with geographical mobility; rather, it served to remind women of their "domestic" duties, now transferred to the contingents of vulnerable refugees. Yet—to complicate matters further—the war disrupted the traditional institutions of rural life, depriving men of direct access to the established peasant community, in which their supremacy was more or less guaranteed. The war encouraged refugees to devise new arrangements for their self-preservation. Women had an opportunity to take the leading role in defining new social and economic duties. Whether on the road or in the refugee camp, there were no ready-made institutions in which patriarchal government was secure. The question then arises: Did refugeedom make the task of establishing women's claim to basic rights more difficult or less?

In another respect, too, we need to think quite cautiously about women and spatial mobility. Whether or not an individual peasant woman had traveled beyond the village in search of work before the war, she continued to retain an attachment to her home. These ties were rudely broken in 1915. During her enforced migration, she was constantly reminded of the various aspects of domestic routine that had conferred one kind of meaning on her life. Makeshift cooking arrangements, temporary housing, and formalized public welfare may all have contributed to feelings of grief and shame. But refugee women normally kept these emotions private, and it is difficult for the historian to catch a glimpse of them, except at moments of acute loss. Perhaps the fact that displacement was so prevalent made them easier to bear. One thing seems clear: only a crude equation of women's domestic sphere with "oppression" could allow us to think of refugeedom as a form of liberation, and only a blinkered approach to displacement could overlook the constant fatigue that resulted from the incessant attention to family members. We are right to be suspicious when male contemporaries gave vent to views about the "devoted" wife and mother, but we should not dismiss the possibility that many refugee women felt a sense of pride and purpose in assuming additional duties—even if the responsibilities of refugeedom were bought at a heavy price.[6]

These questions do not exhaust the relationship between refugeedom and gender. The ascription of gender roles in pre-revolutionary Russia was liable to other kinds of interrogation. Much of the contemporary discourse of refugeedom dealt implicitly rather than explicitly with issues of gender. Narratives of refugee displacement and need did not spell out the gender of the refugee. Sexual identity, like class identity, was frequently a concealed characteristic, one that was subsumed within the broader category of the refugee subject. When publicity was given to gender, it tended to emphasize the need to protect feminine virtue, to sustain women's duties relating to motherhood and domesticity, or to draw attention to the vulnerable female psyche.[7] But this point can be pressed further, with respect to masculinity. The historical record yields few explicit references to male gender.[8] Partly, as already indicated, this reflected the gender distribution of refugees, who were disproportionately female. But maleness was perhaps a non-issue for more subtle reasons. To maintain silence on this score may have been a deliberate device to draw a veil over the de-masculinization of the male refugee. The refugee could be portrayed more comfortably as a victim, where she was female, but to draw attention to the male refugee was to picture him in terms of incapacity or failure. In other words, the male refugee had implicitly been unable to secure the integrity of his family. He had failed to sustain the livelihood of family members. He depended on handouts from charitable institutions. He could be portrayed as a hostage of enemy action, but once he became an innocent and passive victim there was little to distinguish him from his female counterpart. Like the shell-shocked soldier, the male refugee was unmanned.[9]

NARRATING THE EXPERIENCE OF FEMALE REFUGEES

The short stories written by the Russian naturalist Evgenii Shveder demonstrate something of the portrayal of gendered refugeedom. They do not broach the delicate question of masculine incapacity—quite the reverse, in fact.[10] In one story a refugee woman in great distress recounts how she lost everything she owned, including her beloved cat. Her past is tragic, her future insecure: she has no idea of her final destination. Suddenly her husband breaks in, proudly flexing his muscles and announcing that the family will be able to survive thanks to his physical prowess. In the next episode a young mother assures her anxious child that, although evil people have seized their home, they will eventually be able to go back. This theme is developed in the next story, where a mother tells her daughter that their flight provides an opportunity to explore new places; the lights of the big city make an overwhelming impression on mother and daughter. In other stories Shveder resumes the subject of the distraught woman struggling to cope in the face of disease and inadequate medical care. "So many tears, so much woe—why have you not looked kindly upon us?" is the question put to God by one mother as her child lies dying in her arms.[11]

Shveder was not alone in establishing a gendered hierarchy of helplessness. Refugees themselves drew upon personal experience to show how prescribed gender roles might be preserved amid social upheaval. A short story by a Russian priest, Vetlin, tells of the reassurance offered a young girl ("I'm scared") by her brother, who guides her to safety across a river. The boy is brave, determined, and responsible; the girl is vulnerable, innocent, and trusting.[12] A young Armenian peasant farmer, Michael Zaituntsian, described how the Turks had tormented him and separated him from his family. Michael wanted to cry, "but I pulled myself together and refused to cry; I realized that this was the women's way, and that I had to cope differently." He thus went out and killed a Turkish soldier who was holding women and children hostage. Melodramatic accounts such as these helped to restore confidence in the integrity of gender boundaries.[13]

The English nurse Violetta Thurstan also betrayed a keen awareness of distinctions of gender. Thurstan was at pains to distinguish between refugees and to highlight the needs of female refugees: "The old men can be made content with a little tobacco and the company of their old cronies; perhaps, too, they are a little more used to travelling and mixing with the outside world than the women, who seem to miss terribly their accustomed seat near the stove among their familiar household goods." Distinctive needs justified differential treatment. Hence it was vital to restore a sense of purpose among the female refugees, by giving them "household" tasks in order to restore a commitment to domesticity. Women received tiny allowances to enable them to buy food for their dependents; what mattered, according to Thurstan, was not the amount, or the fact that food could have been prepared more efficiently by communal kitchens, but rather the opportunity given to women to remain active and to retain the dignity that went hand in hand with domestic responsibilities.[14]

The children's colonies organized by the Tatiana Committee—with their emphasis on fresh air, contact sports, and baths—reproduced similar distinctions. For a start, the sexes were rigorously segregated. In Voronezh, girls were instructed to make their own beds and to maintain the cleanliness of their living quarters. Outdoor activities were neither neglected nor left to chance: older girls gathered berries on behalf of local peasants, who paid them 50 kopecks for an eight-hour day. Boys were supplied with fishing rods, since "fishing . . . is their favorite pastime." Nothing was said about any domestic chores for them.[15]

Inevitably, refugee women faced other stereotypes. Offers of work made it clear that they were regarded chiefly as a source of domestic service. Opportunities for paid housework presented themselves in towns across Russia, as they had to migrant women before the war. In the village, on the other hand, refugees found it difficult to secure work, especially during the winter months, except as washerwomen.[16] Welfare workers pointed out that many refugee women were likely to find such a position demeaning, by virtue of their social status. In such cases they were persuaded instead to join sewing circles or to spin and weave at home; many of them had to be taught how to perform these tasks.[17] Exhibitions of refugee crafts played up the fact that customers could examine and purchase "items of women's work: pressed flowers, hats, caps, shoes, slippers, and all manner of beautiful handicrafts."[18] But these suggestions did not correspond to the needs and wishes of all women, particularly those from a working-class background, who expressed a preference for paid work in factories producing confectionery, matches, or tobacco, where they would have an opportunity to socialize more freely.[19]

Sometimes the efforts made by refugee women startled contemporary onlookers. Thus newspapers in Petrograd not only publicized a hostel where women continued to keep a watchful eye over their children, but also felt obliged to portray it as a "female kingdom" (*zhenskoe tsarstvo*), in which women also showed an impressive capacity to deal with officialdom. Admiration, amusement, and anxiety all coalesced to form this response.[20] However, contrary images were always more numerous, conveying feminine rage or vulnerability rather than control and power. Stories were told of Russian women in Tbilisi who looted the shops of Armenian merchants in protest at the rise in food prices; this kind of behavior could quite easily be explained—if not justified—in terms of a moral economy that the "housewife" had a duty to uphold.[21]

Other narratives told a yet more terrible tale. A report from Ruzskii uezd, Moscow province, focused on a woman who had been separated from her young baby during the flight east: "This event had unsettled her so much that she dropped everything and went off in an unknown direction." What might, in the circumstances, have been portrayed as a perfectly understandable action served instead to foster a belief in the essential frailty and unpredictability of women.[22] Not surprisingly, stories from the Caucasus exerted a particularly horrific effect. One Russian publicist lamented the fact that "pretty girls and women were shared out among Kurdish beys and Turkish officials."[23] Not sparing the sensibilities of his readers, a young doctor spoke of seeing the graves of Armenian women whose breasts had been cut off. He described how one woman went mad after being forced to witness Kurdish soldiers smash the skulls of her children on the wall of her house.[24]

Only rarely did the contrary image of the heroic female refugee find its way into the contemporary media. The journalist V. Muizhel' published a photograph of the heroic "refugee Sapega," who had prevented German troops from seizing her livestock. She was subsequently awarded the George Medal. More dramatic still was the tale of an anonymous refugee who had tricked a party of German soldiers into thinking that she could direct them back to their base camp near Tarnopol'. Instead of helping them, she took out a bomb that had been concealed in her bag, threw it in their midst, and wounded all eight of them. She was rewarded with her photograph in the local newspaper.[25] But these exceptions prove the general point. The publicity demonstrated that these women had behaved "manfully," unlike most of their fellow refugees.

For young married women, in particular, the main task was to concentrate on improving their mothering abilities. A frequent refrain of contemporary commentaries was that displacement had undermined maternal care, giving rise instead to pathological behavior. Narratives of refugeedom were riddled with tales of desperate mothers who had been unable to prevent the progressive malnutrition of their children, who had failed to prevent the death of their children from infectious disease, or—most shocking of all—who had deliberately murdered their starving or sick children in a fit of madness. Once the refugee population became more settled, an opportunity arose to address the vexed issue of infant mortality, for so long a matter of profound concern to zemstvo doctors. Pregnant women were offered places at the Petrograd "school for mothers," where they received instruction in child care, in the hope that they would learn the need for proper neo-natal care and thus enhance the prospects for the next generation of Russian subjects.[26] In this way, refugee relief was harnessed to self-improvement and eugenics.

VICE AND VICIOUSNESS

More frequently, female refugees were deemed to be in need of protection, not from the enemy or from tsarist officials, but rather from unscrupulous and mercenary or lustful individuals. By virtue of their sex, women were believed to be exposed to specific dangers.[27] Refugee women turned to prostitution out of a desperate need to feed themselves and their dependents. In the words of the veteran zemstvo physician Dmitrii Zhbankov, "For want of a piece of bread, hungry refugee women are drawn into debauchery."[28] Sometimes their husbands or fathers forced them to sell their bodies for sex.[29] The hazards began the moment refugees left their homes and traveled to the Russian interior. The train journey was invested with particular risks:

> Attention female refugees! The editor of *Iugobezhenets* considers it his duty to make refugee women aware of the need to be extremely careful when dealing with men who offer their services and protection during the journey. These people move in groups through trains where they make the acquaintance of young refugee girls, passing themselves off as respectable citizens. But when the train reaches its final destination they demonstrate their cunning by leading their victims to dens of iniquity.[30]

Graphic stories reached the Special Council about the vulnerability of refugee girls to the temptations of the urban milieu. Their protection from "lascivious actions" and sexual abuse (*liubodeianie*) required vigorous and urgent intervention by the Russian Society for the Protection of Women (Russkoe obshchestvo zashchity zhenshchin, established in 1901) and Russia's Roman Catholic Society.[31] Predatory brothel keepers reportedly scoured the ranks of refugees in Petrograd for potential prostitutes. Welfare workers commented on the depressing ease with which grasping madames gained access to women's refuges.[32] Violetta Thurstan paid particular heed to the moral condition of young refugee women. She applauded the intervention of female students in Petrograd who had "done admirable work in keeping the young girls straight and out of temptation."[33] Overcrowding posed moral as well as physical dangers. Where numbers could not be reduced, it mattered that refugees should at least be segregated according to sex. So alarming did educated society find prostitution before 1914—Aleksandr Blok was moved to describe St. Petersburg as "a gigantic brothel"—and so widespread was the link made between prostitution, crime, and disorder that it is hardly surprising to find so much attention given to preventive measures during wartime.[34] Leading lawyers such as A. F. Koni advocated the creation of a team of refugee guardians, employed on the railways and specially trained to keep an eye on refugee women who might be the subject of unwelcome advances by pimps when the train stopped at a station—who might, in the colorful euphemism of the time, become the target of unscrupulous men engaged in the "recruitment of live goods" (*verbovka zhivogo tovara*).[35]

Yet there remained some ambiguity about the link between refugeedom and prostitution. Not all contemporaries pinned the blame on those who organized commercial sex. There was also a belief that young women offered themselves all too willingly to prospective customers, choosing "debauchery" as a means of economic survival.[36] The chief means of deterrence—salvation from commercial sex—and of moral improvement was, first and foremost, to learn a trade. If women could not or would not marry in wartime, at least they could be encouraged to acquire some legitimate income and avoid the temptation to sell their bodies. Young girls could be taught to sew and cook, allowing them to acquire a sense of self-respect.[37]

Wherever possible, young women were to be housed either in sheltered accommodation or with their parents. But it was easier to make this recommendation than to put it into practical effect. The government's advisers were well aware that the housing problem was likely to get worse. One solution was to promote the building of more workhouses and rural "colonies" where young women might live in greater seclusion. In addition, they could learn the virtues of hard work and receive appropriate training, enabling them to ply a trade or to work in cottage industry when they left.[38]

These approaches suggest that contemporary opinion about prostitution had undergone yet another shift. After 1905, most reformers pinpointed the need for the individual to exercise sexual self-restraint, rather than for the state to regulate prostitution along traditional bureaucratic–police lines. During the war, the scale of population displacement suggested to Russia's liberals that private control would not suffice. A definite place must be found for benevolent public supervision of those "at risk," who could not and should not be expected to assume sole responsibility for their actions, given the intense and overwhelming impact of refugee-dom.[39]

Other stories emphasized the dangers that lurked in the sprawling urban settlements. *Vestnik iuga* in Ekaterinoslav reported the dramatic tale of a young refugee couple who had found their way to Moscow. Instead of finding happiness, they met with tragedy. The young woman's partner spotted her embracing another man in a cinema, and in a fit of jealous rage, he shot her and then turned the gun on himself. The implicit moral of the story was that displacement and deracination made it all too easy to lose one's self-control.[40]

Sometimes the very silence of the surviving sources speaks of the almost casual way in which the fate of young refugees might be decided. In May 1917, the officials who administered children's homes on behalf of Sobezh considered an unusual request from one I. S. Ermolov, a resident of the small town of Pereslavl'-Zalesskii, who asked to be allowed to take home "one young girl between two and five years of age" from the local monastery. Is it only because of a modern sensibility that one is shocked at this bold and peremptory proposal—with its very precise specification of age and gender—and unwilling to accept that it was prompted by an innocent wish to help? Does the fact that the officials at Sobezh passed the proposal to the monks for a decision imply that they too had reservations which they were unable or unwilling to voice? Did Ermolov have a more innocent motive, perhaps to substitute a refugee child for a daughter who had died in infancy—a surprise "gift" for a distraught mother? Whatever the motives of those involved, one is entitled to wonder at Ermolov's presumption that young girls could be procured in this manner, and struck by the vulnerability and utter powerlessness of refugee children.[41]

The published record gives little indication of the extent to which Russian and non-Russian women suffered serious sexual assault, whether from soldiers (enemy or otherwise) or from civilians. Stories gathered by the tsarist police and corroborated after the war spoke of attacks by Cossacks on Jewish women in and around Vilna and Minsk, but these were of course concealed from the Russian public.[42] Newspapers carried articles from time to time, warning women of the fate that might befall them if they encountered unscrupulous men and dropped their guard.[43] The one notable exception concerns Armenian victims of Ottoman atrocities. "Armenian women have, against their will, become victims of the animal instincts of men who pursue them without any shame, like a hunter in pursuit of its prey."[44] A contemporary report from the provincial town of Erzindzan told of "countless" Armenian women who had been raped by Turkish troops. Most of those who had become pregnant could not bear the humiliation and sought an abortion. In desperation, one young mother had smothered her newborn infant.[45] "Those who are unfamiliar with the history and psychology of the Armenian people will regard this behavior as fanatical and barbaric, but those of us who have seen the hatred toward Muslims instilled in the hearts of Armenian women understand that it is connected to the wish to be rid of all contact with their former captors."[46] Armenian reporters also drew attention to the predatory and outrageous behavior of the Kurdish population of western Armenia, who held thousands of Russian women and children captive in appalling conditions where sexual exploitation was rife.[47] Contemporaries asked their readers to understand why, in these circumstances, some Armenian women might commit suicide: "This is not surprising when one takes into account the religious and moral upbringing of Armenian womanhood. The outrage inflicted on her honor and dignity is not just a huge crime but an earthly catastrophe [*zemnoe bedstvie*]," to which death was the only response.[48]

THE CARE OF REFUGEES AS A GENDERED RESPONSIBILITY

The claim to feminized expertise was founded on carefully drawn images of the particular qualities and experience of predominantly middle-class women. In this respect, the activities of professional women in the years before the war now created the possibility of still greater intervention designed to "protect" women. Inevitably, there were limits to intervention. Few towns could as yet boast an active branch of the Russian Society for the Protection of Women. Only Petrograd and Kiev were regarded as sufficiently organized and vigilant, and even they faced an uphill struggle to obtain adequate resources. Besides, these well-meaning volunteers also confronted the problem of how to secure the compliance of refugees. Not all refugees took kindly to a moral crusade against sexual promiscuity that sometimes masqueraded as a campaign against prostitution.[49]

Female physicians acquired important responsibilities during the war, not least because of the preponderance of women and young children among the refugee population. For instance, doctors such as E. P. Unanova, E. E. Burgardt, and M. F. Korsak were sent to the Caucasus by the Pirogov Society in order to attend to the needs of Armenian refugees.[50] This represented a significant extension of female access to the professional sphere.

Middle-class women did not limit their activities to monitoring the sexual conduct and physical well-being of refugees in their care.[51] They also extended the scope of charitable activity in which they had engaged before the war. The war inspired a multitude of "ladies' committees," "ladies' circles" (*damskie kruzhki*), and "maidens' societies" (the latter in the Caucasus), which collaborated with other agencies, such as the Tatiana Committee, and arranged programs of welfare and work on their own account.[52] In Tver', the ladies' circle set up kitchens and canteens, helped refugees find somewhere to live, and created sewing circles to keep female refugees occupied. Its leading light, Sofiia Mikhailovna Biunting, had a background in good works, having chaired for several years the long-established local charity Dobrokhotnaia kopeika (literally, "the Obliging Kopeck"). The chronicler of all this hectic activity felt it necessary to emphasize that the volunteer workers showed not only sympathy toward refugees but also feminine qualities of "tenderness and love."[53] E. V. Kolobova, wife of a local official in Ekaterinoslav, set up a refugee committee, in part with funds donated by white-collar workers at the South Russian Dnepr Metallurgical Company.[54] From the Urals town of Ekaterinburg came a report of the devoted work of Nina Vladimirovna Smirnova, who found housing for a hundred refugees at the local copper mine and never missed an opportunity to assist refugees.[55] In Novgorod, the local Tatiana Committee encouraged women to volunteer as assistants whose task would be to supervise workshops, inspect housing, check the financial status and needs of refugees, and organize collections of money. Once again, the correspondent judged it insufficient to catalogue the practical steps that women had taken on behalf of the refugee population. The "female element" had developed a "sensitive and compassionate relationship" with the refugee population.[56] In the Caucasus, several "Armenian maidens' societies" (*obshchestva armianskikh devits*) had been active since the winter of 1914, calling upon "all Armenian girls to offer material and moral support to refugees."[57] Parties of girls went from house to house at Christmas, singing hymns and collecting money for the aid of "homeless, helpless, hopeless little children."[58]

Several diocesan committees joined in the celebration of feminine public activism. In Simbirsk, the aptly named Anna Nikolaevna Benevolenskaia—the widow of a priest who lived opposite the railway station—was praised for her readiness to alert the local committee to the imminent arrival of trainloads of refugees. This "elderly, energetic, and cultivated woman" was held up as an example to all readers of the diocesan journal.[59] She appears to have answered the call published in *Zhenskoe delo* for women to frequent railway depots and see for themselves the plight of refugees: "Go to them and extend a friendly hand of assistance; give them not only a piece of bread, clothing, and shelter, but also love and tenderness. Who, if not women, can understand the suffering of the mother . . . ?"[60] Orphaned and homeless children deserved particular care: "The world is full of kind people, and it is to be hoped that our mothers, looking at their own children, will not forget those who stand in need of a mother's tenderness, as well as food and shelter."[61]

This level of commitment did not satisfy Russian nationalist opinion. One jaundiced commentator drew a distinction between the energetic enthusiasm of Polish and other non-Russian female volunteers and Russian women. "There is no shortage of kind-hearted welfare workers [in the Polish national organization in Petrograd]. . . . When one Russian woman volunteered her services, she was turned away by the Poles because large numbers of Polish women were willing to contribute to the welfare of refugees."[62]

Monarchical authority also served to reinforce prescribed gender roles among those who volunteered to assist refugees. It is worth emphasizing that one of the chief agencies for refugee relief was named after the tsar's daughter, who embodied the virtuous ministry of Russian women and whose contribution to refugee relief included the comfortably "feminine" task of sewing fabrics that were subsequently auctioned to raise money.[63] Tatiana was held up as a dutiful daughter and a model representative of the Romanov dynasty. The visits she and her family made to provincial towns and villages provided an opportunity to arrange simple demonstrations of royal benevolence and popular loyalty. Typically, those who staged such occasions chose a young refugee girl to present an icon or gifts of sewn fabric, and to pray for the future health and happiness of the royal family.[64] Here the Russian public was invited to forget descriptions of the degenerate and sordid atmosphere of the court, to set aside suppositions about the routinized world of the Petrograd bureaucracy, and to focus instead on the pure and selfless spirit shown by the tsar's daughter.

No one, however, should confuse these orchestrated expressions of loyalty with the genuine emotion conveyed in letters to Tatiana and her officials, particularly when families had been reunited. "Thank you, dear Tsarevna, for finding my daughter for me. I kiss your hand and foot for having brought us back together. . . . For now, farewell, Tsarevna Tatiana. Thank you for your labors," wrote one grateful refugee woman. Anna Khmurchik, *bezhenka,* wrote, "My husband Martyn Petrovich and our children have been found, for which I thank you from the bottom of my heart."[65] Jan Konopli promised to pray eternally to God for the health and longevity of all those who had given him precious news of his family. Filipp Kukharchuk wrote, "I have suffered grievously, but you understood my misfortune and my unhappy soul and found my sister for me."[66] We should acknowledge the sincerity of such sentiments, while not being surprised that the Tatiana Committee sought to exploit the propaganda value of such messages. At stake, after all, was the prestige and even authority of the royal family. In the words of the Voronezh branch of the committee, "The name of the Tsar's daughter will live on for many years as a protector of the unfortunate and the miserable."[67] At a time when the popularity of the Empress Alexandra had dwindled beyond hope of recovery, it is worth remembering that at least one of her daughters kept alive the association between royalty, humanitarianism, and "femininity."

CONCLUSION

The careful designation of the rules of engagement between refugee (and non-refugee) men and women confirms the point made by R. I. Moore in his compelling study of pollution fears in medieval Europe: "If new social boundaries are being established it will be appropriate to consider whether heightened vigilance over sexual matters may be one means of securing them."[68] Manifestations of such watchfulness were already evident before the outbreak of world war, in the regulations that governed Russian prostitution, as well as in the fear that the migrant was a prime site for the propagation of sexually transmitted disease. Now, however, the danger was much more extensive; to fail to exercise sufficient vigilance was to expose Russia's towns and villages to an influx of sexually active—maybe also uninhibited—refugee women, as well as to the predatory actions of pimps and brothel owners. From this point of view, rules about sexual segregation, sexual conduct, and sexual hygiene also revealed underlying fears about threats to the security of other boundaries in the Russian empire.

The war prompted a flurry of activity among middle-class Russian volunteer workers and female professionals. In retrospect, it is not difficult to detect a contrast between the portrayal of their attributes and those of the refugee. Intervention reflected refinement and dutiful benevolence, whereas the refugee population manifested coarseness, confusion, helplessness. Yet for all their commitment to the tasks of welfare, Russia's women did not achieve much prominence either on the Tatiana Committee or in the public organizations. Contemporary publicity material demonstrates this quite clearly. Women were largely invisible in the written accounts of organized refugee relief. Although they figure in the photographic record as clerical staff, actively engaged in registering refugees, handling requests to trace missing persons, or (like Lenin's sister) helping to find lost luggage, they remain in the shadows, dutiful yet anonymous assistants to male officials. No women sat on the central Tatiana Committee in Petrograd, at least not until after the February revolution. Nor did the democratic impulses unleashed by revolution raise their public profile.[69] Energetic fundraising or social work did not qualify women for anything other than subordinate status on the home front. For the most part, women were employed as volunteer workers, whose role could easily be accommodated within the existing convention of the "angel of mercy."[70]

Refugee women faced all manner of hardships and prejudices, and it is frustratingly difficult for the historian to address them with anything like the attention that they deserve.[71] No opportunities appear to have been afforded them to tell their stories in their own words. It is striking that the questionnaire drafted by the Tatiana Committee at the beginning of 1917 made no explicit mention of female refugees.[72] Only rarely did their actions receive any publicity, and only then for their propaganda value in wartime. If refugees in general have been hidden from history, refugee women were doubly banished, except insofar as they were deserving supplicants or pitiful victims, whose "nakedness" impressed itself so clearly upon contemporaries.[73] Strategies for their "protection" also cordoned women off from the gaze of historians. By extension, the same is true of gender issues as a whole. Refugees were identified as women when they conformed to prevailing stereotypes of vulnerability; the (de-)masculinized refugee was all but invisible.

6.

◦∞◦

REFUGEES AND THE LABOR MARKET

*In Russia, where the abundance of human resources appeared to be
inexhaustible, no steps have been taken to regulate or even to register
the labor force; and, as a consequence, two years of war have brought
the shortage of workers into sharp relief.*

—F. A. IVANOV, 31 MAY 1916

*It is psychologically beyond the strength of the merchant to join the
ranks of the unskilled, and for the professional musician to go down
the mine. . . .*

—V. M. VORT, "PROMYSHLENNYI TRUD I BEZHENTSY"

*Migrant workers are immortal; immortal, because continually
interchangeable. They are not born; they are not brought up; they do
not age; they do not get tired; they do not die. They have a single
function—to work. All other functions of their lives are the
responsibility of the country they came from.*

—JOHN BERGER, *A SEVENTH MAN*

None of Russia's refugee population were "immortal" in the sense in which John
Berger characterizes the status of migrant workers in western Europe. Refugees
were not "continually interchangeable," and they certainly aged, fell sick, and (in
some cases) died before they were able to go "home." For the most part they did
not have a background in the industrial economy. The search for work was normally an incidental attribute, not a condition of their spatial mobility.[1] All the same,
we must be alert to the prospect that refugees might have sought paid employment
as a means of maintaining carefully acquired skills and sustaining a sense of personal dignity and worth. This is not how it seemed to many jaded observers, who
regularly criticized refugees for avoiding work wherever possible. Even some sympathetic onlookers believed that there was some truth to this accusation, although
they accepted that exhausted and demoralized refugees were understandably reluctant to enter the labor market.

The possibility that refugees could work in order to support themselves and
their dependents did not figure prominently in public discussions of the consequences of the first wave of population displacement in the summer of 1915.[2] Most
government officials and public activists devoted their time to the alleviation of
individual physical suffering or to public health issues. Contemporary reports also

made much of the fact that the majority of refugees were not able-bodied and would need to be supported by productive workers from among the settled population. Indeed, most refugees tended to be young or old, and disproportionately female; as dependents or women with family responsibilities, they were deemed unsuitable for war work.[3] No more than one-fifth of all refugees were believed to be capable of productive labor, and in the case of Armenian refugees the proportion was thought to be less than 5 percent. Officials nonetheless devoted a good deal of time to the discussion of measures that might encourage this minority to respond to offers of paid employment.[4]

During the early months of 1916, when the situation in the labor market became more critical, the potential role of refugee labor began to command more space in the local and national press, as well as in the deliberations of the Special Council for State Defense, the chief executive agency for the administration of the war economy.[5] A shortage of labor, particularly in the agricultural sector and to a lesser degree in the coal mines of south Russia, helped to concentrate the minds of government officials. Members of the Special Council were understandably more concerned with production and with public finances, rather than with the right to work, and it was from these perspectives that employment became an issue.[6] Another argument—less frequently advanced—in favor of promoting employment among refugees was that they could substitute for "undesirable" elements in the labor force. A tendentious article in the prestigious Petrograd newspaper *Birzhevye vedomosti*, entitled "Yellow Labor and the Refugees," took the view that it would be "criminal" to continue to employ Chinese and Korean workers in Russia's Far East when there were "fit, healthy, energetic, and enthusiastic" Slavic refugees who could take their place.[7]

Whatever the justification for finding them jobs, refugees who could work sometimes featured in official discussions as a broadly undifferentiated pool of potential labor.[8] Zemstvo and municipal activists, in closer touch with the profile of the refugee population, tended to adopt a more nuanced perspective, which governed their approach to the question of refugee employment. An article in the leading mouthpiece of big business advocated a detailed statistical breakdown of the refugee population by sex, age, nationality, and occupation, but this idea was not pursued.[9] The results of more limited inquiries tended to reinforce the earlier view that relatively few refugees could (or should) participate in the labor market.[10]

FINDING WORK

Some of the first reports of refugees' search for work yielded sanguine assessments of their job prospects and praised their initiative in the absence of organized attempts to find them work. Polish refugees in Odessa had established workshops as early as July for the manufacture of buttons and other "fashion items." Many Latvian refugees quickly found work as agricultural laborers during the summer of 1915, as shoemakers, blacksmiths, joiners, cooks, and chambermaids: "They are welcomed everywhere with enormous respect."[11] Refugees in Siberia were taken on as domestic servants and farmworkers, or collected timber for the railways in Tomsk and Irkutsk; in Arkhangel'sk, the governor reported that refugees worked as auxiliary (*podsobnye*) members of the peasant family farm.[12] In the central industrial region there was sustained demand for carpenters, construction workers, and unskilled labor; by contrast, demand for servants and tailors had already been satisfied. Refugees with a trade found work easy to come by in Ivanovo-Voznesensk. In Perm', employers pleaded for unskilled laborers, as well as for skilled engineers, cooks, and chambermaids, but without much success. Refugees from Riga arrived in Nizhnii Tagil and found work as fitters, joiners, and blacksmiths. In Kazan', refugees from Minsk worked as bakers, tailors, shoemakers, and carpenters, as well as in the local abattoir.[13] The Tatiana Committee applauded the initiative of craftsmen who settled in Smolensk, where they made models of human body parts for use by medical students.[14]

Finding work remained a rather hit-and-miss affair. The published record yields abundant evidence of sharp practice by local merchants and householders who sought to take advantage of the weak bargaining position of refugees. A shopkeeper in Petrograd advertised for a 45-year-old woman to become a domestic servant and look after three young children, tasks for which he was prepared to pay a paltry five rubles a month. Although the local refugee relief committee turned him away in disgust, this kind of detailed, paternalistic concern for the individual welfare of refugees became more difficult to sustain once the numbers of refugees increased.[15] In Kiev, refugees from Russian Poland and the southwest congregated in the overcrowded Podol'sk district, where contractors adopted uncompromising methods: "The recruiting agent goes to the refuge, chooses the fittest member of the family, and takes him away without leaving any means of contact address; young children, the elderly, and the infirm are simply abandoned." Little could be done in the short term to obviate these practices.[16]

Part of the problem, as the employment office of Sobezh discovered, was quite simply that refugees were dispatched from the front to the Russian interior without due regard for the prevailing conditions of supply and demand: "The main obstacle to finding jobs for refugees is that they have been dispersed in a highly uneven fashion among the local population. We need to take steps to promote the progressive resettlement of refugees." The public organizations planned to establish a network of labor exchanges across the country, and to advertise vacancies to refugees as soon as they were announced. Those who took up offers of work would, along with family dependents, be entitled to free transport.[17]

These ambitions were thwarted as part of the state's general onslaught on public organizations. It was left instead to local municipal dumas to establish labor exchanges. Partly they were conceived as a means of undermining the sharp practices described above; more prosaically, they offered a place where refugees could meet and relax over a glass of tea and a newspaper.[18] Such attempts to organize work for refugees did not meet with universal approval: "It may be that instead of unemployed refugees the result will be a mass of unemployed local workers."[19] Nor did the actual practice of organizing employment exchanges always proceed smoothly. Mine owners in Ekaterinoslav expected to fill 22,000 job vacancies from among the refugee population, but most of those who turned up had experience only with agricultural field work, and only 1,000 positions were filled. In Penza, by contrast, there were 100,000 vacancies for agricultural laborers, but the refugees who arrived were too old or too young to undertake the backbreaking work.[20] Employers also behaved thoughtlessly, by advertising vacancies in several different exchanges without informing staff when the post was filled; as a result, refugees sometimes turned up expectantly, only to find that their journey had been in vain.[21] The solution, according to *Promyshlennost' i torgovlia,* was to resettle refugees more systematically—precisely the point made by Sobezh.[22]

Another solution to the problem of refugee unemployment lay in public support for "work relief" (*trudovaia pomoshch'*). This movement had developed during the later nineteenth century as a state-sponsored means of encouraging voluntary societies to establish "houses of industry" for unemployed workers. By 1905 there were around 150 such houses, supplemented later by instructional workshops for apprentices.[23] In the Transcaspian oblast, local authorities opened workshops to train refugees in useful crafts. Many other provinces and towns did the same.[24] National committees and local branches of the Tatiana Committee also embraced the doctrine of work relief. The propagation of this idea during the war served to emphasize that refugees fell into the category of the "deserving poor" who needed to be found temporary gainful employment prior to their eventual return to the labor market.[25] But these and other initiatives were always vulnerable to abrupt and arbitrary action by the Russian army. Refugees in Kiev, many of them Poles from Galicia, complained that they had succeeded in finding work with great difficulty, only to face deportation by the military authorities, in order to make way for Russian troops. This was a constant risk, and it jeopardized attempts to organize the refugee labor market.[26]

In the agricultural sector, the availability of a pool of refugee labor helped to offset the drain of manpower to the army, which became a matter of grave concern to the tsarist government by the spring of 1916.[27] The Special Council for Refugees noted that "the labor of all manner of people is valued in the rural economy, including women and children."[28] Up to 800,000 refugees were believed capable of making themselves available for work, although only 354,000 were employed in Russian agriculture by October 1916. Their numbers had dropped to 250,000 by 1917, still an impressive total. From the government's point of view, this result represented a triumph over refugees' perceived reluctance to move to relatively remote rural settlements.[29] It was also achieved in the face of frequent obstruction by Russian army commanders; in late September 1915, for instance, General Ivanov ordered the evacuation of refugees from Poltava and Chernigov, where they were urgently needed to harvest and process the sugar beet crop.[30]

The most important contribution made by refugees was as a source of labor on privately owned farms and estates, around 6 percent of which employed refugees. According to one source, by 1916 refugee labor amounted to around 8 percent of the total labor force in the private farm sector. By contrast, refugees contributed no more than 1 percent to the labor on the peasant family farm, despite the drain on manpower caused by the draft of second-category reservists during the autumn of 1915.[31]

Notwithstanding the modest share of refugee labor in the peasant economy, contemporary observers of the rural scene set great store by the anticipated influx of refugees into the village. The newcomers were thought likely to introduce superior farming methods to the Russian peasantry and to improve the general level of rural civilization. "Latvians have long forgotten what it means to suffer from a harvest failure or to have a shortage of bread," boasted their spokesmen.[32] From Riazan' came a plea that Latvian farmers be encouraged to impart something of their "advanced culture and knowledge" to the backward Russian peasantry.[33] The Russian village also stood in sore need of craftsmen—blacksmiths, tailors, carpenters, and so forth—whose numbers had been depleted by conscription.[34] A priest from Simbirsk expressed the hope that refugees would throw themselves wholeheartedly into village life; he had high expectations of one poor but adept blacksmith who might be able to teach one of the villagers this "not exceptionally difficult trade."[35] Indeed, he continued, these hopes had already begun to be realized: "Even in this lonely backwater [*zakholust'e*] the refugee movement has brought something new. The refugees who have arrived in the village, no matter how poor they may be, have shown the local population that there are shortcomings in their way of life and daily practices, that it is conceivable to live a better life, that it is possible to work a good deal more productively. Each of these half-starved refugees tells the peasantry that they—the refugees—cannot work as the peasants do here."[36] In another account, Polish refugees from Chelm province challenged Russian peasants in Riazan' to adopt improved farming methods: "A straw-cutting tool [*solomorezka*] is needed. 'D'you expect me to use an axe to cut straw for my horse?' asks the farmer from Chelm, in a waspish tone. 'It'll take just an hour or two with a cutter and a good man, rather than everyone wasting a whole day for no reason.' These bold words make an enormous impression on the local peasantry. 'Look, 'ere's a real farmer. . . . You shan't go far wrong with 'im.'" The author looked forward to the day when villages in Russia's black earth region would have not only their strawcutter, but steam power, electricity, schools, and a theater as well.[37]

Such optimistic visions of economic and cultural improvement proved somewhat premature and fanciful, although they were endorsed by some Russian peasants, one of whom expressed his admiration for the energy and inventiveness of refugee farmers and the craftsmanship of women weavers from Latvia.[38] Relatively few peasant farmers could find useful jobs for refugees who turned up at the *dvor*.[39] More to the point, most refugees balked at the idea of settling permanently in the village. The governor of the Priamurskii krai observed that some refugees contributed to the peasant economy to only a limited extent "because they feel themselves to be temporary residents, and are not likely to become accustomed to the special conditions of local life and work; besides which their tolerance level and state of mind render them of doubtful productive use as workers on peasant farms."[40] But perhaps this is to miss the essence of the question. The hopes that were pinned on settlement of the refugees helped at the same time to give them a better public image, something that was badly needed amid the growing charge that refugees shirked work.

The government encouraged the creation of a more active labor market in agriculture by arranging for the unrestricted movement of refugees who took up offers of work on distant farms. However, some relief committees were understandably eager to retain refugee labor in their locality. In Voronezh, for example, the local committee objected to government proposals to send refugees to the Caucasus, claiming instead that they were badly needed in the central black earth region.[41] It is interesting to reflect on the willingness of the tsarist state to promote population displacement, this time for economic rather than military purposes.[42] Nevertheless, the Special Council refused to entertain suggestions that the state assign refugees to particular jobs.[43]

Where refugees declined to work or (what amounted to the same thing) to move to rural areas, the government nevertheless planned to remove their entitlement to relief after one month had elapsed.[44] Some members of the Special Council objected that this was too rigid and rigorous a measure, others that refugees had no excuse to turn down the offers of work that were likely to come their way within four weeks. In the event, the government continued to pay a food allowance to all those under 14 years of age, as well as to refugees with dependent children (this entitlement was limited to one carer per household).[45] Significantly, the council also agreed that refugees who worked in the agricultural sector should continue to receive relief. This decision went ahead even though concern had been expressed that the government was subsidizing local landowners, who might offer low wages to refugee labor, knowing that refugees received state benefits. Other objections were couched in terms of comparability with those households that had lost breadwinners to the army, and that received only one form of benefit; but the majority opinion held that it was not unreasonable to pay additional benefits to refugees who worked in agriculture.[46] But it was also motivated by official concern that many refugees were refusing to respond to other inducements to settle in rural locations, where their labor was sorely needed. In practice, however, local authorities appear to have been reluctant to enforce instructions to deprive refugees of relief, and thus to leave themselves exposed to the charge that refugees were made to suffer twice over.[47]

There are some indications that refugees resisted these renewed attempts at manipulation. In the western provinces of the Russian empire, such as Minsk, Mogilev, and Vitebsk, refugees formed labor teams (*rabochie druzhiny*), usually according to nationality. These gangs concluded contracts with local landowners for the hire of farm animals and agricultural equipment; some were even headed by a professional agronomist. Their organization suggests an initiative that sits uneasily with prevailing images of passivity in the labor market.[48] Refugees began to organize themselves into artels in order to counter the prevalent tendency to employ them at the lowest possible wage: they were otherwise being offered jobs as laborers at around one-third of the going rate for local workers. In Nizhegorod province and Tambov, several thousand refugees joined these gangs.[49]

The use of refugees as a source of labor in the industrial economy met with a number of difficulties. Although on one level Russian industrialists might have been expected to welcome any source of labor that helped to compensate for the sudden mobilization of workers in 1914 and 1915, the availability of refugees did not prompt universal rejoicing. On the contrary, their presence in the interior frequently exposed a deep vein of prejudice. Many employers expressed disquiet about the government's intention to recruit refugees into manufacturing industry. Some industrialists doubted refugees' commitment and suitability for industrial work. Members of the Moscow War Industry Committee stated that "attempts to attract refugee workers into industrial enterprises have not met with any success to date, since this group runs off home at the first opportunity; in addition, their ignorance of the language and their unsuitability for local conditions constitute serious obstacles to their mass recruitment."[50] In Tula the provincial governor complained that refugees had behaved in a "criminal" fashion, by agreeing to take on factory work and receiving an advance on their wages, only to renege on the contract and abscond at the earliest opportunity. This, he duly noted, represented a "threat to public order."[51]

There were other reasons why refugees did not figure prominently in the expanding industrial economy. Only a small minority had any background in mining or manufacturing. By the end of 1915, around 3,200 refugees had registered with the local labor exchange in Saratov, but of these only 337 had experience of working in a factory.[52] They were outnumbered by unskilled workers and white-collar workers, for whom job opportunities were much harder to come by. Among Polish refugees in Petrograd, fewer than 10 percent were employed in factories; on the other hand, several thousand obtained work in small workshops.[53] Ukrainian refugees from Galicia fared somewhat better, finding work as weavers, whose colorful designs reportedly made a big impact on the population of Siberia.[54] Russians, Poles, and even Germans were reportedly taken on in the flour mills, paper factories, and timber yards of Simbirsk province.[55] Armenian refugees were regarded as "excellent craftsmen" who needed to be found appropriate employment.[56]

In the south Russian iron and steel industry, refugees were easily outnumbered by other categories of newly recruited workers. Of the 9,150 workers who had recently been engaged, only 1,500 were refugees.[57] By 1916, only 3 percent of the labor force in ferrous metallurgy were refugees, while in coal mining the figure was a mere 1 percent. The authorities appear to have deliberately prevented refugees from entering mining districts, in order to reduce the risks from infectious diseases.[58] It may also be that industrial managers were eager to downplay the potential contribution that refugees could play in defense production, in order to strengthen their hand in bargaining with the government over the exemption of qualified workers from the military draft. Employers were, however, justified in pointing to the shortage of skilled labor in the industrial economy; few refugees could offer the requisite skills and experience that were badly needed as the mobilization of industry gathered pace.[59] The armaments industry appears to have made use of refugees who did have the needed skills: nearly 1,000 refugees were employed, for example, at the Samara Fuse Factory, in addition to those scattered throughout munitions factories in the mid-Volga region.[60]

DEBATING THE REFUGEE WORK ETHIC

Other observers offered a different perspective, recognizing that "we cannot possibly deal with refugees solely from a market point of view," because "most refugees are psychologically disturbed."[61] Tikhon Polner wrote that able-bodied men, "finding themselves in strange places without future prospects, and having suffered untold hardships, had lost all energy and simply given up the struggle in hopeless resignation."[62] The local Catholic priest in Iaroslavl' told his colleagues on the provincial relief committee that the experiences suffered by refugees "have inflicted the most terrible shock on the psyche and produced profound emotional disturbances," which he drew upon to explain why refugees might take time to adjust to their new surroundings and respond positively to offers of work.[63] A report from Minsk spoke of the "shock to one's morale and the profound exhaustion" experienced by refugees, who took the view that "it's all the same to us, we'll go wherever they chase us."[64] Violetta Thurstan expressed alarm about the "inertia" induced by a loss of confidence and self-respect, insisting that these were quite distinct from "slacking and shamming."[65] In the words of M. Strikis, a member of the Latvian National Committee operating in Penza,

> Refugees have not been driven from their homes with kindness and consideration. On the road, "enterprising" people bought their draft animals at bargain prices. At each new place, refugees encountered people seeking to exploit them. People who enjoyed a comfortable life back home are now obliged to look for work. Families have been broken up; the domestic hearth has been left in ruins. All this has fostered among refugees a mood of apathy and a complete indifference to their new surroundings.[66]

In a similar vein, Iugobezhenets, the commission responsible for refugee relief in the southern provinces, advocated the recruitment of refugees for agricultural work, not only because of the need to improve the food supply, but also because they could derive pleasure and spiritual satisfaction from cultivating the land. Physical work would lighten the load of refugeedom.[67]

It was recognized that refugees would respond only if they were treated fairly. The charge of "exploitation" figures quite often in discussions of the employment prospects of refugees, and was used to rebut claims that refugees were malingerers. A debate in Rostov on 23 September 1915 revealed that refugees were loath to accept work because of the miserly rates of pay that were being offered, not because they were inherently work-shy. Spokesmen from Novocherkassk and from Romanovsk discovered that refugees were eager to work, because "we offer human conditions of work and don't disregard the needs of the family." Refugees should be able to support their dependents and even be able to put some money aside for when they would return to "their devastated nest" (*razorennoe gnezdo*).[68] Notwithstanding the above, many refugees, particularly in Petrograd, were forced to work at whatever wages were offered, once the authorities decided to cancel welfare benefits as an inducement to them to leave town. Not wishing to leave, hundreds of refugees stayed on to find poorly paid work in the urban economy.[69]

Little account was taken of the potential for labor organizations to mitigate some of the worst effects of the war on working-class refugees. In contrast to other belligerent economies, tsarist Russia never took the opportunity to enlist organized labor in the war economy. It was left to the public organizations—war industries committees and the unions of towns and zemstvos—to articulate an alternative vision of collective action in pursuit of better conditions of employment. A congress of VSG and VZS activists meeting in Khar'kov at the end of 1915 resolved that, "in the interests of the improved morale of refugees and their protection from such things as the exploitation of their miserable situation . . . it is imperative that they be closely connected to the settled working population, by means of the complete freedom of trade union and other labor organizations."[70] Such a radical reformulation of the issues found no favor with tsarist officials, and these bold ideas fell victim to the general bureaucratic assault on the public organizations, which was discussed earlier.

More frequently publicized than the victimization of refugees by potential employers was the charge that refugees shirked work.[71] (Some hostile observers nevertheless managed to hold two contradictory opinions at once—that refugees were "lazy," and that they competed with local people for jobs.)[72] Refugees and relief organizations alike were sensitive to this charge. One welfare worker wrote, "Whoever knows these people, whoever is close to them, knows that one should give credit to the work done by these involuntary travelers upon whom so much blame is constantly placed."[73] Others pointed out that most refugees of working age were women with young children, and that statistics did not support the view that refugees were work-shy.[74] Members of the Union of Zemstvos noted that some able-bodied refugees had good reason to reject offers of work, so that they could devote their time and energy to the search for family members from whom they had been separated.[75] Other valid reasons for turning down the offer of a job included its unsuitability (particularly in view of the refugee's qualifications), the lack of appropriate work clothes and footwear, or illness within the family.[76]

Nonetheless, several provincial relief committees (as in Iaroslavl') drew up plans to withdraw allowances from refugees who declined to accept a job, although this measure did not include women who were looking after young children. Eventually, the committee decided to create a positive rather than a negative incentive: refugees would receive an allowance, but ought not to suffer a decline in their living standards as a result of refusing work.[77] In Petrograd the city authorities at the outset sought to withdraw housing from refugees who declined offers of work; those who did not obey the order to leave would be handed over to the police.[78] These stringent initiatives followed the lead given by the Special Council for Refugees, which resolved in January 1916 that refugees who turned down the offer of work should forfeit state benefits, a move that was described as "very radical."[79] However, the government subsequently retreated. The Soviet government would later encounter similar problems. Under the stringent conditions imposed by civil war, the Bolsheviks introduced regulations designed to punish able-bodied refugees who refused to work, while continuing to support those who were physically unable to work.[80]

The published record yields other glimpses of refugees' attitudes and behavior. The journal of the Union of Zemstvos reported the views of refugees who attended the Petrograd district and city labor exchange, claiming that they had a right to be given work: "Refugees are firmly convinced of their entitlement to complete support on the part of the state, which has forced them—in their words—from their place of origin."[81] A determined group of Galician refugees expressed the view that they should not have to work at all: "We have been forcibly expelled from our homes and villages, so let others feed us now, educate our children, and give us clothes—we have no wish to work."[82] But such a forthright expression of opinion appears to have been quite unusual.[83] For many refugees, the right to work—provided that work was available at a "living wage," and that it did not entail fresh separation from family members or prevent their subsequent return "home"—conferred dignity and purpose.

ASPECTS OF DIFFERENTIATION IN THE REFUGEE LABOR MARKET

The relationship between refugees and economic activity became clear from the discussions that took place about the relaxation of residence restrictions on Russian Jews. The minister of trade and industry urged that Jews be allowed to settle not only in towns, but also in rural areas, in order to permit them to reestablish businesses that had been disrupted by the retreat from the western provinces in the summer of 1915. He was accused by colleagues of underestimating the degree of animosity that would arise between Jewish merchants and Russian peasants, and overestimating the capacity of police to maintain public order.[84] However, it became an accepted view in government that "the transfer of Jewish businesses from the western periphery will give impetus to the development of industry, and will ensure a rise in the local economy. . . . Jews will stir up the merchant guild, which has become lazy under protectionism."[85] By this means, the government agreed, some good would come from the enforced abolition of the Pale of Settlement. Refugees had a role to play not just in the expansion of production, but also in challenging the complacency of Russia's mercantile estate.[86] But not all Jewish refugees owned a business. More difficult was the plight of Jewish craftsmen and laborers who were urged to find work in order not to become a burden on Jewish charitable organizations Various efforts were made to ensure that "ruined artisans" among Russia's Jewish population were able to make ends meet.[87]

Refugees who had forfeited well-paid jobs in the professions or as members of the artistic intelligentsia fared particularly badly in the wartime labor market. The governor of the Amur district expressed the widely held view that "difficulties have been encountered in the organization of jobs for those engaged in intellectual labor."[88] The Special Council for Refugees discussed the possibility of arranging government loans for refugee *intelligenty,* but did not pursue the suggestion, on the grounds that relatively few applicants would have the necessary collateral, without which the scheme could not proceed. Besides, it was not always easy to identify the "genuine" *intelligent* as opposed to the ordinary peasant, whose needs were more limited.[89] Local relief workers drew attention to the loss of dignity that formerly well-heeled (*samostoiatel'nye,* literally "independent") refugees faced once they had exhausted their savings and were obliged to accept more menial positions in Russia's urban economy.[90] On several occasions local authorities manifested little sympathy for the plight of *intelligenty.* Count I. I. Tolstoi, the mayor of Petrograd (and by no means hard-hearted or unsympathetic to the needs of refugees), argued that the city council needed to be selective in the aid it could give; refugee schoolteachers and other members of the Latvian "intelligentsia" came low on his list of priorities, even though their prospect of finding work must have been limited.[91] The Polish Refugee Committee operated a special office for the relief of the professional intelligentsia; detailed records were kept of individuals' previous experience and qualifications, in the hope that the committee could find them appropriate work.[92] But many educated refugees would have understood the anguish that lay behind the advert placed by Osip Grigor'evich Oprysk in a newspaper in August 1916: "Refugee (Galician), now destitute, knows Russian, Polish and German, seeks employment in an office."[93]

CONCLUSION

The participation of refugees in productive economic activity betrayed an element of state coercion, cloaked in the need to prevent the state budget from spiraling out of control. This strategy—which never amounted to a complete withdrawal of assistance to refugees who turned down work—appears to have paid dividends. By the summer of 1916 the Special Council was congratulating itself on the fact that "the acute and hopeless situation in which refugees found themselves has by now largely disappeared," because the labor market had absorbed those who were able and willing to work.[94]

However, we should also direct our attention to refugees' sense of self-interest. Some "able-bodied" refugees deliberately refrained from entering the labor market, because they had no wish to become part of the local economy. To do so would have been to become embroiled in established networks of economic activity, and thus to lay the basis for their incorporation into an "alien" economy. These men and women wanted to go back "home," not to sink deep roots into their new habitat.[95] This self-denial may have meant a temporary loss of dignity and a forfeit of the tenuous material security conferred by work; but such deprivation was thought worthwhile if it emphasized the refugee's claim to welfare in the short term and ultimately to repatriation.[96]

Such determination only made it more imperative, so far as some observers were concerned, that the settled population take advantage of the skills and civilization of the newcomers while they remained in the village. It is difficult to tell whether hopes of cross-cultural contact were realized. But their articulation serves to remind us that refugeedom could be given a positive meaning, as in the following testimony:

> As I left the village of Guliushevo and reflected on the conversations I had had there, I took away the conviction that the Russian narod is beginning to wake up to the fact that its own welfare and material prosperity cannot be created if people do not shift themselves. Not for nothing is there a popular saying: "Water doesn't flow under a settled stone."[97]

To be sure, the perception of refugees as potential *Kulturträger* never supplanted more negative images that had become embedded in the popular consciousness and public discourse throughout 1915 and 1916. The growing economic crisis would only intensify such sentiments, giving credence to the suggestion that refugees imposed an intolerable burden on the host society. But the above quotation has a more remarkable subtext. In drawing attention to cultural differences between refugees and non-refugees, it simultaneously highlights perceived ethnic characteristics. These and other dimensions of refugeedom form the basis for the following chapter.

7.

∽

REFUGEES AND THE CONSTRUCTION OF "NATIONAL" IDENTITY

*What form has the contact between nationalities taken? What
relations have been established between the representatives of different
nationalities and the settled population? What innovations have
foreigners [inorodskie gruppy] introduced into Russian life, and what
will they absorb from the Russian people? What impressions will they
take from this enforced journey into a strange land, if they are obliged
to return home? How many of them will put down roots in new
places?*
    —"REFUGEES," *UFIMSKIE EPARKHIAL'NYE VEDOMOSTI*, 1 APRIL 1916

*Most of those who hitherto called themselves "Russian" are now
beginning to think of themselves as Poles, Jews, Ukrainians,
Armenians, Latvians, rather than as Russians.*
    —EDITORIAL, *SPUTNIK BEZHENTSA*, 26–28 SEPTEMBER 1915

*One cannot circumvent the national phase of social development
and pass directly to a non-national cosmopolitanism. . . . Today's
cosmopolitan types, if they reject their own people, will not embrace a
non-national state of the future, but will instead be submerged in a
different oppressor nation.*
    —J. RAINIS, *JAUNAIS VARDS*, 5 FEBRUARY 1917

The enforced resettlement of population during the First World War from areas
threatened by the enemy was termed a "national migration" by eyewitness accounts. Slavic peoples—Ukrainians, Poles, and Belorussians, as well as "Great Russians"—made up the majority, but a substantial proportion of the refugee population were Jews, Latvians, Lithuanians, and Armenians, who constituted a veritable
"mixture of racial types" (*raznoplemennaia pestrota*).[1] This "national migration" had
profound consequences. From a purely demographic point of view, some provincial "Russian" towns were transformed into polyglot and "international" centers, a
refuge for people who frequently professed non-Orthodox faiths and who sought to
cultivate non-Russian cultures.[2] More significant still, in view of the notorious suspicion in official quarters of non-Russian cultural and political organizations, population displacement created a new framework for political activity. Refugees were

afforded access to a broader national community, built on the foundations of a common sense of violation and loss and sustained by the need for collective effort to regain what had been forfeited in wartime. The struggle to overcome individual hurt was more likely to succeed if it could be harnessed to a collective struggle that validated itself in national terms. Defilement was a vital component in contemporary political discourse, as if the patriotic elite "arrived at their sense of . . . nationality by diminishment."[3]

The question of national identity also requires us to pay some attention to the attitudes and actions of the settled communities that played host to the refugee minority. Conceivably the encounter stimulated national sentiment, either because host communities respected popular culture, religion, and language, or because they behaved in ways offensive to "national" dignity and culture.[4] Armenian refugees accused their Azeri and Kurdish neighbors of profiting from their plight. In a dramatic outburst, one Georgian nationalist expressed the view that Armenians in search of a safe refuge in Tbilisi threatened to "infiltrate the Georgian population . . . raising the prospect of our forcible de-nationalization."[5] Refugees sometimes faced prejudice and anger, as a result of mistaken ethnic identity; Latvians complained of the hostile reception given them by ignorant officials or local residents who took them for Germans. In such circumstances the best defensive response was to take pride in one's Latvianness and find strength in a collective ethnic difference.[6] Some accounts implied that displacement would lead to cultural contamination, unless refugees took appropriate steps to protect themselves from vice. "Becoming separated from [home life], Latvians are drawn into late-night parties, drinking, gambling, and, even worse, depravity. . . . Books, newspapers, good theater, singing and playing music, lectures and so forth will guard against the numbing of one's mind."[7]

To complicate matters further, the settled community and the displaced sometimes shared a common ethnicity. The challenge implied in this discovery was taken up by self-appointed patriotic spokesmen, who proclaimed that refugees reminded "settlers" of the culture they had left behind, sometimes reluctantly, in search of a new life in Russia. Poles or Latvians who had been forcibly exiled could not be blamed for abandoning their homeland, but other settlers occupied a more ambivalent position in the minds of national leaders. A prominent Latvian newspaper suggested that the war had roused Latvians in Siberia from a deep torpor: "Refugees, having a higher intellectual development and superior standards of culture, have begun to create a more vital atmosphere. Interest in the latest developments in the war have turned the apathetic Siberian into an assiduous newspaper reader. Imperceptibly, closer contacts with the motherland have been established." All that remained, it was implied, was to reclaim the old settler communities for a new Latvia.[8]

Thus, well-meaning expressions of concern could have profound consequences. Where members of host communities (like nationalist leaders) urged refugees to return to their place of origin, they contributed to the realization that a "homeland" beckoned, and that it could be peopled—even governed—by a reconstituted national community. But refugees did not need to have experienced oppression, degradation, or neglect in their temporary home in order to be conscious of their ties to a lost land. To have been forcibly uprooted was itself a potent reminder that one could take pride in one's roots. Some observers found it slightly comical that non-Russian professionals—doctors, dentists, and engineers—had longed to live in Moscow before the war. Now, everything had changed: "It is touching to see how these people demonstrate affection for their 'accursed' backwoods. Tears fill their eyes as they speak about their previous existence where, not so long ago, they vegetated in such a disagreeable fashion. Now they dream of nothing more enticing than to return to this place."[9]

REFUGEEDOM AND NATIONALITY

A link between refugeedom and nationality was inscribed in the evolving structures of refugee relief. To be sure, the degree to which administrative arrangements reflected ethnic difference was a sensitive issue. The national dimension of refugeedom provoked some unease in official circles, yet little could be done to prevent the efflorescence of relief organizations catering to specific nationalities, whose efforts were grudgingly accepted by government as a means of lightening the burden on hard-pressed officials and on the public purse. In Russia's provincial towns, too, local authorities often welcomed the intervention of national committees as a means of relieving the strain on municipal budgets and concentrating on provision for the indigenous population.[10] Contrasts were sometimes drawn between the speed and efficiency of the national committees and the hesitant manner in which local authorities handled refugee relief.[11] The national committees also served another purpose so far as the government was concerned: they represented an alternative to the public organizations, whose leaders asserted a claim to organize refugee relief and resettlement throughout the empire.

It was difficult to avoid the need to identify refugees' nationality when competing claims were being made to look after their interests. Refugees were given a green book registering their name, place of origin, and ethnic affiliation, with the aim of deterring fraudulent claims for assistance from more than one national committee.[12] National committees not only transacted their business with refugees in their native language, but also devoted much of their time to arranging for tuition in the mother tongue. The Latvian organization Dzimtene created a network of schools for refugee children, with a curriculum designed to assist children in coping with their new circumstances by including instruction in Latvian and Russian language and composition, religious study (Lutheranism and Russian Orthodoxy), as well as math, nature study, singing, and gymnastics. Where schools near the front had closed, money was also earmarked to provide Latvians with instruction in their own homes.[13] Similar initiatives were launched on behalf of Armenian refugees.[14] In Khar'kov, the municipal education office established the principle that non-Russian children were entitled to the same kind of education that they would have received in their place of origin. School inspectors sometimes tried to ban the use of the national language, but the MVD did not attempt to prevent the establishment of private "national" schools.[15] The main difficulty they faced was not the obtrusive school inspector, but rather an insufficiency of good-quality staff. National committees struggled to overcome such limitations; like other activists, they hoped that schooling would stem the rising tide of juvenile crime and immorality.[16]

Many non-Russian refugees demonstrated a tendency to "integrate" themselves to some extent into the local community. In Riazan' province, home to some 68,000 refugees by the end of 1915, Lithuanian, Polish, and Latvian refugees made use of local medical services, attended local schools (where they learned Russian), and—in the case of Poles—worshipped in local Catholic churches. Refugees often found quarters in Russian neighborhoods. Officials who toured provincial towns expecting to find refugees in tight-knit groups sometimes complained that they had to look much harder in order to contact ethnic minorities. In Vladimir, the diocesan committee went out of its way to allocate housing on a non-national basis. Amid the welter of different facilities created by national committees for specific ethnic groups—canteens, apartments, clubs, schools, and orphanages—one should not lose sight of this reality.[17] Of course, practice was not uniform throughout the country. In Vologda and Novgorod, refugees were housed according to nationality, and in Tula, refugees who had been mixed asked instead to be placed with members of the same nationality.[18] Jewish refugees also tended to live a more self-contained existence. But they too attended local clinics and hospitals, and Jewish dignitaries supported the teaching of Russian in Jewish schools, now that Jews were allowed to settle in the Russian interior.[19] It would be a mistake to think that refugeedom automatically entailed the creation of fresh ghettos in provincial Russia.

Large towns appear to have taken in refugees from varying national backgrounds without causing intense inter-ethnic conflict. The authorities in Taganrog asserted that its inhabitants contributed to collections for refugee relief "without making distinctions of nationality."[20] Paustovsky recalls that "Moscow absorbed a stream of refugees from Poland, Belorussia and the Baltic countries [sic]. Their quick, sibilant accents mingled more and more often with the sing-song intonation of the natives."[21] One member of the Union of Zemstvos reported in February 1916 that Latvian refugees from Riga had settled in the town of Briansk, where they "hardly differ from the local population in their customs and behavior."[22] But not all reports spoke in such positive terms; the provincial governor of Tula noted that "the formation of national committees caused murmurs of dissatisfaction among Russian refugees, because the Poles, Lithuanians, and others received much larger allowances than they did."[23]

Relations between refugees from different national minorities appear to have become strained when refugees began the process of going "home." The issue of return and resettlement generated antagonisms because some spokesmen claimed a leading role for the "citizens' committees," whose members were anxious to exclude members of other minorities from taking part in the debate about resettlement. In March 1916, the Duma deputy Jan Garusevich came under fire for suggesting that the repatriation of refugees to liberated Polish provinces should be entrusted to so-called citizens' committees, from which Russians, Jews, and Lithuanians were to be excluded. The latter may have been a populist attempt to regain the initiative from the elite-dominated national committees.[24]

"WANDERING" JEWS AND JEWISH REFUGEEDOM

Abrupt physical displacement had an uneven impact. It entailed particularly profound social and political consequences for the Jewish population of imperial Russia. In a crucial sense the war liberated Russian Jewry, by forcing the tsarist government to recognize that it could no longer continue to sustain the Pale of Settlement—in other words, that it was more important to defeat the real enemy than to maintain administrative controls over the Jewish population of the Russian empire. Certainly, Jews continued to suffer all manner of military harassment and physical abuse.[25] However, once it was recognized that the movement of Jewish refugees could no longer be controlled by government agencies, the Pale of Settlement dissolved itself. The First World War yielded a kind of emancipation that was no less meaningful for the restrictions that remained.[26]

The opening phase of this process came during the dramatic retreat from Poland and Galicia in 1915, when the government reluctantly conceded that "Jewish war sufferers"—both those who had fled and those who had been deported—should be allowed to settle outside the Pale. Voronezh, Tambov, and Penza were the first provinces to be "opened" to Jewish refugees. On 15 August 1915, the government extended this privilege to Jews who wished to move to other towns and cities in the heart of the empire.[27] In a revealing demonstration of the depth of prejudice, the government refused to allow Jews to enter Petrograd and Moscow; nor were they permitted to settle in the Caucasus or on Cossack land.[28] Furthermore, and consistent with traditional official beliefs that Jews and peasants should be kept apart, Jewish refugees were forbidden to settle in villages. The government also forbade Jews to buy land or other real estate in the towns, as if to demonstrate that this relaxation of administrative constraint did not betoken a weakening of the ban on permanent Jewish settlement in the urban areas of European Russia. In April 1916, the government rejected appeals from local branches of the unions of zemstvos and towns that Jews be allowed to settle in villages, in order to relieve overcrowding in urban areas.[29]

Leading Jewish spokesmen had no illusions that the circular of 15 August necessarily implied political emancipation, but they were nevertheless impressed by the potential gains that might be made.[30] The practical results of this new dispensation for Jewish settlement were that two-fifths of all Jewish refugees moved to areas of the Russian empire that had previously been closed to them. Of these, around 17 percent found themselves in the provinces of central European Russia, a further 14 percent settled in the Volga region, and 7 percent moved to Siberia, the Urals, or the far north. Large numbers evidently remained in the old Pale of Settlement. This nevertheless marked a profound change in the geographical distribution of the tsar's Jewish subjects. Town dwellers in the Russian interior who had previously scarcely set eyes on Jews now rubbed shoulders with Jewish refugees.[31]

More ambitious schemes for Jewish resettlement were also contemplated. The progressive economist Boris Brutskus maintained that hundreds of thousands of refugees could establish a "Jewish center" in Siberia, helping "to transform this region into a powerful developing country."[32] Others took a more cautious line, warning that the streets of Siberian towns were not paved with gold or well provided with schools and synagogues. Serious reservations were also expressed by nationalists who regarded the Pale of Settlement as the nexus of Jewish solidarity: "We need to consider this from a national, not a narrow refugee [*uzkobezhenskaia*], point of view." It was unwise to promote the dispersion of Jews throughout the Russian empire, still less to tolerate the potential "assimilation" of Jews in the Russian interior.[33]

Notwithstanding the perpetuation of civil disabilities, some members of the tsarist government sought to promote a more liberal regime. The industrialist A.D. Protopopov, appointed minister of the interior on 16 September 1916 and noted for his moderately progressive views, hoped to integrate Jews more fully into Russia's economic life.[34] Perhaps this was indicative of a broader shift in official opinion, in which the old certainties—at least, those that stretched back to the "temporary" May laws of 1882—were crumbling before social reality. Some members of the tsarist elite kept up a rearguard action: a meeting of provincial governors in May 1916 expressed the hope that the Pale could be reestablished after the war. But they were fighting a losing battle, not so much against a tide of liberal opinion within

Russia or of international disquiet as against the impact of population displacement. For a vocal lobby inside and outside the Duma, only full civic equality would render Russia "indestructible." But most officials were swayed less by such appeals than by difficult and unpleasant wartime realities that challenged old modes of thought and action.[35]

Ministers had their own reasons for addressing the "Jewish question" without delay. They feared that Jewish refugees would be provoked into radical action by the evidence they encountered on the road of the lavish lifestyles of army commanders. The government was also obliged to take some account of public opinion. A deputation of leading figures from the Jewish banking community called upon Shcherbatov in the summer of 1915 and urged him to denounce the actions of Ianushkevich.[36] Finally, several ministers argued that the government could not ignore intermittent expressions of concern from allied governments about the deportation of Jews, particularly in view of the desperate need for additional credits to sustain Russia's war effort. As Krivoshein put it, "One cannot fight a war against Germany and against the Jews," a view that led the right-wing minister of transport, S. V. Rukhlov, to declare that "Jewish bankers buy for their compatriots the right to make use of the misfortunes of Russia for further exploitation of the bleeding Russian people."[37]

These remarks should alert us to the ways in which contemporaries ascribed specific characteristics to refugee minorities, thereby constructing a dominant image that served multiple purposes. Government ministers viewed Jews as potential revolutionaries, troublemakers, spies, or parasites, or as the clients of foreign creditors upon whom the Russian war effort depended. They remained wedded to traditional fears about the impact on local Russian communities of Jews in desperate need of food and shelter. They feared the outbreak of pogroms once Jews "invaded" peasant villages in the Russian interior. As we saw earlier, these potent images were also widespread in the tsarist army.[38]

Well-meaning professionals exposed their own prejudices. Thus, Violetta Thurstan wrote that "Jewish refugees do not suffer so acutely from the terrible homesickness that attacks the refugees of other countries; they are wanderers by nature or sub-conscious instinct, and are not so rooted to one particular soil as those with a heavier sense of nationality. They settle down more quickly . . . and take more easily to new work. . . . Another compensation for them is the extraordinary generosity shown by many Jews to their co-religionists." Thurstan also swallowed the assumption that "many Jews . . . have on the whole German sympathies," repeating the belief that the impoverished Jew supplemented his income by selling information to the enemy. Her own access to the front—she had earlier served as a nurse in Russian Poland—doubtless meant that Thurstan had imbibed the prejudices of military commanders.[39]

What of the initiatives taken by Jews themselves? A full answer to this question would require proper attention to international assistance provided by Jews in the United States and elsewhere, something that is beyond the scope of this study. Jews overseas rallied behind fragile communities that stood in sore need of financial, administrative, and moral support. Particularly significant here was the Joint Distribution Committee headed by Felix Warburg in New York, which channeled around 10 million rubles to Russia's Jewish refugees between 1914 and 1917.[40]

More important for our purposes is to trace the extent of Jewish self-help initiatives within the borders of Russia. To what degree did displacement promote new opportunities for action—or were Jews paralyzed by virtue of having been "promiscuously amassed into communities of fear"?[41] In the first phase of the war, a group of wealthy activists—mostly bankers and lawyers in Petrograd—established the Central Jewish Committee for the Relief of War Victims (Evreiskii komitet pomoshchi zhertvam voiny, EKOPO). EKOPO enjoyed the backing of four influential organizations: the Society for the Propagation of Enlightenment among Russian Jews (ORPME), the Society for Handicrafts (ORT), the Jewish Colonization Association, and the Society for the Health of Jews. The latter body, established in 1912, included a number of men who would play a leading role in Soviet health care, such as M. M. Gran, S. Frumkin, and V. I. Binshtok. During the war it effectively acted as the health wing of EKOPO, to which it gave a more democratic complexion, without satisfying the more radical Jewish organizations.[42]

Other spokesmen praised Jewish agencies for having set aside political differences: "Now one flag has been raised, the Jewish banner."[43] The claim was made that refugeedom yielded educational benefits, by "mixing" Jews together and demonstrating the need for them to find a common language of communication. "The wave of refugees has united all shades of Judaism and all languages. Jews who hitherto did not know or understand one another have been brought together. Mutual antagonisms have disappeared, to be replaced by excellent fraternal relations." Given everything else that Russia's Jews had suffered before and during the war, the author of these sentiments may perhaps be forgiven this degree of hyperbole.[44] To be sure, the cultural and economic distance between the poor Jew from the shtetl and the small and more privileged Jewish communities in Moscow and Petrograd remained difficult to bridge. Besides, the tiny Jewish populations in towns beyond the Pale of Settlement were anxious about the impact the new arrivals would have on the attitude of the dominant Christian citzenry; relations between resident Jews and Jewish refugees were thus sometimes frosty.[45] But important changes were taking place within Jewish society. The concerns of established Jewish residents began to dissipate once it became clear that the newcomers would not provide the pretext for fresh pogroms. Their privileged position was increasingly challenged. For one thing, the voluntary 5 percent levy to support needy refugees made it difficult to avoid calls for greater accountability. For another, the war brought to prominence several hundred Jewish relief workers who bridled at the condescending approach adopted by the affluent elite in Petrograd.[46] Finally, Jewish refugees demanded that their voice be heard in decisions that affected their livelihood. Relief workers encouraged refugees to become more assertive in the face of well-meaning but elitist initiatives. In recognition of the fact, EKOPO agreed in August 1916 to co-opt representatives from among refugees themselves.[47] As the official history of EKOPO acknowledged, "Small oases have become major centers of Jewish settlement, and the newcomers have demanded the right to participate in communal life."[48]

Each provincial town, including those formerly outside the Pale of Settlement, boasted a Jewish society. These were loosely linked to EKOPO, because the Ministry of the Interior refused it permission to establish local branches. Many of them gave glowing accounts of their contribution to refugee relief and their support of Jewish cultural life. The Iaroslavl' Jewish Society celebrated its first anniversary in August 1916 in a "festive" atmosphere, praising the work of Jewish youth and noting its "cultural-national importance." Its members congratulated one another on their attempts to maintain a register of Jewish refugees. As in other refugee organizations, professional men were in the forefront; the Iaroslavl' committee was chaired by E. D. Neushtadt, a local gynecologist. The committee organized an employment exchange, a trade school, and an ongoing cultural program, and it kept Jewish children supplied with clothes and shoes. Jewish committees took great pains to ensure that refugees were given kosher food.[49]

Popular prejudice and official hostility continued to provide the framework within which Russia's Jewish refugees struggled to survive. The use of Yiddish in public places led some Russians to think that German was being spoken, and this compounded the fear of Jewish otherness. Some municipal authorities made it clear that Jews should not venture outdoors.[50] The furious governor of Vladimir province met the first party of 600 Jewish refugees to arrive at the main railway station and gave permission for just 60 of them to disembark; the rest were sent farther north.[51] The governor of Tambov obstructed the distribution of allowances to Jewish refugees, giving as his reason the support they received from Petrograd's Jewish committee.[52] Typical of bureaucratic unwillingness to renounce old attitudes was the decision by the minister of the interior in April 1916 to erect obstacles in the way of Jewish refugees who wished to return to their former homes. "The issue of permits to Jews is unacceptable," wrote Stürmer, "because Jews are not suited to agricultural work, and because the army needs to be protected from espionage."[53]

The perpetuation of bigoted attitudes such as these was one bitter dimension of Jewish refugeedom, complicated still further by the caution and even contempt shown toward poor newcomers by well-established Jewish residents. Yet we should not lose sight of the assertion of Jewish solidarity and self-defense that culminated in the view that Russia's Jews formed "a single national unit." From this standpoint, "refugeedom, national scourge though it is, has been of some service to us."[54]

ARMENIANS, REFUGEES, AND THE MEANING OF "ARMENIA"

The construction of Armenian refugeedom entailed at least one set of assumptions similar to those held about Jews by tsarist officials and the educated public alike. Like the Jews, Armenians were regarded by others as an ethnic group that had already been "scattered." Leaders of the Armenian community themselves alluded to the centuries-old diaspora. They had no obvious "home," being distributed across two empires and at least two continents. Furthermore, Armenians were believed to be an inherently mobile people. Their evident proclivity to migrate and to form dispersed settlements served as an obstacle to official recognition of the plight of Armenian refugees. In due course, the Armenian diaspora was expected to come to their rescue, relieving the burden placed on central government. Allied to this purported characteristic was the belief that Armenians and Jews shared a common flair for business; their calling was to trade in money and manufactured goods. This perceived commercial "guile" encouraged the view that both groups survived at the expense of others. Such beliefs fostered a more jaundiced attitude within tsarist society toward humanitarian relief for Armenian refugees.[55]

The similarity between Jewish and Armenian refugees does not end there. Jews had become refugees because they were viewed as potential spies by the Russian military leadership. Armenian refugees were a product of the belief, widely held among the Ottoman military leadership, that the Armenian community either was or had the potential to become a fifth column that would stop at nothing to hamper the Turkish war effort and engage in spying and sabotage, in order to maximize the prospect of a victory by Russia over its historic enemy. Nor did Armenians escape the opprobrium of the tsarist state. A century of Russian rule in the Caucasus had instilled in tsarist officials a residual suspicion that Armenians would always manifest a degree of untrustworthiness toward any host society, wherever they resided and whoever ruled them. Whether they were deemed "wanderers," "wily" businessmen, or "spies," Jewish and Armenian refugees alike found themselves victims of deep-seated prejudice.

Progressive members of the Russian cultural elite rallied to the cause of Armenian refugees no less vigorously than they did with respect to Russia's Jewish population. Paul Miliukov called upon Russians to speak of Armenia in the same breath as "valiant" Belgium, Serbia, and Poland.[56] Maxim Gorky edited a collection of Armenian literature, which appeared in 1916. The poet Valerii Briusov gave lectures and readings on the history of Armenia and its poetry, which he subsequently published. These and other leading literary figures—including the symbolists Zinaida Gippius and Fedor Sologub—also contributed regularly to the leading journals devoted to Armenian affairs, *Armianskii vestnik* and *Armiane i voina*.[57]

Philanthropic relief efforts mobilized Armenian society in the Caucasus. Dozens of committees, some of them active since the beginning of the war, organized programs of relief. Although they were frequently accused of acting entirely independently of each other, this charge was not entirely fair.[58] Welfare and relief agencies developed expertise in specific fields. By the end of 1916, the Caucasian Armenian Benevolent Society (KAVO) concentrated on the supply of foodstuffs. The Union of Towns took charge of public health, screening refugees for infectious diseases and building seven new hospitals to cope with those in greatest need. Orphanages were built and maintained by the Armenian Central Welfare Committee, by the Armenian "Maidens' Committee" (Komitet armianskikh devits), and by "Fraternal Aid committees" in Erevan and Etchmidzian, the latter under the aegis of the Catholicos.[59] But the limited resources were thinly spread. The Union of Towns was overwhelmed. Erevan, with just one hospital and only a handful of doctors and medical orderlies, was simply not equipped to deal with the thousands of physically and mentally scarred refugees who congregated there in the summer of 1915.[60]

Armenian refugees complained about the treatment they received from their Russian Armenian neighbors, who were urged to show greater compassion and generosity. Communities in the Transcaucasus and farther afield that had managed to escape from the war relatively unscathed—one critic mentioned Tbilisi, Baku, Astrakhan', and the Crimea—were accused of failing to respond sufficiently energetically to the "huge national need" manifested by Armenian refugeedom.[61] However, this accusation needs to be treated with some caution. An offer by Armenians in the Crimean town of Simferopol' to build an orphanage for refugee children was eventually turned down, because "to take Armenian orphans outside the borders of the Caucasus and bring them to a strange and unfamiliar place is undesirable." Armenian particularism, if such it can be called, entailed costs.[62]

Members of the Armenian elite in Moscow and Petrograd rendered assistance to the refugee population, although they were frequently charged with indifference to the plight of refugees.[63] An Armenian committee in Moscow was headed by a member of the Cadet party, Aleksandr Khatisov, the wartime mayor of Tbilisi (which, like Baku, had a large Armenian presence), and a leading politician in his own right.[64] Khatisov was joined by other Armenian liberals, including Moisei Adzhemov and M. I. Papadzhanov, both members of the Cadet fraction in the Duma. Nor were the citizens of Tbilisi quite so lethargic as was suggested. The local Armenian bourgeoisie had done little, prior to 1914, to suggest that they would be willing leaders of a national movement; the Armenian cultural intelligentsia was a more promising source of national mobilization. Now, however, many Armenian businessmen and professional men occupied positions of influence in Tbilisi, which formed the geographical core of relief efforts. Local relief workers urged that yet more use be made of the patriotic intelligentsia, in order that they could lead refugees farther north, to places of greater safety and comfort.[65] Armenian peasants were also praised for their willingness to help refugees, even though their own economic situation was precarious.[66]

More disconcerting was the attitude of the tsarist government toward the Armenian community. Nicholas II's proud boast to the Armenian Catholicos Kevork V in May 1915 "that a most brilliant future awaits the Armenians" soon rang hollow. Russian government ministers objected to the suggestion that Russia should "take risks for the sake of restoring Armenia." Tsarist officials were ordered to disarm Armenian refugees. The regime clamped down on Armenian political activity and imposed press censorship. Grand Duke Nicholas, dismissed as commander-in-chief of the Russian army and—in October 1915—offered the consolation prize of becoming the new viceroy for the Caucasus, liquidated the Armenian volunteer units in December 1915 with the dismissive comment that "there is no Armenian question, any more than there is a Iakut question."[67]

According to Richard Hovannisian, these tactics formed the prelude to the anticipated incorporation of Turkish Armenia into the Russian empire. The commander of Russia's army of the Caucasus let it be known privately that Russia wanted to "populate the border regions with a Russian element," and not allow Armenian refugees to settle on the territory seized from Turkey. Russian colonists from the Kuban' and Don region were earmarked for a kind of Cossack *cordon sanitaire;* refugees from Ottoman Armenia were ordered to surrender to the Russian authorities the title deeds to their property.[68] In a cynical observation, a Russian dignitary wrote that "the destruction of the Armenian nation has at least had one positive aspect from a political point of view, namely that the Turks have left us an Armenia without Armenians."[69]

Armenian political leaders had their own agenda, which entailed first and foremost the physical protection of the Armenian community from renewed Ottoman attack, as well as from epidemic disease. But they coupled this program with a challenge to the tsarist administration in which they joined forces with Russia's public organizations. At a banquet hosted by the unions of towns and zemstvos in Moscow on 13 March 1916, timed to coincide with the new session of the Duma, Armenian politicians received a rousing ovation. Khatisov announced that the government could not set the "Caucasian nations" against one another or against Russia, because they were now united against a common foe—the "arrogant and shameless tsarist bureaucracy" that had failed to deal with the refugee problem. Only self-government within a reformed polity could offer the Caucasus a way out of the deepening social and economic malaise: "There is no question of separatism:

the Caucasian peoples see their salvation as bound up closely with that of Russia." Finally, Khatisov made explicit the link between refugeedom and national organization: "We have been ready [for the decisive political transformation] for a long while, and we need only a signal for everything that is hidden to become visible."[70]

Russia's liberals supported this broad strategy. The Cadet activist M. M. Shchepkin argued that the territory liberated from Ottoman rule should be administered by "local cadres, and fundamentally by representatives of the Armenian intelligentsia." He went on to suggest that the unions of towns and zemstvos "should do everything in their power to help the newly freed population see the advantages of Russian rule. It would be extremely dangerous to introduce a police-administrative system. Rather, it is necessary to substitute one of a public character, permitting broad local initiative and practical public supervision." Armenian refugees should be encouraged to return to their farms, not just to improve military security—the farmers could supply the local army with food and provisions—but also to emphasize that "Armenia was for Armenians."[71]

Russian military successes during the first half of 1916 helped to boost the Armenians' confidence. The Russian army occupied Erzerum in mid-February, captured the coastal town of Trebizond in April, and took Erdindzan four months later. The region around Lake Van was in Russian hands by the summer, although "there remained no one to liberate."[72] Reports spoke of a steady stream of returning refugees in the wake of the tsarist army (up to 600 men per day "spontaneously" made the trip from Djulfa to Van in the late spring of 1916).[73] But they entered a wasteland. The agricultural economy was in ruins, with fewer than six thousand goats and cows left out of a prewar herd of one million. Not one shop or market stall survived intact in Van, a thriving market town before the war. Most dwellings had been damaged beyond repair. In Kars oblast and Erevan province alone, 30 million rubles was needed in order to rebuild shattered farms. In consequence, "we who live in the twentieth century have had to turn to forgotten forms of barter exchange and a natural economy." Armenian relief workers praised the selfless humanitarianism of Armenian villagers who offered shelter to those in need. But private charity on a short-term basis was insufficient; collective action by Armenian farmers themselves was imperative.[74]

The Armenian political elite mobilized in support of the demand for greater security in the aftermath of the terrible events in Turkish-held Armenia during the previous year. In May 1916, the tsarist government approved the convocation of a special Armenian congress in Petrograd, the first occasion on which the regime had tolerated public discussion of the "Armenian question" outside the Caucasus itself. The meeting brought together 150 Armenian and other representatives, including Armenian Cadet members of the Duma, Dashnaks (members of the Armenian Revolutionary Federation, socialist in outlook), Social Democrats, and Socialist

Revolutionaries, as well as representatives of the Armenian community in Russia and the United States. Headed by S. G. Mamikonian, the congress was opened by G. F. Tigranov, who had been mandated by the Armenian colony in Paris.[75] Delegates confined themselves to formal discussion of relief efforts, including the care of orphans and the education of refugee children (40 percent of Armenian refugees were under the age of 17). They also heard a patriotic opening speech from Mamikonian, who declared, "It is better to eat Russian hay than Muslim bread."[76]

One of the chief concerns of Armenian political leaders was to bring the Turkish perpetrators of genocide to justice, although this seemed a remote prospect. An additional goal was to liberate any surviving Armenian refugees who remained in Turkish hands. Some national patriots spoke of putting an end completely to the Ottoman state, "this twentieth-century anachronism." As one journalist put it in 1915, "Those sacrifices that we have made during the war give us the right to hope for corresponding political compensation."[77] As troubling a conclusion as it may seem, refugeedom—the product of genocide—had a partially positive outcome, providing unforeseen scope for political agitation, allowing political leaders to capitalize upon a wave of public sympathy, and—by forcing the Armenianness of refugees into the official consciousness—challenging established modes of rule in the Russian empire. Nevertheless, the practice of genocide constituted what has rightly been called an "unambiguously grisly episode" in twentieth-century history.[78]

POLISH REFUGEES: LEAVING "GOD'S PLAYGROUND"

Unlike the Jews or Armenians, Poles initially found themselves being courted by Tsar and Kaiser at the outbreak of the First World War. Poland's strategic position, which (together with the effects of the 1863 rebellion) had exposed it to the oppressive attention of tsarist rulers throughout the nineteenth century, now appeared likely to work to its advantage. The commander-in-chief of the Russian army, Grand Duke Nicholas, issued a manifesto that spoke of the freedom of the Polish nation, "joined in one under the scepter of the Russian Tsar." Unluckily for the tsar, other rivals vied for the political loyalties of the Polish people, weakening the impact of this unprecedented step. German occupation forces established a civilian administration in Warsaw and Lublin and made positive overtures, restoring the old University of Warsaw, allowing the Polish legions to parade in public and, above all, recognizing the old Kingdom of Poland, which had disappeared in 1863.[79]

Military misfortune meanwhile turned the "tsar's scepter" against ordinary Polish citizens. When the Russian army left Warsaw in August 1915, its inhabitants were forced out of the city, on the basis that they were pro-Austrian. According to Shcherbatov, "No exceptions were made, even for minors. All these arrested people have been sent to the rear and imprisoned. . . . The Poles are outraged . . . they are requesting a reexamination of this action." The Russian army not only had failed to protect Poland from invasion, but also had rendered intolerable the plight of many Polish civilians through its crude use of force against supposedly disloyal elements.[80] It was as if the events of 1863 were being played out again, only this time without any evidence of Polish "disloyalty." The army's actions compounded other grievances. Patriotic leaders protested that attempts to form a guerrilla force had been thwarted (some units were instituted following Pilsudski's initiatives in Galicia). Ianushkevich remained implacably opposed to the formation of wholly Polish units within the imperial army, but in 1915 the tsarist government reluctantly authorized the creation of a Polish division, "in response to incessant petitions by enterprising nationalist politicians." Although only a few thousand troops served in the "Polish legion"—which formed part of the imperial Russian army, conducted its business in Polish, and wore the imperial uniform—the implicit message behind these initiatives was that the defense of Poland could best be conducted by the Poles themselves.[81]

Political discussions continued among refugees who fled the German invasion. The lawyer and Cadet politician Aleksandr Lednicki, a member of the First Duma in 1906, supported the continued territorial integrity of the Russian empire in the interests of victory over Germany. Like Roman Dmowski, the leader of the Polish National Democratic Party (PNDP), Lednicki feared that a more radical stance would generate renewed repression by St. Petersburg and destroy any hope of constitutional reform.[82] Both men took an active part in refugee relief, forming a Polish National Committee (PNC) in Warsaw in order to aid victims of the war. After the fall of Warsaw, Dmowski moved its operations to Petrograd, and subsequently to Lausanne, where he denounced his pro-German political opponents (he also accused Polish Jews of supporting the German cause). The PNC enjoyed financial support from Britain via the "Great Britain to Poland Fund," as well as from Switzerland, France, Italy, and the United States.[83]

Two organizations dominated the relief of Polish refugees on Russian soil. One was a "citizens' committee" under Prince Lubomirski (Tsentral'nyi obyvatel'skii komitet gubernii tsarstva Pol'skogo), which engaged in welfare work and rapidly became the focus of local and national political activity. It placed particular emphasis on the needs of Polish farmers who settled in the Russian countryside.[84] The other was the Polish Society for the Aid of War Victims, founded by Lednicki and chaired by the energetic Polish engineer V. V. Zhukovskii—Duma deputy, leading member of the Association of Trade and Industry, and member of the Special Council for State Defense, the Special Council for Refugees, and the Central Committee of the Central War Industry Committee. The overall coordination of their activities lay with a confederation of Polish organizations, representing committees active throughout the empire, in Belorussia, the south, the Volga provinces, the Urals, and Siberia. The citizens' committee divided European Russia into 38 districts and the rest of the country into 5 districts, with a full time staff of more than 300 officials, not including priests, doctors, feldshers, and teachers employed on the committee's behalf. The Polish committee was far larger, with a huge total of around 25,000 staff assigned to 237 offices.[85]

These organizations took up the cases of Polish refugees who had been mistreated by the Russian army, including those who had been deported from Galicia during 1915.[86] They established a network of day schools, boarding schools, and orphanages, in Moscow and in other cities and towns. They promoted a vigorous program of educational, cultural, and religious activity.[87] Refugees set up newspapers, of which the best-known were *Echo Polskie* and the PND newspaper *Gazeta Polska*. The national committees appealed to local communities to institute a levy on their members, in order to raise funds.[88] Schools and evening classes proved very popular; there was even talk of a "national university" in Moscow, a proposal that would have been inconceivable before the war. Polish refugee communities organized displays of handicrafts, not only to show that they were willing and able to work hard, but also to demonstrate to local people the distinctive characteristics of Polish arts and crafts. Strenuous efforts were made within the organized refugee community to establish the prospects of finding work, something on which the Polish citizens' committee prided itself.[89]

Such initiatives underlined the need for national solidarity and served "not only to look after the body but also to preserve the refugee's soul for Poland."[90] Yet the national committees resented any suggestion that they should restrict themselves to cultural and educational activities. The Polish intelligentsia were determined to play a full part in all aspects of Polish refugee life, even if this exposed them to the charge of national particularism: "Only continuous and close contact with the national group, whether in the distribution of allowances, the allocation of accommodation, the supply of clothing, the search for work, the offer of medical treatment, the satisfaction of all material and spiritual needs—only this can guarantee, secure, and preserve refugees on behalf of the motherland."[91]

But what meaning attached to the "motherland," and what part did Polish refugeedom play in its articulation? Following the First Congress of Polish Relief Organizations, held in Moscow in early August 1915, Zhukovskii, Lednicki, and Swencicki proclaimed Poland to be an "outpost of Slavdom" whose inhabitants had made an "incalculable sacrifice" in the interests of the tsarist state, protecting Russia from the German onslaught at the price of becoming a wasteland. They spoke of the destruction of Polish national wealth and a "centuries-old culture." Polish farmers had been forced to leave land that they had tilled for generations, and now saw it being appropriated by German colonists. The congress also asserted the indivisibility of Poland: "Poles have never recognized the division of their homeland into three parts and have always regarded themselves as one people; we believe that the Russian people will share this point of view and will not look differently on the fortunes of Poles who are subjects of the Russian, Austrian, and German empires."[92] No mention was made of the Polish landed elite (*szlachta*); the appeal to national sentiment seemed instead to be founded on an alliance between the intelligentsia and the peasantry.

Russians were asked to accept that Polish refugees not only had no desire to leave their homes but also wished to seek temporary shelter close to their home, rather than in "far-off Siberia." Poles were owed support by virtue of the sacrifices they had made, but any assistance had to take account of national peculiarities. Well-meaning proposals to promote permanent settlement thousands of miles from their homeland should be resisted. Even less acceptable was the propensity of some zemstvos to disperse Polish refugees without regard for religious and educational needs that could be met only by the maintenance of cohesive settlements. "Under this system, the refugee will become a completely passive subject, and this will have an extremely demoralizing effect," wrote the Polish Citizens' Committee in October 1915. Poles themselves had a responsibility to mitigate the impact of refugeedom: those who had long since settled in European Russia or Siberia were asked to do their utmost to support new schools and kindergartens for refugee children.[93]

Imperial officials shared the concerns of national patriots that Polish refugees should be discouraged from moving to Siberia in large numbers and acquiring farmland there. The Special Council was prepared in principle to earmark land for refugee settlement, but it made an exception with respect to Polish settlers, who "from a national point of view . . . are lost from their homeland, which is presently undergoing such a difficult period of the greatest misfortune."[94] These expressions are a sign of imperial commitment to an ethnically homogeneous territory, in which Polish peasants were expected to remain loyal to the tsarist state. In this respect there was little to separate the official viewpoint from nationalist sentiment or the self-expressed views of refugees themselves. A correspondent for the newspaper *Sibirskaia zhizn'* wrote that the dream of Polish refugees was "to return to their native hearth"; if asked about the possibility of settling in Siberia, they replied, "Herman can be chased off and we'll go home."[95]

LATVIAN REFUGEES: AVERTING DIASPORA

In the Baltic lands, too, the self-styled leaders of the Latvian intelligentsia made strenuous efforts to rally members of the "national community," shaming those who neglected their patriotic duty to contribute to the cause of refugee relief.[96] The process of counting, organizing, and administering Latvian refugees amounted to the formation of an embryonic political authority. The most important organization was the Latvian Central Welfare Committee (LCWC), whose leaders included Pastor Vilis Ia. Olavs, A. Bergs and the liberal lawyer Janis Cakste, subsequently president of independent Latvia.[97] These men linked the welfare of Latvian refugees to the political struggle. They denounced the restrictions placed by the tsarist state on Latvian cultural development and demanded the extension of self-government to Latvia. They appealed to the Russian government to abolish the privileges enjoyed by the "Kurland barons," who were accused of collaborating with the German occupation forces. The LCWC also alerted Latvian and Russian society to plans by the Reich's occupying forces to assign farmland to German immigrants. Along with evidence that German troops destroyed Latvian property, this appeared to support the nationalist view that Latvia had been singled out for devastation.[98]

Refugeedom mobilized the Latvian cultural and professional elite. From its base in Petrograd, the LCWC coordinated the activities of more than one hundred separate Latvian refugee welfare organizations, which employed around two thousand staff, including schoolteachers, doctors, agronomists, engineers, journalists, and tax inspectors.[99] The key Moscow branch was chaired by Janis Zalitis, lawyer and Progressist member of the State Duma (he also sat on the Tatiana Committee). Like other national organizations, the LCWC maintained schools, hostels, and orphanages ("We shan't forget the young victims of war!"), extended loans to refugees, offered specialist legal advice, helped refugees to establish contact with family members, and sponsored a program of Latvian drama.[100]

Underlying Latvian national consciousness was a pronounced fear that the close bonds between Latvians in Latgale and Vidzeme would be severed permanently unless they resisted dispersion. Suspicions were aroused that the tsarist authorities deliberately steered Latvian refugees to remote parts of the empire.[101] Siberia in particular appeared to be the graveyard of Latvian identity. Distressing reports were already circulating that Latvians who had settled in western Siberia before the war had ceased to read Latvian books and newspapers, and drowned their sorrows in drink.[102] Other observers felt that the blame for the dilution of Latvianness should not be pinned wholly on the migrant population. In an extensive article, "Our Previous Mistakes," Kristaps Bachmanis dwelled on Latvians' migration to the Urals and Siberia in the 1880s and 1890s: "Did we bother to get to know these 'outcasts' who had moved away from Latvia? Did we try hard enough to seek to maintain their links with the fatherland? Why did we forget them? We should be discovering the threads that would bind these emigrants together with Latvia's culture and future prospects."[103] For the younger generation of Latvian patriots, the war represented an opportunity to bring together Latvian settlers and the flower of modern Latvia, with refugees as the instrument of mediation.[104]

The fear of national disintegration was articulated by the leading Latvian parliamentarian, Janis Goldmanis, in a speech to a congress of Latvian delegates in Petrograd at the end of August 1915. Goldmanis took as the theme for his address "the forms and means of saving and preserving the Latvian people who face the lot of the Jews—to be scattered across the entire globe." He saw no point in encouraging Latvia's young sons to fight to defend farms and fields if they could not be repopulated with "people who think and act in a Latvian manner." Hence it was vital that refugees should refrain from buying or renting plots of land in Russia and Siberia, lest they forget where their roots properly lay.[105] These arguments were carefully constructed and cleverly formulated, reminding Latvians of the bitter conflicts that had taken place ten years earlier, when the Baltic German landlords fought to keep Latvian laborers and peasants from seizing their estates. To abandon Latvian territory at this juncture would be to betray those who had paid with their lives during the great agrarian revolts in 1905–1906. The wartime discourse was closely tied to fears of imminent German colonization. In the longer term, the doctrine espoused by Goldmanis seems to anticipate the interwar government's ideological commitment to the Latvian peasantry as the backbone of independent statehood.[106]

What of the perceptions held of Latvian refugees and the day-to-day experiences they encountered? They were frequently mistaken for Germans, since they shared the same religion and often bore Germanic surnames. From Khar'kov came a cry that "even the local intelligentsia cannot distinguish between Latvian refugees from Kurzeme and Germans."[107] At the same time, there was also a more benign aspect to inter-ethnic encounters. Non-Latvian observers were impressed by their work ethic, which made Latvians attractive as agricultural laborers. Latvians were portrayed as solid and respectable citizens who were committed to family solidarity. The Petrograd newspaper *Birzhevye vedomosti* reported that Latvian refugees expressed unease over the separate accommodation arranged for men and women, but that the community was "even somewhat joyful" at the knowledge that it could remain close-knit. New ties were forged between Latvian families who lived together and whose members helped one another to find work. If they had to move far from home, at the very least they resolved to create temporary "colonies" where they could retain a sense of Latvianness. Outsiders thus shared the patriotic assumption that Latvians would emerge from refugeedom with an enhanced sense of collective worth.[108]

However, these broadly liberal perceptions and desires bypassed more radical peasants and workers, whose own politicization had been deeply influenced by the events of 1905. Workers who remained on territory under German occupation took part in the revolutionary movement, despite the threat of summary execution. Workers from the big engineering plants in Riga left to join the army or to find work in the rear, contributing to a revival of social-democratic activity in towns

and cities across European Russia. The revolutionary impulse was also strengthened by the formation of the famous Latvian brigades, two units in which around
40,000 Latvian soldiers served. This suggests that some refugees responded to displacement by engaging directly in radical political activity.[109]

LITHUANIAN REFUGEES: BETWEEN GERMANY AND RUSSIA

In 1914 and 1915, the German army overran the provinces of Suwalki, Kaunas
(Kovno), and much of Vilna, home to the bulk of the empire's Lithuanian population. Vilna, a large, cosmopolitan city, lost almost one-third of its inhabitants during the first year of the war; when the Germans occupied it, they found only
140,000 residents. The invaders created a "Lithuanian military district," containing
a much-depleted population. Few Lithuanians demonstrated any great enthusiasm
for the new administration, the infamous *Land Ober Ost*.[110] In Vilna, Suwalki, and
Kurland, the German military authorities imposed a ruthless regime. The German
high command intended in due course to annex these territories; Kurland in particular inspired hopes of energetic colonization by German farmers. In the short
term, around 150,000 civilians were left homeless and destitute by the destruction of farms or their sequestration as billets for German troops. The harshness of
General Ludendorff's regime prompted talk of "partisan warfare" against the German occupation. Diplomatic maneuvers complicated matters still further. As the
war dragged on, the prospect of Lithuania's reincorporation into the Russian empire
receded. But what would be the fate of Lithuania? Germany's dramatic promise in
November 1916 of a Polish state raised fears that Lithuania would be swallowed up
by its neighbor. This prospect helped to promote a national movement that Germany was powerless to curb.[111]

The leaders of the Lithuanian community in Russia took the view that they had a
responsibility both toward refugees and toward their fellow citizens who remained
in Kaunas and Vilna. The Duma deputy and lawyer Martynas Ycas, subsequently
minister of finance in the postwar Lithuanian government, had already formed a
committee in Vilna in July 1914 to help Lithuanian refugees and other "victims of
war . . . regardless of nationality."[112] This body became the basis for the Lithuanian
Welfare Committee (LWC) in Petrograd. Ycas remained at the helm, trying to fight
off a leftist challenge to his supremacy, while a rump committee headed by Antanas
Smetona was left behind in Vilna to "help war victims and represent the Lithuanian
people." From the Russian capital came the familiar charge that local communities and church leaders had not done enough to alleviate the plight of refugees.[113]
The accusation was not wholly justified; the LWC engaged in intense educational
and cultural activity in the major places of Lithuanian refugee settlement, such as

Voronezh, Iaroslavl', Tambov, and Ekaterinoslav. Catholic priests also played an important part in refugee relief.[114]

Like their Latvian counterparts, the Lithuanian leadership devoted particular attention to the need to prepare refugees for their return to the homeland. Courses in agronomy and agricultural reconstruction were taught with this in mind.[115] Lithuanian architects and engineers made plans to redesign and reconstruct homes and public buildings that had been damaged or destroyed, "emphasizing the desirability of re-creating a consistently Lithuanian style."[116] In the meantime, it was important that "the Lithuanian narod, which has now been scattered to various parts of Russia, should not be allowed to fragment" and to fall victim to "moral degradation."[117]

Against this background Ycas called upon Lithuanians in other countries, particularly the United States, to contribute to a fund in support of the refugee population. In October 1916, Woodrow Wilson gave the collection maximum publicity, and $200,000 was collected in a single day. The appeal to the Lithuanian community in America may have helped compensate to some extent for the lack of support given the Lithuanian cause by the Vatican, which regarded the Catholic population of Lithuania as essentially part of Poland.[118]

Little work has been done on the experiences of Lithuanian refugees during the war years. It appears that they faced some animosity from local officials in the Urals, where several thousand Lithuanians moved during the autumn of 1915. Some were treated as virtual prisoners of war; the American Red Cross complained that its representatives were unable to visit their camps. Why they should have been singled out for particularly harsh treatment is a subject that requires further investigation. There appears to have been a deep-seated anti-Protestant element in this region, with some officials complaining that Lithuanian pastors were inherently subversive.[119]

Although there does not appear to be any direct evidence that Lithuanian refugees were at the forefront of moves either to establish greater national autonomy or, still less, to seize the opportunity eventually to institute an independent state, nevertheless their presence in the Russian interior was undoubtedly significant in several respects. Ycas himself boasted that the LWC "unearthed the buried name of Lithuania" and drew attention to the "separate and distinctive character" of the Lithuanian people.[120] Whatever the truth of these assertions, the mere fact of displacement forced the existence of Lithuanians to the attention of Russian peasants and townspeople, who might never have stopped to think of the multinational character of the Russian empire or the place of "Lithuania" within it. What rights they should enjoy and what respect should be accorded individual national cultures were questions that could not easily be avoided in the circumstances. It made little sense to treat Lithuanian refugees as a version of their Russian counterparts when they spoke a different language and professed a different religion.

Lithuanian national relief committees conferred legitimacy on established movements in support of greater cultural freedom and political autonomy; their leadership gained experience in managing budgets and administering programs for national welfare. As in other instances, the Lithuanian committees were able to tap a deep well of genuine suffering and seek to give it a "national" form. Through their encouragement of non-refugees to contribute to refugee welfare, a sense of national community was cultivated among both groups. When the central government reduced funding, they embarked on ambitious cultural programs in order to raise funds and propagate the message of national struggle. They promoted a culture of gallantry and sacrifice, which has played an important role in some national movements.[121]

RUSSIANS AND RUSSIA'S REFUGEES

What of Russian identity? The war unleashed contradictory impulses in Russian society. On the one hand, the subjects of the tsar were invited to serve the cause of the "motherland" (*rodina*), which implied an attachment to the lands over which he ruled; in other words, the war united all subjects of the Russian empire (*rossiiskaia imperiia*) in the "great patriotic war."[122] As one patriotic newspaper put it, "The names Rus', Russia [*Rossiia*], Russian have a sanctified importance. They are not merely descriptions, but programs of action. They signify the unity and indivisibility of Russia."[123] This viewpoint tended to blur distinctions between Russians and non-Russians, while privileging the status of Russians within the empire.

On the other hand, there was clearly a sense in which the values of "Russianness"—specifically Russian culture, the centrality of Orthodox faith—were threatened by states (Germany, Austria-Hungary, Turkey) whose dominant nationalities were obviously non-Russian. Russia's enemies had the capacity to deal a serious if not fatal blow to its preeminent position within the imperial polity. These values might also be subverted by refugeedom, given that non-Russians were now a more powerful presence in European Russia, the Urals, and Siberia. A priest from the Urals perhaps had this in mind when he spoke of "the terrible portrait of Rus' in flight," his poetic language drawing attention to a time when Russia did not have to contend with strangers in its midst.[124]

A recent study of popular culture, including *lubki* (woodprints), posters, cartoons, peepshows, and the cinema, finds evidence that Russians voraciously consumed stories about their enemies and allies, but is hard pressed to find any substantial "internal" patriotic images and themes. Russians were reminded of their military heroes, Suvorov and Kutuzov. Customized right-wing and official propaganda tended to be stale and unimaginative. Portrayals of the imperial family had less resonance than the traditional figure of the brave Cossack or the contemporary intrepid Russian aviator, to whom ordinary Russians responded more enthusiastically. There was a broad popular attachment to Russian cultural tradition, but certainly not to the person of the tsar. Perhaps, too, the emphasis in some quarters upon the restoration of Russian refugees to their "hearths" and "nests" stimulated the same kind of feelings that such evocations were meant to convey for non-Russian nationalities.[125]

We may look to refugeedom for the crystallization of Russianness. Refugeedom reinforced the sense of otherness, reminding Russians—whether as refugees or as part of the settled population—what they were not, as well as what they were. At first glance, the derivation of Russianness from a negative perception of the enemy might be seen most clearly with respect to the official program to expropriate the farms of ethnic Germans, many of whom had settled in the empire for several generations without losing their attachment to Lutheranism and the German language. As a result, according to one scholar, they "lived alongside rather than among" their Russian and Ukrainian neighbors.[126] Russian nationalists demanded the seizure and redistribution of their property; it was doubtless no accident that many of the most tireless campaigners originated from Volynia, where German farmers had been settled for more than a generation.[127] In the Duma debates on the "German question," the arch-conservative A. N. Khvostov charged that German settlers had forced Russian peasants to move to the Siberian taiga and therefore deserved to have a taste of their own medicine. Shcherbatov maintained that German settlers should reject their own culture, in order to become "true sons of the fatherland."[128] Yet popular enthusiasm for this assault on their property was not restricted to Russians; Ukrainian and Belorussian refugees did not hesitate to take over German farms. Punitive and uncompromising policies were greeted by Russian and non-Russian subjects of the tsar alike, for whom German settlers could never be loyal members of the political community.[129]

In more troubling ways, refugeedom challenged Russians to confront their own inadequacy. Russian nationalist politicians believed that national committees had thrown down the gauntlet. Whereas non-Russians imposed a levy on settled communities in order to assist refugees, no Russian neighborhood had yet followed their lead.[130] A correspondent to the Iaroslavl' newspaper found it shameful that Jews and Catholics had devoted resources to the relief of suffering among their flock, whereas the local Russian community displayed no such commitment: "Can we call ourselves Christians?" she asked. Russians owed duty and loyalty to Christ and to the traditions of Russian Orthodoxy.[131] Other kinds of anxiety emerged when Russian conservatives examined the activities of the public organizations. For example, Urusov charged that the Union of Zemstvos discriminated against Russians, by favoring Jews, Poles, and Latvians with housing in town, whereas Russian refugees were forced to settle in the countryside. The Union of Zemstvos countered the accusation by pointing out that Russian refugees were disproportionately peasant farmers. More to the point, "All *zemtsy* are Russians and are incapable of behaving unfairly toward their own people. . . . All refugees are given the same kind of attention and assistance."[132]

Russian refugees had first to be identified. Neither language, religion, nor customs rendered them immediately visible; on the street they were indistinguishable from the non-refugee poor. This posed an immense challenge to those who would give assistance. There were other complicating factors as well. Russian refugees could not necessarily count on solidarity from communities that prided themselves on their authentic Russianness. To take the most famous group, Old Believers reportedly looked askance at the newcomers and treated them with undisguised hostility when they looked for work in their settlements.[133]

If there were firm beliefs as to the constitution of Russianness, they were surely tested by the eruption in the Russian interior of "borderline" minority groups.[134] What limits did Russians set on their toleration of ethnic difference? One means of exploring this crucial question is to consider the ways in which invidious comparisons were made between the provision made for Russian and non-Russian refugees, some of whom received relief payments from the government and from national organizations as well. This dualism created great bitterness among Russian nationalists.[135] From Ekaterinburg came complaints that Russian Orthodox refugees had been "cheated" in comparison with Jewish refugees, who received money from several quarters. "The Jewish refugee strolls around in a comfortable suit and galoshes, while the Russian has to make do with cast-offs and felt boots." It was left to the local bishop to try to assuage these feelings of relative neglect.[136] An article in April 1916 in the newly founded *Golos Rossii,* edited by the conservative Prince M. Andronikov, drew attention to the prevalence of Russian refugees on the streets of the capital—a sure sign, he maintained, that they lacked the kind of welfare provision available to Jews, Poles, and Latvians. How, the editor asked, could Russian society tolerate this negligent state of affairs? "National pride" required nothing less than adequate relief of the peasant, "beneath whose torn coat the spark of God is alight and a true Russian heart is beating." With the onset of spring, more fortunate members of the Russian narod had an opportunity and a duty to come to his aid.[137]

The moderate nationalist newspaper *Sputnik bezhentsa* correctly forecast a patriotic Russian backlash against the feverish growth of non-Russian refugee organizations. According to an editorial in September 1915, "The day is not far off when Markov and Zamyslovskii will demand an exclusively 'Russian' organization."[138] Russian refugees wrote from Ufa asking when they would be offered material and spiritual assistance to match the provision made to Poles, Armenians, and Jews:

"The Jews have their synagogues, rabbis, people to tend their cemeteries, and doctors; we miserable Orthodox refugees have to make do with Father Thomas."[139]

Specifically Russian organizations for refugee relief duly followed, building upon a growing sense that the Russian refugee population had been neglected by Russia's "public men" in their headlong rush to assume political supremacy. Certainly the main organizations adopted an avowedly conservative outlook.[140] Most significant among them was the All-Russian Society for the Care of Refugees (Vserossiiskoe obshchestvo popecheniia o bezhentsakh, or VOPB), formed in September 1915 by Senator A. A. Rimskii-Korsakov.[141] The society aimed not only to provide for the material needs of Russian refugees, but also to support those who wished to return to their homes. Although it gave priority to Russians, Rimskii-Korsakov indicated that he would not turn down requests from refugees of other nationalities if they had been left stranded.[142] By the beginning of 1916, the VOPB had fifty-four branches throughout Russia, offering clothing, footwear, shelter, and schooling to more than 400,000 refugees. Typically, each branch included prominent religious figures, the provincial governor, the local representative of the State Bank, and other worthies.[143] Despite these initiatives, however, complaints were still being lodged in the late summer of 1916 that refugees of Russian nationality were finding themselves at a disadvantage compared to the non-Russian population.[144]

All the same, wartime displacement provided Russian refugees with an opportunity to assert their own Russianness in order to navigate the "cosmopolitan crossroads of human and other traffic."[145] Refugeedom offered the same kind of opportunities for Russian nationalists as it did for leaders of the non-Russian patriotic intelligentsia. The potentially far-reaching consequences of this process were well articulated by *Sputnik bezhentsa,* whose editor anticipated a time, not far off, when extreme nationalists would say, "We were right all along when we stated that Russia is home to many who are Russian only by virtue of their passport, as well as home to those who are genuinely Russian—that is, not only to those who regard Russia as the place where they are registered, but also to those who regard it as their cultural and spiritual homeland."[146]

"LITTLE RUSSIANS," AWKWARD REFUGEES

Official discourse denied the existence of a distinct Belorussian language and affirmed the belief that Ukrainian was a dialect of Russian. As they had for generations, tsarist officials "remained suspicious of the separatist potential of Ukrainian language and culture."[147] But the state was powerless to prevent Belorussians and Ukrainians from creating their own dedicated organizations, thereby preventing their amalgamation into the category of Russian refugees. A small Belorussian elite formed the "West Russian Society" (Zapadno-russkoe obshchestvo), which operated out of Minsk during the autumn of 1915 and which claimed to attend to the needs of 100,000 Belorussian and Russian refugees.[148] Beyond this initiative, the Belorussian peasantry would have to wait until after the February revolution for any further acknowledgment of their needs.[149]

The situation in Ukraine was a good deal more complicated, especially given the influx of Ukrainian refugees from Galicia, where opportunities for political activity had been more extensive before the war. These refugees were now taken under the wing of the "Russian People's Council of Carpathian Rus'," a shady group whose leaders reportedly had close contacts with Russia's Black Hundreds.[150] There appears to have been some truth to this charge. The council dedicated itself to the promotion of loyalty to Russia, opening its doors to those "who willingly disclosed their Russian national consciousness [sic] or in some measure demonstrated that they were well disposed toward Russia and the Russian people."[151] In reality, relief efforts fell far short of the rhetoric. In Rostov, Ukrainian refugees complained that they were given only cold food, that they were forced to sleep on cold floors, and that allowances arrived erratically. Dudykevich, the local organizer of the Russian People's Council, blithely told a visiting journalist, "These are refugees, after all, and they can hardly count on the comforts of home." Not surprisingly, some of the older refugees expressed the hope that an alternative organization would care for them instead.[152]

A very different, pro-nationalist organization, the Society for the Assistance of the Population of South Russia, operating out of Kiev, offered support to refugees from Bessarabia, Volynia, Lublin, Chelm, Bukovina, and Galicia. Its spokesman drew attention to the needs of Ukrainian intellectuals, politicians, and businessmen who had incurred the wrath of the Russian army in the summer of 1915, and whose physical condition had rapidly deteriorated.[153]

Unofficially, then, the plight of "refugee Ukrainians" (*bezhentsy-ukraintsy*) did not go unreported.[154] But moderate and extreme Russian nationalists alike pounced on any attempt to draw attention to the Ukrainianness of refugees. A proposed Ukrainian society in Moscow aroused the ire of the editor of *Sputnik bezhentsa*, who demanded that it be renamed the "Little Russian Society"; to adopt the term "Ukrainian" meant to accept that they were a "non-Russian people."[155] Yet his anger and unease betrayed the fact that the war facilitated the dissemination of Ukrainian views. One of the chief outlets was the monthly journal *Ukrainskaia zhizn'*, published in Moscow by Ia. A. Sheremetsinskii. In an unsigned article, "To Flee or Not to Flee?," the author argued that there might be advantages to staying put if one was Ukrainian:

In favor of remaining behind is the centuries-old culture that previous generations have created there. Not everywhere will become a war zone. Our own culture will remain; so, too, should those people who can preserve it. . . . Even if the enemy should strike deeper, individuals may be killed and individual property may be destroyed, but the land, its culture, its *"didivshchina,"* its *"bat'kivshchina,"* will survive. For although people change, are born and die, nevertheless the *"bat'kivshchina,"* the *krai*, will survive—these last forever.[156]

Given this rival vision of the future, supporters of the status quo believed that much more needed to be done for "Galician" refugees to convince them of the need to remain loyal to the Russian cause:

The great events and shocks of recent months have shattered the spiritual world of many of these ignorant people. They don't understand what has happened and are easily led astray by various unknown political adventurers who make all kinds of dishonest attempts to win them over. . . . We should have taken advantage of the presence of refugees in Russia in order to awake in them the slumbering national awareness and to explain to them the fate of the Russian people and of the "Russian faith" in Galicia. We need to make them devoted sons and daughters of the holy Orthodox Church and the common mother of great Rus', and devoted believers in their noble Russian Tsar.[157]

This rhetoric underlines the unease felt by Russians about the proselytizing opportunities presented to Ukrainian patriots. The author, Professor P. E. Kazanskii, did his utmost to encourage Ukrainian children in Odessa to learn to speak (and to pray in) Russian, and to sing the Russian national anthem. Adults were offered a similar diet of lectures (on the "unity" of the Russian narod), songs, and Russian hymns. Not content with religious instruction, Kazanskii arranged for Ukrainian refugees to take part in a dramatic ceremony in Odessa's cathedral, enabling them to renounce the Uniate church and convert to the "faith of their fathers," and thereby to become Russian by nationality and Orthodox by faith. When they returned home, Kazanskii urged, they should keep the faith and avoid the temptation to succumb to the "Papal yoke."[158]

The contact between Russians and Ukrainian refugees did not always imply such a one-way relationship. Refugeedom also offered an opportunity to engage with religious and cultural differences between Ukrainians and Russians, without implying that the former had everything to learn from the latter. A brief ethnographic account of 1,500 Ukrainian refugees from Volynia who had settled in Saratov makes this clear. According to a local priest, these refugees were distinguished by the modesty of their dress and footwear, and by their "slow-wittedness," which made them ill suited for work. Yet at a spiritual level these country cousins had something to teach their Russian neighbors. Although both groups were Orthodox, the Volynian refugees were much more devout. Other reports contrasted the boisterous and often insolent Russian peasant youth with the quieter and more compliant Ukrainian teenage refugees.[159]

There were virtually no opportunities for Ukrainians to conduct independent educational and cultural programs among the Ukrainian population; besides, the tsarist government closed many of the *prosvita* associations in 1915, hoping to stifle separatist sentiment and nip any political activity in the bud.[160] (It should be noted that such activity certainly took place in Austria-Hungary, where Ukrainian patriots enjoyed some scope to proselytize among the huge prisoner-of-war population.) Well-meaning observers challenged the legitimacy of past political affiliation, on the grounds that "the Galician question, in regard to refugees, has become one of morality rather than politics; sorrow and sympathy are needed, not slogans and political programs." This kind of attitude subtly asserted that it was inappropriate for refugees to engage in political activity. One author proceeded to argue that Galician refugees actually regarded themselves as Russian, but that their aspirations had traditionally been thwarted by Austria-Hungary.[161] More crudely still, Russian nationalists denounced manifestations of "mazepism," or treachery to the tsarist cause. This prejudice sometimes conditioned the response of local Russian people to refugees. A correspondent for the newspaper *Priazovskii krai* reported that 500 young refugees from Galicia had settled in Rostov, only for some of them to be bullied for being "mazepists" (a reference to the Cossack hetman who collaborated with the Swedes and led a revolt against Peter the Great in 1708). Their offense had been to answer truthfully that they professed the Greek Catholic (Uniate) faith. What made the taunts worse was that they came from their companions who had decided to espouse the Orthodox religion, explaining that "in Russia everyone has to be Orthodox."[162]

CONCLUSION

Let us now attempt to summarize the ways in which refugeedom confirmed, modified, or subverted the perceived attributes of ethnicity. Particularly interesting are the remarks of the Dashnak theorist Nikol Aghbalian, a member of the Armenian National Council, who blamed what he took to be their modest level of national consciousness on the fact that "the Armenian people were not a compact element in their native lands but lived in the midst of other peoples, each with distinct aspirations. Constant friction with those neighbors had hindered Armenian progress." Did the migration of some Armenian refugees to towns and villages in the north Caucasus and European Russia enhance this sense of national dispersion?

Or did the events of 1915–16 challenge the stereotype of a scattered people, by concentrating Armenian refugees in ethnically more homogeneous communities? The latter seems to fit the facts more comfortably.[163] Comparable anxieties began to be articulated with respect to Latvians and Lithuanians; notwithstanding prewar emigration, these communities had scarcely been conceived in terms of a diaspora. Now their spokesmen feared that the war had forced them to scatter. Latvian patriots discovered pockets of settlers who needed to be incorporated into the incipient nation. It was imperative to avoid further dispersion, which would destroy national solidarity and condemn these nations to the status of Jews. From this point of view, the prospect of diaspora status may have intensified rather than diminished national consciousness. Religious belief, affiliation, and practice probably worked to the same end.

Most of imperial Russia's national minorities could count on material and other assistance from communities in self-imposed or voluntary exile overseas. Thus, the rhetoric of an Armenian diaspora took on a new aspect. Some Armenian patriots argued that the diaspora was transcended in wartime: "Armenians, scattered throughout the entire world, are becoming a solid and strong unit, before which the cruel enemy trembles."[164] Latvians and Poles derived financial support from scattered "colonies," particularly in the United States. Yet none of this provided much comfort to national leaders who wished to promote a close connection between settlers and soil. A revived homeland required the application of labor, not just overseas aid.

Refugeedom did not paper over the political divisions among the self-appointed leaders of the empire's national minorities. Indeed, by forming part of broader debates about the meaning of imperial rule, refugeedom may have helped to intensify political division. From the refugees' point of view, however, the experience of war appears simultaneously to have contributed to the growth of national consciousness and to the promotion of a degree of inter-ethnic political cooperation, without doing anything to diminish a specific sense of betrayal and oppression at the hands of Russian officials. True, such cooperation—including, of course, cooperation with Russians on the boards of the public organizations—may have been short-lived. But we should not deny its capacity to mitigate some of the worst effects of population displacement.[165]

It is a difficult task to reconstruct the meaning of national identity for ordinary refugees. Theoretically, "the individual does not require the mediations of family, community, region, or class to be a member of the nation. Nationality is understood precisely as an attribute of the individual and the whole, not of the intermediate associations."[166] In the specific circumstances of late imperial Russia, refugee associational activity may have crystallized national particularism by helping to generate a sense of what "the whole" entailed, as an alternative to that other whole represented by the imperial polity. One could also make the case that national identity was "reflexively constituted" as the opposite of other national groups brought together by refugee displacement. In other words, refugees became accustomed to forms of action and ways of thinking that had previously been impossible to conceive.[167]

Collective action helped to bridge the gap between the educated national elite, refugee members of the national intelligentsia, and the "common" refugee. It was no longer possible to retain the conventional sharp distinction between members of the educated intelligentsia and the "dark" narod, because they had suffered a common exposure to the dehumanizing and debilitating consequences of refugeedom. All of them could empathize with the sense of trial and tribulation, as well as with the destruction of "national" assets. Non-refugee members of national minorities bound themselves together by the common "tax" levied on the entire community. By virtue of the disruption caused to other relationships by war, refugeedom created a situation in which nationality could assume a peculiar significance, even becoming prior to other kinds of solidarity.[168] Refugeedom conferred respectability upon the rhetoric of national consciousness and imparted vitality to actions that were couched in a national idiom. Refugees were mobilized for a crusade in support of national regeneration and, ultimately, the creation of nationhood.

—◯—

8

REVOLUTION AND REFUGEEDOM

All these endless horrors, this misery, these incredible sufferings, these hundreds of thousands of abandoned prisoners of war, these famines, these millions of helpless refugees are the result, direct or indirect, of the war.
— FRIDTJOF NANSEN, "NO MORE WAR"

Refugees as a distinct phenomenon are dissolved in the general calamity afflicting the entire population at the front.
— S. I. ZUBCHANINOV, 12 DECEMBER 1916

We must impress all our activity upon the public, collect all documentary material relating to refugees, arrange reports, write down our memoirs, and then deposit everything in an archive. Only then will our work be complete.
— A. B. NEIDGARDT, 15 MAY 1917

The marginal position occupied by refugees made them invisible guests at the festival of the Russian revolution. Class affiliation came increasingly to dominate political loyalties and social behavior, leaving refugees ever more in limbo. Refugees lacked any defined corporate representation. They thus did not occupy center stage during the tumultuous events of 1917. In one sense the revolution passed them by, as neither the February nor the October revolution impinged directly on refugees. The revolution of February did not produce a refugee Soviet, nor did the Bolshevik revolution yield any decree to match the extraordinary paper chase that set about the transformation of property relations. To remain a "refugee" was to risk oblivion. Yet this litany of negatives overlooks the lives actually lived by refugees, the administrative agencies that attended to their welfare, and the political context that governed their prospects of resolving the question of their permanent place of residence. The revolution did have an impact; refugees did speak. It is for the historian to listen to what they were saying.

The revolution in February 1917 inevitably placed a question mark over the future of at least some of the agencies engaged in refugee relief work. Whether the public organizations, defeated in 1915, could resume their attempt to establish supremacy over the administration of refugee relief remained uncertain. But an assault by the unions of towns and zemstvos upon the entrenched positions occupied by such agencies as Severopomoshch' and the Tatiana Committee was only to be expected.[1] Even before the abrupt and ignominious collapse of the tsarist regime, the existing arrangements for the relief of refugees in the Russian empire had come under intense scrutiny. In part this reflected the fact that the administration of refugee relief was necessarily subject to the same process of reevaluation that affected other areas of political activity. In part it was a result of the mounting economic crisis and the need to look for ways to curb the growth in public expenditure. Contemporaries began to recognize that refugees would continue to require support in peacetime; this made them aware of the need to keep administrative arrangements under constant review.[2]

Pressure mounted in 1917 for the democratization of the established system of refugee relief. "The ruling classes and the spokesmen of countless government departments keep telling us that the care of refugees, like the war itself, is a national affair. Well, if this is the case, give the people themselves the chance to speak their mind," said the progressive newspaper editor V. Muizhel' in November 1916. "Citizens' committees" created an opportunity for the disaffected Russian public to become involved in welfare provision. But, as Muizhel' recognized, public enthusiasm for the plight of refugees could not be taken for granted. He admitted that "we must explain to the narod exactly who refugees are, and then the people will begin to understand the entire tragedy of refugees' plight." Muizhel' envisaged the transfer of responsibility from the tsarist bureaucracy to Russia's public organizations, but his position neatly captured one of the dilemmas inherent in democratization. There was a risk that, against the background of economic crisis, the narod would refuse to commit sufficient energy and resources to refugee relief. Popular sympathy for the plight of refugees might easily evaporate.[3]

No less troubling for the new government, the military offensive launched by Kerenskii in June 1917 quickly ran into difficulties, prompting a fresh influx of refugees.[4] This raised the prospect that Russia's new rulers would, like the old regime, be overwhelmed by the scale of displacement, allowing little time for reflection about the principles and procedures of refugee relief, including arrangements for the eventual repatriation of those who wished to return to their homes. In the meantime, refugees old and new were urged to keep up their spirits, no matter how far from their homes they had traveled.[5] This injunction was easier to utter than to enforce. Most refugees had spent nearly two years far from home and were anxious that their sojourn in the Russian interior not be extended any longer than was necessary. However, they soon understood the magnitude of the forces unleashed by the social revolution that gathered momentum during the second half of 1917. This upheaval would ultimately have a profound effect on their own fragile condition. Radical measures undertaken by Russia's citizens after the Bolshevik revolution, in particular the seizure and redistribution of privately owned land, confirmed that refugees did not belong in the world of the Russian village and threatened to expose them to hunger and exploitation.

THE TWILIGHT OF THE OLD REGIME

The material support offered to refugees had first to be safeguarded. The value of relief payments made to refugees, and the categories of people entitled to such relief, became matters of great concern as the economic crisis deepened in the last months of 1916. The government sought to limit entitlements, in order to reduce pressure on the state budget. Higher rates of inflation meant that the norms laid down in 1915 bore little relationship to refugees' needs twelve months later. Many refugees were also vulnerable to illness as the real value of relief declined. With the onset of winter, they could no longer count on the prospect of paid employment as a means of supplementing state benefits.[6] These anxieties were echoed by refugees themselves, such as Armenians in Erevan who complained that they had not received an allowance for two months.[7] Other voices spoke instead of the intolerable burden that refugee relief imposed. In a characteristic comment, liberal members of the Special Council feared a backlash by local taxpayers, "from whom extremely unwelcome excesses are to be expected."[8] Not for the first time, refugeedom was inextricably tied to questions of public order. At the beginning of 1917, the allocations made to provincial authorities were slashed by up to 50 percent, causing widespread dismay and reviving claims that some national committees were better placed than others to provide refugees with adequate funds.[9]

Divisions also opened up over the role of various relief organizations. As we saw in chapter 2, leaders of the Union of Zemstvos and the Union of Towns criticized the way in which the Tatiana Committee had usurped responsibility for collating and processing information about the refugee population. Opposition to the "bureaucratization" of refugee relief now gathered momentum. During the autumn of 1916, the activities of the two special commissioners for refugee relief, Zubchaninov and Urusov, also attracted critical comment. The scope and scale of Severopomoshch'—by 1916 it had direct responsibility for around 550,000 refugees—came in for particular criticism.[10] Operating with a great deal of autonomy (far too much for the liking of the Union of Zemstvos), Severopomoshch' had established a range of services that were reportedly being used not just by refugees but by the Russian army as well.[11] The overhead costs of both agencies were also regarded as excessive.[12] An element of pique was almost certainly involved, insofar as the unions of towns and zemstvos and national committees in the northwest vied with Severopomoshch' for control over welfare provision. These altercations were doubtless recalled when the time came to settle accounts. Minister of the

Interior Khvostov accepted that it was appropriate to wind up the organization and transfer its operations to local authorities, which could look after schools, orphanages, and feeding points; the Red Cross should meanwhile assume responsibility for medical care.[13] Zubchaninov did not dispute the fact that his task as a commissioner for refugees had been completed, but he sensibly urged that proper attention be given to the needs of all civilians, refugees included, in the vicinity of the front.[14]

Urusov decided in the meantime to go before he was pushed. Handing in his resignation in September 1916, he pointed out that—as a result of the Russian advance during 1916—the Special Council planned to reduce his responsibilities and confine Iugobezhenets to just two provinces, as against the seventeen he had administered originally.[15] The editor of *Iugobezhenets,* Urusov's mouthpiece, signed off in sentimental style: "We are convinced that our recent work has been of no little service to refugees and that, thanks to our paper's good offices, more than one mother has, with tears of gratitude, clutched to her breast her newfound child."[16] But their political enemies did not weep for Urusov and Zubchaninov. Thus, in the final weeks of the tsarist regime, liberal and nationalist politicians appeared to have scored a minor victory over the plenipotentiaries engaged by the Ministry of the Interior.[17]

Other issues also dogged the tsarist government and showed how difficult it was to solve "the refugee question." The unforeseen flight from their homes that refugees had been forced to endure was mirrored in their subsequent refusal to bow to official demands that they stay put in their new location for the duration of the war. Many instances came to light of refugees who took advantage of the Brusilov offensive to attempt to return "spontaneously" to their homes in the western borderlands, even though this rendered them liable to the withdrawal of their allowances. Military commanders feared that this impulsive drift would play havoc with troop transport and supply trains, and they were no less alarmed about the potential for refugees to spread disease in the shifting and volatile military theater. Accordingly, government and military officials announced that homeward journeys would have to await formal approval; the General Staff took the view that refugees could in principle return to localities that had once been occupied by the enemy, provided they were not accompanied by family dependents and that they were physically able to engage in productive labor.[18] However, attempts to stem the tide of returning refugees appear to have been unsuccessful. This was an ironic reversal of fortune. At an earlier stage of the war, refugees had borne the brunt of military arbitrariness (*proizvol*); now they had the capacity to wreak a kind of revenge on the leadership of the Russian army, by unwittingly obstructing military movement and the health of troops.[19]

Return raised a fresh set of problems. One issue concerned the administrative arrangements for monitoring resettlement. The government had originally envisaged that this responsibility would be assumed by Zubchaninov and Urusov, and subsequently by local authorities. Where towns lacked a self-governing body, local citizens' committees were charged with overseeing the return of refugees.[20] Nor did the public organizations hold back. The Union of Towns discussed arrangements for the return of refugees to their places of origin in terms of a "systematic, clear plan . . . so that the forthcoming return movement of refugees will not turn into the same kind of spontaneous and miserable phenomenon that occurred during the difficult circumstances of last year."[21] It was taken for granted that such administrative planning should be entrusted to the public organizations, in conjunction with the national committees, rather than to the Special Council. Once again, educated society was on the offensive.[22]

"Spontaneity" implied other risks from the point of view of public officials. Senator Neidgardt—as chair of the Tatiana Committee, a rather unlikely figure to be concerned with peasant farming in Russia's western borderlands—argued that returnees should be discouraged from buying building materials, lest this obstruct the task of land settlement (*zemleustroistvo*) after the war. Far better, he maintained, that farmers make temporary use of timber and scrap iron, for example from abandoned trenches, rather than making long-term investments in advance of government plans for rural reconstruction. Government should "plan" for the resettlement of refugees, specifically by rebuilding farms to the highest possible standards, including fireproof materials, stronger structures, and better sanitation. Plenty of local professional experts were likely to be on hand for this task.[23]

It took a long time before government and society began to consider the respective rights of returning refugees and the settled population.[24] Should the Special Council ignore the needs of civilians who had not left their homes, but whose health and material condition gave no less cause for concern than that of refugees who planned to recover their property?[25] The former had also suffered the consequences of enemy occupation; they too were victims of war and could legitimately claim compensation or assistance from the tsarist state. It was agreed that aid should be given on an equal basis to both sections of the population, because in the vicinity of the front, "the very concept of 'refugee' is inappropriate, in view of the impossibility of distinguishing refugees from the settled population." Both groups were equally vulnerable to deteriorating living conditions. The Special Council came to the conclusion that, in principle, compensation should be extended not only to those who had been forced to leave their homes in 1915, but also to those who had departed voluntarily and whose property was currently in the hands of the enemy. In addition, compensation could be claimed by farmers whose land was being or had been fought over; the only condition was that they had to be able to demonstrate that military action had prevented them from farming their land.[26] However, although in this instance the authorities blurred the distinction between refugees and the settled population, in other respects it had not lost its meaning.

REFUGEES IN "FREE RUSSIA"

Following the overthrow of the tsarist regime in February 1917, the provisional government rapidly instituted important changes to the existing administrative arrangements for refugee relief. At the first meeting of the newly constituted Special Council for Refugees, the deputy minister of the interior promised a fresh start, in the hope of cementing greater trust between central government, public organizations, and national committees. One means of improving public confidence in the Special Council was to ensure that, at a time of mounting inflation, government monies were released promptly to those responsible for meeting refugees' needs.[27] A. A. Isaev, a member of the Petrograd Regional Union of Towns, called upon the council to become more broadly representative of Russian society by giving seats to the Moscow Central Cooperative Union and the Petrograd Soviet of Workers' and Soldiers' Deputies. He also urged the convocation of a nationwide commission that would bring together all organizations involved in refugee relief.[28]

As expected, the Special Council proceeded to abolish the office of special commissioner for refugees and to transfer his functions to the unions of zemstvos and towns. These measures aroused little passion or debate. Far more controversy was sparked by a proposal to abolish the Tatiana Committee. V. A. Gerd launched a fierce attack on Neidgardt and his colleagues, accusing the committee of a campaign to stifle the public organizations from the outset. However, Gerd found himself in a minority, perhaps because the intemperate nature of his onslaught alienated some of his colleagues who lined up to speak on behalf of the Tatiana Committee. Jewish, Polish, and Belorussian members maintained that "under the old regime the Tatiana Committee had managed to organize matters on a public footing, indicating that healthy instincts were alive and well within it." Neidgardt himself pointed out that the committee currently had 130,000 orphaned children in its immediate care, as well as a further 167,500 whom it subsidized indirectly. He pleaded the case for the men and women who staffed its 1,217 offices—three-quarters of them "public activists." He expressed pride in the fact that most of the committee's money went directly for refugee relief. He insisted that the Tatiana Committee had held firm to the principle that assistance should be offered to all those in need, regardless of nationality, and that local committees should be autonomous. Finally, he emphasized that the committees had been responsible for collecting nearly 13 million rubles in voluntary contributions: "Not one association or society in Rus' can boast such a degree of civic generosity."[29] A few days later, Isaev once more took up the cudgels on behalf of the anti-Tatiana lobby, arguing that a permanent resolution of the refugee problem belonged, as a matter of "state significance," to the Special Council. Once again, Sliozberg and others rallied to the defense of the Tatiana Committee, which, according to its spokesman, had reunited or established contact between half a million refugees, including 20,000 children.[30]

The Tatiana Committee survived these onslaughts at the cost of abandoning some of its favorite programs and yielding to the popular mood for greater glasnost and democratization. The key decisions were reached at a congress of its provincial representatives, held in Petrograd in April 1917. In a sharp break with tradition, the participants were elected by local committees; they included 6 women out of a total of 81 delegates. They agreed that it was now imperative to include new workers "from all sections of the population," to secure representation from public organizations, and—significantly—to invite refugees themselves to participate. Nor did democratization stop there. After a bad-tempered debate, the conservative-minded leadership reluctantly accepted that those who worked on its behalf had the right to be paid for their services, thereby opening the way for the participation of broader sections of the population.[31]

Pressure mounted for yet more thoroughgoing change. In early April 1917, representatives from the public organizations and national committees were invited to Moscow to attend a congress devoted to the relief of refugees.[32] The delegates voted in favor of the democratization of the Special Council, by recommending the inclusion of two representatives from the Petrograd soviet, as well as two each from the Confederation of Cooperatives and the All-Russian Peasant Union. They advocated the creation of a new executive board to administer finances, to maintain a register of refugees, and to arrange for their repatriation. In what amounted to a much more radical departure from tsarist practice than these decisions, the congress decided to arrange for "the participation of refugees themselves in the work of the Special Council." True to the spirit of bourgeois revolution, the congress resolved to liquidate any organization involved in refugee relief that did not conform to the need for a "public profile"; "all refugee organizations shall be built on democratic foundations."[33] The congress sent a pointed message of congratulation to Prince L'vov: "We are convinced that children of the old Russia will forget the misfortunes brought about by crimes inflicted by the state, to which it gave the hypocritical label 'refugeedom'; and that in this reborn country we shall acknowledge a motherland for whose freedom it will be both easy and honorable to lay down our lives."[34]

Among its specific proposals, the congress laid down ground rules for agencies responsible for refugee relief. It affirmed that "the state has an obligation to assist refugees, [but] the refugee does not have an inalienable right to receive an allowance. Relief should be regarded exclusively as a guideline, and the amount of assistance that is given may fluctuate from one instance to another, in accordance with individual need."[35] Everyone applauded the principle of work relief, in the interests both of economy and of instilling a sense of self-worth among refugees. In some respects, then, the statement simply reaffirmed the principles by which the old Special Council had operated, in its attempts to avoid writing a blank check to relief organizations. At the same time, it is possible to detect a new emphasis. A distinctive kind of surveillance was being articulated, representing the abandonment of the older bureaucratic form of tutelage (*opeka*), as practiced by provincial governors and special commissioners who had attended to generalized categories of need. Refugees were promised instead a new respect for the person, while at the same time each individual was to be scrutinized to establish his or her entitlement to relief. The corollary of this fresh approach was that the citizen-subject should aspire to become more self-reliant.[36]

The new emphasis on the individual citizen was coupled with an invocation of patriotic duty, as in the public appeal issued by the Special Council at the end of March 1917. Echoing similar rallying cries from the provisional government to workers and soldiers, the appeal is worth quoting in full:

> Refugees! Russia and all the nationalities that inhabit it have been reborn, and you who are henceforth free citizens believe steadfastly that with God's help the enemy will be crushed and forever expelled from our borders! On that joyful day you will once more enter your native land, cast upon its soil the first handful of seed, and begin to rebuild your devastated property.
>
> There is no effort and no labor that mighty and free Russia will not expend in order to bring that day nearer! And in this task a large share falls to you, for the most part tillers of the land. Our valiant defenders—the army and its various ranks, your sons and brothers—need above all military provisions and bread. With these basic necessities, the army will triumph. As farmers, your public duty with the onset of spring is to devote all your energy to the cultivation of the land. In your experienced and capable hands, the land will become bountiful. God grant you the means to enrich Russia with new harvests and thereby supply the army and people, yourselves included. The provisional government is anxious to help you in any way possible to apply your productive labor. Each uezd has a special committee comprising local people, which will help you with advice and information about land that is available to rent, . . . about the possibilities for the hire of labor, the creation of an artel, and which can advise on the rent of land or the means of beginning work on the terms that are most suitable to you and your families.
>
> The onset of work is at hand. Prepare yourselves and tell the committees at once about your wish to start work. Your contribution to food production this year is your great public service to the country. May God grant you strength![37]

This striking accent on the obligations of citizenship is a departure from previous messages, which conveyed above all else the drama of displacement and the magnitude of the relief effort; refugees were now invited to think not what their country could do for them, but what they could do for their country. No less significant is the assumption that refugees should suppress any anger toward the Russian army for the wrongs that troops had inflicted on the civilian population in 1915, and should instead concentrate on the task at hand, since only a military solution would restore their homes and property.

Meanwhile the calamitous Kerenskii offensive and the ensuing German advance prompted a further influx of refugees to Kiev and other towns in the eastern regions of Ukraine. General Kornilov, commander of the southwestern front, entertained the hope that civilians would be discouraged from leaving their homes, "in view of present circumstances and bearing in mind the experience of refugee movement in 1915." Others took a less sanguine view of the impact of injunctions such as these.[38] The renewed displacement was thought to be the likely result not just of military setbacks, but also of the inability of the government to feed the population of Russia's northwest. The public organizations discussed with Stavka the need to look after as many as one million additional refugees. Civilian and military authorities alike agreed that refugees should be sent to Siberia, the north Caucasus, and the Don oblast, avoiding Moscow, Orel, Kursk, and Ekaterinoslav "at all costs."[39]

The plight of those who had already found refuge in the Russian countryside provided evidence of a steady deterioration in their circumstances. Whatever initial warmth and sympathy they had met with now began to evaporate during the critical months of economic collapse. During the winter there were calls for Armenian refugees to be moved from the countryside in Orel and sent back to the Caucasus.[40] In Voronezh, local land boards reported that peasants had intimidated and in some cases physically attacked refugee families. Local government officials and militias were asked to intervene in order to improve the relations between villagers and refugees.[41] The peasant/non-peasant nexus generated enormous tension and conflict, providing yet another manifestation of the maelstrom in rural Russia that was to persist beyond the *annus mirabilis* of 1917.

RUSSIA'S MINORITIES AND NATIONAL MOVEMENTS, 1917–1918

Other displaced groups suffered at least as much, and were perhaps even more vulnerable to the shifting economic and political conjuncture. The provisional government indicated little willingness to adopt a more liberal approach to the needs of the German farmers who had been unceremoniously expelled from Volynia and other provinces. By the beginning of 1917, their economic position had become precarious. Financial assistance from the MVD via the Department of Police had declined, and now it ceased entirely. The formerly prevailing view—convenient for a government whose own financial situation was deteriorating day by day—held that all German settlers, being wealthy, could sell some of their property if and when necessary.[42] They were thus thought to have much less of a claim to financial support than "real" refugees.[43] Nevertheless, humanitarian considerations prompted a review of the treatment of German settlers. The winter of 1916 had been particularly harsh. Reports reached Petrograd of the shortage of food in Samara and the likelihood of popular disturbances as the local population attempted to drive 142,000 Germans out of the lower Volga region in order to reduce competition for food. The Special Council eventually decided to renew financial aid to the settlers, on the understanding that its level should be fixed at 50 percent of the allowances paid to refugees. When this failed to improve their situation, the government encouraged the Volga Germans to move yet again, this time to the neighboring province of Orenburg, where the harvest had been abundant. The Special Council could scarcely conceal its impatience with the settlers.[44]

In this respect the change of government in February 1917 had little impact; indeed, the vigorous prosecution of the war effort by Kerenskii, along with the growing economic crisis in the country, may unintentionally have reinforced popular anti-German sentiment. However, other important changes were also taking place. First, German settlers could take some comfort from the government's decision on 21 March to proclaim the equality of all citizens, regardless of national or religious affiliation. Second, members of the German community in cities such as Moscow, Odessa, and Saratov were able to engage openly in political activity, although this exposed sharp differences of strategy between left and right. In Moscow, for example, a national-liberal elite campaigned for an exclusively nationalist platform, whereas other towns favored cooperation with all democratic parties in "free Russia" that would hopefully extend educational and cultural autonomy to national minorities. Third, forcibly displaced German settlers were no longer condemned to remain passive, and the most determined families even managed to make their way back home during the autumn months.[45] The revolution therefore brought about opportunities for personal and political action that had previously been inconceivable.

More troubling was the prospect that political instability might prompt concerted violence against Russia's Jewish refugees. Hans Rogger has suggested that popular attacks against Jews became more common after the end of the monarchy (as in 1905, peasants and townspeople ascribed the misfortunes of Russia to the malignant influence of Jewish revolutionaries and students). The decision by the provisional government to grant full civil liberties to Jews signaled a profound change in official attitudes, but did nothing to convince popular opinion of the need to treat them as equal members of society. Indeed, by altering their status without establishing a secure hold on Russian society and local institutions, the new government may have helped to create the conditions for more serious outbreaks of violence than at any time since the pogroms of 1905–1906. Jews were once more targeted as profiteers, self-serving revolutionaries, and favorites of the new regime. Where neither the writ of government nor that of the Petrograd soviet ran, pogroms began to multiply. But the extent of assaults upon Jewish refugees must remain a matter of conjecture.[46]

A full examination of the impact of revolution on the myriad national refugee organizations has yet to be made. Even so, some broad trends seem clear enough. In each case, the revolution lifted the lid on political intrigues that had earlier been masked by the need for national elites to set aside any differences and to cooperate among themselves. Another important consideration was the political community to which patriotic leaders were now free to appeal. Since so many potential constituents had been displaced, much attention was devoted to the means whereby they might once again be gathered together. Finally, ethnic leaders could appeal beyond their chosen constituency to international patrons.

After the February revolution, leaders of the Latvian Central Welfare Committee continued to support the Russian war effort, but they sought a fair price for this stance.[47] The dominant political mood was summed up in the call for a "free Latvia in a free Russia." Earlier calls for self-government no longer satisfied popular opinion. Latvian public organizations, as well as the newly formed Latvian National Democratic Party (LNDP), demanded autonomy and a national parliament (*Saeima*) to be elected on the basis of universal suffrage, without distinction of nationality, gender, class, and religion.[48] Yet the optimistic vision of a "free Latvia" was sharply qualified by the realization that the war had scattered so many of its potential citizens. The progressive newspaper *Dzimtenes Atbalss* bemoaned the loss of Latvia's cultural and intellectual elite: "The only people to have returned are men on the make, slackers and the kind of women who have a bad name. . . . Latvia is beset by lethargy, military discipline, money, and cheap favors. . . . There is only one solution, and that is for the Latvian intelligentsia to go back home." Latvian patriots nevertheless derived some comfort from reports of refugees' commitment to a sense of Latvianness, such as their celebration of the midsummer festival (23 June), which provided an opportunity to listen to songs and speeches in favor of a united and free Latvia. Such exuberance encouraged the LNDP in its wish to propagate the "national idea" among a receptive refugee population.[49] Unhappily for Latvia, the late summer of 1917 brought further disaster. German troops entered Riga on 21 August. The Russian 12th Army retreated in disarray, looting and mistreating the local population as they did so. The number of refugees swelled yet again.[50]

Members of the Latvian Refugee Committee in Petrograd, notably Goldmanis and Zalitis, finally succeeded in October 1917 in making arrangements for a Latvian national council as a forum for all political groups.[51] The inaugural meeting of the Latvian Provisional National Council (LPNC) took place at the end of November, with representatives from thirteen parties and other organizations; social democratic groups (including the now victorious Bolshevik party) refused to attend. This "democratic bloc" resolved to establish an independent state and convene a Latvian constituent assembly to determine its political structure. Delegates declared that Latvia was "united and indivisible and included Latgale, Vidzeme, and Kurzeme," and resolved to "bring refugees home." But what kind of home? Ten thousand copies were printed of a rousing declaration on national independence:

> We shall be slaves to no one. It is time to plow with Latvian hands the lands whose borders until now have been determined by foreigners, by Russians, Poles, and Germans, all of whom have plundered and divided our fatherland. . . . One part of the nation is beyond German barbed wire, another part is in Russia; some have become refugees, some serve in a foreign army. Mother Latvia wants to bring together and unite in love all its fragmented people and unite them in one single and organic whole. . . . Let the LPNC be the star showing the way to a free and united Latvia.[52]

Local Latvian refugee organizations responded at once. Much to the surprise of the leaders of the LPNC, refugee committees in Khar'kov, Tver', Iaroslavl', Vitebsk, and Tomsk threw in their lot with the National Council.[53] The new Bolshevik government tried to hamper its work, but independent newspapers continued to publicize the council's activities. As a result of the relatively free flow of information, local Latvian refugee groups sent messages of support as well as cash to the LPNC. The council in turn advised refugees to avoid purchasing land or taking part in its redistribution: "No Latvian should give up hope of returning to the fatherland and securing land there." Latvian leaders in Tbilisi proclaimed their intention of meeting the needs of Latvian refugees in the Transcaucasus and uniting them to work for a free and independent Latvia.[54]

However, other developments contributed to the radicalization of Latvian political life. Social democratic organizations refused to have anything to do with the patriotic intelligentsia, and they were joined by the Committee of Landless Peasants, the Cultural Bureau in Moscow, and the pro-Bolshevik branch of the Congress of Refugees in Kurzeme. The Bolsheviks enjoyed widespread popular support among the Latvian riflemen and workers who had been evacuated to industrial centers in European Russia. Among these groups, the Bolshevik seizure of power met with enormous enthusiasm.[55] Their anti-war stance contrasted sharply with the strategy of moderate socialists and liberals, who looked to international support as the best guarantee of future statehood. "Bolshevism would have been the eventual victor in Latvia but for the German intervention which gave the nationalists an initial chance to create their own republic."[56]

Lithuanian activists placed themselves at the head of a national movement that faced an uphill struggle against other contenders for the loyalty of the Lithuanian population. A congress of refugees' organizations in May 1917 took the radical step of demanding independence, prompted by Germany's declaration of a Polish state. Parallel initiatives were launched in German-occupied Lithuania. A conference held in Vilna in September 1917 repeated the claim for an independent Lithuanian state. The leading spokesman was the lawyer Antanas Smetona, who had chaired the relief committee in Vilna since 1915. Smetona now took the lead in creating a provisional Lithuanian council (*Taryba*). As in Latvia, this authority succeeded in mobilizing moderate liberal opinion, as well as some groups on the left of the political spectrum. But the appeal of Bolshevism spread rapidly among Lithuanian peasants, soldiers, and refugees. In October 1917, the new government "bolshevized" the Central Lithuanian Welfare Committee.[57] Inevitably, the October revolution did not put an end to political instability, which was fueled by continued fighting at the front and by diplomatic intrigue. Eventually, in March 1918, the German government recognized the claims of Lithuanian "independence." This was something of a fiction, given that German troops continued to occupy Lithuanian territory.[58] Lithuanian refugees who remained on Soviet territory found it virtually impossible to move back home, whatever their political sympathies or affiliation. They played little direct part in determining the immediate structure of the new state.

In Ukraine, as elsewhere, the February revolution encouraged the population to look forward to the end of the war and to think that social justice might soon be realized. Few people gave any thought to national independence; much more important was the prospect of greater freedom to propagate Ukrainian culture. However, political activity quickly began to assume a more radical complexion. In Kiev, Hrushevsky and Vinnichenko created a new council (Rada), which followed the general pattern of declaring allegiance to the new regime in Petrograd, while demanding cultural autonomy. Procrastination by the provisional government, anxious as always to postpone constitutional decisions until after the war, led Ukrainian activists to issue the "First Universal" in June 1917, calling for a Ukrainian legislative assembly, on the grounds that "no one can know better than us what are our needs and which laws are best for us."[59]

A number of points can be made about the new Ukrainian politics of 1917 and its relation to refugeedom. First, some of its leaders (such as the journalist Semen Petliura) had played an active part as members of the "third element" in the Union of Towns and the Union of Zemstvos, where they had become impressed by the size of the displaced Ukrainian population. Second, delegates to numerous conferences in Ukraine included refugees ("newcomers"), such as those from Galicia, who kept the spotlight on the complex problem of Ukrainian territorialization. There was thus a direct link between refugeedom and the development of national politics during 1917.[60] On the other hand, Ukrainian activists acknowledged that the social basis of their support in Khar'kov and other towns remained weak, not only because the existing proletariat was already "russified," but also because the war had brought about the "denationalization" of towns and cities; urban Ukraine was Bolshevik, not nationalist. The authority of the Rada ran more adequately in rural areas, but the village population looked for agrarian reform above all else, and this did not necessarily entail benefits for refugees, of whatever nationality.[61]

International diplomacy, as in the Baltic, helped to resolve the status of Ukraine. Ukrainian nationalists attended the Brest-Litovsk negotiations from a position of strength, demanding the inclusion of Chelm, Galicia, and Bukovina in the "popular republic of Ukraine." Bolshevik military advances forced the Rada delegates to compromise, but the support of Germany was decisive; at the end of January 1918, Germany and its allies recognized the independence of Ukraine, in the hope of securing large supplies of food and raw materials. Independence, however, did not bring peace, any more than it did in the Baltic. The Bolsheviks occupied Kiev, symbolic capital of Ukraine, helping to provoke further involuntary displacement of civilians. Revolution and counter-revolution yielded a fresh harvest of refugeedom.[62]

In Belorussia, the revolution created opportunities for national organization that had simply not existed under the old regime. The establishment of a Soviet government in Minsk in October 1917 exposed a power struggle, similar to that in Ukraine, between the Bolsheviks and a nationalist coalition. But the German advance rapidly put paid to the Soviet government and replaced it with a puppet regime, headed by the conservative politician A. S. Skirmunt, whose authority rested largely on the uncertain support of the German army. A congress of refugees that met in Moscow in July 1918 bitterly denounced the division of Belorussia following the Brest-Litovsk treaty in March. Delegates acknowledged that "we did not know until now that we were Belorussians," a lack of consciousness that was blamed on the "dark masses" and the lack of a full-fledged patriotic intelligentsia. Much remained to be done to create a progressive stratum and to educate the Belorussian *narod*. In the short term, Belorussian refugees suffered from poor organization and inadequate finance, especially when compared to other national minorities such as Latvians and Poles. Again, however, the international context was crucial in highlighting the meaning of "Belorussia." The congress demanded the "reunification" of the country and its incorporation into the new RSFSR. Only then would refugees be free to go "home."[63]

The collapse of the tsarist government was greeted with enthusiasm among the Armenian community, as throughout the entire Transcaucasus. Local political leaders not only hoped that thousands of refugees from Turkish Armenia would now be resettled without hindrance, but also anticipated a decisive Russian onslaught against the Ottoman state.[64] Under the new administrative arrangements, and against a background of increasing shortages and social instability in the Armenian countryside, many Armenian survivors of the genocide felt sufficiently reassured to move back to their original settlements; perhaps as many as 150,000 did so.[65] In May 1917, a second congress of Armenian activists assembled in Petrograd to discuss the economic and social problems that were confronting Armenia. More than a third of the delegates belonged to different refugee relief organizations, whose efforts it was hoped to coordinate more effectively. The congress had originally been scheduled to convene in the autumn of 1916, in either Erevan or Etchmidzian, in order that delegates could be drawn from local activists, and that others could see at first hand the devastation of the regional economy. But this proved impossible, and as a result, the congress was deemed by some reporters to "lack weight and authority." Those who attended the meeting in Petrograd called for a network of societies to revive the shattered economy, to establish a proper education system, and to offer full security to the returning refugees.[66] Ozakom (the Special Transcaucasian Committee) was subordinated to a new commissar for the occupied territory, who reported directly to the government in Petrograd; the fate of refugees was thus "removed from the arena . . . of Transcaucasian rivalries."[67]

The fragility of these hopes was exposed by the progressive erosion of popular support for the provisional government and the transfer of popular allegiances within Russia to the Bolshevik Party, whose commitment to peace "without annexations" obviously had serious implications for Armenian security.[68] The beleaguered Armenian leaders, faced after the Bolshevik revolution and the Brest-Litovsk treaty with the loss of Russian patronage, and the withdrawal of any support from Georgia or Azerbaijan, were obliged to declare independence, not as a hallmark of national strength but as a sign of national isolation. With the defeat of the central powers, however, Armenia was offered a respite from Ottoman aggression and an opportunity at the Paris peace talks to entertain the grand vision of a greater Armenia.[69]

In the longer term, the political and military turmoil in Armenia between 1915 and 1920 prompted a shift in population to the Caucasus, and thus a rethinking of the geographical meaning of Armenia among the patriotic intelligentsia. But the new Bolshevik regime had no truck with the idea of a separate Armenian state. For the Bolsheviks, refugeedom belonged to the panoply of issues that could be "solved" only internationally. According to Ron Suny, war and revolution undermined the careful efforts that had been made over several generations to create a conscious Armenian nationality. Territorial and population losses played their part, along with the reduction in the size of the Armenian bourgeoisie and cultural intelligentsia in centers such as Tbilisi and Baku. Neither an institutional nor a social basis existed for the articulation of Armenian nationality. However, Suny's argument seems to operate best as a characterization of Armenian vulnerability after 1918. During 1915–17, the refugee problem served as a basis for the articulation of Armenian-

ness. Yet it remains difficult to link refugeedom to nation-building in a straightfor-
ward manner. Armenian political opinion, as elsewhere, was sharply divided. The
Dashnaks enjoyed some popular support, including among Armenian peasants and
many refugees, but many members of the professional intelligentsia sided with the
Armenian Populist Party. All the same, the convocation of the Armenian National
Congress in Tbilisi in October 1917 brought agreement over the need for a demo-
cratically elected legislative body that would act on behalf of all Russia's Armenians.
No less significant, delegates to the congress had been chosen from local cultural,
charitable, religious, and political organizations, demonstrating the association between refugeedom and national political mobilization.[70]

   The foregoing remarks suggest that refugeedom had the capacity to mobilize
and, in some instances, even to unite political opponents; it certainly helped to
inspire collective "national" endeavor and to create opportunities for the practice of
government. Refugeedom trained national elites in the conduct of politics and administration. This was evident in the aftermath of the peace treaties and the creation of the successor states. The first cabinet to be appointed in Latvia included
Mikelis Valters (minister of the interior), Janis Goldmanis (minister of agriculture),
and Janis Zalitis (minister of war), each of whom had played a prominent role in
refugee relief work. Janis Cakste became president of Latvia. Many statesmen had
a background in parliamentary politics before the revolution, but it was arguably
their active involvement in refugee relief that brought them more closely before the
public.[71] We can see this pattern in other cases as well. The leader of the Lithuanian
refugee relief effort in Russia, Martynas Ycas, became the first finance minister in
the new Lithuanian state.[72] Aleksandr Khatisov was for ten months the prime minister of independent Armenia. These men could begin to fashion a fledgling civil
service from the plethora of refugee relief organizations.[73]

   What of the potential citizens of these states? Did they share the vision of national regeneration? Desperation, combined with an element of national pride, best
sums up the popular mood. In May 1919, a group of Polish teachers in Riazan'
complained of their desperate material plight, but added that their wish to return
to Poland was prompted by grander ambitions: "We have a natural wish to go back
to our native country, where a new and brighter future awaits us in free Poland. . . .
we are anxious to reestablish contact with our families who remained behind there,
and we have a passionate desire to serve our homeland during the difficult time of
its founding."[74] In the newly founded Baltic states, too, hard work and self-reliance
were the keys to national construction. As Vieda Skultans has recently pointed
out, in Latvia "the master narrative of the independence period . . . put so much
emphasis on working to rebuild life."[75] By speaking the language of national loss,
homecoming, and restitution, these refugees repaid their debt to national relief

agencies with interest. What refugeedom could not do, however, was to invent nationhood.

FROM REVOLUTION TO CIVIL WAR

The political upheaval that took place in Russian society during the autumn of 1917 did not leave refugees untouched. An attempt to channel mass energies toward a defense of refugees' interests culminated in an inaugural congress of the "All-Russian Union of Refugees" that took place in Petrograd at the beginning of September. The delegates claimed to speak on behalf of as many as 150,000 refugees. They had much to complain about. Refugees received a mere pittance, and even then on an irregular basis; in Minsk, for example, they were now entitled to just 15 kopecks. Food supplies were also held up. There was widespread suspicion that welfare agencies looked after their own. In Smolensk, Vitebsk, Kurland, Volynia, Voronezh, and Moscow, refugees went without clothes and shoes, whereas "the friends and acquaintances of the relief committees receive whatever they need, and more besides." Purely material issues were thus not their sole grievance. The entire apparatus of refugee relief offered too much scope for favoritism, corruption, and speculation. An overhaul was required, in order to make it more accountable and democratic.[76]

The provisional government—by now in its death throes—took an unsympathetic line. Deputy Minister of the Interior Bogutskii spoke to the congress and indicated that the government had spent generous sums on refugee relief. He urged the congress to consider the problem from the "state's point of view," a tactic that had already been tried with workers, soldiers, and peasants, with a conspicuous lack of success. Refugees were in no mood to make "sacrifices"; delegates demanded not only higher and more regular allowances, but also exemption from taxes for three years when they returned home. When Bogutskii made an off-the-cuff suggestion that refugees should move to sparsely populated areas such as the Altai, the delegates derided this as a trivial response. In their view, "the *chinovniki* have caroused while refugees starved."[77]

The tone of the congress was broadly in line with current Bolshevik opinion about the social revolution. Delegates castigated unnamed "opponents" who sought to divide refugees from their "class allies" among the working class and the poor peasantry. Unhappily, however, attempts to forge this kind of alliance were not blessed with conspicuous success. Particularly disheartening was the dismissive response of the executive of the Soviet of Peasant Deputies, which refused to recognize a deputation from the Union of Refugees, on the grounds that it was "regarded as an all-estate body which includes well-off people" (*soiuz vsesoslovnyi sostoiatel'nykh liudei*). In short, the congress was caught between a bureaucratic apparatus that had scarcely begun to acknowledge the pressure for democratization, and a representative body of the Russian peasantry which understood the world of refugeedom as one of relative privilege rather than desperate need. Nor was this the only difficulty that confronted the Union of Refugees. In asserting the need for a separate organization to represent refugees, and to prevent the relief effort from being dominated by bureaucrats and clerics, their leaders were bound to be confronted by the Bolsheviks' intransigent aversion to autonomous organizations.[78]

Russia's new leaders quickly gave notice of their wish to exert state control over population displacement. One of the first steps of the Soviet regime was the creation of a refugee section within the new People's Commissariat of Internal Affairs.[79] These arrangements lasted until April 1918. Following the Brest-Litovsk treaty (3 March 1918), the Bolshevik government established the Central Board for POWs and Refugees (Tsentral'naia kollegiia po delam plennykh i bezhentsev, or Tsentroplenbezh). Headed by Iosif Unshlikht, who reported directly to Sovnarkom, Tsentroplenbezh devoted much of its energy to the repatriation of around 4 million Russian prisoners of war and the return of 2.5 million German and Austrian prisoners held on Russian soil.[80] Tsentroplenbezh was given the task of establishing the size and location of the displaced population, providing proper medical care, and unifying the existing administrative apparatus.[81] During the summer of 1918, its central bureau received nearly one thousand delegates, representing 540,000 refugees, allowing Tsentroplenbezh to build up a picture of the magnitude of the displaced population in different localities, the progress of registration and repatriation, the availability of food and other resources, the material and physical condition of refugees, and the conduct and attitude of local people toward the refugee population.[82]

Unshlikht and his team spent much of their time drafting plans for the re-evacuation of refugees. Soviet Russia was divided into six territorial zones, the first of which included those provinces that were suffering most acutely from food shortages. It was imperative to clear these provinces of refugees. The next priority was to evacuate the frontier zone: Pskov, Novgorod, Vitebsk, Smolensk, and Mogilev. This would make it easier to move refugees from the east of the country to the western borderlands.[83] Those traveling to the Baltic states were ordered to cross the border at Sebezh, Polotsk, or Pskov; Ukrainian refugees were to travel via Briansk or Kursk, and Poles and Belorussians via Orsha.[84] The collegium also stipulated in precise terms what personal belongings they could and could not take with them.[85]

These plans did not proceed as smoothly as Unshlikht evidently had intended them to. At the end of May 1918, Tsentroplenbezh was obliged to issue a public statement, urging refugees to follow its instructions and to refrain from voluntaristic attempts to make the journey west. Anyone who has followed the concerted efforts of previous administrations to curb the spontaneous movement of refugees and to bemoan the impulsive desires of refugees will recognize the note of bureaucratic frustration and desperation in the following appeal:

> Citizen-refugees: we hear, see, and sympathize with the fears that you are experiencing. Here in Russia life is difficult for you, sometimes even unbearable. Here there is hunger, cold, and loneliness. Conditions in the homeland may also be squalid and difficult, but over there is everything you grew up with and to which you became accustomed. We understand all this and sympathize with your fervent wish to leave behind this strange land and return to everything that is near and dear to you.
>
> But comrades, please understand that the return journey is as much in your own hands as it is in ours. . . . The movement of people toward the frontier, which is now taking place spontaneously throughout Russia, and which is being accomplished by individuals at their own risk and cost, brings with it pernicious consequences. The border crossing points are already overflowing with thousands of starving, homeless, and sick people. Beware of following their example.[86]

Around half a million refugees were thought to have left the territory of the RSFSR by October 1918, in order to go "home." Many did so "spontaneously."[87] But this still left some three and a half million people registered as refugees, only one-fifth of whom were deemed to have "assimilated themselves" (*assimilirovalis'*) and to wish to remain on Russian territory.[88] Many refugees were desperate to return to Poland and the other successor states, although others awaited greater stability or more radical political changes on home soil before they intended to return. Sometimes, as we have seen, refugees gave as a reason the wish to participate in national reconstruction. On other occasions, domestic rather than public considerations played a part. As late as August 1919, two brothers, Matvei and Aleksei Osipovich Maksimshchikov, wrote of their forced evacuation from Grodno to Riazan' in 1914. Their father had died before the war, and their mother was left in charge of the family farm. But she could no longer cope on her own and the farm had fallen into disrepair: "With the onset of autumn and winter, she is threatened with starvation and death." Matvei and Aleksei appealed to be allowed to go home: "We are sure that our request will not remain like a voice crying in the wilderness."[89]

Unhappily, the majority of refugees found it almost impossible to exercise any real freedom of choice. The closure of the frontier with Lithuania upset the plans of the brothers Maksimshchikov, as it did those of many others. Much depended also on the attitude of the German authorities who manned the border crossing points. Wealthy refugees were able to bribe German guards, and there was an active black market in travel documents.[90] The mouthpiece of Tsentroplenbezh told of obstructive German officials on the frontier who allowed refugees to congregate

in atrocious conditions in transit camps, fearing that they would export the proletarian revolution to central Europe.[91] Worse still, witnesses claimed that German
officers were surreptitiously scouring the makeshift settlements on Soviet territory,
in order to recruit able-bodied workers for farms in Prussia. Many desperate refugees availed themselves of this opportunity to move closer to their ultimate destination. Tsentroplenbezh lodged an official protest against a practice that had "introduced to Russia the customs and morals of Negro slave plantations."[92]

The new government decided at the outbreak of the civil war to clarify the status
of refugees. A decree issued on 27 July 1918 stipulated that all "permanent residents of Russian localities" whose original homes were in territory occupied by the
enemy or ceded to foreign states by the Brest-Litovsk treaty, but who currently
resided on the territory of the Russian Federation—in other words, "those known
as 'refugees'"—were considered to be Russian citizens, and therefore liable for military service in the Red Army.[93] This became one option. According to one account,
"The combination of ideological pressure and a difficult material situation induced
many refugees and prisoners of war to accept recruitment into the Red Army or
Red Guards."[94]

Simultaneously, the new government abolished all national committees for refugee relief. Their cultural, educational, and training programs were handed over to
the People's Commissariat for Education (Narkompros). So, too, were the hundreds
of orphanages and "children's colonies" that operated in their name. Where appropriate, Narkompros was instructed to consult with the Commissariat for Nationalities (Narkomnats).[95] Canteens and feeding stations were transferred to local soviets, unless refugees were being repatriated, in which case the collegium for POWs
and refugees assumed responsibility. Narkomzdrav, the People's Commissariat for
Health, took over mobile clinics, hospitals, barracks, and sanatoriums. The assets
of all existing refugee organizations passed to the relevant people's commissariats.[96]
Tsentroplenbezh expressed reservations about this administrative reorganization,
which had sown confusion and brought no real advantages to the poorest refugees.[97]

REFUGEES IN A COLD CLIMATE

Rhetoric of proletarian revolution apart, much of the Bolshevik discourse of refugeedom had a familiar ring. Refugees still found themselves treated in condescending fashion. In Saratov, the local collegium of Tsentroplenbezh spoke of "this
terrible scourge . . . an enfeebled and exhausted mass . . . which for the most part
supports itself by begging," and which was rife with typhus.[98] Those at the overcrowded border town of Orsha were described as a bedraggled, hungry, and dis-

eased multitude, waiting for the chance to return to the "forbidden paradise that is their homeland." They were urged to remain calm and patient, and not to leave their temporary shelters, lest they jeopardize their own health and safety or, worse still, "exacerbate the catastrophic situation of those impatient souls who find themselves behind German barbed wire."[99] At the small border town of Sebezh, refugees were thought likely to vent their frustration on Soviet guards or on local farmers.[100] Like prisoners of war, for whom Tsentroplenbezh also assumed responsibility, refugees were perceived as a threat to public order and as a vector for infectious disease; hence the constant need for vigilance, cleanliness, disinfection, and—where appropriate—isolation.[101]

Worse still, refugees were exposed to the animosity of the settled population. This needs to be set against the background of the profound social changes that were taking place on territory controlled by the new Bolshevik state. The large number of refugees who had not returned to their homes were now swelled by hundreds of thousands of demobilized soldiers who used whatever means of transport were available in order to make their way home. Returning soldiers were eager to participate in the wholesale seizure and redistribution of arable land, to which the Bolsheviks had given their blessing in the Decree on Land. Although the subsequent Law on the Socialization of the Land (April 1918) entitled refugees and other in-migrants to a share in the resources now at the disposal of the peasantry, villagers for the most part divided up the privately owned land among themselves. Where refugees did receive land, it tended to be of poor quality.[102] A. Okninskii, a former tsarist official who held a position with a volost executive committee in Tambov province during 1918, wrote in his memoirs that refugees and other in-migrants who plied a useful trade were allowed to stay on; others were encouraged to leave. Those who remained behind found themselves in desperate straits. Villages no longer had need of their labor once the soldiers returned.[103] The hospitality extended by many peasants to refugees in 1915 and 1916 proved to be temporary: "Village and volost assemblies now pass resolutions, refusing to offer refugees any help whatsoever, lest the latter decide they wish to settle permanently in the peasants' midst."[104] The village community turned inward. There remained a clear dividing line between peasant and refugee.[105]

Nor did urban Russia offer any better sanctuary. Townspeople charged inflated rents, in the hope of forcing refugees to make way for the influx of people from Moscow and Petrograd who were desperate for a local base from which to scour the countryside for food.[106] Many refugees bemoaned the hostile reception they received: "We refugees, living in a strange land for four years . . . find that the local people have no time for us. . . . We have had to sell our last shirts and jackets in order to buy firewood and bread."[107] They could not always count on the new Soviet administration to come to their aid. Some boards demanded that Tsentroplenbezh take urgent steps to remove refugees from their impoverished territory.[108] Other local satraps scarcely bothered to conceal their aversion to the presence of refugees, and informed them that they should work for a living and not become "parasites."[109] Some made sure that refugees were singled out for backbreaking building work or snow-clearing duties.[110] But it was unrealistic to expect everyone to find a job, and many refugees were in any case physically incapable of work. Not surprisingly, they remained suspicious of officialdom. In Tsaritsyn', refugees refused to take up an offer of accommodation in camps, preferring to remain in tents and railway cars, where they believed they were at less risk of instant deportation to more remote regions.[111]

Shortages of food caused the greatest friction. Everyone, whether employed or not, needed access to food rations. Refugees evidently had to fight for their share. In Balashovsk uezd, Saratov, local people refused to sell bread to refugees at the fixed price. Refugees complained that they now had to pay for a drink of water, or to work an entire day for a glass of milk. There were other instances in which peasants sold them rotten potatoes and milk that had gone sour. By way of explanation, the author suggested that "refugees are regarded as newcomers, present in the uezd only on a temporary basis, and not entitled to be taken into account in the distribution of food."[112] Local food supply commissioners and village soviets were blamed for ignoring the needs of refugees. During the harsh winter of 1918, Tsentroplenbezh wrote to a district office in Riazan', reminding it that food should be distributed to refugees on the same basis as to other local residents: failure to comply with this order would render officials liable to "the full force of revolutionary law."[113] Even "our bourgeois opponents don't deny refugees the right to food," wrote one local collegium.[114] "The separation of refugees into any kind of special group is completely inadmissible," asserted the collegium in February 1919, denouncing the practice in Saratov province of dividing the population into "ours" and "not ours."[115]

The infant Bolshevik government was acutely aware of the often fraught relationship between the settled and the displaced population. Refugees were reminded of the sacrifices that "hungry, cold, worker-peasant Russia" had made, "sharing its last scrap of food with you refugees, whom it considers to be comrades, proletarians."[116] This pointed homily was implicitly designed to excuse (or at least explain) the animosity now being shown by local people, but also to remind refugees of their obligation to contribute to the local economy. In Saratov, the provincial board of Tsentroplenbezh instructed its officers to explain to local inhabitants that refugees found themselves in the villages of the Volga for "political reasons," adding, "Everyone has a duty to show special consideration to refugees and not to subject them to any kind of persecution."[117] In a similar vein, other authors sought to play down the difference between refugees and non-refugees, arguing that hunger recognized no distinction, and declaring that they had a common cause in defending the gains of proletarian revolution.[118] The context was troubling for the new regime as it struggled to cope with mounting shortages and a tense political atmosphere. Recognizing the limits of rhetoric, and acknowledging that some refugees felt alienated from the regime, the Bolshevik government urged them to emphasize that "power to the Soviets means power to you as well."[119]

In the longer term, the most visible aspect of Russian refugeedom was its pan-European dimension. Following the collapse of anti-Bolshevik resistance in 1919 and 1920, around 860,000 Russian refugees who had abandoned Soviet territory found themselves scattered across Europe and the Far East.[120] Several public organizations looked after their needs. The Union of Towns and Zemstvos (Zemgor) was reestablished for purely civilian purposes; its volunteers maintained a range of services for émigrés, including child care facilities, instruction in foreign languages, and employment training.[121] Among the Armenian community, the American-Armenian organization Near East Relief and the British Society of Friends of Armenia were prominent in organizing humanitarian assistance and help with relocation. The Armenian community itself continued to provide material support through the Armenian Benevolent Union, a cultural organization originally established in 1905. Political leadership, which extended to the claim to represent refugees, was vested in the Central Committee for Armenian Refugees and the Armenian National Delegation, which together constituted in effect a government-in-exile.[122]

After extended military confrontation and diplomatic uncertainty, Soviet Russia concluded treaties with Latvia, Poland, and other successor states.[123] By this stage there was an enormous amount of ground to make up. The territory of the fledgling Polish state was home to more than one million displaced persons, including Poles, Germans, Jews, Belorussians, and Ukrainians, who were found by the American Relief Administration to be "living like ground-squirrels in dugouts, trenches and caves, and lacking food, clothing and everything necessary to keep themselves alive," and whose status was entirely uncertain.[124] Meanwhile, on Soviet territory, more than 650,000 Polish citizens required repatriation from Russia, half of them from Siberia; by the beginning of 1922—long after the end of the Polish-Soviet war—around 375,000 still remained on Russian territory. Some were prisoners, but the vast majority were described as refugees. The rate of repatriation of Latvians in 1921 had been faster, for obvious reasons. Some 130,000 had returned home by December, leaving an estimated 35,000 individuals (including 25,000 refugees) still awaiting repatriation. Around 50,000 Lithuanians had left Russia during 1921, but 55,000 remained (45,000 of them refugees). These figures did not take into account those on Ukrainian territory, of whom there were an estimated 253,000, mostly Polish displaced persons. A total of one million people fell into the category of those awaiting repatriation.[125]

Other displaced persons were less fortunate. In December 1922, the new Soviet state withdrew diplomatic recognition and protection from the Russian exiles who were scattered across Europe and the Far East. This had profound consequences for hundreds of thousands of people, who, as an official of the League of Nations put it, "cannot travel, marry, be born, or die without creating legal problems to which there is no solution."[126] In a sensitive recognition of the consequences of this absence of legal protection, a spokesperson for the Russian refugee organizations in London wrote of the humiliation that refugees experienced and the "heavy burden upon their lives" imposed as a result of the new arbitrariness shown by the successor to the old regime. Many Russian refugees believed their exile to be a temporary condition: they expected that the imminent overthrow or collapse of the Soviet state would restore their entitlement to Russian citizenship. They were mistaken. Urgent steps were taken under the leadership of Fridtjof Nansen to make passports and identity documents available to refugees, in order that they should not be returned involuntarily to the Soviet Union. By 1923, thirty-nine governments recognized the right of holders of the "Nansen passport" to cross international boundaries, provided that they did not thereby adopt another nationality. This measure, according to a recent account, facilitated the "more equitable distribution of Russian refugees."[127] The American journalist Dorothy Thompson wrote in 1938, "The Nansen certificate is the greatest thing that has happened to the individual refugee. It returned to him his lost identity."[128]

CONCLUSION

The revolution of 1917 did not liberate or empower Russia's refugees, although it created plenty of political opportunities for the leaders of national committees. Refugees faced long months and even years of further exile, amid military dangers and economic collapse. The dramatic political upheavals in 1917–21 produced many more refugees, either by displacing them internally or by forcing them to leave the country in order that they might escape the consequences of revolution and civil war. On many occasions, internally displaced refugees complained to Tsentroplenbezh that they had been abandoned and forgotten by the new administration.[129] "We have spent four years suffering in the depths of Russia," wrote one anguished group of refugees in January 1919, in a typical lament, "and we remain at the mercy of fate."[130] This suggests that this "time of troubles" bred passivity rather than instilled self-confidence. Even so, the evidence is mixed: refugees also continued to press the case for better treatment and for repatriation. Tsentro-plenbezh did not stand in the way of delegations of refugees who raised these issues at the highest levels.

Social revolution inevitably affected the prospects for refugees. In Russia's villages, they were excluded from the redistribution of land and other assets, which confirmed their status as outsiders. This sense of exclusion strengthened the wish to return home. But "home" had itself been transformed during the long years of war and revolution. "Home" might mean a sovereign state—stable, perhaps, but perhaps prepared to extend a welcome only to politically conservative elements among the refugees. Not all refugees were prepared to curb their appetite for radical change. Many hoped that the social and political revolution would not leave the "homeland" untouched. Delegates to the Congress of Belorussian Refugees in July 1918 looked forward to the day when landlords (many of them Polish or German) and "kulaks" would be dispossessed, allowing the poor refugee to return to a land with better social and economic prospects. Thus, land redistribution in the successor states might work to the advantage of refugees, whereas in the Russian interior it was liable to promote continued suffering and social exclusion.[131]

The political activism of the patriotic professional intelligentsia in refugee organizations and national committees enabled them to claim a share in the leadership of the national movements that burgeoned after February 1917. By this means they could also prepare for their subsequent participation in the short-lived "bourgeois" governments of Latvia, Lithuania, and Armenia during 1918 and 1919, and for the leading role they played in the new successor states that came into being in 1920–21. Administrative practice within the national organizations, each of which had sections dealing with agriculture, law, education, health, and statistics, demonstrated the emergence of incipient departments of state.[132] The formation of independent states obviously did not bring to an end the "refugee problem." Tens of thousands of non-Russian displaced persons sought to return to their homes and to establish some semblance of normality following years in the rapidly unraveling and poverty-stricken former Russian empire. The men who ruled in the successor states—Poland, Latvia, Lithuania, and (briefly) Armenia—thus had unfinished business to transact. Refugeedom gave them ready-made institutions, trained personnel, and direct experience of rule.

There is nevertheless more to the study of refugees after revolution than the elaboration of administrative measures or the effect on refugees of the transformation of rural life that followed the Decree on Land, important though these issues are in their own right. Did refugees believe that the revolution ultimately brought about significant changes in their status, *qua* "refugees"? Did revolution resolve their position in society by giving them a different and more purposeful role to play in the new social and political order, for instance by enrolling them in new state organizations such as the Red Army or in the local and district soviets? This seems doubtful. Refugees became absorbed in negotiations with harassed officials over food supply and the prospects of repatriation. They displayed little inclination to contribute to Bolshevik state-building. Notwithstanding the rhetoric of proletarian solidarity, refugees perceived themselves—and were perceived—as outsiders.

More broadly, the revolution and its aftermath entailed a qualitatively different kind of disruption. Millions of peasants and workers in European Russia, whose communities had been immune from wholesale relocation during the First World War, were now exposed to the selfsame forces of displacement that had earlier beset the population of Russia's troubled borderlands. The Russian civil war unleashed widespread spatial mobility throughout the entire country. Peasants and townspeople had encountered refugees during the world war; now, in a sense, they themselves were to experience displacement at first hand. By these various means, the revolution universalized refugeedom.

CONCLUSION:

⌇

THE MEANINGS OF REFUGEEDOM

Refugeedom is an unprecedented phenomenon. It is a new form of civic status [novyi vid grazhdanskogo sostoianiia].
—EDITORIAL, SPUTNIK BEZHENTSA, 24–25 SEPTEMBER 1915

Understanding displacement as a human tragedy and looking no further can mean that one gains no insight at all into the lived meanings that displacement and exile can have for specific people.
—LIISA MALKKI, PURITY AND EXILE

In this book I have been concerned with a social group that appeared in the public arena virtually overnight. Refugees in wartime Russia posed a clear challenge to social convention. They tested the validity of the officially sanctioned categories of *soslovie,* whereby each individual was ascribed to a specific estate. Because so many refugees lacked property, occupation, and income, their presence was also difficult to reconcile with more modern kinds of class affiliation and identity. Refugees surrendered whatever social standing they had possessed before the war. Other losses were still more perceptible. Established family ties had been ruptured, apparently beyond repair. Refugees needed as a matter of urgency to be found somewhere to live and to secure the means of subsistence. Their physical condition rendered not only them but also the settled population vulnerable to infectious disease. Refugees represented an unprecedented social problem, defined in terms of liminality and loss, damage and danger.

The old regime did not explicitly create a new *soslovie* to cope with wartime realities. What purpose would this have served, when refugees were expected to return to their homes and assume their former roles in society? No one thought that an individual would remain a refugee for the rest of her or his life; this possibility dawned on Europe's consciousness only after the First World War. All the same, displaced people lost their place in the social hierarchy. Having forfeited their ascribed status, they were lumped together in a hastily devised category for which there was no precedent in Russian history.[1] Some contemporaries believed that refugees themselves "created an entirely new *soslovie*." But this group bore little resemblance to other estates: "Their social position has not been resolved. The result has been a kind of nomadic group [*kochiushaia massa*], and a highly unusual one at that."[2] Often the emphasis was on the loss of tangible assets; to be deprived of one's sense of belonging clearly entailed a loss of one's home ("hearth," "fireside," and "nest" were common appellations for the abandoned home). Those who in peacetime had been economically secure were now threatened with downward social mobility. Stripped of their property, "wealthy householders have been turned into homeless vagrants."[3] The loss of official documentation that so concerned tsarist bureaucrats, policemen, and public lawyers testified to a double deprivation, of formal status as well as property. Once the war was over, documents might be restored to the erstwhile refugee, but displaced people would find it more difficult to recover social position. Whether the state had an obligation to intervene in these circumstances, and to compensate for the various losses incurred by refugees, was an issue that remained unresolved through 1917.[4] But the main point is that those in authority had only a vague idea where the refugee "belonged." This uncertainty allowed different agencies to rush to fill the vacuum on behalf of the displaced population.

Secondly, and in a different vein, refugeedom also subverted more modern kinds of group affiliation and identity, such as those that attached to occupation and to class in a developing capitalist economy. These were relatively recent and quite fragile shifts in consciousness, reflecting the speed and intensity of industrialization and the volatile character of political life. During 1917, class difference became the all-important signifier of one's political stance. Yet the sharp edge of class position was quickly blunted during the civil war, when industrial production collapsed and the cities emptied, leaving behind a diverse group of petty traders, artisans, and day laborers who struggled to survive.[5] Russian society by 1920 comprised millions of peasant households—in Moshe Lewin's words, "the class [*sic*] that survived the upheaval best"—as well as a motley group of urban survivors, characterized by Victor Serge as "a grey crowd of thousands of people who are neither workers nor rich nor poor nor revolutionaries nor absolutely ignorant nor truly educated."[6] Needing to identify their enemies and supporters, the Bolsheviks imposed class labels, which were crude and inappropriate instruments of social categorization in a world that had been turned upside down.[7]

Something of this topsy-turvy society was already anticipated by the onset of refugeedom in 1915. Old and new claims alike to social identity yielded to a more fluid and contingent characteristic. To be a refugee was to stand outside established boundaries of society, to be waiting on the margins of social life in the hope or expectation that one's status would be resolved. It meant becoming accustomed to a new category that might prove temporary or might yet endure. Refugees mocked modernity no less than they ridiculed the social conventions of tsarist Russia. Their liminality challenged traditional categories, but it also confused those who anticipated an orderly shift to modern forms of social organization. The stories they told did not fit snugly into the grand narratives of class that were beginning to be fashioned in pre-revolutionary Russia. The assumption that class affiliation and class identity would triumph over time was tested to the limit.[8]

Their physical presence in the Russian interior forced government officials, political leaders, members of the public organizations, relief workers, clergymen, and peasants to come to terms with the reconfiguration of space and the redefinition of social order. Well-publicized attempts by refugees to make contact with relatives from whom they had been separated were given an extra dramatic edge by the realization that Russia was an "immense land."[9] Yet how often did contemporary commentators attempt to establish the "limits" of population settlement in Russia's towns and provinces, and even to engage in fine statistical calculations of the capacity of each region?[10] Few could escape the presence of refugees in Russia's disturbed polity and society, which prompted a fresh approach to the relationship between people and territory. This relationship assumed an especially acute form in the contested lands of Armenia, where the Ottoman genocide erased hundreds of thousands of Armenians: while Russia's towns swelled with refugees, entire villages were sacrificed to competing visions of "Armenia."

One can speculate further about the wider meaning of displacement. Expressions of official and public disquiet may have concealed deeper fears about the historical consequences of the unrelenting spatial mobility unleashed by war.[11] I am thinking in particular of the well-cultivated memories of the significance for Russian history of the Mongol invasion. The prevailing cultural convention in nineteenth- and early-twentieth-century Russia emphasized plunder, pillage, and destruction, as well as the rupture of contacts with western European culture that Mongol domination of Russia implied. From this point of view, the incursion of "hordes" of dispossessed and displaced refugees can hardly have been a prospect that Russia's rulers faced with any degree of enthusiasm or equanimity. The point should not be pushed too far. We must remember that spatial mobility was the *sine qua non* of the formation of Russia; colonization accompanied the territorial extension of the empire. But there remained a clear distinction between the broadly organized movement eastward of Russian settlers, on the one hand, and, on the other, the unfettered, "spontaneous," and unwelcome incursion of "alien" elements into Russian space during the war.[12] Nor was the analogy with events in Russia's distant past lost on some witnesses: "The migrations that accompanied the Tatar invasions do not remotely compare with the magnitude of what is happening now," asserted the eminent Cadet Nikolai Shchepkin.[13]

We should thus pay close attention to the discourse of displacement. In one formulation, the refugee "problem" was characterized as a "state tragedy"; in another, as a "social catastrophe."[14] It was often likened to the biblical Exodus.[15] Some witnesses believed that the "boundless ocean" of refugees could never be properly navigated.[16] More typically, contemporary observers used language that was directly reminiscent of disaster, of river banks being broken—thus flood (*navodnenie*), deluge or torrent (*potok*), wave (*volna*), avalanche (*lavina*), deposit (*naplyv*), lava (*mnogomillionaia lava*)—and of fertile land being laid waste by hordes of locusts.[17] These metaphors were all the more powerful, given the familiar, widespread, and paralyzing impact of recurrent natural disaster on the Russian landscape and the national economy. How did the construction of these metaphors affect refugees? How did the rhetoric of menace condition the response of welfare agencies and settled communities? A recent anthropological account of refugeedom in modern Tanzania reminds us that "the territorializing metaphors of identity—roots, soils, trees, seeds—are washed away in human flood-tides, waves, flows, streams, and rivers. These liquid names for the uprooted reflect the sedentarist bias in dominant modes of imagining homes and homelands, identities and nationalities."[18] This language inspired civic leaders to devise and promote "rational" measures to cope with refugee relief, implying not only that government had failed to prevent chaos, but also that refugees needed to be protected, resettled, disciplined, and re-territorialized. Refugees found it difficult to devise an alternative discourse.[19] It did not help that they were excluded from the provincial Tatiana committees, from the zemstvos, and from many other organizations devoted to refugee relief.

Nowhere was the reconfiguration of space more evident than with respect to the empire's Jewish population. So much has been written about the disabilities, indignities, and violence that Jews suffered at the hands of the tsarist state and the tsar's Russian subjects that it is easy to overlook the extraordinary change in their status that the war brought about. Unlike other refugees, Russia's Jews had previously enjoyed little scope to choose their place of residence. The war did not weaken the stereotype of the "wandering" Jew, but it largely wrecked the capacity of the tsarist state to dictate where Jews should and should not settle. In distributing themselves across large parts of the empire, Russia's Jews broke the bounds of imperial Russia and walked toward a kind of freedom. Jews were no longer physically quarantined, and they escaped the conditions that in other times and places made genocide possible. Some local Russian residents were sufficiently well disposed toward the newcomers that Jewish refugees described them as "saintly creatures" (*pravedniki*).[20] Meanwhile, government ministers, albeit reluctantly, conceded that the Pale of Settlement had disintegrated.[21] No minister publicly supported the "pogrom mood" that characterized sections of the Russian army. There was thus a fundamental political constraint on more extreme manifestations of prejudice against Jews.

Other national minorities also enjoyed a kind of liberation. Their enforced relocation—bemoaned by the patriotic intelligentsia as a loss of attachment to the homeland—was accompanied by a demonstration of their ability to invent institutions that substituted for older forms of association, some of which were retained or modified to suit the new circumstances. Polish refugees abandoned their farms, but they were exposed to a new world of work and collective association. Latvians evacuated Kurland, but they maintained settlements elsewhere that augmented their sense of national pride. Jews were driven from Galician towns and from the shtetls of Russian Poland, but their world was reinvented in Jewish schools and workshops in the central industrial region or in eastern Ukraine. Armenians asserted the antiquity of their history by organizing exhibitions of archeological finds and cultural artifacts; sympathetic supporters publicized Armenia's literary and artistic heritage. Far from being dissolved, collective identities grew stronger as a result of the need to devote resources to the tasks of survival, cultural improvement, and reproduction.

In Petrograd, leaders of national committees harnessed their wagons to the cause of refugees, but their activities in the capital should not blind us to the enormous range of local endeavor and personal initiative, much of which had the consequence of undermining localized identities, overcoming a sense of isolation, and strengthening national feeling. The aim throughout was to recapture the homeland symbolically, in the interests of an ethnic group whose suffering was dramatized in the national media. It behooved all members of the national community to preserve national customs, to sustain the native language, and not to permit the dissolution of their ethnic identity by mingling promiscuously with Russian peasants or, still worse, settling permanently in the Russian interior and becoming "assimilated."

Much remains to be done to explore the impact of refugeedom on national minorities in the long term. Evidently, the energies of the patriotic intelligentsia who stood at the forefront of the national committees were transferred to the administration of independent polities in the aftermath of the Bolshevik revolution. The practice they gained in organizing budgets and managing public institutions could be put to use in the enterprise of state-building. But this does not tell us very much about popular perceptions of national identity and national difference. One obvious place to begin is with an examination of the perceptions of eastern Europe that crystallized as a result of the occupation of the Baltic lands during the war. Did their wartime experiences reinforce broader understandings of "Russia" that were held by German administrators and academics who contemplated fresh opportunities to "civilize" the barbarian after the war? Did the complex encounters between Russia's various nationalities generate enduring images of ethnic difference that helped to determine social behavior and political action? As Geoff Eley has pointed out, "It was in encounters of this kind, as the German officers, soldiers and civilian personnel recorded their reactions to the ways and appearance of the peoples of the East (Poles, Lithuanians, Ukrainians and above all the reviled *Ostjuden*) that the radical-right racism of the interwar period had many of its origins." In this instance a specific ideology of racial supremacy was linked to the more general case of "cultural dissonance."[22] How cultural dissonance worked itself out after the war in terms of the relations between Ukrainians and Jews, or between Lithuanians and Poles, is something beyond the scope of this study. Certainly it is a subject that deserves to be properly researched in the light of wartime population displacement.

Nor, in this connection, should we overlook the impact of refugees on the world of the Russian village. Peasants had long been accustomed to spatial mobility.[23] Before 1861, serfdom entailed enforced relocation for many individual peasants or even entire communities. Peasants were obliged to disgorge young men into the arms of the recruiting officer, and they had to come to terms with the likelihood that their sons would never return. Other peasants were allowed to work "abroad" for cash in the expanding economy, sometimes for months or even years at a time. But these decisions affected people who were already members of the village community. Refugeedom represented an intrusion of unfamiliar faces, a rupture of the "impermeable skin" of household and commune, in a process that peasants themselves could neither monitor nor wholly control.[24] The evidence suggests that, to begin with, peasants broadly welcomed refugees insofar as they represented a useful addition to the family labor force who could be incorporated into the household as farm servants. But peasants were equally well aware that refugees imposed a burden on the village economy. Refugees who could not work for their keep challenged the limits of peasant tolerance; few villages were sufficiently prosperous or secure that they could offer refugees food, fuel, and shelter without threatening the already dangerous margin of subsistence. Their presence might jeopardize the relaxation of material hardship that the war had brought about for some peasant families. From a sociological point of view, it may be argued that the stronger and more resilient the community, the more receptive it was likely to be to the sudden incursion of strangers in its midst. Conceivably, some communities may have regarded the care of refugees as a means of consolidating their own administrative and moral superiority as self-governing agents over state officials, who had now brought further misery and humiliation to the Russian (and non-Russian) population. In other words, peasants had the opportunity to assert themselves as more active subjects in a sociopolitical system whose leaders had formerly deigned to act as if they knew what peasants needed.[25]

Recent work on social theory invites us to challenge essentialist approaches to social identity, and to reflect on the ways in which the subject is constructed.[26] From this perspective, it cannot be taken for granted what it "means" to be a refugee, as if there were some irreducible, unproblematic, and ultimately recoverable characteristic that underpinned the status of refugee. This is not to overlook attempts that were or are made to universalize or essentialize the refugee—a project implicit not only in the construction of refugeedom, but also in the notion of "refugee studies"—but it does alert us to the suggestion that the term "refugee" conceals multiple differences of ethnicity, gender, age, occupation, and social status, which were and are obliterated in the process of constructing refugeedom. As we have seen, such distinctions were drawn in the course of formulating strategies for refugee relief. "Educated" refugees could sometimes pay a premium to escape the more debilitating consequences of enforced flight and were frequently found superior housing, lest they be forced to mix with the lower orders. Young refugee women were afforded special attention lest they fall into the "trap" of vice and commercialized sex. Working-class organizations (sick clubs, trade unions, cooperatives) mobilized themselves in order to attend to the needs of plebeian refugees.[27]

Furthermore, it cannot be assumed that the possession of common attributes—their status as "displaced people"—automatically conferred a sense of common experience, let alone that it triggered joint action. Russia's refugees were at times socialized within a broader context than the refugee community. Local relief agencies sometimes went out of their way to encourage closer contact between refugees (at least those who were not "diseased") and the native population, in the hope that the encounter would prove mutually beneficial. Some refugees appeared willing to renounce their peculiar status and to adjust to Russian provincial life. Several thousand committed themselves to settle on farms in distant corners of European Russia and Siberia, rejecting the status of temporary residents in an attempt to discard the label of refugee and to become "invisible." Others, particularly non-Russian refugees, opposed attempts to settle them on remote farms, where carefully cultivated urban solidarities could easily be ruptured, and from which subsequent "liberation" might be rendered difficult. These varied histories show how difficult it is to arrive at a summary of refugee ambitions, even when they were amalgamated into a common narrative by public organizations and government or national committees, all of whom at various moments discovered the "pleasure of speaking for the oppressed."[28]

The construction of a shared narrative that had the capacity to inscribe or invent a common awareness of affliction, and to prompt collective endeavor, proceeded most obviously at the level of ethnicity.[29] Many refugees found in the language of ethnicity a powerful means of counteracting the negative discourse to which population displacement inevitably gave rise. Specific institutional arrangements were devised by Jews, Poles, Latvians, and Armenians for members of their own group. Such initiatives contradicted—although they did not completely supplant—attempts to "collectivize" refugees. The rhetoric of relief allowed the claim that Latvian refugees had different "needs" from those of Armenians, Russians, and Jews.

Patriotic leaders feared the emergence of a hybrid culture that obliterated national peculiarity. National committees sometimes ended up imposing "their own sense of opposition onto a world of continuous shades of difference and similarity."[30] In this regard, the common narrative was reinforced by shared experiences in hastily improvised schools, workshops, orphanages, clubs, canteens, and barracks. Here, to repeat, membership implied some sense of what it meant to be Polish, Latvian, Armenian, or Jewish. Much of the cultural and educational activity that took place in these institutions encouraged the belief that each nationality "always and every-where possessed a core of discernible, ethnically determined qualities" (including, one may add, the quality of praising national saints and popular heroes, perhaps now including individuals who attended to the needs of the suffering refugee population) and sought to validate "historically sanctified claim[s]" to particular lands.[31] Hence, to emphasize the point made earlier, the importance of promoting a sense of loyalty to the homeland by reminding refugees that they should not settle permanently in the Russian interior and thus contribute to a dilution of the ethnic whole.

Yet ethnicity—whatever the exponents of nationalism said—was not necessarily an exclusive, let alone a fixed, attribute. While it was capable of overriding other forms of identity, ethnicity could itself be overridden, above all by the claims of class consciousness that exercised such a compelling force during 1917. Besides, the purportedly homogeneous characteristics of ethnicity were open to hybrid in-fluences from other contiguous nationalities, each of whom had the capacity to challenge and "contaminate" the others.[32] From this point of view, the constant emphasis on loyalty to nation and homeland can also be read as uncertainty on the part of the patriotic intelligentsia about the entire national project.[33]

During the war, the opportunities for proselytization expanded considerably, but nervousness about ethnic dispersion increased with each wave of displacement. Indeed, as Eley has argued, "where the working class was divided from the local-regional bourgeoisies by ethnic differences it was often easier to mobilize it for revolutionary politics, and in this sense the Russian-cum-Russified working class of the western borderlands acted as a Bolshevik wedge into the anticipated popular hegemony of the respective nationalist movements."[34] This rendered the nationalist project problematic. Patriotic leaders mapped one route to liberation, but not all refugees necessarily understood this cartography; those of modest means thought of the "homeland" in terms of class structure and economic oppression, whereas the elite recollected in more pastoral terms.[35]

To sum up, refugeedom presented emerging national elites with a golden opportunity to agitate and organize, but "defeat" stared them in the face by virtue of national dispersion and the competing appeal of revolutionary socialism. National self-determination was not built upon refugeedom but followed the politics of diplomacy. Lithuania, Latvia, and Armenia escaped into nationhood as a result of great-power intervention and patronage. This is not to overlook the ways in which war and refugeedom contributed to the radical "hardening of the perceptions of national difference" that underpinned postwar political projects in many of the successor states.[36] Nor—to labor the point—should we neglect the role of refugeedom in giving the intelligentsia direct access to a constituency and contributing to the socialization of refugees as "members" of a national community.

No less important, collective action was crucial in helping to dispel the demeaning aspects of refugeedom that might otherwise have been internalized. At times, therefore, it was important for refugees to emphasize how ubiquitous and painful was the refugee experience, since it was in these terms—as "victims of war"—that charitable assistance might be unlocked. The possibility also arose of deriving dignity and pride from the condition of being a refugee, reducing the shame associated with dependence on charity.[37] Refugees who sought information about their loved ones or who advertised their services normally signed their messages as *bezhenets/bezhenka*. (Lest it be thought that this was a stylistic device imposed by the editors of the newspapers in which these notices appeared, it should be noted that some refugees chose not to use this appellation.)[38] Sometimes refugees defined themselves in opposition to others, particularly to those they deemed to be permanent social outsiders. When one of the refugees in a short story by Evgenii Shveder compares himself to "Gypsies, tramps [*brodiagi*]," the author allows fellow refugees to rebut this affiliation, pointing out that Gypsies never had property and lacked roots, unlike the refugee, who had suddenly been deprived of both.[39]

Refugees sometimes chose instead to dissolve their identity in the larger collective struggle. One rhetorical device was to assert that they fought for the same cause as Russian soldiers. In his "Thoughts of a Refugee," V. Tkach from Chelm managed simultaneously to renounce self-pity and to link his personal fate to public fortune: "My suffering is nothing compared to the dangers experienced by those who defend the fatherland. . . . I no longer think of myself as an insignificant, superfluous refugee, but as a citizen of my homeland, called upon by my privations to save our common heritage."[40]

Thus a search for the archetypal "refugee" will be fruitless; she or he assumed human shape in the minds of some relief workers and tactically astute refugee leaders who constructed an archetype for their own purposes. We cannot hope to find that "experience" automatically generated a uniform refugee consciousness. Many refugees were able to manage various kinds of identity and to avoid the "heroization of a single collective identity."[41] Vera Krinitskaia, who was forced to leave her home in Warsaw, described herself as "a refugee [*bezhenka*], an *intelligentnaia*, a Russian."[42] The historian should accordingly be aware of the multiple meanings that attached to the refugee construct.[43]

We also need to explore more fully the implications for the individual of the move from an established community to a new world: "from a security based on a repetition of sameness, to a much less certain security that can only be based on efforts to live the good life without any ability to predict the outcome of our actions in an ever changing context."[44] To what extent did their "new world" entail the abandonment of community? In this connection, more work needs to be done to relate ideas about "social memory" to the concrete experience of ruptured communities.[45] As one theorist succinctly puts it, "If we are to play a believable role before an audience of relative strangers we must produce or at least imply a history of ourselves: an informal account which indicates something of our origins and which justifies or perhaps excuses our present status and actions in relation to that audience."[46] Paul Connerton points out that there was no need for this kind of presentation of the self in established communities, which relied on daily practice, shared knowledge, and gossip to create a common awareness of social space and a sense of continuity.[47] Of Russia's refugees it was said that "the threads that tie them to their own region, with its own specific cultural and social conditions, are becoming ever weaker."[48] War disrupted—although it did not destroy—the capacity of individuals to "remember in common."[49] I hope to have shown that refugees began, in difficult circumstances and in a short space of time—albeit from different perspectives—to devise new forms of remembrance that helped to restructure broken lives and to reform shattered communities. The remarkable initiatives taken in 1916–17 by the Tatiana Committee, whereby individual refugees were encouraged to find their voice and to articulate their experiences, suggest the emergence of a project whose purpose was to confound the anonymity of "refugeedom" and to lay the basis for a dignified assertion of the self. The dispossessed refugee could at least recover the property of memory and perhaps begin to fashion fresh hopes and aspirations from the pain of remembering.[50]

Refugees could not always count on collective action or memory in order to negotiate the perilous shoals of an unfamiliar settled society. They frequently fell back on their own personal resources; sometimes they asserted the primacy of self over community.[51] Even the most resilient individuals were obliged to adjust to unaccustomed forms of self-presentation. An acute observer grasped this point in a discussion of the "soul" of the refugee:

> Not so long ago, these people lived a full and independent working life. They had the right to be just like us—that is, indolent, rude, and ungrateful. Now they have lost this prerogative; their poverty and helplessness oblige them to be meek and grateful, to smile at people they don't like, to answer each and every question, without the right of asking questions in turn, to submit to the authority of people they don't respect and have no wish to know, to accept disadvantageous terms from anyone who seeks to exploit their mishaps and destitution.[52]

The author expressed admiration that, in her experience, at least, refugees had not lost a sense of self-worth.

We cannot, therefore, hope to provide a straightforward answer to the question: What did it mean to be a refugee? The question needs to be reformulated: How did various meanings come to be attached to the state of refugeedom? One way of thinking about this process is to consider refugeedom as the source of yet another kind of antithesis in early-twentieth-century Russia. Scholars have frequently commented on the emergence of polarities in revolutionary Russia that derived from class "position," and from the opposition between "educated society" and the "dark masses." I myself have alluded to these distinctions. I have also been at pains to pinpoint some of the polarities of ethnic affiliation. In his classic study of war and memory, Paul Fussell introduces another dimension—what he terms "the versus habit"—that destroyed ambiguity and thrived on binary opposition, pitting British against Germans.[53] Did refugeedom confirm this habit, by inculcating a sense that refugees were "not like us"? Did their difference condemn them to be strangers? Or did it weaken this practice, by demonstrating the existence of a social group that was neither purely friend nor purely foe, neither wholly familiar nor wholly foreign, part of neither the front line nor the home "front"? It seems to me undeniable that refugeedom introduced ambiguity; whether Russians became accustomed to the liminality of refugees is more difficult to establish, because within a few years, other projects of social (re)construction and state-building took pride of place. Did anyone remember refugeedom during the chaotic collectivization drive, when an even more concerted state-driven process of population displacement transformed the Soviet economy, in part by targeting supposedly antagonistic social categories?[54]

We also need to take into account the susceptibility of individuals to the organizing, surveillance, and information-gathering capacities of external authorities, whether of the state, the locality, or professional agents. Deported German colonists were brutally repressed as a group, but what is equally striking is that many individuals readily volunteered details about their personal qualities and political opinions, in an attempt to deflect the government from its intended course.[55] Refugees were counted, examined, photographed, described, organized, confined (for their "protection" and that of local residents), and even—as in official publicity material or in Violetta Thurstan's vivid account—put on display for the benefit of visiting dignitaries and well-wishers.[56] Relief agencies devoted enormous time and energy to the dissemination and completion of forms that registered refugees; many of the displaced—particularly if they had not previously had a passport for internal travel—were encountering such documentation for the first time. This paperwork had a benign purpose in part, because it formed the necessary prelude to attempts to reunite families that had been torn apart by war. But it also gave voluntary agencies and semi-official bodies such as the Tatiana Committees and national organizations unprecedented practice in the registration and accumulation of detailed information about individuals. Relief workers now assumed responsibility for maintaining files on millions of refugees. Hesitantly at first, then with huge enthusiasm and energy, relief agencies developed greater administrative capacity and sophistication. Refugees lined up obediently at welfare offices to supply personal details that were a condition for receiving money or improving the prospects of being reunited with family members. The person of the refugee, one might say, belonged to an impersonal agency, to an unsurpassed extent. Whereas the tax official or recruiting officer had not been directly concerned about an individual's obligation to pay taxes or serve the tsar—what mattered was the levy on a village, not its precise apportionment or the individual liability—the new agencies had a direct and immediate interest in the person over whom they claimed jurisdiction or competed for control.[57]

It should by now be apparent that refugeedom also implied a project for social reconstruction. Public organizations and Tatiana committees established "colonies" for refugee children and adolescents, with the aim of turning them into good citizens and healthy adults, and channeling anti-social behavior in a positive direction.[58] Psychologically disturbed "victims of war" received professional attention in new mental hospitals. Children with disabilities were sent to special schools. The "mentally defective" offspring of refugee parents needed particular attention from expert medical authorities.[59] In the process of drawing these distinctions, liberal practitioners sought to create new categories and communities, which they justified in terms of improved social welfare, public order, and their own sense of public duty. However, there was little in this project to suggest that they welcomed or understood the possibility for refugees to take the initiative or to assume personal responsibility for their own welfare. In a similar vein, when individuals were given the dignity of a personal name in the published record, it was not to allow them a voice, but rather to emphasize that no one would be overlooked in the project of constructing a better world.[60] In preparing to intervene on behalf of categories of refugees, and in adopting what has been termed an "over-socialized view of human nature," government agencies and public organizations anticipated practices that subsequently became commonplace during other emergencies.[61]

The work of Michel Foucault is very suggestive in this regard. What is stimulating about the Foucauldian approach is the possibility of being able to trace the emergence of an entirely new discourse, a "rupture" in prior ways of thinking about the individual and the group in early-twentieth-century Russia, as well as being able to reflect upon the creation of new taxonomies of social order. The refugee demanded action by the tsarist government; but refugees also invited non-governmental (even anti-governmental) agencies to assert the wisdom, benevolence, and efficiency of action by "educated society," or the self-appointed leaders thereof, and thereby to constitute themselves as an "interest."[62]

If the category of refugee is more problematic than often appears to be the case—if our knowledge of refugees is "discursively organized"—what role is there for the study of the impact of formal political structures on refugee status and organization? As has often been pointed out, Foucault argued that the exercise of power took many forms, which extended beyond the exercise of formal political domination by the state or by a ruling class. In his view, power must be related to the process whereby knowledge is accumulated and classification takes place at micro-social levels of kinship, family, and the body. For Foucault, power was not "a system of commands and force radiating from a center" that can be conceptualized as "the state."[63] Toward the end of his life, Foucault became interested in what he termed "governmentality," or the practice of government, where neither overt force nor pure acquiescence operates in the relationship between rulers and ruled. This concept embraced "the ensemble formed by the institutions, procedures, analyses, and reflections, the calculations and tactics, that allow the exercise of this very specific albeit complex form of power, which has as its target population, as its principal form of knowledge political economy, and as its essential technical means apparatuses of security."[64]

I hope to have shown that refugeedom represented a discrete process of knowledge accumulation and classification in wartime Russia. The tsarist state played a central, although not exclusive, role in this process. The state began by exercising traditional and overt instruments of power, which soon exposed it to criticism and obloquy. This subsequently yielded to an intense scrutiny by the "educated public" of the refugee subject. Early efforts by the unions of towns and zemstvos to seize control of the administrative apparatus did not come to fruition. But to focus exclusively on this failure is to miss crucial aspects of Russia's wartime history. The First World War created a moment and a space in which non-governmental agencies established a "disciplinary regime." In constructing and refining refugeedom—inscribing upon the canvas of refugeedom their own vision of Russia's future—they also crystallized their own sense of purpose. Professional bodies, municipalities, national committees, and peasant communities were all involved in the process of constructing refugees as a distinct subject. So too were refugees themselves. This seems to be compatible with Foucault's project, which was intended to challenge prevailing assumptions about the primacy of class, economic interest, and state power, without dismissing politics *tout court*. In one of his last interviews, Foucault pointed out that his work was devoted to "thinking about the relations of these different experiences [i.e., madness, crime, sexuality] to politics, which doesn't mean that one will seek in politics the main constituent of these experiences or the solution that will definitively settle their fate."[65] One should add refugeedom to these "experiences." Foucault insisted on the need to demonstrate how a collective definition of a political problematic came to be created and what this entailed for the subjects of the altered discourse.[66] His work invites us to attend to the politicization of discourse, a process that was particularly critical at a moment of national emergency. In wartime Russia, the power struggle was all-pervasive. Social identities were at stake, but so too were the political future of Russia and the social practices that its rulers were prepared to tolerate. Refugeedom dramatized these political struggles and social practices in novel and unexpected ways. Whether refugees themselves derived any consolation from the construction of refugeedom remains an open question.

APPENDIX 1:
REFUGEE POPULATION STATISTICS

⁓

No study of refugeedom would be complete without a consideration of what Aleksandr Blok called "the heat of cold numbers." Attempts during the war to estimate the numbers of refugees were complicated by the poor relationship between central and local authorities, by the plethora of agencies involved in refugee relief, and by the specific characteristics of the refugee population.

It is important to distinguish between the number of refugees at a given time and the overall flow of refugees. An estimate of the refugee population on a given census date is obviously not equivalent to the total number of people who had experienced refugeedom. The pool of refugees was continuously being depleted and then replenished, not just because of renewed German or Austrian military incursions and Russian retreats, but also by the exhaustion of savings among the better-off Polish or Latvian families who were forced to seek public assistance and who were thus enumerated for the first time. Meanwhile, refugees disappeared from view because they no longer qualified for the public assistance that in the eyes of most relief agencies defined their status as refugees.[1]

The starting point for any estimate of the size of the refugee population must be the reports prepared by the Tatiana Committee. These bulletins were regularly cited in the Duma and in the press.[2] A survey carried out on its behalf on 20 December 1915 yielded a total of 2.076 million refugees in European Russia. The viceroy of the Caucasus reported that there were 221,000 refugees on 1 January 1916 in the territory he administered, giving a figure of 2.297 million assisted refugees on Russian territory at the end of 1915. The Tatiana Committee regularly updated its estimates. A census of the refugee population in the middle of December 1916 put the total number at just under 3.2 million.[3]

Notwithstanding its heroic efforts, the Tatiana Committee did not provide an accurate picture of the total refugee population. Its statisticians were concerned only with individuals who qualified for public assistance; they took no account of those who relied upon their own resources.[4] For this reason, in Demosthenov's view, "for the whole of the empire the number of war refugees must have been far in excess of three millions."[5] In addition, some critics believed that the committee frequently enumerated family units rather than individuals. M. M. Gran, working after the revolution in the offices of the People's Commissariat for Health, maintained that the "real" number of refugees on relief was closer to 9 or 10 million (this assumed, conservatively, a mean family size of three members). Gran inflated this to 15 million, to allow for those "better-off refugees" who received no public assistance.[6]

The general criticisms of the Tatiana Committee's data, although not the revised figures quoted by Gran, were endorsed by the well-known Soviet demographer Evgenii Volkov, in his standard treatment of Russian demographic history between 1850 and 1930. Volkov argued that Stavka's decision to prevent the enumeration of refugees in a 15 kilometer zone at the front may have excluded up to 600,000 refugees.[7] Taking into account the Tatiana Committee's census results, allowing for under-registration, excluding around registered 121,000 refugees who had since died, and including refugees in the front zone, Volkov arrived at a provisional total of 3.848 million refugees as of 15 December 1916, compared to his estimate of 2.897 for 1 January 1916. Military developments on the western front and in the Caucasus during the latter part of 1916 probably produced a further influx of refugees, and Volkov accordingly put the refugee population at 5.256 million on 1 January 1917.[8] The collapse of the June offensive in 1917 produced additional refugees, suggesting to Volkov that the refugee population reached 6.391 million on 1 July 1917.[9]

Volkov suggested, moreover, that these figures needed to be inflated by 17.8 percent to take into account the forcibly displaced population (primarily Jews and Germans), predominantly from urban settlements, who left for the Russian interior without any prospect of assistance and without being registered by official relief agencies. Applying this coefficient to his revised estimates of the refugee population (but not to those in the 15 km zone), and making some assumptions about the distribution of refugees in 1914 and 1915, Volkov arrived at the following totals:

Table One
The Refugee Population According to Volkov
(USSR pre–1939 territory)

Year	Cumulative total	Annual increase
1915 (1 Jan.)	892,600	(1914) 892,600
1916 (1 Jan.)	3,306,000	(1915) 2,413,400
1916 (1 July)	4,425,700	(1916) 2,778,200
1917 (1 Jan.)	6,084,200	(1917) 1,337,200
1917 (1 July)	7,421,400	

Source: Volkov, *Dinamika,* pp. 72, 75.

To be sure, Volkov's methods are not altogether satisfactory. The allocation of nearly 900,000 refugees to the second half of 1914 may not be justified, given what is known about the impact of military action on the civilian population. In addition, he appears to have minimized the extent of refugee displacement during 1915 and to have exaggerated its scale during 1916. His suggestion that the first six months of 1917 witnessed an increase of more than 1.25 million displaced persons is also questionable. But the total he arrived at for July 1917 is compatible with other sources, and I am inclined to accept it as a reasonable approximation.

Fragmentary data on the size of the refugee population after the October revolution appeared in the official Soviet record. Tsentroplenbezh put the number of refugees on Russian (i.e., Soviet) territory at just under 4 million on January 1918.[10] But this was just a fraction of the total refugee population. In January 1918, large parts of the former tsarist empire (including Ukraine, Russian Poland, and the Baltic provinces) were in the hands of the German armies, and no estimates are currently available for the refugee population in these lands.

The main source on the geographical origin and ethnic composition of the refugee population in European Russia is again the Tatiana Committee. According to a survey conducted in July 1916, around 31 percent of refugees had come from Grodno (Lithuania), and 24 percent from Volynia in Russia's southwest. A further 11 percent came from Chelm province, and 6 percent from Kovno (Kaunas).[11]

The distribution of refugees by nationality presents some difficulties of interpretation. As noted in the text, the authorities did not distinguish between Russians, Ukrainians, and Belorussians. In official accounts and in the reports prepared by the unions of towns and zemstvos, the Jewish refugee population appears to have been very modest, at around 5 percent of the total in mid-1916. By far the majority (67.2 percent) were "Russians," with a further 11 percent Polish and 4.6 percent Latvian. Armenians, Lithuanians, Estonians, and "others" made up the remainder.[12] The ethnic composition of refugees in Petrograd was quite different. A census conducted at the end of February 1916 counted 100,700 refugees, 21 percent of whom were Russian, 23 percent Polish, 23 percent Latvian, 7 percent Lithuanian, and 4 percent Jewish (with 20 percent unidentified).[13] However, a survey conducted in Kursk province in the autumn of 1916 revealed that the refugee population was 34 percent "Ukrainian," 25 percent Polish, 12 percent Belorussian, and only 17 percent Russian.[14] Nor should we overlook the presence in European Russia of other nationalities. Several thousand Rumanian and Serbian refugees made a temporary home in Odessa, Kiev, Moscow, and other urban centers.[15] By the beginning of 1917, around 15,000 Greek refugees had arrived on Russian soil, fleeing from Palestine and settling in towns in Bessarabia.[16]

Figures published in the spring of 1916 by the Union of Zemstvos revealed some differences between refugees who settled in urban areas and those who settled in the countryside. Compared to the "Great Russian" population, relatively few non-Russians settled in rural localities:

Table Two
Distribution of Refugees by Nationality and Place of Residence
(percent)

	"Great Russian"[1]	Polish	Jewish	Latvian	Other	Total
All	67.5	13.2	6.4	4.9	8.0	100
Urban	52.5	19.2	14.2	5.7	8.5	100
Rural	80.0	9.0	1.5	1.4	8.2	100

[1]Including Ukrainian and Belorussian.
Source: Izvestiia VZS, 37–38, 15 April–1 May 1916, p. 149, sample of 526,000 refugees.

Few robust data have come to light on the social origin of refugees. A census of 18,041 refugees in Novgorod revealed that 75 percent belonged to the peasant *soslovie,* and 18 percent to the lesser middle-class *meshchanstvo.* Two percent were merchants, 2.7 percent noblemen, 1.6 percent officials, and 1.3 percent priests.[17]

According to the historian of the Union of Zemstvos, "The overwhelming majority of refugees consisted of women, children, and the aged."[18] He put the proportion of adult males at 22 percent, a figure that probably errs on the high side, in view of the fact that the underlying data excluded the Armenian refugee population. Information on the age distribution of refugees reveals significant gender variation. Around half the female refugee population was between 17 and 55 years of age, whereas fewer than 40 percent of males belonged to that category. Forty percent of female refugees were younger than 17 years, compared to half the male population:

Table Three
Percentage Distribution of Refugees by Age

	male	female
up to 7 years	19.5	15.6
7–14	21.7	17.1
14–17	9.2	7.4
17–55	38.4	50.0
over 55 years	8.6	7.6
unknown	2.6	2.3
Total	100	100

Source: Izvestiia KTN, 17, 1 February 1917, p. 13. The census data referred to 1.218 million persons in 38 provinces of Russia.

Data on the ultimate destination of refugees are not very satisfactory. According to one source, as of May 1916, 26 percent of refugees had stayed in the general vicinity of the front lines, while 41 percent had made their way to "central Russia." The remainder presumably went to Siberia, central Asia, and to the southern provinces of the empire.[19]

APPENDIX 2:
QUESTIONNAIRE ISSUED BY THE TATIANA COMMITTEE, JANUARY 1917

1. Point of departure.
2. Type of place: village, town, or hamlet.
3. Living conditions of refugees prior to their departure.
4. Circumstances of departure. Did refugees leave of their own free will, or were they forcibly removed for some reason? Were there any instances of refusal to obey the order to evacuate, and if so, what were the consequences?
5. How did refugees occupy themselves at home, and what was their economic status?
6. The composition of the refugee's family before departure from the permanent place of residence, and its present composition. The causes and circumstances of the separation of family members. If the refugee subsequently found members of his family, by what means and under what circumstances?
7. By what means did the refugee travel, how long did the journey take, and what stops were made?
8. Who accompanied the refugees? Were they organized into groups with a guide? What feeding points did they pass? Which organizations offered help, and what were the sanitary conditions en route?
9. How did the local population relate to refugees as they passed through, and how did refugees relate to the local population?
10. Did any memorable events happen to the refugees during their flight, and if so, what were they?
11. Did the refugees settle immediately in a given place? If not, why did they have to move on?
12. In what condition were the refugees when they arrived at their final destination? Were they able to salvage any of their property? If so, what precisely?
13. What losses did refugees suffer in terms of the destruction of sown area, buildings, movable property? Did they receive any compensation, and from whom?
14. The attitude of local authorities to refugees.
15. The attitude of the local population to refugees.

16. The relationship of refugees to one another; relationships between refugees of different nationalities.
17. Do the refugee and his family earn any money, and from what source?
18. If the refugee has no earned income or it is insufficient, who assists the family? And of what kind and amount is such help?
19. In what kind of housing do the refugees live?
20. Have there been any epidemic diseases among the refugees, and what is their current state of health? Have they received any medical care, and if so, from what source?
21. How do the refugees satisfy their religious needs?
22. Do the refugee's children attend school? If so, of what kind? What is the language of instruction? What arrangements are made for those children who have lost their relatives or do not live with them?
23. Facts concerning the moral condition and the family and social life of the refugee's family.
24. Do the refugees intend to return to their homeland [*rodina*] at the end of the war? Does anyone wish to remain in their new place of residence or move to a new home?

Source: Izvestiia KTN, 15, 1 January 1917, pp. 10–11.

ABBREVIATIONS

BV	*Birzhevye vedomosti*
d.	delo (file)
f.	fond (collection)
GAIaO	Gosudarstvennyi arkhiv Iaroslavskoi oblasti
GARF	Gosudarstvennyi arkhiv rossiiskoi federatsii
GDSO	*Gosudarstvennaia Duma. Stenograficheskie otchety.* Fourth Duma, Session Four (1915–1916), Petrograd, 1915–16
Izvestiia KTN	*Izvestiia Komiteta Ee Imperatorskogo Vysochestva Velikoi Kniazhny Tatiany Nikolaevny*
Izvestiia TsKPB	*Izvestiia Tsentral'nogo Kollegii po Delam Plennykh i Bezhentsev*
Izvestiia VSG	*Izvestiia Vserossiiskogo Soiuza Gorodov*
Izvestiia VZS	*Izvestiia Glavnogo Komiteta Vserossiiskogo Zemskogo Soiuza pomoshchi bol'nym i ranenym voinam*
l., ll.	list, listy (folio, folios)
LVVA	Latvijas Valsts Vestures Arhivs (Latvian State Historical Archive)
op.	opis' (inventory)
RGIA	Rossiiskii gosudarstvennyi istoricheskii arkhiv
RGVIA	Rossiiskii gosudarstvennyi voenno-istoricheskii arkhiv
Sobezh	Sovet otdela po ustroistvu bezhentsev
TP	*Trudovaia pomoshch'*
TsGAA	Tsentral'nyi gosudarstvennyi arkhiv Armenii
UR	*Utro Rossii*
Vestnik VOPB	*Vestnik Vserossiiskogo obshchestva popecheniia o bezhentsakh*
VSG	Vserossiiskii soiuz gorodov
VZS	Vserossiiskii zemskii soiuz

NOTES

The Bibliography provides full bibliographical information for all sources cited in shortened form in the Notes.

INTRODUCTION

1. Gay, *The Cultivation of Hatred*, p. 515.
2. McNeill, *The Pursuit of Power*, p. 318.
3. Eksteins, *Rites of Spring*, p. 288.
4. Fussell, *The Great War*, p. 72.
5. Quoted in Woodward, *Great Britain and the War*, p. 39. Between mid-November 1914 and March 1917, "the front lines did not move as much as ten miles in either direction."
6. Stone, *The Eastern Front*, pp. 93–94, 235–40. The Russian army occupied two thousand miles of trenches by early 1917; plans to build additional trenches during 1915 were neglected by lower commands. See Wildman, *The End of the Russian Imperial Army*, pp. xv, 90.
7. But see p. 120 below.
8. On which theme—in particular, on war as a "hideous embarrassment to the prevailing meliorist myth . . . its dynamics of hope abridged"—see Fussell, *The Great War*, pp. 8, 35. On the commemoration of war, see Winter, *Sites of Memory*, pp. 22–53.
9. The total number of displaced persons has been put at 10. 6 million as of 1 January 1917; a year later the total had climbed to 17.5 million, equivalent to 12 percent of the total population. See Volkov, *Dinamika*, p. 104. The standard reference work, Wieczynski, *Modern Encyclopedia of Russian and Soviet History*, contains a brief entry on prisoners of war, but makes no reference to refugees. The first edition of the *Bol'shaia sovetskaia entsiklopediia* contains an entry on "refugeedom" (*bezhenstvo*) by A. Kirzhnits. Published in 1927, this article promises an entry on the post-revolutionary treatment of refugees and prisoners of war, but it never materialized. Later editions of the encyclopedia dropped the entry altogether. Kirzhnits also wrote a short entry on Siberian refugees and exiles, "Bezhentsy i vyselentsy," before he disappeared during the purges.
10. See *Golos*, no. 30, 7 February 1916, and RGIA f. 1322, op. 1, d. 1, l. 8ob., Special Council for Refugees, 14 September 1915.
11. Volkov, *Dinamika*, pp. 71–72. Volkov's figures include displaced German settlers. See also Kulischer, *Europe*, pp. 30–35; Polner, *Russian Local Government*, pp. 159–76; Kohn, *The Cost of the War*, pp. 32–34. For further discussion see Appendix 1.
12. Gaponenko, *Rabochii klass Rossii*, p. 72. Relatively few registered refugees were counted among the industrial labor force. I use quotation marks here to draw attention to the possibility of collapsing the terms "refugee" and "proletariat."

13. *Izvestiia VZS*, 41–42, 15 June–1 July 1916, pp. 121–22; *Izvestiia VSG*, 34, July 1916, p. 219. The proportions were, of course, smaller in Russia's densely populated provinces.

14. Kulischer, *Europe*, p. 32. Kulischer exaggerated the scale of migration to Siberia, but if we include resettlement in the Caucasus and central Asia, his statement is accurate enough. The Siberian migration was also distinguished from refugeedom by the fact that the former was in essence a *response to* a perceived agrarian crisis, whereas the latter *constituted* a crisis.

15. On social stratification in late imperial Russia, see Lewin, *The Making of the Soviet System;* Freeze, "The *Soslovie* (Estate) Paradigm"; and Schmidt, "Über die Bezeichnung der Stände." Elise Kimerling Wirtschafter has made a special study of the *raznochintsy,* who were placed outside the boundaries of established status groups. Wirtschafter, "Problematics of Status Definition." She notes that, "try as they might, policy-makers could never confine that dynamic conglomeration of human beings called 'society' to officially prescribed socio-economic functions." But the state made strenuous efforts to sustain *sosloviia* "as valuable self-regulating administrative units in preparing legislation, regulating social mobility, maintaining public order, and apportioning rights and privileges in relationship to state service," in the words of A. J. Rieber, "The Sedimentary Society," in Clowes et al., *Between Tsar and People,* p. 256.

16. These questions have also been posed by social anthropologists in fieldwork among refugees. See Loizos, *The Heart Grown Bitter;* Harrell-Bond, *Imposing Aid;* and especially Malkki, *Purity and Exile.*

17. Scott, *Gender and the Politics of History,* p. 178.

18. Haimson, "The Problem of Social Identities"; Abbott Gleason, "The Terms of Russian Social History," in Clowes et al., *Between Tsar and People,* pp. 15–27; Rieber, *Merchants and Entrepreneurs,* introduction and pp. 415–27. Haimson suggests that state officials and the intelligentsia both sought to confer identity on social groups, but that "experience" also counted for a great deal.

19. O. [sic], "Itogi goda," *Zhizn' bezhentsev,* 4, September 1916, pp. 8–9.

20. One of the main cooperative unions in Riga planned to issue maps and guides to Latvian refugees, but the mass evacuation in July 1915 rendered this impossible. See *Kratkii obzor deiatel'nosti Pribaltiiskogo Latyshskogo komiteta,* p. 5.

21. This generalization overlooks the fact that inter-district migration was quite widespread within Poland and the Baltic region. According to the 1897 census, between 7 and 9 percent of the rural population lived in a different uezd from the one in which they were born. Kaiser, *The Geography of Nationalism,* pp. 53–55. Besides, long-distance migration had created a sizeable Polish community in St. Petersburg (65,000 by 1910), as noted by Iukhneva, *Etnicheskii sostav,* p. 208. Many Polish *Gastarbeiter* found temporary work on the estates of East Prussia or in the mines of Silesia. See Tudorianu, *Ocherki rossiiskoi trudovoi emigratsii,* pp. 33–91. Yet Russia's ethnic minorities lived for the most part in territorially compact communities. By 1914, for example, 95 percent of the empire's Armenian population resided in the Caucasus, and a similar proportion of the empire's Latvian population lived in the Baltic region. A. Plakans, "The Latvians," in Thaden, *Russification,* p. 269; Ishkhanian, *Narodnosti Kavkaza,* p. 18.

22. Malkki, *Purity and Exile,* p. 4. Malkki argues that the twin ethnic categories of "Hutu" and "Tutsi" are themselves relatively recent constructs and capable of complex (re)definition. See also idem, "National Geographic."

23. Young, "Together in Difference," pp. 158–59.

24. Riley, *Am I That Name,?* p. 111. See Malkki, *Purity and Exile,* pp. 160–61 for a pertinent example among the Hutu "refugees" in Kigoma township: "This trajectory of improvement was linked precisely to the fact that it had become possible for many in Kigoma to escape the refugee label."

25. Many Hutus in the Tanzanian refugee camp at Mishamo defended their status as refugees, not least because it offered a preferable alternative to being amalgamated in Tanzanian society as "immigrants." Ibid., pp. 206–10.

26. Barthes, *Mythologies,* p. 75.

27. Bhabha, *The Location of Culture,* p. 6.

28. Chambers, *Migrancy, Culture, Identity,* chapter 2. For a different approach, see Harvey, *The Condition of Postmodernity,* pp. 295–99.

29. Chambers, *Migrancy,* p. 86.

30. On this topic, see Rose, *Governing the Soul.*

31. Thomas Laqueur, "Bodies, Details, and the Humanitarian Narrative," in Hunt, *The New Cultural History,* pp. 176–204.

32. Neuberger, *Hooliganism.* See also Engelstein, *The Keys to Happiness,* pp. 265–67.

33. Frierson, *Peasant Icons,* pp. 6, 194.

34. Ernest Gellner remarks that in early industrialization, migrants may have to contend with residents who are not only relatively better off but also culturally distinct; thus ethnic and class differences are both sharpened. "For the better-placed category, the culturally distinguishable poor constitute a menace, not only to the social order as a whole, but also in daily life. They are dirty and violent, they make the city unsafe, and they constitute a kind of cultural pollution." Gellner, "The Coming of Nationalism," p. 125.

35. Moore, *The Formation of a Persecuting Society,* p. 100; Douglas, *Purity and Danger,* p. 53.

36. Moore, *Formation,* p. 101.

37. Zolberg et al., *Escape from Violence,* p. 4. For a Christian perspective, see Ferris, *Beyond Borders.* For a philosophical approach, see Shacknove, "Who Is a Refugee?" For legal aspects of refugeedom in contemporary Europe, see Tuitt, *False Images.*

38. Zolberg, *Escape from Violence,* p. 4.

39. Current law in the Russian Federation applies the term "refugee" to those non-Russians who have been displaced from the territory of other parts of the former Soviet Union, and defines as "forced migrants" those Russians who have been forced to leave their homes in other parts of the FSU. See Pilkington, *Migration,* pp. 42–46.

40. "In the increasing complexity of present day society a man is less easily able than ever before to dispense with the normal protection of his state; and the delicate relations of economic life are more easily dislocated, and with more disastrous effects, than the cruder conditions of the past." Macartney, "Refugees," p. 204.

41. Zolberg, *Escape from Violence,* p. 7.

42. Arendt, *The Origins of Totalitarianism,* p. 267. On the durability of "refugeeness" (*prosphygiá*) among Greeks from Asia Minor, see Hirschon, *Heirs of the Greek Catastrophe.* A powerful work which, *inter alia,* sees them as "unwitting agents" of Greek nation state-building is Karakasidou, *Fields of Wheat, Hills of Blood.*

43. Quotations from Zolberg, *Escape from Violence,* pp. 29–30.

44. *The Guardian,* 16 May 1995. In 1992 the refugee population stood at 18 million. See Ferris, *Beyond Borders,* p. vii. Compare the oft-quoted estimate of a total refugee population of 9.5 million in 1926, from Kulischer, *Europe,* pp. 248–49. Figures for 1987 suggest a total

of 15.4 million refugees and 17 million internally displaced. Zolberg, *Escape from Violence,* p. 229.

45. Marrus, *The Unwanted,* pp. 5, 13.

46. Ibid., p. 83. In some fictional accounts, such action has been read as comedy, as in Edith Wharton's short story "The Refugees," where the author parodies the attempts by well-meaning English gentry—"refugee raiders"—to compete among themselves for the right to assist Belgian refugees in 1914. A case of mistaken identity allows the protagonist, "Professor Durand," to humor his rescuer and to permit her the luxury of an "adventure." Wharton, *Certain People.*

47. For a salutary study of the ways in which modern media serve to influence and manipulate popular perceptions of the refugee "problem," see Benthall, *Disasters, Relief and the Media.*

48. Moskoff, *Hard Times,* p. 142.

49. As Zygmunt Bauman points out, obligation can itself have demeaning consequences, exposing the stranger to constant reminders that his or her "form of humanity [is] parochial and shameful." Bauman, *Modernity and Ambivalence,* p. 97. In this context it is revealing that many Russians who move to Russia from the independent states that previously constituted the Soviet Union reject the term "refugee" as a victimizing label. Pilkington, *Migration,* pp. 163–64.

50. Turton, "Conference Report." On the complex issue of "going home," see Malkki, *Purity and Exile,* pp. 259–60.

51. For this theoretical advance, see Zolberg, *Escape from Violence,* p. 263.

52. Marrus, *The Unwanted,* chapter 4; Zolberg, *Escape from Violence,* pp. 6–7; Mayer, *Why Did the Heavens Not Darken?;* and Levene, "Frontiers of Genocide."

53. I am unsympathetic to social scientists who seek to specify the conditions under which displaced people were liable to expressions of "normlessness," "detachment," and even "DP (displaced person) apathy." See Shuval, "Refugees: Adjustment and Assimilation." There is a clear contrast between the treatment accorded refugees in the two editions of this encyclopedia. Macartney, "Refugees," notes the contribution made by refugees to the life of the host society, precisely by dint of their nonconformity, whereas Shuval is eager to establish the conditions under which refugees conform and "assimilate."

54. *Osobye soveshchaniia i komitety voennogo vremeni,* p. 47. See also Gronsky and Astrov, *The War and the Russian Government,* p. 36. The term *bezhenets* was virtually universal, although I have come across the use of the term *izgnannik,* literally "banished person, exile, outlaw," as in *Izvestiia VSG,* 20, December 1915, p. 180. "Ruthenian" was the term used in official Austro-Hungarian documentation to apply to the Slav population of the northeastern part of the kingdom of Hungary; it originally referred to Russians living within the lands of pre-Partition Poland.

55. Thus Simon Schama's assessment of Rousseau's impact on French political and intellectual life. Schama, *Citizens,* p. 161.

56. Lih, *Bread and Authority in Russia.*

57. Smith, "Writing the History of the Russian Revolution," p. 569.

1. WAR AND THE ORIGINS OF INVOLUNTARY DISPLACEMENT

1. Stone, *The Eastern Front,* pp. 95–107, 165–91. Weekly reports of the conduct of the war were carried in the semi-official journal *Letopis' voiny.*

2. S. I. Zubchaninov, Special Council, 10 September 1915. RGIA f. 1322, op. 1, d. 1, ll. 1ob.–2. This view was echoed by the Duma deputy Antonov, *GDSO,* 10th sitting, 14 August 1915, col. 795.

3. Refugees also sought to maintain contact with their civilian relatives who were employed by the Russian army as construction workers in the rear. RGVIA f. 2003, op. 2, d. 860, ll. 40–45, conference at Stavka, 1 October 1915; ibid., f. 2005, op. 1, d. 42, ll. 517–22; ibid., f. 2020, op. 1, d. 131, ll. 211–19, Danilov to Alekseev, 25 August 1915, quoting General Mavrin's decision to conscript males between the age of 18 and 50 for engineering work.

4. Zubchaninov to the commander of the northern front, 8 October 1915. RGVIA f. 2032, op. 1, d. 282, l. 4. See also the description of the situation in Minsk in the telegram from Evert to Alekseev, August 1915. Ibid., f. 2005, op. 1, d. 42, ll. 149–ob. Also Gulevich's report to First Army headquarters on the situation in Grodno, 16 August 1915. Ibid., f. 2042, op. 1, d. 438, l. 75. Latvian politicians endorsed this view in *Kratkii obzor deiatel'nosti Pribaltiiskogo Latyshskogo komiteta,* p. 16. One general suggested that refugees remained close to military encampments in order to scrounge for food, sometimes in exchange for sexual favors. Igel'strom to Evert, 4 July 1915. RGVIA f. 2020, op. 1, d. 131, ll. 131–34.

5. Beliaev to Danilov, 24 July 1915. Ibid., l. 184. Occasionally farm animals were deliberately requisitioned in order to encourage civilians to move to the rear, as General Miller admitted to the governor of Livland on 12 August 1915. Ibid., f. 2032, op. 1, d. 281, ll. 52–ob.

6. Mavrin to the commander of the Kiev Military District, 24 June 1915. Ibid., f. 1759, op. 4, d. 1725, l. 47.

7. Memorandum by Prince N. L. Obolenskii, 30 August 1915. Ibid., f. 2003, op. 2, d. 945, ll. 10.

8. "This will destroy state administration and damage the interests of the people," in Goremykin's words, reported by General Beliaev, 28 August 1915. RGVIA f. 1759, op. 4, d. 1728, l. 5. For the Duma critique see *GDSO,* 10th sitting, 14 August 1915, cols. 795–856.

9. Daniel W. Graf, "Military Rule." These powers were much more extensive than those vested in provincial governors before the war, when (in the aftermath of the 1905 revolution) around 2.3 million inhabitants of the empire were subject to martial law. See Waldron, "States of Emergency."

10. "The main wave of refugees comprises people from provinces that have been completely laid waste by military considerations." *Bezhentsy i vyselentsy,* p. 1; see also Nikol'skii, "Bezhentsy," pp. 22–23.

11. RGVIA f. 2003, op. 2, d. 945, ll. 2–3. A conference on 23 June agreed to destroy food reserves that would otherwise fall into enemy hands, but decided that buildings and woodlands should be destroyed only "for reasons of military necessity." General Ruzskii argued that deportation eased the pressure on available resources at the front, November 1915. Ibid., f. 2005, op. 1, d. 42, ll. 369–70; for the removal of livestock and other assets, see ibid., f. 1759, op. 4, d. 1728, ll. 50–53.

12. Ibid., f. 2020, op. 1, d. 131, l. 6; ibid., f. 2042, op. 1, d. 438, l. 13.

13. As reported in *Bezhentsy i vyselentsy,* p. 54. See also RGVIA f. 2005, op. 1, d. 42, ll. 221–22; ibid., f. 2042, op. 1, d. 438, ll. 88–91.

14. Wolf, *The Legal Sufferings,* p. 50, observed that "the persecutions of Jews in the boundary zone endured until the beginning of the present century." The restriction ceased in 1904, although the state retained a 100 kilometer exclusion zone along the border with

China. See Rogger, *Jewish Policies,* p. 80. A contemporary summary of military repression was published on behalf of the American Jewish committee as *The Jews in the Eastern War Zone.*

15. Evert to Ianushkevich, 18 February 1915. RGVIA f. 2005, op. 1, d. 155, ll. 1–5.

16. Mavrin to the commander of the Kiev Military District, 3 July 1915. Ibid., f. 1759, op. 4, d. 1725, l. 5. See also Danilov's letter to Rausch, governor of Minsk province, n.d. (28 June 1916?). Ibid., f. 2020, op. 1, d. 131, l. 39. Many of the foreign settlers in Volynia, Kiev, and Podol'ia arrived from Germany and Russian Poland during the 1880s, more than a century after Germans and others had been invited by Catherine the Great to colonize the Volga and the southern provinces of Tauride, Ekaterinoslav, and Kherson. Neutatz, *Die "deutsche Frage."*

17. Mendelsohn, *Zionism in Poland,* p. 38. A slightly lower figure is cited in Kirzhnits, "Bezhenstvo," p. 177. Around half were reported to have been forced to move to Warsaw on the orders of the Russian army. "Iz 'chernoi knigi,'" p. 217. Early attempts by the newly formed Union of Towns to identify the extent of civilian needs in Russian Poland, including on-the-spot surveys by the eminent economist S. N. Prokopovich, were reported in *Izvestiia VSG,* 9, March 1915, pp. 76–77.

18. *Kratkii obzor deiatel'nosti Litovskogo obshchestva,* pp. 2–3.

19. Senator A. B. Neidgardt, quoted in GARF f. 651, op. 1, d. 39, l. 15.

20. "Iz 'chernoi knigi,'" pp. 209–10. See too the plaintive telegram from the Jews of Ianovsk to the commander of the northwestern front in May 1915, appealing against deportation on the grounds that that they were loyal to tsar and fatherland, and "pure in the eyes of God and our neighbors." RGVIA f. 2020, op. 1, d. 128, l. 4.

21. The canard about Jewish treachery is found in Thurstan, *People,* p. 150. The British ambassador Sir George Buchanan reported that "there cannot be the slightest doubt that a very large number of Jews have been in German pay and have acted as spies during the campaigns in Poland." Quoted in Levene, "Frontiers of Genocide," p. 93.

22. "Vyselentsy," *Ukrainskaia zhizn',* 4–5, April–May 1916, p. 130. The author pinned the blame on "police sergeants and secret agents, not always recruited from the best elements in society. This sows national discord and promotes an atmosphere of denunciation. None of this helps to secure the front; rather, it disorganizes the rear."

23. Details in "Iz 'chernoi knigi,'" pp. 214–19, 231–42; "Dokumenty o presledovanii evreev," pp. 247–48. See also Nelipovich, "V poiskakh 'vnutrennego vraga.'"

24. "Dokumenty o presledovanii evreev," p. 250.

25. This figure is cited by Kulischer, *Europe,* p. 31. Kulischer adds that of this total, 190,000 Jews were evacuated from Kurland, Kovno, and Grodno. Lower estimates appeared in *Evreiskaia zhizn',* 5, 2 August 1915, p. 34.

26. They were members of the SVU, or "Union for the Liberation of Ukraine," formed in August 1914. Details in Oleh S. Fedyshyn, "The Germans and the Union for the Liberation of the Ukraine, 1914–1917," in Hunczak, *The Ukraine, 1917–1921,* pp. 305–22.

27. Brylkin to the commander of the southwestern front, 1 September 1916. RGVIA f. 2005, op. 1, d. 43, ll. 47–51; *Ukrainskaia zhizn',* 10, October 1915, pp. 103–104; Doroschenko, *Die Ukraine und Deutschland,* p. 181.

28. *Evreiskaia zhizn',* 9, 30 August 1915, pp. 30–31.

29. B. D. Brutskus, "Ekonomicheskoe polozhenie evreev i voina," *Russkaia mysl',* 4, 1915, pp. 27–45. Typical examples of the declarations that hostages were forced to sign, and of protests against this practice, are printed in "Dokumenty o presledovanii evreev," pp. 256–57.

30. One of Ianushkevich's orders read as follows: "As soon as some substantial change in the locations and movements of our troops occurs, and whenever we temporarily evacuate one or another district, the enemy, because of the intervention of Jews, adopts cruel measures against the loyal non-Jewish population. In order to protect the population faithful to us from the reprisals by the enemy and to safeguard our troops against the treason which the Jews employ along the entire front, the Supreme Commander of the Russian armed forces considers it necessary that Jews be banished as soon as the enemy retreats." Baron, *The Russian Jew,* p. 158. N. N. Ianushkevich, by origin a Pole, became chief of staff at the outbreak of war. He accompanied Grand Duke Nicholas to the Caucasus when the commander-in-chief was dismissed from his post in August 1915; there he continued to inflict further misery on the local civilian population.

31. *Ukrainskaia zhizn',* 10, October 1915, pp. 103–104; "Dokumenty o presledovanii evreev," pp. 247, 251; Kazanskii, *Galitsko-russkie bezhentsy,* pp. 5–8.

32. Ananov, *Sud'ba Armenii,* p. 21; Hovannisian, *Armenia on the Road to Independence,* pp. 41–42. A "Committee to Aid Refugees Regardless of Nationality" was formed in Baku in February 1915. *Bezhenets* (Baku), 23 February 1915, and *Mshak,* 3, 6 January 1915, p. 5.

33. Some leaders of the Armenian community rallied to the Ottoman cause when war broke out, but they refused to organize anti-tsarist revolts across the border. Somakian, *Empires in Conflict,* provides the context.

34. RGIA f. 1276, op. 17, d. 477, ll. 1–2; RGVIA f. 2005, op. 1, d. 66, ll. 118–ob.

35. *Mshak,* 2, 4 January 1915, p. 3. The Petrograd Armenian Church council immediately sent 25,000 rubles to Etchmidzian, where many refugees gathered. Ibid., 47, 4 March 1915, p. 3. The Armenian mayor of Tbilisi recalled that "the flux of the refugees impeded the free movement of the armies, giving rise to anti-Armenian feelings." Khatisov, "Memoirs of a Mayor," p. 110. Somewhat lower figures are cited in Arutiunian, "Pervaia mirovaia voina i armianskie bezhentsy," p. 20.

36. Chief of Railway Police Administration of the Transcaucasus, 10 January 1915. RGVIA f. 2005, op. 1, d. 66, ll. 118–ob.

37. Neidgardt, 15 December 1914, as reported in *Komitet,* p. 244.

38. Wildman, *The End of the Russian Imperial Army,* p. 89.

39. Corrsin, "Warsaw: Poles and Jews," p. 145.

40. See Nikol'skii, "Bezhentsy," pp. 15–17 for a description of the sudden evacuation of civilians, postal workers, and civil servants from Kozenitsa to Ivangorod, thence to Siedlice and Brest-Litovsk.

41. The plight of refugees in the city was reported in *BV,* 14953, 9 July 1915; see also the debates in the municipal Duma, in LVVA f. 2736, op. 1, d. 38, l. 55ob., d. 39, l. 44ob. A Latvian agricultural association complained that the refugee population—"loyal to the tsar"—suffered more hardships than the Jews. RGVIA f. 2005, op. 1, d. 42, ll. 39–40.

42. Ibid., f. 369, op. 1, d. 39, ll. 28–33ob., Shakhovskoi to Council of Ministers, 11 December 1915. See also Buchanan, *My Mission to Russia,* vol. 1, p. 237; Cherniavsky, *Prologue to Revolution,* p. 95.

43. Ibid., pp. 147–48, 168–72, 228–30. By the beginning of September, ministers were resigned to the loss of Kiev and discussed the painful business of having to abandon saints' relics in the Kiev-Pechora Monastery to German troops. Details in "Materialy o plane evakuatsii goroda Kieva, 1916" (RGIA library, file 2415).

44. *Izvestiia VSG,* 17, September 1915, p. 5, reprinted in *Bezhentsy i vyselentsy,* p. 5; the union passed the telegram on to the war ministry with an urgent request for funds to attend

to refugees' needs. See also *Russkoe slovo,* 153, 4 July 1915, the first occasion on which this leading national newspaper mentioned refugees.

45. Alekseev to Danilov, 3 August 1915. RGVIA f. 2042, op. 1, d. 438, l. 4.

46. *Zhizn' bezhentsev,* 4, September 1916, pp. 8–9.

47. Shveder, "*Bezhentsy,*" p. 18. The *khata* is a typical Ukrainian cottage.

48. The story is told of a young Jewish woman whose daughter was killed by a German raid on Lodz. Her husband eventually caught up with her in Warsaw. "Tragediia bezhenki," *Vestnik iuga,* 14 May 1915. The widespread fear of enemy behavior is recounted in Bachmanis, *Latvju tauta beglu gaitas,* p. 76.

49. Danilov acknowledged as much in a letter to the governor of Minsk province dated 24 June 1915. RGVIA f. 2020, op. 1, d. 131, l. 15.

50. LVVA f. 5626, op. 1, d. 82, l. 5, Latvian Committee to Aid War Victims, Refugee Section, to Zubchaninov, 16 August 1915.

51. See the remarks of S. I. Zubchaninov at a conference at Stavka, 1 October 1915. RGVIA f. 2005, op. 1, d. 42, ll. 517–22.

52. Zubchaninov to Northwest Army Headquarters, 26 August 1915. RGVIA f. 2042, op. 1, d. 438, ll. 182–83.

53. Ibid., f. 2005, op. 1, d. 42, ll. 78–ob., Bankowski to Skirmunt, 17 July 1915; ibid., ll. 424–28, memorandum from Zubchaninov, 20 August 1915.

54. Ibid., ll. 19–ob. The army reported that a further 75,000 refugees settled in the province itself.

55. RGIA f. 1322, op. 1, d. 13, l. 70ob. G. V. Viktorov to Zubchaninov, 16 September 1915, RGVIA f. 2042, op. 1, d. 440, l. 112. Roslavl' lay at the intersection of two major railways, the Brest–Moscow line and the Riga–Smolensk–Orel line.

56. Kovalevskii et al., *Ekonomika Belorussii,* p. 180. Karl Baedeker, *Baedeker's Russia 1914,* and Lubny-Gertsyk, *Dvizhenie naseleniia,* pp. 74–76, are my sources for urban population in 1914, although Baedeker's figures are not always reliable.

57. A. M. Smirnov-Kutacheskii, "Bezhentsy-galichane," *Russkaia mysl',* 9, 1915, pp. 125–39; *Ukrainskaia zhizn',* 10, October 1915, pp. 103–104; RGVIA f. 13273, op. 1, d. 29, ll. 10–11ob.; ibid., f. 2003, op. 2, d. 845, ll. 1–13. The description of Ianushkevich appears in "Dokumenty o presledovanii evreev," editor's introduction.

58. *BV,* 14963, 14 July 1915; *Izvestiia VZS,* 21, 15 August 1915, pp. 49–52; *Ekaterinoslavskaia zemskaia gazeta,* 1 September 1915; *Rech',* 114, 27 April 1916. Twenty-four thousand refugees arrived in the city of Ekaterinoslav during the week beginning 23 August 1915.

59. RGIA f. 1322, op. 1, d. 1, l. 25ob.

60. RGVIA f. 13273, op. 1, d. 24, l. 36.

61. RGIA f. 1322, op. 1. d. 1, ll. 260–ob., Special Council, 5 March 1916.

62. Ibid., l. 1, 10 September 1915. The origins of the Special Council for Refugees are discussed in chapter 2.

63. Ibid., l. 3; *GDSO,* 10th sitting, 14 August 1915, col. 807. Nikol'skii, "Bezhentsy," p. 22, relates how he heard stories of Cossack brutality toward Polish refugees.

64. See also the remarks of Senator A. B. Neidgardt quoted in GARF f. 651, op. 1, d. 39, l. 25, and summarized in *BV,* 14999, 1 August 1915: "Refugees are divided into two categories: those forcibly displaced by the authorities, and those who flee from their native towns and villages under the influence of fear and panic." The minister of the interior's

response is discussed below. Polish political leaders referred to *vyselentsy*. See *UR,* 230, 21 August 1915.

65. "Iz 'chernoi knigi,'" pp. 268–69, 277–85; exceptional instances of a "soft" approach are noted on p. 272. Jews were once again accused of communicating with the enemy by various elaborate means, such as airplanes and an underground telephone system, and even sending gold concealed in the wings of geese that were directed toward enemy lines.

66. "Dokumenty o presledovanii evreev," p. 249; "Iz 'chernoi knigi,'" p. 221. See also Graf, "Military Rule," pp. 399–400, and Zipperstein, "The Politics of Relief," p. 24. The term "cleansing" reappears in the context of the Armenian genocide; it definitely implied ethnic cleansing. *Armianskii vestnik,* 17, 22 May 1916, p. 22; 7, 12 February 1917, p. 20.

67. Details in "Iz 'chernoi knigi,'" pp. 274–85; and Strazhas, *Deutsche Ostpolitik,* p. 81. Brief allusions to the summary execution of Jewish "spies" are to be found in Knox, *With the Russian Army,* vol. 1, pp. 120, 145–46.

68. Graf, "Military Rule," p. 400.

69. RGVIA f. 2020, op. 1, d. 128, l. 25, n.d. Danilov instructed provincial governors to return deported Jews to their homes, although at the same time he insisted on the need to take hostages from among rabbis and the wealthy members of the local Jewish community.

70. Telegram from Bonch-Bruevich, 29 September 1915. RGVIA f. 2032, op. 1, d. 282, l. 13; see also the comments by Ia. M. Fridman at the Special Council, 24 October 1915. RGIA f. 1322, op. 1, d. 1, l. 42ob. Plehve retorted that the Special Council had always accepted that strategic considerations might justify compulsory deportation.

71. RGVIA f. 2005, op. 1, d. 42, ll. 333–ob., telegram from the Jewish *kahal* in Skala, Tarnopol', to Ivanov, 16 October 1915.

72. Nelipovich, "V poiskakh 'vnutrennogo vraga,'" p. 59.

73. *GDSO,* 5th sitting, 3 August 1915, cols. 360–61, 423. A right-wing deputy from Khar'kov accused German religious minorities of espionage, singling out Stundists and Adventists. See Neutatz, *Die "deutsche Frage,"* p. 429; Striegnitz, "Der Weltkrieg und die Wolgakolonisten."

74. RGVIA f. 2005, op. 1, d. 28, ll. 5–7. Ibid., f. 2020, op. 1, d. 126 for messages to the governor of Riga from Baltic Germans appealing against deportation.

75. Ibid., f. 2005, op. 1, d. 28, ll. 5–7ob., chief of Odessa Military District to Ianush-kevich, 25 October 1914. The nationalist Purishkevich believed that German settlers pointed out potential bomb targets to the German army. Ibid., l. 164.

76. *Novoe vremia* outdid itself on 30 December 1914 with the following comment: "Let us hope that we shall soon get rid of these poisonous spiders that suck the best juices from our land and systematically undermine the Russian state idea." Quoted in ibid., d. 24, l. 346.

77. Ibid., d. 28, ll. 84, 89, 92. Measures directed against foreign nationals were discussed by the Council of Ministers between 17 October and 14 November 1914. Ibid., d. 24, ll. 109–21ob.

78. Telegram from General Ivanov to the governors of Volynia and Podol'ia, 19 June 1915. RGVIA f. 1759, op. 4, d. 1725, l. 46; ibid., f. 2005, op. 1, d. 28, l. 137.

79. Ibid., ll. 132, 227–29, "Special Commission for Measures to Purify Lands in the North and Southwestern Fronts," 24 June 1915. For the story of one family of settlers, see Krueger, *Die Flüchtlinge von Wolynien,* p. 25.

80. RGVIA f. 2032, op. 1, d. 281, ll. 75–76, 83–84. This file contains petitions submitted against deportation. Mariia Westfal, a 43-year-old resident of Riga, petitioned on the

grounds that as a disabled woman, she would be "sent to certain doom." She also volunteered the information that her three daughters had all married respectable Russian citizens who served in the army. Her request was finally turned down in March 1917, and she was ordered to pay stamp duty on the correspondence. Ibid., ll. 308–22.

81. Some German colonists asked that Stavka draw a distinction between those who had settled in the eighteenth century and the "newcomers" who arrived during the 1880s. Ibid., f. 2005, op. 1, d. 28, ll. 238–39, letter to Ianushkevich dated 5 December 1915.

82. Kondrat'ev, *Rynok khlebov,* p. 124.

83. The frontier was defined as up to 150 kilometers from the western borders (from Finland to the Black Sea), and included the whole of Poland. Details in Lindeman, *Prekrashchenie zemlevladeniia,* p. 191; Nolde, *Russia in the Economic War,* pp. 103–15; Rempel, "The Expropriation of the German Colonists."

84. Order issued by General Ivanov, 19 June 1915. RGVIA f. 2005, op. 1, d. 28, l. 137; *Vestnik VOPB,* 18, 15 May 1916, p. 10; *Iugobezhenets,* 16, 27 February 1916, p. 1.

85. RGIA f. 1322, op. 1, d. 16, ll. 48–49.

86. Schechtman, *European Population Transfers,* p. 216.

87. RGVIA f. 1759, op. 1, d. 1725, l. 46.

88. RGIA f. 1284, op. 194, d. 22–1915, l. 3. The governor of Kherson reported that "Jews and German colonists have declined to respond to the draft, and this has aroused hostility among the local people." Ibid., d. 41–1915, l. 20.

89. Grave, *Burzhuaziia nakanune fevral'skoi revoliutsii,* p. 137, quoting a police report dated 30 October 1916.

90. Nelipovich, "Rol' voennogo rukovodstva," p. 272.

91. The state auditor called for Ianushkevich's dismissal. The foreign minister called him a "narcissistic nincompoop," and the minister of the interior prescribed valerian, concluding with the rhetorical question, "How does the Chief of Staff plan to buy the heroism of non-landowners?" Cherniavsky, *Prologue,* pp. 22–26.

92. *TP,* 4, 1916, p. 356.

93. *GDSO,* fifth sitting, 3 August 1915, cols. 497–508.

94. "The faces of the refugees were gray, their movements slow and feeble. It seemed as if they were all covered by a mask of unutterable stiffness and appalling indifference." Bachmanis, *Latvju,* pp. 76, 171.

95. To put this in context, the 1897 census counted 1.3 million Latvians in the three main provinces of Latvian settlement, namely Livland (Vidzeme), Kurland (Kurzeme), and Vitebsk. See Netesin and Krastyn', "Ekonomika Latvii," pp. 268–69.

96. Netesin, *Promyshlennyi kapital Latvii,* pp. 201–202. According to the Ministry of Transport, two-fifths of all evacuated factories were relocated in Moscow and its environs, a further third in Khar'kov, and 10 percent in Petrograd and the Volga region respectively. RGVIA f. 369, op. 1, d. 307, ll. 195–7ob.

97. Netesin, *Promyshlennyi kapital Latvii,* pp. 206–207; Burdzhalov, *Vtoraia russkaia revoliutsiia,* p. 261.

98. Riga and the surrounding region accommodated between 200,000 and 250,000 refugees in the autumn of 1915. Around 110,000 were Latvian or Lithuanian, 55,000 were Polish, and the remainder were Russian. See Nikol'skii, "Bezhentsy," pp. 78–79.

99. LVVA f. 5626, op. 1, d. 82, ll. 20–21, September 1915. Carpenters were valued at 20 rubles, and carters at 30 rubles; the contract stipulated a fee of just 10 rubles for unskilled laborers. I have been unable to determine the result of this scheme.

100. Kirakosian, *Zapadnaia Armeniia*, pp. 420–26; Arutiunian, "Pervaia mirovaia voina," pp. 26–41.

101. Somakian, *Empires in Conflict*, pp. 82–83, points out that the Armenian protest at Van (in April 1915) followed rather than preceded the massacre of unarmed civilians by the Turkish authorities.

102. In October 1915, the Special Council for Refugees talked of a "systematic and premeditated massacre [*izbienie*], having as its goal the complete destruction of the Armenian nationality in Turkey." RGIA f. 1322, op. 1, d. 1, l. 26ob. The analogy with St. Bartholomew's Day appears in Osherovskii, *Tragediia armian-bezhentsev*, p. 10. See also Dadrian, *The History of the Armenian Genocide*, pp. 221–22.

103. Turkish scholars deny that state policy toward the Ottoman Armenians was prompted by racial motives. In support of this contention, one can cite the harsh punishment of Syrian Muslim dissidents during 1915, showing that the internal security of the Ottoman empire remained a major consideration. Kedourie, *England and the Middle East*, p. 63fn. The fact remains that the "disloyalty" of some Armenian dissidents was transformed into statewide measures against the entire Armenian community.

104. There are various estimates of the total number of victims. In September 1915, the Russian foreign minister received reports that around 1 million Armenians had been massacred. Somakian, *Empires in Conflict*, p. 94. According to Leo Kuper, between 800,000 and 1 million Armenians were killed or starved to death. Arnold Toynbee calculated that 600,000 were killed in 1915 alone, 600,000 survived on Turkish soil—many of them to fall victim later on to massacres in Smyrna and Constantinople—and 600,000 escaped abroad, of whom 182,000 crossed into the Russian Caucasus. Other estimates suggest that the figure was closer to 1.5 million, equivalent to one-half of the total Armenian population of the Ottoman empire. Kuper, *Genocide*, pp. 113–14; Melson, *Revolution and Genocide*, p. 146. Dadrian, who provides an account of earlier massacres in 1894–96 and 1909, adheres to a figure of 1 million Armenian deaths during the war. The events of 1896 were recalled, and their impact on Armenian children recounted, in Iu. Veselovskii, "Deti obezdolennogo kraia," *Vestnik vospitaniia*, 27, 1916, no. 3, pp. 179–97.

105. *Izvestiia VSG*, 29–30, 1916, p. 215 (a much higher estimate than the one given earlier in ibid., 17, 1915, p. 88), endorsed by Ananov, *Sud'ba Armenii*, p. 23.

106. Report of the governor of Erevan to MVD, 21 January 1916. RGIA f. 1322, op. 1, d. 16, l. 38.

107. Walker, *Armenia*, pp. 193, 203. Other sources suggest that the chief beneficiaries were Kurdish farmers. Osherovskii, *Tragediia*, p. 10.

108. Report of a meeting convened by the MVD, 14–16 September 1915. RGVIA f. 2005, op. 1, d. 42, ll. 20–21. The dismissive response by front commanders to parliamentary complaints is contained in ibid., d. 155, ll. 1–5, Evert to Ianushkevich, 18 February 1915; ibid., ll. 6–13ob., Brusilov to Stavka, 14 June 1916; ll. 28–ob., unnamed officer to Stavka, 22 March 1917.

109. *Golos*, 224, 2 October 1915.

110. RGIA f. 1322, op. 1, d. 1. l. 14ob.

111. Cherniavsky, *Prologue*, pp. 232–33, minutes of meeting of Council of Ministers, 2 September 1915. I have modified the translation.

112. RGIA f. 1322, op. 1, d. 1, l. 14ob.

113. Ibid., l. 4, Special Council, 10 September 1915. A similar view was expressed in the Duma by Swencicki. *GDSO*, 10th sitting, 14 August, cols. 800–801.

114. RGIA f. 1322, op. 1, d. 1, l. 13ob., Special Council, 22 September 1915. This minority view was supported by P. P. Stremoukhov, but the suggestion that the state should commit itself to refugee relief in an open-ended way found no favor.

115. Cherniavsky, *Prologue,* pp. 168, 170–71, minutes of the Council of Ministers, 24 August 1915; RGIA f. 1322, op. 1, d. 16, ll. 48–49, report of provincial governor, 8 February 1916.

116. Paléologue, *La Russie des Tsars,* vol. 1, pp. 335–36. Latvian relief workers complained to the commander-in-chief of the northwestern front about the proposed evacuation of refugees. LVVA f. 5626, op. 1, d. 82, ll. 25–26ob., 26 September 1915.

117. *Sputnik bezhentsa,* pp. 8–9. Refugees were to travel along a designated route; local commissioners would stipulate places to eat, rest, obtain medical treatment, etc.

118. S. V. Rukhlov to Stavka, 30 September 1915. RGVIA f. 2005, op. 1, d. 42, ll. 518–19; summary of discussion at Stavka, 1 October 1915, ibid., f. 2003, op. 1, d. 860, ll. 40–45; Stavka to Ruzskii, 28 September 1915, Ibid., f. 2032, op. 1, d. 282, ll. 1–2. In December 1915, Alekseev instructed the commanders of the northern, western, and southwestern fronts to call a halt to further deportation of German settlers, in view of the "disarray" of rail transport. Nelipovich, "Rol' voennogo rukovodstva," pp. 276–77.

119. See the description of conditions on the Riga–Orel line in Nikol'skii, "Bezhentsy," pp. 52–53. The resourceful Nikol'skii managed to obtain two trains and seventy wagons from the military authorities in order to move two thousand refugees each day from Roslavl' to the east. However, they continued to arrive at the refugee camp at a far higher rate.

120. Sidorov, *Ekonomicheskoe polozhenie Rossii,* pp. 590–92.

121. RGIA f. 1322, op. 1, d. 1, l. 1ob.; Nikol'skii, "Bezhentsy," pp. 47–48.

122. RGVIA f. 2005, op. 1, d. 42, l. 271, Alekseev to VZS, undated; *Izvestiia VZS,* 21, 15 August 1915, pp. 75–76, reporting the situation in Orenburg and pleading for additional medical personnel.

123. "Iz 'chernoi knigi,'" pp. 242–43. It was a further sign of military paranoia that the commander of the northern front ordered Jewish railwaymen to leave the town of Toropets in October 1915, along with all other refugees. RGVIA f. 2032, op. 1, d. 282, ll. 11–12.

124. The Ministry of Transport blamed conditions on the conscription of railway personnel, and suggested that many refugees wanted to be kept on the move. RGIA f. 1322, op. 1, d. 1, l. 26, sixth session of the Special Council for Refugees, 3 October 1915.

125. An editorial in *Severnyi bezhenets* (Novgorod), 4, 2 February 1916, urged its readers to recognize how easily families could be separated; parents were not to be blamed. See also *Zhizn' bezhentsev,* 5, October 1916, pp. 6–7.

126. *Bezhenets,* 4, 1 November 1915, quoting a party of refugees traveling to Zlatoust in the Urals.

127. Some lines were commandeered by the army or were impassable. See the memoirs of Iakov Vol'rat, "Begstvo ot germantsev i skitaniia," *Izvestiia Tatianinskogo komiteta,* 19, 1917, p. 17.

128. On the plight of refugees who traveled in open wagons, see I. Nikol'skii, "Itogi zabot Simbirskogo eparkhial'nogo upravleniia o bezhentsakh," *Simbirskie eparkhial'nye vedomosti,* 23, December 1915, pp. 918–31.

129. For an unsympathetic and uncritical account of refugees as a hindrance to retreating troops, see Lobanov-Rostovsky, *The Grinding Mill,* p. 156. The author relates how he hired two refugees to carry his baggage after his horse became too exhausted to continue. As

in other testimonies, refugees were portrayed as a ragged nuisance, in contrast to heroic soldiers.

130. RGIA f. 1322, op. 1, d. 1, l. 36ob., Zubchaninov to Special Council, 20 October 1915; ibid., f. 1276, op. 12, d. 1411, ll. 1–4, and testimony of Nikol'skii, "Bezhentsy," p. 48.

131. Alekseev to Danilov, 28 August 1915. RGVIA f. 2005, op. 1, d. 42, l. 156; governor of Mogilev to N. Obolenskii, 21 September 1915. Ibid, ll. 286–87.

132. RGIA f. 1322, op. 1, d. 16, ll. 48–49. Desperation also took a verbal form: "This is not Russia, this is cholera," stated one indignant refugee, reported in *Russkaia mysl'*, 9, 1915, p. 127.

133. RGIA f. 1322, op. 1, d. 1, l. 1ob., Urusov to Special Council, 10 September 1915. The Progressist newspaper urged that state and society cooperate in order to allocate refugees "to those places of the European empire which pessimistic military minds, even in their most gloomy prognostications, do not expect the enemy to penetrate." *UR*, 209, 31 July 1915.

134. The difficulties faced by the Ministry of Agriculture (GUZZ) in evacuating livestock are described by A. V. Krivoshein in a letter to Alekseev, 5 October 1915. RGVIA f. 2003, op. 2, d. 860, ll. 10–11ob.

135. RGVIA f. 1759, op. 4, d. 1728, l. 39. Typically, Jews were nonetheless blamed for having persuaded refugees to part with their livestock. "Dokumenty o presledovanii evreev," pp. 268–69.

136. RGIA f. 1322, op. 1, d. 13, l. 70ob. Understandably, refugees took their best animals along and left the weakest beasts behind. Nikol'skii, "Bezhentsy," p. 59. But they were often obliged to dispose of their horses before continuing on their journey. The anonymous author of "Zapiska bezhentsa," *Severnyi bezhenets*, 17, 4 May 1916, p. 2, noted that horses were being sold for 15 rubles, a tenth of their value. A survey of 1,050 families conducted by the Union of Zemstvos at the front found that the number without horses had risen from 271 to 712. The number of horses at their disposal fell from 1,309 to 479. Even more dramatic was the decline in the number of cattle; only 28 cows remained, compared to 1,924 before the enemy advance. Details in *Zhizn' bezhentsev*, 5, October 1916, pp. 6–7.

137. *Russkaia mysl'*, 9, 1915, p. 126.

138. Among the peasantry of Smolensk province, the value of fixed structures (residential and farm buildings) averaged between 717 and 1,262 rubles, depending on the district. The corresponding range for the value of farm equipment went from 82 to 100 rubles per household. Kerblay, *Oeuvres choisies*, p. 86.

139. The total estimated value of peasant assets in January 1914 was 9.9 billion rubles. Vainshtein, *Narodnoe bogatstvo*, p. 403. Of course, not all refugees' assets were permanently lost.

140. *BV*, 14987, 26 July 1915; ibid., 14993, 29 July 1915.

141. *Ekaterinburgskie eparkhial'nye vedomosti*, 8, 21 February 1916, p. 62.

142. *Rech'*, 207, 30 July 1915.

143. Zubchaninov report to Stavka, 14–16 September 1915. RGVIA f. 2005, op. 1, d. 42, ll. 519–ob. This estimate includes 250,000 refugees in the southwest provinces.

144. RGVIA f. 2020, op. 1, d. 131, l. 39, Danilov to Rausch, n.d.

145. *Ukrainskaia zhizn'*, 1, January 1916, p. 93. In an interesting reflection of early usage, the Ukrainian Society for War Victims drew a distinction between three groups: (1) refugees; (2) deportees (*vyselentsy*), including lawyers, university teachers, students, doctors, and engineers; and (3) hostages (*zalozhniki*), among whom were political figures, bankers, mayors, and town councilors. RGVIA f. 13273, op. 1, d. 27, ll. 10–11ob.

146. B. M. El'tsin, in *Trudy vneocherednogo Pirogovskogo s"ezda,* p. 66.

147. Ibid., p. 66.

148. Contemporaries were well aware of the distinction. Mikhail Lemke, a correspondent attached to Stavka, observed that "*bezhenstvo* is not a well-chosen term, but it has acquired a legal form. Those who 'ran' [*bezhali*] were the propertied classes, whereas the masses were chased away by force from their farms and hearths, deprived of everything. 'Refugees' managed to bring along their capital assets, enabling them to live a new life; the forcibly displaced [*vygontsy*] crawled along with half their family, having buried the others along the way; they are empty-handed, hungry, sick." Lemke, *250 dnei,* p. 265. The fact remains that the term *bezhenets* became virtually universal.

149. *Spisok tsirkuliarov komiteta,* p. 14.

150. Shchepkin, *Bezhentsy i organizatsiia pomoshchi im,* pp. 1–2; *Ocherk deiatel'nosti Petrogradskoi oblastnoi organizatsii,* p. ix.

2. THE POLITICS OF REFUGEEDOM

1. Levine, *The Russian Revolution,* pp. 77–78, argued that "the bureaucracy had no vigor left." See also Pares, *The Fall of the Russian Monarchy,* pp. 189, 195, 219, 351, 355.

2. Florinsky, *The End of the Russian Empire,* chapter 6. Paul Miliukov asserted that "the present time is the most effective for the rebirth of all-powerful public organizations under the flag of . . . aid to war victims." Quoted in Pearson, *The Russian Moderates,* p. 25.

3. Pearson, *The Russian Moderates,* chapter 3; Hamm, "Liberal Politics"; Diakin, *Russkaia burzhuaziia,* pp. 96–109. The left Cadets temporarily dropped their demand for a government answerable to the Duma.

4. *BV,* 14979, 22 July 1915.

5. *Rech',* 200, 23 July 1915, quoting N. I. Opochnin. This followed a meeting with Zubchaninov, the recently appointed commissioner on refugees in the northwest.

6. Shcherbatov was appointed in June 1915, replacing the reactionary N. N. Maklakov. According to one scholar, the aristocratic Shcherbatov was "much more popular but also less competent" (his previous administrative experience having been confined to the director of state stud farms). Lieven, *Nicholas II,* p. 222. He lasted only four months in his post, giving way to A. N. Khvostov. Stürmer succeeded him in turn on 3 March 1916 and held office until 9 July, when he was replaced by A. A. Khvostov.

7. V. A. Bobrinskii was vice-chairman of the Nationalist fraction in the Duma (he is not to be confused with his cousin G. A. Bobrinskii, governor of occupied Galicia in 1914–15). Witte described him as "a decent but somewhat odd and unbalanced man," who had moved to the right after the revolution in the countryside during 1905–1906. Harcave, *The Memoirs of Count Witte,* pp. 60, 574fn.

8. For example, on 23 December 1915, the governor of Mogilev province ordered groups of refugees to leave the town within twenty-four hours. RGVIA f. 13273, op. 1, d. 24, l. 36.

9. These exchanges were reported in *BV,* 14981, 23 July 1915. The ministry's department was headed by A. I. Tyshkevich. For another comment on the analogy between refugeedom and *pereselenchestvo,* see N. Ezerskii, "O merakh pomoshchi bezhentsam," *Vestnik Penzenskogo zemstva,* 37, 24 September 1915, pp. 662–64.

10. Pearson, *Russian Moderates,* p. 55; Graf, "Military Rule."

11. Cherniavsky, *Prologue,* p. 40 (modified translation). This is a summary of cabinet

discussions made by A. N. Iakhontov, deputy chief of chancellery of the Council of Ministers from May 1914 until October 1916.

12. Ibid., pp. 39–40 (modified translation). The comment about a recent compromise clearly refers to the dismissal of Ianushkevich and his replacement as chief of staff at Stavka by Alekseev. RGIA f. 1276, op. 19, d. 1148, l. 2. Similar language, describing the "flood of refugees which was to inundate the entire country," is used by Levine, *Russian Revolution,* p. 76.

13. Cherniavsky, *Prologue,* p. 46. Krivoshein regarded the movements of barbarians in late antiquity as the "first migrations."

14. Ibid., p. 122. Compare the very different view he espoused in September, when he spoke of refugeedom as a purely "spontaneous phenomenon."

15. Paléologue, *La Russie des Tsars,* vol. 1, pp. 335–36.

16. *GDSO,* Session Four, 5th sitting, 14 August 1915, cols. 800–805; *Izvestiia VSG,* 19, November 1915, p. 33, reporting debates at the third congress of the Union of Zemstvos.

17. RGIA f. 1322, op. 1, d. 1, l. 4ob.

18. Katkov, *February 1917,* p. 193. Rumor had it that the grand duke had personally convinced his cousin to sign the October Manifesto in 1905.

19. For example, General Ivanov refused to allow Jewish civilians to return to their homes in the autumn of 1915. RGVIA f. 2005, op. 1, d. 42, ll. 333–ob.

20. The Union of Zemstvos was officially established on 30 July 1914, and the Union of Towns on 16 August. There was no obligation on the part of any zemstvo to join the new union, although only the notoriously conservative Kursk zemstvo refused to participate. Florinsky, *End of the Russian Empire,* p. 125.

21. Theoretically, the Red Cross had responsibility for the care of sick and wounded in the vicinity of the front, leaving the unions to concentrate on relief operations in the Russian interior, defined as east of a line drawn from Moscow through Orel to Khar'kov. But this distinction was not rigidly maintained. Miliukov, *Political Memoirs,* p. 314.

22. A. Novikov, "Zemskii soiuz na fronte," *Zhizn' bezhentsev,* 4, September 1916, pp. 5–6. The zemstvo union supplied medical and nursing staff, hospital trains, equipment, bedding, and bandages. See Gleason, "The All-Russian Union of Zemstvos," pp. 369–70.

23. During the war, the Union of Zemstvos sought a much greater role in military procurement, with the result (in Miliukov's words) that its chairman, Prince G. E. L'vov, became "a kind of Muir and Mirrelees"—a sarcastic reference to Moscow's fashionable department store. Miliukov, *Political Memoirs,* pp. 313–16.

24. In fact, Octobrists gravitated toward the Union of Zemstvos; the VSG did indeed attract many Cadet activists. Pearson, *Russian Moderates,* p. 28.

25. *Izvestiia VSG,* 17, September 1915, pp. 5–18. Of course the MVD had a duty to evacuate its staff from the frontier provinces to the Russian interior. The governor of Vilna and his staff were moved to Tula. Other administrative personnel were transferred as follows: from Grodno to Kaluga; Kovno to Vitebsk; Kurland to Iur'ev; Livland to Riga; Suwalki to Riazan'; Chelm to Kazan'; Warsaw to Petrograd; Volynia (uezd) to Zhitomir. "Spisok pravitel'stvennykh uchrezhdenii.," RGIA library file 2416.

26. Alekseev to Ivanov, 10 November 1915. RGVIA f. 2005, op. 1, d. 42, ll. 453–ob.; Ivanov to Alekseev, 3 February 1916, ibid., ll. 454–ob. The committees included village elders.

27. Danilov to Sivkin, 28 June 1915. Ibid., f. 2020, op. 1, d. 131, l. 30; Novikov, "Zemskii soiuz"; *Izvestiia VSG,* 17, September 1915, pp. 5–6. Those who had been forcibly

displaced—Jews and Germans—were not regarded as deserving of relief, either by the military or by most members of the public organizations. For general discussion of the relationship between the army and the Union of Towns and Zemstvos, see *Kratkii ocherk deiatel'nosti Vserossiiskogo Zemskogo Soiuza,* pp. 40–46.

28. *Izvestiia VSG,* 17, September 1915, p. 6. By the middle of August, M. V. Chelnokov, on behalf of the Union of Towns, was asking for 10 million rubles at once, and a monthly grant of 6 million. In January 1916 the VSG petitioned for 22 million rubles to see it through the first three months of the year. RGVIA f. 13273, op. 1, d. 16, ll. 30–31.

29. N. N. Shchepkin went to Kobrin, A. G. Meier to Orel, Kursk, and Ekaterinoslav, N. N. Polianskii to Pskov, Vitebsk, and Vilna, A. O. Bonch-Osmolovskii to Smolensk and Mogilev. N. M. Kishkin was dispatched to the southwestern front. *Bezhentsy i vyselentsy,* p. 10.

30. A summary of the conference proceedings on 30 July, with N. Shchepkin, N. Astrov, A. Meier, and S. Bakhrushin in attendance, is provided in *Izvestiia VSG,* 17, September 1915, pp. 14, 21. See also General Ivanov to Ianushkevich, 29 July 1915. RGVIA f. 2005, op. 1, d. 42, ll. 118–19.

31. *BV,* 15035, 19 August 1915, quoting A. N. Kulymanov. A representative of the Tatiana Committee also attended. The Ministry of the Interior sent along A. Tyshkevich as an observer.

32. Ivanov to Ianushkevich, 29 July 1915. RGVIA f. 2005, op. 1, d. 42, ll. 118–19.

33. George, "The All-Russian Zemstvo Union," pp. 146–48; Katkov, *February 1917,* p. 200. The tsar's own antipathy to the public organizations is well known. Lieven, *Nicholas II,* p. 216.

34. RGVIA f. 2049, op. 1, d. 447, ll. 29–29ob. See also Danilov to Ianushkevich, 25 June 1915. RGVIA f. 2020, op. 1, d. 131, ll. 20–ob.

35. As army headquarters, northern front, acknowledged in March 1916. RGVIA f. 2032, op. 1, d. 283, ll. 29–30ob.

36. Danilov to Evert, 25 March 1916. RGVIA f. 2049, op. 1, d. 447, ll. 45–46. See also ibid., f. 2020, op. 1, d. 131, ll. 20–ob., and Danilov to governors of Warsaw, Chelm, Grodno, Lomzha, Lublin, and Zhitomir, 13 July 1915. Ibid., l. 116. The army chiefs had few kind words to say about Severopomoshch' (see below). The commander of the Second Army struck a critical note toward the VSG, and advocated the creation of a single welfare agency at the front, preferably under the direction of the Red Cross. Ibid., f. 2049, op. 1, d. 447, ll. 6–7.

37. Katkov, *February 1917,* pp. 78–81. Alekseev had formerly been chief of staff on the southwestern front.

38. P. A., "Evrei v obshchestvennykh organizatsiiakh," *Evreiskaia zhizn',* 7, 14 January 1916, pp. 1–3; Ia. R., "Evrei v obshchestvennykh organizatsiiakh," ibid., 3, 22 January 1917, pp. 3–4; "Dokumenty o presledovanii evreev," pp. 248–49, 266, 272; RGVIA f. 2005, op. 1, d. 66, ll. 271–ob., editor of *Zemshchina* to Grand Duke Nikolai Nikolaevich, 22 April 1915, complaining of the "pacifist yid newspapers" promoted by the public organizations. The first and second elements were respectively zemstvo officials and elected deputies.

39. S. I. Zubchaninov's remarks on the rivalry between voluntary organizations and government are recorded in RGIA f. 1322, op. 1, d. 13, l. 69.

40. Shchepkin, *Bezhentsy,* pp. 6–8.

41. In May 1916, Boris Stürmer, the then minister of the interior, charged that "the

founders i.e. [i.e., of the unions] began work before the limits and actual permissibility of such work attracted the attention of the government." Reported in *Izvestiia VSG,* 33, June 1916, pp. 6–13. For a criticism of the public organizations along similar lines, see the remarks of Deputy Minister of the Interior N. V. Plehve, quoted in Polner, *Russian Local Government,* p. 166.

42. *BV,* 15037, 20 August 1915, quoting K. N. Anufriev.

43. *Bezhentsy i vyselentsy,* p. 2; *Izvestiia VSG,* 17, September 1915, pp. 16, 34–37, reporting on a conference held on 8 August with representatives from the Union of Towns and municipal authorities; and *Izvestiia VZS,* 28, 1 December 1915, pp. 68–69.

44. A. N. Sysin, "Rol' pravitel'stva i obshchestva v dele pomoshchi bezhentsam," *Trudy vneocherednogo Pirogovskogo s"ezda,* p. 73. Inevitably some doctors felt that the Pirogov Society should keep out of politics.

45. M. M. Shchepkin, "Pomoshch' bezhentsam," *Izvestiia VSG,* 19, November 1915, pp. 78–99, and idem, *Bezhentsy i organizatsiia pomoshchi.* Like many members of the Central Committee of the Union of Towns, Mitrofan Shchepkin belonged to the Constitutional Democrat Party (Cadets). He is not to be confused with Nikolai Shchepkin, a leading Cadet politician, who was executed by the Bolsheviks in 1919 and who also played an active part in the Union of Towns.

46. RGVIA f. 13273, op. 1, d. 64, l. 78; d. 20, ll. 91–97, questionnaire issued in November 1915, asking for information about local initiatives for refugee relief. Sobezh acted separately from the executive committees of VZS and VSG; in this respect it was similar to "Zemgor."

47. Sysin headed the public health division of Sobezh; he worked for Narkomzdrav after the Bolshevik revolution. Bakhrushin took charge of the children's division; a graduate of Moscow University's history faculty, he later became a distinguished Soviet historian. Baron Vrangel' was responsible for feeding points. Ibid., f. 13273, op. 1, d. 16, l. 2; d. 64, l. 78. The archivist who compiled the inventory to this *fond* proudly noted that Lenin's sister, N. I. Ul'ianova, worked in the subsection that handled inquiries from refugees about lost luggage, until it closed in July 1916.

48. Ibid., f. 13273, op. 1, d. 16, l. 11, journal 46 of executive committee of VZS, 15 November 1915, complaining about the actions of the special commissioner, Prince Urusov, appointed by the MVD (see below), who "sent waves of refugees along a route where nothing has been provided for them."

49. The Tatiana Committee was probably modeled after the long-established Department of Institutions of the Empress Maria, which administered several hundred charities, orphanages, hospitals, and schools. Members of the committee were appointed by Tatiana (1897–1918) in consultation with and following the approval of her mother, the Empress Alexandra Fedorovna. The main personnel included Senator Aleksei Borisovich Neidgardt (chairman), Vladimir Vasil'evich Nikitin (deputy chairman), and Vasilii Ivanovich Drury (secretary). (Drury appears to have been an American citizen.) Other members of the Central Committee included representatives from the financial and industrial community, spokesmen for Russia's national minorities, as well as representatives from the Russian Society for the Protection of Women. Four government ministers sat *ex officio*—War, Foreign Affairs, Transport, and Finance. Attendance lists are in RGIA f. 1276, op. 12, d. 1382, ll. 73–75, 407–408, and in the large volume issued in 1916 to celebrate the first fifteen months of the Tatiana Committee. *Komitet,* 1916. The first volume contains details of the Central Committee, as well as of

activities undertaken by provincial committees. A second volume listed the committee's personnel. Previous initiatives taken on behalf of the imperial family are described in Lindenmeyr, *Poverty*, pp. 75–76.

50. GARF f. 651, op. 1, d. 39, l. 11.

51. "Many categories of war sufferers have not fled their normal abode, but are in great distress on account of the war, whether inside Russia's borders or in those regions of Russia that are currently occupied by the enemy." A. B. Neidgardt, 11 October 1915. RGVIA f. 13273, op. 1, d. 37, ll. 13–14ob.

52. Thurstan, *People*, p. 105. See also RGIA f. 1284, op. 194, d. 26–1917, l. 9, for the role of the Tatiana Committee in Tula province. The committee at first did not operate throughout the empire, and the lack of a branch in the Caucasus hampered relief operations until 1916. See ibid., f. 1322, op. 1, d. 1, l. 3ob. The institutions maintained by the committee in Petrograd are listed in ibid., f. 1276, op. 12, d. 1382, ll. 52–55. For the situation in Novgorod, see *Severnyi bezhenets*, 6, 17 February 1916, p. 1.

53. *TP*, 2, 1916, pp. 152–53. Other members of the imperial royal family also lent their names to refugee relief initiatives; for example, the Dowager Empress Maria Fedorovna placed the royal train shed at Gatchina (near Petrograd) at the disposal of Polish refugees.

54. S. Andreevskii, "Kratkii ocherk bezhenskogo dvizheniia i mer," *Severnyi bezhenets*, 7, 24 February 1916, pp. 1–2. Neidgardt proudly announced that he intended to enlist the services of "priests, the nobility, civil servants, public figures, and charitable persons of either sex, and people of all faiths and nationalities." RGVIA f. 13273, op. 1, d. 37, ll. 13–14ob.

55. Neidgardt conceded that the Tatiana Committee would operate according to the principle of glasnost, but his statement did not reassure the public organizations. Ibid.

56. *Bezhentsy i vyselentsy*, pp. 2, 25. The Tatiana Committee was, for example, criticized for helping Jewish refugees in some towns but not in others.

57. Ibid., p. 40. In a conciliatory gesture, the spokesman from the ministry acknowledged that the unions should adopt a long-range view of refugee relief.

58. For a preliminary assessment by the Chief Committee of the Union of Zemstvos of the size and distribution of the refugee population, see *Izvestiia VZS*, 28, 1 December 1915, pp. 75–82.

59. The tsarist secret police concluded that "the recruitment of these people is conducted without any attempt to verify their political loyalty." Quoted in George, "The All-Russian Zemstvo Union," p. 278. The author also draws attention to the portrayal by conservative commentators of the "zemstvo hussars," who were accused of dodging the draft by finding a comfortable job with the voluntary organizations, a smear that appears not to have stuck, although Wildman, *The End of the Imperial Russian Army*, pp. 102–103, surprisingly gives some credence to this view. Other critics complained that privileged parents found jobs in Zemgor for their sons in order to evade the draft. Similar charges were leveled at Severopomoshch', the government agency for the relief of refugees at the front. See Nikol'skii, "Bezhentsy," p. 27.

60. Gleason, "The All-Russian Union of Zemstvos"; idem, "The All-Russian Union of Towns."

61. The council issued instructions to this effect on 26 November 1915, requesting provincial governors to cooperate with the Tatiana Committee. The spokesman for the Tatiana Committee, V. F. Solntsev (deputy chairman of the Registration Bureau, and an official of the MVD's statistical committee), pointed out that its officials had collected data on more than 1 million refugees since August 1915. *TP*, 1, 1916, p. 54.

62. "The Tatiana Committee, relying on local administrative agencies, has absolutely no forces at its disposal to undertake such complex statistical tasks." L'vov to Khvostov, 18 December 1915. RGIA f. 1276, op. 19, d. 1223, ll. 1–5.

63. Nikitin to L'vov, 11 October 1915. RGVIA f. 13273, op. 1, d. 37, l. 15. In a nice gesture, L'vov eventually sent some old issues of *Izvestiia VZS*.

64. For discussion of L'vov's letter in the Special Council on 6 February 1916, see RGIA f. 1322, op. 1, d. 1, ll. 209–14; *Izvestiia VZS*, 33, 15 February 1916, pp. 80–83. L'vov's position was supported in the Special Council by M. M. Fedorov. It appears that Khvostov had already made the decision at the end of November 1915, in order to prevent the unions from using registration as a pretext to enhance nationwide coordination of their activities. See *Otchet o deiatel'nosti osobogo otdela,* pp. 63–64. For the link between data collection and control of the refugee population, see the remarks in *Izvestiia VZS,* 37–38, 15 April–1 May 1916, pp. 144–48. Locally, many zemstvos and municipalities cooperated with the Tatiana Committee. In a final show of pique when (in September 1916) its own information office was closed down, Sobezh sent the Tatiana Committee a large number of boxes containing the names of 320,000 individuals who had made inquiries about missing persons and 179,000 addresses, by which time the committee had already made considerable progress along similar lines. RGVIA f. 13273, op. 1, d. 37, ll. 77–78.

65. Shchepkin, *Bezhentsy,* p. 56. Gronsky grudgingly conceded that the Tatiana Committee was "an active and energetic institution." Gronsky and Astrov, *War and the Russian Government,* p. 31.

66. *Rech',* 194, 17 July 1915; *GDSO,* Session Four, 10th sitting, 14 August 1915, cols. 795–856, for the debate on the proposed Special Council for Refugees.

67. RGIA f. 1276, op. 19, d. 1148, ll. 1–2; Goremykin to Nicholas II, 1 July 1915. RGVIA f. 2005, op. 1, d. 42, ll. 1–2. Averbakh, *Zakonodatel'nye akty,* vol. 2, pp. 721–24; *Russkoe slovo,* 162, 15 July 1915. Zubchaninov was a marshal of the nobility from Pskov. Urusov, whose base was in Ekaterinoslav, entered state service in 1885 and rose to the rank of provincial governor in 1901. RGIA f. 1276, op. 12, d. 1424, l. 3. Shcherbatov, who replaced the reactionary Maklakov on 7 July, secured the agreement of the Council of Ministers to these appointments at its meeting on 24 July. Another commissioner acted on behalf of refugees in the Caucasus. From November 1915 on, this post was held by General V. M. Tamamshev. See *Armianskii vestnik,* 6, 6 March 1916, p. 11.

68. RGIA f. 1322, op. 1, d. 13, ll. 67–69, summary of report by A. Khvostov, received by the Special Council, 3 December 1916. Zubchaninov also enlisted the help of two Duma deputies from Ekaterinoslav and Pskov (respectively G. V. Viktorov and A. I. Zarin), as well as several other men, including the MVD official E. A. Nikol'skii, whose memoirs I draw upon in what follows.

69. Urusov launched a newspaper by the name of *Iugobezhenets.* It was edited by A. Ia. Kryzhanovskii in Odessa. Thirty-six issues appeared between November 1915 and October 1916.

70. *TP,* 1, 1916, p. 50; ibid., 8, 1916, p. 270. The rivalry between Severopomoshch' and the public organizations is evident in Shchepkin, *Bezhentsy,* p. 18, and in Nikol'skii's memoirs, "Bezhentsy," pp. 27–28, where the author betrays his anti-Semitic credentials by complaining that the Union of Towns was "bursting at the seams with Jews" seeking to escape conscription. Urusov complained to the Ekaterinoslav Union of Zemstvos that it favored non-Russian (read: Jewish) refugees, by pursuing a policy of settling Russians in the countryside. See *Izvestiia VZS,* 40, 1 June 1916, pp. 103–13; *Rech',* 68, 10 March 1916.

71. *Trudy vneocherednogo Pirogovskogo s"ezda,* p. 75.

72. *BV,* 15009, 3 August 1915. One of Shcherbatov's assistants, A. I. Tyshkevich, implied that the "flexible" (i.e., arbitrary) behavior of special commissioners at the front could not be tolerated in the rear, where a "systematic" (i.e., law-governed) relief effort was required. Ibid., 15013, 8 August 1915.

73. Cherniavsky, *Prologue,* pp. 175, 182, 215–16.

74. *Osobye soveshchaniia,* pp. 47–60. The decree was issued on 30 August 1915. The statutes stipulated that anyone who had been forcibly relocated by the police could not be regarded as a refugee, thereby excluding political exiles. German colonists were also excluded from consideration. On the need to maintain diplomatic channels, in order to allow refugees to keep in touch with relatives on enemy-held territory, see RGIA f. 1291, op. 124, d. 39, ll. 7–12.

75. *BV,* 15015, 9 August 1915. A few days later, fifty-four Duma deputies appealed to the viceroy of the Caucasus to take urgent steps to alleviate the suffering of "sick, hungry, and terrorized" Armenian refugees. RGIA f. 1276, op. 5, d. 1027, ll. 4–4ob.

76. Ibid., f. 1322, op. 1, d. 1, ll. 11–12ob., Special Council, 19 September 1915. Only the first sitting of the Special Council was actually chaired by the minister, Prince Shcherbatov; subsequent sessions were chaired by his deputy, N. V. Plehve, and later by Prince V. M. Volkonskii and A. I. Pil'tse. The minister's absence from the deliberations of the Special Council resulted in a letter of protest in September 1916, signed by five of its members. Ibid., d. 13, ll. 45ob.–46ob. The recently appointed minister of the interior, A.D. Protopopov, the fourth to fill this post since the establishment of the Special Council, pleaded pressure of work.

77. Both chambers requested and were allocated a further two seats in June 1916; the state auditor also became a member at this time. Averbakh, *Zakonodatel'nye akty,* vol. 4, pp. 546–47. But a proposal by Plehve and Stishinskii to give a seat on the Special Council to each provincial governor was defeated. *UR,* 223, 14 August 1915.

78. *Osobye soveshchaniia,* para. 22. He was also entitled to co-opt refugees, although there is no evidence that this became policy. I have found no information about the person appointed to the post. Further bureaucratic initiatives followed. In October 1915, the minister of the interior appointed twelve regional plenipotentiaries, charging them with the task of "unification of the work of local authorities and organizations," including private charities. They were based in Vologda, Tver', Kostroma, Riazan', Tambov, Voronezh, Kazan', Orel, Khar'kov, Samara, Saratov, and Cheliabinsk. Most of them were ex-governors from the occupied territories, such as P. P. Stremoukhov from Warsaw, now in charge of refugee relief in Iaroslavl' and Kostroma. RGVIA f. 2032, op. 1, d. 283, ll. 20–22; *Sputnik bezhentsa,* pp. 6, 42–43; *Bezhenets,* 5, 8 November 1915.

79. The seating plan for the Special Council makes plain that their marginalization was physical as well as metaphorical. RGIA f. 1276, op. 19, d. 1148, ll. 45ob.–46.

80. By the beginning of September, the VSG and VZS received requests from local unions for financial assistance totaling 871,000 rubles, but had been able to allocate less than a tenth of this amount. *TP,* 8, 1915, p. 237. In December 1915, N. M. Kishkin informed Sobezh that the VZS executive could no longer finance the activities of local zemstvo unions. RGVIA f. 13273, op. 1, d. 16, ll. 23–24.

81. M. V. Chelnokov, mayor of Moscow and chairman of the Union of Towns, decided to stay on. *Izvestiia VZS,* 30–31, January 1916, pp. 261–62. For L'vov's resignation, see the vitriolic exchange of correspondence in ibid., 35–36, p. 339; *Izvestiia VSG,* 27–28, p. 352.

He refused to answer Neidgardt's letters seeking the cooperation of Zemgor in the process of registration of the refugee population. *Otchet o deiatel'nosti osobogo otdela,* pp. 32–35.

82. *Osobye soveshchaniia,* para. 10. In practice, many municipal councils cooperated with the provincial governor.

83. Complaints were made in September 1916 about the behavior of the governors of Kaluga and Ekaterinoslav provinces. RGIA f. 1322, op. 1, d. 13, ll. 45ob.–46ob.

84. *Bezhentsy i vyselentsy,* pp. 2–3.

85. Ibid, p. 4.

86. *TP,* 8, 1915, pp. 237–28. Bakhrushin maintained that up to 12 million refugees might eventually flee to the Russian interior. *UR,* 218, 9 August 1915.

87. "Zemstvo i bezhentsy," ibid., 234, 25 August 1915; *Izvestiia VZS,* 28, 1 December 1915, pp. 68–71. The commission advocated that the new body should collect information about the numbers of refugees and advise provincial authorities about their possible destination.

88. RGVIA f. 13273, op. 1, d. 62, l. 21.

89. V. Muizhel', "Zemskii soiuz i bezhentsy," *Zhizn' bezhentsev,* 3, September 1916, pp. 5–6.

90. I. I. Vol'skii, in *Trudy vneocherednogo Pirogovskogo s"ezda,* p. 63.

91. V. M. Bogutskii, "Mediko-sanitarnye meropriiatiia pomoshchi bezhentsam," *Izvestiia VZS,* 28, 1 December 1915, pp. 87–89; I. Dagaev, "Bezhentsy v Sibiri," *TP,* 6, 1916, pp. 11–29. See also *Izvestiia VSG,* 41–42, February–March 1917, p. 279, for a similar conclusion reached by M. Tarasenko in his survey of Siberian municipal life during 1916. By contrast, Latvian refugees found a warmer welcome among Latvian settlers in Siberia, according to *Latviesu beglu apgadasanas centralkomitejas zinojums,* 24, 1916, p. 6.

92. *TP,* 6, 1916, p. 17.

93. This point was made by Janis Zalitis in an interview for *BV,* 14995, 30 July 1915. The Union of Towns and Zemstvos also argued that the refugee question required the creation of volost guardianships (*volostnye popechitel'stva*), a sensitive claim in view of the protracted struggle before 1914 to make the case for a volost zemstvo.

94. Bogutskii, "Mediko-sanitarnye meropriiatiia."

95. Hamm, "Liberal Politics." It is, however, difficult to agree with Hamm (p. 467) that "without the Bloc the public organizations would have been hindered even more in their activities."

96. *Bezhenets,* 1, 4 October 1915. The final issue appeared on 28 December.

97. *Kratkii ocherk deiatel'nosti,* 1916, p. 46; Polner, *Russian Local Government,* pp. 161, 165–66, 176; Diakin, *Russkaia burzhuaziia,* pp. 258–60; Pearson, *Russian Moderates,* p. 126; Gleason, "The All-Russian Union of Zemstvos," p. 372.

98. The property office closed in July 1916, and its work was transferred to the Tatiana Committee. The labor exchange was shut down in the same month. The statistical office closed in December 1916. RGVIA f. 13273, op. 1, d. 16, l. 45; ibid., d. 20, ll. 206, 211, 213, 238. Sobezh itself survived until August 1918, although its surviving responsibilities for forty-five children's homes and eight children's hospitals had by then all but disappeared. An important part in the care and welfare of refugee children was played by the historian M. I. Rostovtseff. Ibid., d. 16, ll. 101–103.

99. "If the Union of Zemstvos lacks resources [for refugee relief], this is because it has pursued a passive political course up until now and has not been sufficiently aggressive in demanding funds." S. V. Ivanov to the Executive Committee of the VZS, 2 December 1916.

Ibid., l. 84. A telegram sent on 19 May 1917 from the "Committee of United Employees of the Union of Zemstvos" to L'vov, Kerenskii, and the Petrograd soviet complained about the "chaos" (*razrukha*) sown by the executive committee of the VZS, and about the hostility shown by the latter toward any attempts by employees to organize. Ibid., op. 4, d. 2, l. 100.

100. Gleason, "The All-Russian Union of Zemstvos," pp. 374–75.

101. Arkin, in *Trudy vneocherednogo Pirogovskogo s"ezda,* p. 63; Sysin, "Rol' pravitel'stva," pp. 72–75.

102. Note the view of one delegate to the third congress of the Union of Zemstvos, 7–9 September 1915, reported in *Izvestiia VSG,* 19, November 1915, pp. 32–35." "We should not think of the refugee question as a special issue; rather, it needs to be seen in broad sanitary and medical terms, although the refugee phenomenon is complicated by some of its economic features, such as concern for livestock." Most delegates disagreed with this assessment, arguing that "the refugee question was huge and exceptional in its magnitude and humanitarian implications."

103. An article in the journal of the Union of Towns concluded that the refugee movement had gradually assumed a "chronic" rather than a "spontaneous" form. Cited in *TP,* 1, 1916, p. 49.

104. Shchepkin, *Bezhentsy,* p. 19.

105. See the contrast drawn in *TP,* 6, 1916, p. 15.

106. Ibid. Compare *Izvestiia VZS,* 27, 15 November 1915, pp. 63–64, for the view that private charity should yield to state provision.

3. RESETTLEMENT AND RELIEF OF REFUGEES

1. For a list of organizations as of 11 September 1915, and the facilities they supported on the northern and western fronts, see RGVIA f. 2042, op. 1, d. 440, ll. 92–94.

2. *Spisok organizatsii.*

3. S. Bakhrushin, quoted in *Bezhentsy i vyselentsy,* p. 1. The parliamentarian Dymsha spoke of his fears of "war in the provinces" (*mestnaia voina*) when large numbers of refugees entered Russia's overcrowded towns. *GDSO,* 10th sitting, 14 August 1915, col. 807.

4. RGVIA f. 13273, op. 1, d. 24, l. 36.

5. Nikol'skii, "Bezhentsy," p. 26.

6. L. N. Iurovskii, in *Bezhentsy i vyselentsy,* p. 49.

7. RGIA f. 1322, op. 1, d. 13, ll. 69–71. For a more upbeat assessment, see *Iugobezhenets,* 1, 1 November 1915, p. 1.

8. Nikol'skii, "Bezhentsy," pp. 65–68, describes his attempts to assist up to 200,000 "hypnotized" refugees from Roslavl' to Kaluga province.

9. For their opposition to Urusov and Zubchaninov during the autumn of 1915, see *Izvestiia VSG,* 19, November 1915, pp. 32–35. Nikol'skii, however, makes no mention of obstruction by the voluntary organizations in his memoirs.

10. Quoted in *Zhizn' bezhentsev,* 7, October 1916, p. 6.

11. B. D. Brutskus, "Gde ustroit nashikh bezhentsev?" *Evreiskaia nedelia,* 18, 1915, pp. 1–14; ibid., 19, pp. 12–15.

12. Nikol'skii, "Bezhentsy."

13. Aerial attacks on refugees were reported in *BV,* 14953, 9 July 1915. They are also mentioned by Nikol'skii, "Bezhentsy," p. 54, and by E. P., Sviashchennik, *Bezhenstvo,* pp. 2–3.

Nikol'skii was disgusted by refugees who lined up for soup on arrival at their destination and proffered a chamber pot.

14. Nikol'skii, "Bezhentsy," pp. 42–43; *Bezhentsy i vyselentsy,* p. 50. For similar reports from the Caucasus, see *Armianskii vestnik,* 6, 6 March 1916, p. 10.

15. *Vestnik VOPB,* 15, 24 April 1916, pp. 11–12.

16. Ibid., 10, 6 March 1916, pp. 8–9. See also the telegram from General Orlov to Danilov, 4 August 1915, reporting that "there are no feeding points [in Bialystok]; the refugees are starving, and soon the local population will starve too." RGVIA f. 2042, op. 1, d. 438, l. 1.

17. "Sostoianie bezhentsev," *Gorizont,* 180, 12 August 1915, p. 3.

18. Paustovsky, *Slow Approach,* pp. 113, 115–16, 135–41. Paustovsky was employed as a medical orderly by the Union of Towns.

19. Igel'strom to the commander of the northern front, 23 June 1915. RGVIA f. 2020, op. 1, d. 131, ll. 46–47.

20. Knox, *With the Russian Army,* vol. 1, pp. 305, 322–23, accompanied by photographs opposite pp. 310, 330.

21. Anon., "Obshchii obzor," *Izvestiia VSG,* 29–30, April 1916, pp. 211–18.

22. Ionnisian, *Polozhenie bezhentsev v Aleksandropol'skom raione,* p. 6.

23. *Gorizont,* 185, 19 August 1915, p. 3; ibid., 194, 29 August 1915, p. 3. By late summer, 150 refugees reportedly died there each day; on some days the figure reached 400. According to one report, around 60,000 Armenian refugees died between 1915 and early 1917. *Armianskii vestnik,* 9, 26 February 1917, p. 10.

24. *Ashkhatank,* 29, 1916, p. 4; N. M. Kishkin, "Bezhenskii vopros na Kavkaze," *Izvestiia VSG,* 17, September 1915, pp. 83–89; A. A. Aganasian, "Ocherednye nuzhdy bezhentsev Vanskogo raiona," ibid., 29–30, April 1916, pp. 243–49; *Mshak,* 213, 29 September 1915, p. 3. See also Price, *War and Revolution.*

25. Quoted in Drampian, *Martiros Sergeevich Sar'ian,* p. 32.

26. P. Abelian, "Bezhentsy v Tiflise," *Armiane i voina,* 5, June 1916, p. 72; ibid., 9, November 1916, p. 128. The plight of Armenian refugees was also discussed in the Special Council on 3 October 1915. RGIA f. 1322, op. 1, d. 1, ll. 26ob.–27. The eyewitness ("Leo") is quoted by Kirakosian, *Zapadnaia Armeniia,* p. 422.

27. *Armianskii vestnik,* 9, 3 April 1916, p. 11.

28. Urusov hoped to streamline the flow of refugees, directing those from Volynia to Kursk and Ekaterinoslav; from Podol'ia to Voronezh, Samara, Saratov, and Astrakhan'; from Bessarabia to Tauride, Khar'kov, and Don oblast; leaving the Urals as a "reserve." *Iugobezhenets,* 4, 23 November 1915, p. 1.

29. *Izvestiia VZS,* 30–31, 1–15 January 1916, pp. 239–41; *UR,* 218, 9 August 1915.

30. RGVIA f. 13273, op. 1, d. 179, ll. 1–7.

31. These fears were not confined to the front. For the situation in the Urals, see *Ekaterinburgskie eparkhial'nye vedomosti,* 35, 30 August 1915, pp. 642–43; ibid., 36, 6 September 1915, p. 645 for the local Okhrana's estimate of 4 million refugees on the move. Municipal authorities sometimes responded by shrugging their shoulders and hoping the problem would go away. The mayor of Moscow, M. V. Chelnokov, at first refused to meet the desperate official who had brought more than a thousand refugees from the Polish town of Kozenitsa to Moscow. When the official—an employee of the MVD's *zemskii otdel*—threw a fit, Chelnokov relented and agreed to provide financial assistance. Nikol'skii, "Bezhentsy," pp. 19–20.

32. *Izvestiia VZS,* 21, 15 August 1915, pp. 74–75; *BV,* 14965, 15 July 1916.

33. Memorandum from MVD to provincial governors, 27 November 1915. RGIA f. 1291, op. 124, d. 39, l. 73.

34. Ibid., f. 1322, op. 1, d. 1, l. 26. From Nizhnii Tagil uezd, the chair of the zemstvo board I. Ia. Cheremnykh told his colleagues in August 1915 that 100,000 refugees were making their way to Perm' province. *Ekaterinburgskie eparkhial'nye vedomosti,* 35, 30 August 1915, pp. 642–43. Around 150,000 refugees from Volynia were expected in Ekaterinoslav, according to *Ekaterinoslavskia zemskaia gazeta,* 28 August 1915.

35. *TP,* 10, 1915, p. 468.

36. *Izvestiia VSG,* 20, December 1915, pp. 167–200.

37. Typhus continued to rage in different parts of Livland throughout the autumn and winter of 1915. Governor of Livland to E. Nikol'skii, 2 March 1916. LVVA, f. 5963, op. 1, d. 2, l. 10. Many refugees traveled east during the hot summer months of July and August, when temperatures exceeded 20 degrees Celsius in the central black earth region. The imminent arrival of autumn brought with it a sharp drop in mean temperatures in European Russia and rendered refugees vulnerable to sudden frosts.

38. Refugees who fled the fighting on the southwestern front had "kopecks in their pockets and not even a change of linen." *Izvestiia VZS,* 21, 15 August 1915, pp. 49–52. For the plight of refugees in the northwest, see *Severnyi bezhenets,* 4, 2 February 1916, p. 1. For the poor physical condition of Armenians see *Gorizont,* 182, 14 August 1915, pp. 2–3.

39. "Mobilizatsiia truda bezhentsev," *BV,* 15105, 28 September 1915. Refugees arrived in Siberia much sooner than expected. Dagaev, "Bezhentsy v Sibiri," p. 11.

40. The estimated refugee population in Ekaterinoslav appears in RGIA f. 1322, op. 1, d. 1, l. 46. For Volynia, see ibid., l. 262ob. Other data from *Izvestiia VZS,* 41–42, 15 June–1 July 1916, pp. 121–22, and RGIA f. 1291, op. 124, d. 39, ll. 4–5.

41. Ibid., f. 1285, op. 194, d. 34–1916, l. 8. More than 100,000 refugees passed through the transit point at Cheliabinsk in October alone.

42. *Izvestiia VSG,* 20, December 1915, pp. 185–86; *Bezhentsy v Tomskoi gubernii;* this reference work contains the names of 6,500 families, each listed by name, place of origin, current place of residence, and total number of dependents, as of 1 May 1916.

43. Their views were aired at the Special Council on 11 November 1915. RGIA f. 1322, op. 1, d. 1, l. 46ob. A general summary of migration during and after the war is provided by Starkov, "Pereselenie v Sibiri."

44. RGIA f. 1284, op. 194, d. 43–1916, ll. 10–13. By contrast, the governor of Dagestan oblast reported that he knew of only 127 refugees. Ibid., f. 1276, op. 17, d. 463, l. 6. In Sakhalin, refugees "praise the local climate, the abundance of timber, the fertility of the soil, and the opportunity to hunt and fish." *Iugobezhenets,* 32, 20 July 1916, p. 2.

45. Gronsky and Astrov, *War and the Russian Government,* p. 240.

46. RGVIA f. 1759, op. 4, d. 1744, ll. 1, 9, telegrams dated 12 and 25 September 1915. According to the governor, there were already 28,000 refugees in Simbirsk, in addition to 15,000 POWs and *vyslannye,* and 100,000 troops, equivalent to 30 percent of the native population.

47. RGIA f. 525, op. 2/225/2747 1916, d. 462, 13ob.–16. This kind of behavior was even more evident with respect to Jewish refugees.

48. RGIA f. 1322, op. 1, d. 16, l. 10. For remarks about the uneven distribution of refugees throughout Siberia, see *Izvestiia VSG,* 20, December 1915, p. 197.

49. *Izvestiia VZS,* 33, 15 February 1916, p. 77.

50. RGVIA f. 2042, op. 1, d. 438, l. 45; ibid., f. 2020, op. 1, d. 131, l. 6.

51. Ibid., f. 1759, op. 4, d. 1744, ll. 17, 27. Similarly, on the northern front, refugees were ordered out of Toropets in October 1915. Farmers were sent to Viatka in the Urals, Jews to Nizhnii Novgorod. Those who were prepared to pay for their own travel could go "wherever they wished," provided they kept well away from the front. Ibid., f. 2032, op. 1, d. 282, ll. 11–12.

52. Report from General M. Manakin, 24 October 1915. RGIA f. 1322, op. 1, d. 1, l. 40. The remaining 150,000 were prisoners of war.

53. Ibid., ll. 259–60, Special Council, 5 March 1916; ibid., ll. 282–86, Special Council, 19 March 1916.

54. *Izvestiia VSG,* 33–34, June 1916, p. 295.

55. Ibid., 20, December 1915, p. 235; ibid., 33–34, June 1916, p. 296. Similar steps were taken by the authorities in Moscow. See *TP,* 8, 1916, p. 267.

56. Thurstan, *People,* pp. 98–99. Elsewhere she described the tenements as "filthy, damp, and overcrowded." Thurstan papers, unpublished letter, January 1916.

57. *Izvestiia VSG,* 33–34, June 1916, pp. 297, 299–300.

58. The improved nutritional intake among soldiers and the peasantry is discussed in S. S. Demosthenov, "Food Prices," in Struve, *Food Supply,* pp. 330–31, 347–49. As they moved east, soldiers sometimes sold bread, jam, sugar, and tea to refugees. See Nikol'skii, "Bezhentsy," pp. 39–40.

59. Ibid., p. 55 (one funt is equivalent to 0. 41 kilograms). Nikol'skii makes much of his triumphs over minor bureaucrats.

60. The Russian Red Cross was active in setting up mobile canteens at the front. *TP,* 4, 1916, pp. 352–53. For another description of food offered at transit points (tea, one funt of white bread, one funt of black bread, a quarter of a funt of meat, two bowls of soup, and occasionally kasha), see *Komitet,* p. 250. RGVIA f. 2042, op. 1, d. 440, l. 127. On the lack of hot food for Armenian refugees, see *Gorizont,* 211, 22 September 1916, p. 3.

61. Offer, *The First World War,* p. 39.

62. *Ukrainskaia zhizn',* 1, January 1916, p. 100; Kazanskii, *Galitsko-russkie bezhentsy,* pp. 6, 20.

63. Prison accommodation, as well as space in a hurriedly cleaned juvenile detention center, was found in Stavropol'. Monasteries opened their doors to refugees in Kostroma, Simbirsk, and Kursk. See L'vov to Samarin, 5 August 1915. RGVIA f. 13273, op. 1, d. 24, l. 9; L'vov to the minister of justice, 5 August 1915, ibid., l. 12; *Izvestiia VSG,* 20, December 1915, pp. 172, 181–82, 184, 189. The Moscow episcopate reported that refugees were housed in monasteries and church schools. RGIA f. 796, op. 242, d. 2790, l. 21. The use of nunneries is reported in *Irkutskie eparkhial'nye vedomosti,* 21, 1 November 1915, pp. 757–58. Flour mills in the southwest are mentioned in *Izvestiia VZS,* 21, 15 August 1915, p. 50. In Riazan' province, the local hotel quickly became a permanent residence for refugees who were unable to move farther. RGIA f. 1322, op. 1, d. 36, ll. 2, 24. *TP,* 6, 1916, p. 14 noted temporary accommodation in Siberian cinemas; *Russkoe slovo,* 178, 28 July 1915, reported the accommodation of refugees in a circus in Khar'kov. For the use of synagogues, see *Evreiskaia nedelia,* 4, 14 June 1915. Not all went smoothly; Nikol'skii reports that the superior of the monastery in Roslavl' refused to allow part of his premises to be used as a temporary orphanage because it would undermine the single-sex nature of the institution. The orphans were sent to Smolensk instead. Nikol'skii, "Bezhentsy," p. 65.

64. *Izvestiia VSG,* 20, December 1915, pp. 185–86. Tomsk was twice as large as Perm'.

Deep in western Siberia, Tomsk was as distant from Perm' as Perm' was from the front. Some barracks, designed for 60 people, held up to 250 refugees: "The atmosphere is so damp and suffocating that the head begins to spin after a few minutes." *TP,* 6, 1916, pp. 11, 16, 19; *Sputnik bezhentsa,* p. 18.

65. *Izvestiia VSG,* 20, December 1915, p. 178.

66. *TP,* 1, 1916, p. 53. What this meant, apparently, is that the houses were built from door panels, with cracks filled with cinders and peat.

67. *Izvestiia VSG,* 20, December 1915, p. 174.

68. *Golos,* 232, 12 October 1915; 27, 4 February 1916, for the first reports of typhus among refugees in Iaroslavl'. For a graphic account of smallpox, see Paustovsky, *Slow Approach,* pp. 142–55. Mortality from measles among children reached 90 percent [sic] in Siberia according to Dagaev, "Bezhentsy v Sibiri," p. 14. A brief summary is provided by Sysin, "Sanitarnoe sostoianie Rossii."

69. RGIA f. 1284, op. 194, d. 26–1917, l. 9.

70. *Izvestiia VSG,* 20, December 1915, p. 168; *Ekaterinoslavskaia zemskaia gazeta,* 25 September 1915. See also RGIA f. 1322, op. 1, d. 1, l. 41ob., and Nikol'skii, "Bezhentsy," p. 85.

71. RGIA f. 1322, op. 1, d. 1, l. 260.

72. *Izvestiia VSG,* 20, December 1915, pp. 168, 196; *Iugobezhenets,* 5, 30 November 1915, p. 2; Paustovsky, *Slow Approach,* p. 51.

73. *Izvestiia VSG,* 20, December 1915, pp. 177, 196. For an instance of doctors' reluctance to admit refugees to the hospital in Riga, see LVVA f. 5963, op. 1, d. 2, l. 24.

74. RGIA f. 1322, op. 1, d. 1, l. 3ob., Papadzhanov to the Special Council for State Defense, 10 September 1915; ibid., ll. 259–60. See also *Gorizont,* 182, 14 August 1915, pp. 2–3.

75. *UR,* 213, 4 August 1915.

76. *Izvestiia KTN,* 6, 15 August 1916, pp. 6–7, reporting arrangements at the Kiev railway station: "Apart from a feeding station serving 12,000 meals daily there are temporary hostels, baths, laundry, isolation section, disinfection chamber, stores for bedding and warm clothing . . . in a word, everything that the refugee needs during the first few days after his arrival."

77. Lindenmeyr, *Poverty.* On the role of the guardianships of the poor in Siberia, see Dagaev, "Bezhentsy v Sibiri," p. 13.

78. Quoted in Akopian, *Zapadnaia Armeniia,* pp. 193–94. The Armenian press reported that "refugees are generally welcomed by the local population, who provide them with shelter and help them in any way possible, despite the poor harvest this year." *Gorizont,* 242, 28 October 1915, p. 1.

79. *Iugobezhenets,* 24, 16 May 1916, p. 1.

80. There are countless instances. For the situation in Tbilisi, see RGIA f. 1276, op. 17, d. 477, ll. 1–2. See also ibid., f. 1284, op. 194, d. 26–1917, l. 9 (Tula), and ibid., d. 38–1915, l. 10 (Kursk). This is also confirmed by the annual reports of the Russian episcopate, in RGIA f. 796, op. 442, d. 2748, ll. 18–20 (Astrakhan'), and ibid., d. 2758, ll. 46–49ob. (Perm').

81. *Izvestiia VSG,* 20, December 1915, pp. 175–76; *Ekaterinburgskie eparkhial'nye vedomosti,* 35, 30 August 1915, pp. 642–43.

82. *Simbirskie eparkhial'nye vedomosti,* 23, December 1915, p. 926.

83. *Komitet,* p. 92.

84. *Tomskie eparkhial'nye vedomosti,* 17, 1 September 1915, pp. 924–27; ibid., 3, 1 February 1916, pp. 92–93.

85. *Komitet,* p. 260.

86. *Iugobezhenets,* 1, 1 November 1915, p. 4.

87. RGIA f. 1284, op. 194, d. 34–1916, l. 8., report by governor of Ufa province, 15 February 1916. See also ibid., f. 1322, op. 1, d. 16, ll. 56–57; ibid., f. 1291, op. 124, d. 357, ll. 4–5 (governor of Samara to Plehve, 9 December 1915, noting cooperation with the Union of Zemstvos), ll. 8–14 (Kaluga) and ll. 24–27 (Poltava); *Ekaterinoslavskaia zemskaia gazeta,* 25 September 1915.

88. RGIA f. 1284, op. 194, d. 26–1917, l. 9.

89. *Izvestiia VOPB,* 1, December 1915, p. 13.

90. *Ocherk deiatel'nosti komiteta,* p. 17.

91. *Komitet,* pp. 92, 284 (Novgorod); *Ekaterinburgskie eparkhial'nye vedomosti,* 37, 13 September 1915, pp. 650–55.

92. *Irkutskie eparkhial'nye vedomosti,* 24, 15 December 1915, pp. 301–303; *Tobol'skie eparkhial'nye vedomosti,* 35, 15 September 1915, p. 440; *Tomskie eparkhial'nye vedomosti,* 17, 1 September 1915, pp. 529–31; *Saratovskie eparkhial'nye vedomosti,* 1–2, 1–11 January 1916, pp. 26–30.

93. *Vladimirskie eparkhial'nye vedomosti,* 37, 12 September 1915, pp. 745–46; *Ekaterinoslavskie eparkhial'nye vedomosti,* 10, 1 April 1916, appendix; *Ekaterinburgskie eparkhial'nye vedomosti,* 36, 6 September 1915, pp. 645–49.

94. RGIA f. 1284, op. 194, d. 32–1916, l. 4. The population of Nikolaev rose from 118,000 to 150,000 during the war. *Izvestiia VSG,* 34, July 1916, p. 190.

95. RGIA f. 1284, op. 194, d. 34–1916, l. 6; d. 45–1916, l. 10; *Trudy vneocherednogo Pirogovskogo s"ezda,* p. 79.

96. *Golos,* 175, 1 August 1915; ibid., 191, 22 August 1915.

97. Ibid., 190, 21 August 1915; *Izvestiia VSG,* 20, December 1915, p. 188; *Komitet,* p. 416.

98. *Izvestiia VSG,* 20, December 1915, p. 187. Two working-class representatives were subsequently arrested for an undisclosed reason that "did not relate to the activities of the committee."

99. *Bezhenets,* 2, 18 October 1915; *Izvestiia VZS,* 30–31, 1–15 January 1916, pp. 237–38.

100. RGIA f. 1284, op. 194, d. 45–1916, ll. 24, 86; *TP,* 8, 1915, p. 246; ibid., 10, 1915, p. 473.

101. For local lotteries, see RGIA f. 1322, op. 1, d. 16, l. 40; *Izvestiia VSG,* 20, December 1915, p. 167; *TP,* 6, 1916, p. 51 (Khar'kov); *Komitet,* p. 416 (Tver').

102. *Golos,* 221, 29 September 1915.

103. *UR,* 209, 31 July 1915; Thurstan, *People,* pp. 129–36.

104. *Izvestiia VSG,* 20, December 1915, pp. 170–71; RGIA f. 1322, op. 1, d. 1, l. 38ob.

105. *Izvestiia VSG,* 20, December 1915, pp. 170–71; *Vestnik iuga,* 27 August 1915.

106. *Izvestiia VSG,* 20, December 1915, pp. 177, 186.

107. *TP,* 3, 1916, p. 260. By the end of the year, plans were being made to evacuate some of the population, in view of the threat from advancing German troops. RGVIA f. 369, op. 1, d. 39, ll. 28–33ob.

108. *TP,* 8, 1915, p. 245; *Sputnik bezhentsa,* 6, 3–4 October 1915, p. 3.

109. *Izvestiia VZS,* 41–42, 15 June–1 July 1916, pp. 121–22; *Ekaterinoslavskaia zemskaia gazeta,* 25 August 1915; Polner, *Russian Local Government,* p. 169.

110. *Izvestiia VSG,* 34, 1916, pp. 207, 219. See also *TP,* 3, 1916, p. 259.

111. *Izvestiia VZS,* 41–42, 15 June–1 July 1916, pp. 121–22.

112. *Viatskie eparkhial'nye vedomosti,* 35, 27 August 1915, pp. 1070–73.

113. Kazanskii, *Galitsko-russkie bezhentsy,* p. 6. Compare *Bezhenets,* 6, 22 November 1915, emphasizing the public's curiosity about refugees who proved to be "valued guests and interesting conversational partners."

114. *Izvestiia VZS,* 27, 15 November 1915, p. 63.

115. *Vestnik iuga,* 11 September 1915, article by "V. S."

116. Polner, *Russian Local Government,* p. 175. No evidence of disorders is given.

117. *Izvestiia VZS,* 28, 1 December 1915, pp. 145–46.

118. K. Z., "Pechal'naia pravda o bezhentsakh," *Samarskie eparkhial'nye vedomosti,* 14, 15 July 1916, pp. 310–11.

119. *Ekaterinburgskie eparkhial'nye vedomosti,* 52, 27 December 1915, p. 882.

120. Ibid., 37, 13 September 1915, pp. 653–54.

121. *Izvestiia VSG,* 34, 1916, p. 199. See also the discussion in the Special Council on 14 September 1915, where P. I. Georgievskii argued that refugees should receive no more than 20 kopecks per diem, in view of the monthly allowance of 6 rubles given to the families of conscripts. RGIA f. 1322, op. 1, d. 1, l. 8ob.

122. *Golos,* 181, 9 August 1915; ibid., 221, 29 September 1915.

123. *Izvestiia VSG,* 20, December 1915, pp. 182 (Smolensk), 184 (Tver'). Latvian refugees in Moscow and Petersburg told a similar story, of food prices and rents that had been inflated by 50 or 100 percent.

124. *BV,* 15029, 16 August 1915.

125. "This hydra-headed monster will not easily be overcome." *BV,* 15001, 3 August 1915.

126. RGIA f. 1322, op. 1, d. 1, l. 64ob., noting several exceptions, including Volynia and Samara.

127. Testimony of a former Riga factory worker, corresponding from the Sormovo plant at Nizhnii Novgorod, quoted in Netesin, *Promyshlennyi kapital Latvii,* p. 203. For other examples see *Izvestiia VSG,* 20, December 1915, p. 187 (Tula). However, relations could sometimes take a nasty turn; Latvian workers who arrived in Moscow were often taken for Germans and, as a result, cold-shouldered by Russians on the shop floor. *Lidums,* 170, 30 June 1915.

128. *BV,* 15025, 14 August 1915.

129. M. M., "Otzyvchivyi khoziain," *Vestnik VOPB,* 3, 10 January 1916, p. 5.

130. RGIA f. 1284, op. 194, d. 45–1916, l. 10; ibid., d. 38–1915, l. 11.

131. *Irkutskie eparkhial'nye vedomosti,* 12, 15 June 1916, pp. 392–400.

132. *BV,* 15011, 7 August 1915; ibid., 15001, 3 August 1915.

133. *TP,* 6, 1916, p. 13.

134. Dagaev, "Bezhentsy v Sibiri," p. 20.

135. *Vladimirskie eparkhial'nye vedomosti,* 37, 12 September 1915, p. 746.

136. RGIA f. 1322, op. 1, d. 23, l. 2. But see below for the potential role of refugees as *Kulturträger.*

137. Thurstan, *People,* p. 142.

138. RGIA f. 1322, op. 1, d. 16, ll. 45, 60–61, 65, 67, 84.

139. *TP,* 6, 1916, p. 21.

140. *Gorizont,* 18, 24 January 1915, p. 1.

141. *Ekaterinoslavskaia zemskaia gazeta,* 25 September 1915.

142. RGIA f. 1322, op. 1, d. 16, ll. 24 (Ekaterinoslav), 27 (Akmolinsk), 31 (Iaroslavl'), 45 (Stavropol'), 48 (Volynia), 56 (Ufa), 60 (Kiev), 68 (Tula), 85 (Arkhangel'sk), and 86 (Orel). See also *Vestnik Riazanskogo gubernskogo zemstva,* 1, January 1916, p. 76.

143. RGIA f. 1322, op. 1, d. 16, l. 32 ob., letter dated 22 January 1916.

144. Ibid., ll. 20–21 (Enisei province), 24 (Ekaterinoslav), 27 (Akmolinsk), 32 (Mogilev); *Iugobezhenets,* 1, 1 November 1915, p. 4.

145. "Iz zapisok krest"ianina," *Ezhemesiachnyi zhurnal literatury,* 3, March 1916, pp. 231–41. The role of the village assembly is emphasized in *Iugobezhenets,* 2, 9 November 1915, p. 1.

146. *TP,* 6, 1916, p. 21.

147. Cherniavsky, *Prologue,* p. 57. A pessimistic account of the treatment of deported Jews is given in "Iz 'chernoi knigi,'" pp. 243–44, although the author detected some warmth in the response of local people in Voronezh.

148. Graf, "Military Rule," p. 402, simply repeats Iakhontov's record of statements made by Minister of the Interior Shcherbatov to his cabinet colleagues. In his important study of modern refugee movements, Aristide Zolberg maintains that "these unwelcome strangers [i.e., Jews and Volga Germans] were usually set upon by the local population." Zolberg, *Escape from Violence,* p. 286. But he provides no evidence.

149. During the Russo-Turkish War of 1877–78, for example, Jewish merchants were accused of having profited from the war. Peasants suffered from a shortage of work and food, and sometimes pinned the blame on Jewish "profiteers." Hans Rogger, "Conclusion and Overview," in Klier and Lambroza, *Pogroms,* p. 333.

150. Shcherbatov's doubts were disputed by the eminent Jewish economist and public figure M. Fridman, who cited reports of amicable relations between peasants and Jews in Voronezh and Tambov provinces. *BV,* 14983, 24 July 1915; ibid., 14997, 31 July 1915; ibid., 15025, 14 August 1915.

151. *Bezhenets,* 9–10, 28 December 1915. A pronounced strand of anti-Semitism never-theless remained. In May 1916, Russian peasants in Nizhnii Novgorod petitioned the gover-nor to remove Jewish refugees from the village, on the grounds that they were "unsuited for agricultural work." He was asked to supply Christian workers instead. *Evreiskaia zhizn',* 19, 8 May 1916, p. 34.

152. *Izvestiia VSG,* 20, December 1915, p. 178.

153. *Iugobezhenets,* 3, 16 November 1915, p. 1; ibid., 4, 23 November 1915, p. 1. The central government appears to have set a limit of 10 percent on the proportion of refugees in any given province. See RGVIA f. 1759, op. 4, d. 1744, ll. 4–5.

154. *Izvestiia VSG,* 33–34, June 1916, p. 296.

155. "Materialy po voprosu ob evakuatsii," RGIA library, file 2416.

156. RGIA f. 1322, op. 1, d. 1, l. 51ob.

157. Ibid., d. 13, ll. 55–57, Special Council, 15 September 1916; *Izvestiia VSG,* 33–34, June 1916, pp. 296–97, noting opposition from Neidgardt and Senator A. S. Skirmunt, as well as from the Petrograd office of the Union of Towns.

158. RGIA f. 1322, op. 1, d. 1, l. 8ob., Special Council, 14 September 1915. Pavel Ivanovich Georgievskii, a former professor of political economy at St. Petersburg University, headed the statistical section of the MVD.

159. RGIA f. 1322, op. 1, d. 1, l. 192, 195–200; ibid., d. 13, ll. 10–18ob., approved by Khvostov on 2 March 1916. See also the comments of the governor of Tver' to uezd zemstvo boards, 4 November 1915. RGIA f. 1291, op. 124, d. 39, ll. 18–19.

160. Spending totaled 125 million rubles in 1915, 265 million rubles in 1916, and 216 million rubles in 1917 (to 15 October). GARF f. 3333, op. 2, d. 1a, l. 51. Zubchaninov spent around 60 million rubles before his organization (Severopomoshch') was closed down at the beginning of 1917; on behalf of Iugopomoshch', Urusov spent around 36 million rubles. *TP,* 1, 1917, p. 48. The amount spent by the Tatiana Committee (mid-September 1914 to 1 April 1917) was put at 76.2 million rubles, of which 68.2 million came from government grants and the remainder from donations. *Izvestiia KTN,* 20, 15 May 1917, p. 3. The commissioner for Armenian refugees estimated that the government had spent 25 million rubles on their welfare up to October 1916. *Gorizont,* 231, 16 October 1916, p. 1.

161. *Rossiia v mirovoi voine,* p. 98.

162. *TP,* 8, 1916, pp. 265–66, 270–71.

163. RGVIA f. 2042, op. 1, d. 446, ll. 10–12.

164. *Izvestiia VSG,* 20, December 1915, p. 193 (Ekaterinoslav), for details of the financial help available.

165. *Komitet,* p. 454.

166. *Lidums,* 206, 2 August 1915, reporting official attempts to evict Latvian refugees from Samara and Voronezh, on the grounds that they were German settlers.

167. "This is not playing at charity, but a purely Christian act," in the words of a priest from Simbirsk. *Simbirskie eparkhial'nye vedomosti,* 19, October 1916, pp. 502–503.

4. CONSOLIDATING REFUGEEDOM

1. For a reference to compassion fatigue—"the benefactor has become exhausted"—and the need for additional state funding, see *Komitet,* p. 14.

2. *BV,* 14965, 15 July 1915. Compare the comment in *Rech',* 207, 30 July 1915, where a visit to the refuge on Angliiskii prospekt in Petrograd revealed people of "the most diverse condition and status [*sostoianie*], now united by the single general term—'refugees.'"

3. "The business of helping the refugees was transferred from the sphere of charity to that of state support for the daily needs of its citizens." *Komitet,* p. 13. But the state devolved the task of refugee relief onto local authorities and voluntary organizations, all of which could ultimately function only on the basis of public support.

4. *Rech',* 214, 6 August 1918.

5. *Tul'skie eparkhial'nye vedomosti,* 37, 1 October 1915, pp. 504–506; *Vladimirskie eparkhial'nye vedomosti,* 39, 26 September 1915, pp. 797–99. This was evidently a coordinated appeal by the Church authorities.

6. Gourko, *Memories,* p. 124. According to Evgenii Nikol'skii, "Whoever has not been with the mass of refugees who traveled across the Pinsk marshes cannot imagine the sufferings of these unfortunate people." Nikol'skii, "Bezhentsy," p. 43. For a Latvian echo, see *Zinojums,* 51, 22 December 1916.

7. Ionnisian, *Polozhenie bezhentsev v Aleksandropol'skom raione,* pp. 14–15. In a similar

vein, a correspondent wrote, "Refugees! No one who has seen them can utter this word calmly. . . . One morning I shook uncontrollably and could not prevent tears from streaming down my cheeks." S. Aslan'iants, "Bezhentsy: lichnye vpechatleniia," *Armianskii vestnik,* 6, 6 March 1916, p. 10; ibid., 9, 3 April 1916, pp. 10–11.

8. "Dva begstva," *Rodina,* 1, 3 January 1916, p. 5. For the prevalence of biblical analogies likening Hutu refugees to Israelites see Malkki, *Purity and Exile,* pp. 113, 228–29.

9. "Jewish Refugees in a Wood on the Outskirts of Vilna" and "Latvian Refugees in Courland on the Outskirts of Riga," both printed in *Sinii zhurnal,* 39, 26 September 1915, p. 7. "Refugee Types" appear in *Izvestiia KTN,* 11, 1 November 1916, p. 7.

10. *Sinii zhurnal,* 33, 15 August 1915, p. 12; *Zhizn' bezhentsev,* 3, September 1916, p. 3.

11. *Armiane i voina,* 11–12, January–February 1917, p. 160, for photos from Bitlis, "Dante's Hell."

12. *Armianskii vestnik,* 8, 19 February 1917, p. 20.

13. There are around a dozen photographs of refugees in *Letopis' voiny.* See, in particular, no. 71, 24 December 1915, p. 1131, and no. 91, 14 May 1916, p. 1449. Photographs of the registration process were published in ibid., no. 53, 22 August 1915, p. 845. Most of the photographs were taken by Aleksandr Bulla and Iakov Shteinberg.

14. *Iugobezhenets,* 10, 12 January 1916; *Izvestiia KTN,* 4, 15 July 1916; ibid., 6, 15 August 1916; ibid., 18, 15 February 1917.

15. *Golos,* 237, 17 October 1915, letter signed "Do-na"; Krueger, *Die Flüchtlinge.* See also the comments in Harrell-Bond, *Imposing Aid,* p. 371; and Benthall, *Disasters.*

16. *Golos,* 240, 21 October 1915.

17. *Izvestiia VSG,* 20, December 1915, pp. 186–87.

18. *Zhizn' bezhentsev,* 1, September 1916, p. 1.

19. *Sputnik bezhentsa,* 5, 1–2 October 1915, p. 3.

20. *Vestnik VOPB,* 19, 22 May 1916, pp. 14–15. A shorter appeal to trace the 14-year-old daughter of Pamfil Lukashchuk—originally from a village in Volynia, last seen in Ekaterinoslav on train no. 30 (destination unknown)—appeared in *Ekaterinoslavskaia zemskaia gazeta,* 10 November 1915.

21. *Vestnik VOPB,* 12, 20 March 1916, p. 10.

22. *BV,* 14987, 26 July 1915.

23. For an example from Smolensk, see *Izvestiia VSG,* 20, December 1915, p. 183.

24. *Mshak,* 78, 16 April 1915, p. 4; ibid., 267, 3 December 1915, p. 3.

25. RGIA f. 525 op. 2/225/2747, 1916, d. 427, ll. 142–43. The program for this concert (12 January 1916) included a beautiful watercolor depicting the flight of refugees. The Tatiana Committee auctioned priceless porcelain donated by the imperial factories. Ibid., l. 50. A few days earlier, a grand celebration had taken place in the Mariinskii Theater, where the famous ballerina Matil'da Ksheshinskaia (1872–1971) performed national dances and scenes from Tchaikovsky's *Eugene Onegin.* (These entertainments were lent a certain piquancy by the fact that Ksheshinskaia had been Nicholas II's mistress before his marriage to Alexandra.) Fireworks and a lottery capped the evening. Tatiana and her mother, Empress Alexandra, donated some of their own handicrafts in order to raise money. Ibid., f. 1276, op. 12, d. 1382, ll. 57–62.

26. Ten issues of *Bezhenets* appeared between early October and the end of December 1915, under the editorship of D. G. Muntianov. For *Severnyi bezhenets* (34 issues appeared between 12 January and 31 August 1916), published by the Novgorod branch of the Tatiana

Committee, see *Komitet,* pp. 259, 283, where it is described as operating according to the principle of "complete glasnost." *Vestnik Vserossiiskogo obshchestva popecheniia o bezhentsakh* announced its arrival in December 1915 as "an organ that will allow refugees to speak to one another, to express their needs and wishes, and to help find one another in this immense land of ours." *Vestnik VOPB,* 1, December 1915, pp. 1–2. *Iugobezhenets* served largely as the official organ for Prince Urusov, although it carried notices of missing persons. It contained none of the stories, reminiscences, poems, and diverse material found in other newspapers. *Sputnik bezhentsa* enjoyed a shorter life; just six issues appeared in September and October 1915, selling at 10 kopecks and with a print run of around 2,600. The editor complained in the final issue that *Russkoe slovo* had run a vendetta against what it termed a "superfluous" paper.

27. *Saratovskie eparkhial'nye vedomosti,* 1–2, 1–11 January 1916, p. 26; see also *Izvestiia VZS,* 29, 15 November 1915, pp. 61, 63.

28. RGIA f. 1322, op. 1, d. 1, l. 2, Zubchaninov to Special Council, 10 September 1915; Smirnov-Kutacheskii, "Bezhentsy-galichane."

29. A. A. Isaev, "Bezhentsy na staroi i novoi osedlosti," *UR,* 234, 25 August 1915; Starkov, "Pereselenie v Sibiri," pp. 29–37; *Vestnik Penzenskogo zemstva,* 37, 24 September 1915, pp. 662–64 (N. Ezerskii).

30. *BV,* 14985, 25 July 1915.

31. Gronsky and Astrov, *War and the Russian Government,* p. 231. For collective departures (including references to refugees' *zemliachestva*), see *TP,* 10, 1915, p. 469; *Severnyi bezhenets,* 17, 4 May 1916, p. 2; and *Zhizn' bezhentsev,* 4, September 1916, pp. 8–9, where the author comments on the wealthy "substratum" of refugees who quickly threw in their lot with fellow villagers during the long march eastward.

32. *Bezhentsy i vyselentsy,* p. 51; Neuberger, *Hooliganism,* pp. 8, 66.

33. RGVIA f. 13273, op. 1, d. 39, ll. 2–3, Wladyslaw Grabski, on behalf of the Central Committee for the Provinces of Russian Poland, to the VZS, 11 September 1915.

34. RGIA f. 1322, op. 1, d. 1, l. 65. Nikol'skii, "Bezhentsy," p. 25, described the situation in Chelm province, suggesting that once they reached Roslavl', the priests abandoned their flock and ran off. Russian suspicion of Catholic priests had a long pedigree.

35. RGIA f. 1322, op. 1, d. 1, l. 288ob., Special Council, 26 March 1916. Other kinds of community also remained intact. The renowned orchestra sponsored by the Warsaw Fire Service reconstituted itself in Moscow, where its reputation for a fine sound and disciplined playing commended itself to a new audience. *UR,* 211, 2 August 1915.

36. *Vestnik Riazanskogo gubernskogo zemstva,* 1, January 1916, p. 71.

37. Thurstan, *People,* p. 108; Nikol'skii, "Bezhentsy," p. 52; Paustovsky, *Slow Approach,* p. 128, described "a mob of hungry refugees battling its way to the stew pots. . . . Men were tearing the bowls from each other's hands, women shoving greyish bits of hot stewed pork into babies' mouths." The government perspective is given in RGIA f. 1276, op. 12, d. 1411, ll. 1–4.

38. *Golos,* 242, 23 October 1915; Thurstan, *People,* p. 163.

39. Polner, *Russian Local Government,* p. 162.

40. The Union of Zemstvos urged the need for "planning," but maintained that regulations for refugee resettlement should be implemented "in a flexible and elastic manner, free from the superfluous formalism of administrative practice." *Izvestiia VZS,* 37–38, 15 April–1 May 1916, p. 144.

41. See Levine, *The Russian Revolution,* p. 76, for one of many contemporary descriptions, and the additional comments in Hutchinson, *Politics and Public Health,* pp. 117–20. The incidence of highly infectious diseases (cholera, dysentery, measles, scarlet fever) among refugees was put at between 1 and 4 percent in Petrograd and Moscow. Cholera generated high mortality, reaching 37 percent during the second half of 1915. Mortality rates among Jewish refugees reached 47 per thousand, compared to a prewar rate of between 15 and 21. *Trudy vneocherednogo Pirogovskogo s"ezda,* pp. 75, 79, 83.

42. P. I. Fedorov, "Bezhentsy v Sibiri," *Izvestiia VSG,* 31–32, May 1916, pp. 250–73.

43. RGIA f. 1284, op. 194, d. 37–1916, l. 10ob.

44. *BV,* 14987, 26 July 1915. The party of Gypsies had traveled from Tukums, a small town 50 kilometers west of Riga.

45. *Izvestiia VZS,* 21, 15 August 1915, p. 76.

46. *Iugobezhenets,* 5, 30 November 1915, p. 2. Doctors in Moscow maintained that fewer than 5 percent of refugees who settled in the city suffered from serious infectious disease, such as measles, dysentery, and scarlet fever. But mortality levels were high among those affected. *Trudy vneocherednogo Pirogovskogo s"ezda,* pp. 75–76.

47. *Severnyi bezhenets,* 3, 26 January 1916, p. 2. For the situation in Kiev in the autumn of 1915, see *Ukrainskaia zhizn',* 10, October 1915, pp. 101–102. There is a biographical portrait of Whittemore in the *Dictionary of American Biography.* Whittemore was a "man of independent means," whose greatest triumph was his work on the mosaics of Santa Sophia in Constantinople, which he carried out with the approval of Kemal Atatürk, no less. Whittemore appears as "X" in Graham Greene's story "Convoy to West Africa," and as "Professor W." in Evelyn Waugh's account of the coronation of Emperor Haile Selassie, in *When the Going Was Good.* His portrait was painted more than once by Henri Matisse, a personal friend.

48. See also *Iugobezhenets,* 5, 30 November 1915, p. 1. For the desperate situation in Livland, see LVVA f. 5963, op. 1, d. 2, l. 10.

49. RGIA f. 525, op. 2, d. 437, ll. 177–82; f. 1276, op. 12, d. 1382, ll. 114–20. Extracts of his report were published in *Izvestiia VSG,* 29–30, 1916, pp. 326–30. "Dry infection" was Whittemore's preferred method for dealing with lice; "fleck typhus" could be prevented by inoculation.

50. Thurstan, *People,* pp. 53, 55.

51. *Armianskii vestnik,* 9, 26 February 1917, p. 10. Erzerum had been captured in February 1916.

52. *TP,* 6, 1916, pp. 14–15.

53. Knox, *With the Russian Army,* vol. 1, p. 323.

54. Hutchinson, *Politics and Public Health,* pp. 121–32.

55. *Izvestiia VZS,* 28, 1 December 1915, pp. 87–89; *Trudy vneocherednogo Pirogovskogo s"ezda,* pp. 75–6.

56. Doctors did not confine themselves to the physical condition of refugees. Delegates to the extraordinary congress of the Pirogov Society in April 1916 complained about the "exploitation" to which refugees were subject by unscrupulous employers. Ibid., p. 76.

57. The Tatiana Committee also relied on medical and nursing personnel, who did not necessarily share the views of, and certainly did not come from the same background as, the Central Committee in Petrograd. *Izvestiia KTN,* 2, 15 June 1916, p. 10.

58. E. P., Sviashchennik, *Bezhenstvo,* p. 3. For an eyewitness account, see Nikol'skii,

"Bezhentsy," p. 40. Similar concerns about the psychological consequences of abrupt displacement were voiced by a congress of public organizations in Khar'kov in November 1915. RGVIA f. 13273, op. 1, d. 62, l. 21.

59. *Izvestiia VSG,* 20, December 1915, p. 172; Nikol'skii, "Bezhentsy," p. 42.

60. A. I. Khatisov, "Poezdka po mestam," *Izvestiia VSG,* 17, September 1915, pp. 90–95.

61. Thurstan, *People,* p. 6. In an unpublished letter (dated January 1916) she described a visit to a "lunatic asylum" in Moscow, where a hundred refugees had gone "mad from the strain and want of food." Thurstan papers.

62. N. M-skii, "Bezhentsy," *Golos,* 203, 5 September 1915. Compare the remarks in Harrell-Bond, *Imposing Aid,* pp. 284–89, noting the neglect of mental health issues in refugee studies.

63. The objections were raised by the well-known geographer V. P. Semenov Tian-Shanskii. The deal that Bekhterev eventually struck with the Tatiana Committee stipulated that 10 percent of the beds might be occupied by private patients. RGIA f. 1276, op. 12, d. 1382, ll. 135ob., 187–88, 340–41.

64. *Izvestiia VSG,* 20, December 1915, p. 180, on refugees' refusal to be separated; Thurstan, *People,* pp. 98–99.

65. RGIA f. 1322, op. 1, d. 1, l. 3, Special Council, 10 September 1915.

66. *UR,* 202, 24 July 1915.

67. GAIaO f. 485, op. 1, d. 1182.

68. "Spisok detei bezhentsev," March 1916. RGVIA f. 1759, op. 4, d. 1780, ll. 3–38. In February 1917 the Tatiana Committee celebrated the fact that it had successfully dealt with the 500,000th request for help. *Vestnik VOPB,* 49–50, 12 February 1917, p. 9. "From all corners of Russia, we have received the most moving expressions of joy and gratitude." See also *Otchet o deiatel'nosti osobogo otdela,* p. 4, where the committee reminded its readers that it fulfilled not only "charitable," but also "state" responsibilities.

69. M. F. Zamengof, "Brak, sem'ia, i prestupnost'," *Zhurnal Ministerstva iustitsii,* 2, 1916, pp. 143–74. For examples of this discourse in prewar Russia, and for other perceived causes of criminal activity, see Neuberger, *Hooliganism,* pp. 181–98, 204–209. Implicit in the statements of other commentators was a belief that population displacement on this scale would also undo the positive effects of prohibition. M. Figurin, "Ob umenshenii prestupnosti za vremia voiny i o vozmozhnykh prichinakh etogo," *Zhurnal Ministerstva iustitsii,* 3, 1916, pp. 181–98. For evidence that Latvian refugees in Siberia had taken to drinking cheap substitutes for alcohol, see *TP,* 1, 1916, pp. 59–60. Education in the dangers of drink was regarded as the chief weapon in the struggle against alcohol abuse.

70. S. Bakhrushin, "Bor'ba s detskoi prestupnost'iu v sviazi s voinoiu," *Izvestiia VSG,* 29–30, 1916, pp. 54–65. Some urban centers had virtually been taken over by children, as in Irkutsk, where two-fifths of the population was believed to be under the age of 14 by the beginning of 1916. Fedorov, "Bezhentsy v Sibiri," p. 262. The subsequent treatment of *besprizorniki* is described by Ball, *And Now My Soul Is Hardened.*

71. RGIA f. 1322, op. 1, d. 1, l. 17ob.

72. Ibid., f. 1276, op. 12, d. 1382, ll. 252ob.–253, memorandum from Neidgardt to local committees, 7 March 1916. *Izvestiia KTN,* 6, 15 August 1916, p. 7, reports on the activities of the Kiev branch of the League for the Protection of Children and the local Froebel Society, noting that the refuge boasted facilities corresponding to "the latest demands of hygiene." Similar views are expressed by P. Spasskii, "Bor'ba s detskoi prestupnost'iu," *Severnyi*

bezhenets, 8, 2 March 1916, p. 1; ibid., 9, 9 March 1916, p. 1. Spasskii advocated a good dose of military instruction as well as hard work.

73. *Izvestiia KTN,* 10, 15 October 1916, pp. 14–15, for a detailed description of several such colonies in Voronezh, where the children had "a hale and healthy appearance." Orphanages were also established under the aegis of Severopomoshch'. *Zhizn' bezhentsev,* 9, October 1916, pp. 6–9; 10, November 1916, pp. 5–8.

74. *Izvestiia VSG,* 20, December 1915, p. 172.

75. P. Spasskii, "Sel'skie priiuty-iasli," *Severnyi bezhenets,* 10, 16 March 1916, pp. 1–2; *Izvestiia KTN,* 10, 15 October 1916, p. 14–15.

76. *Irkutskie eparkhial'nye vedomosti,* 18, 15 September 1916, pp. 606–15; ibid., 21, 1 November 1916, pp. 720–23. The text used in the seminary was *Mir bozhii* ("God's world") by Grechushkin.

77. Graham, *Russia,* p. 52.

78. *Kratkii obzor deiatel'nosti Pribaltiiskogo Latyshskogo komiteta,* p. 2.

79. *Golos,* 181, 9 August 1915.

80. *Izvestiia VZS,* 21, 15 August 1915, pp. 50–51.

81. *Komitet,* p. 421.

82. *Vestnik VOPB,* 2, 3 January 1916, p. 3.

83. *Golos,* 237, 17 October 1915.

84. *Moskovskie vedomosti,* 234, 11 October 1915. Other newspapers frequently lampooned refugees with pretensions to privileged accommodation or treatment. See *BV,* 14987, 26 July 1915.

85. *Moskovskie vedomosti,* 240, 18 October 1915. The correspondent concluded by suggesting that Poland would be a wealthy country after the war, given the cash that Russian soldiers had spent on visits to prostitutes.

86. The author mentioned Nizhnii-Novgorod and Irkutsk as towns where this had happened. Iu. V-n, "Bezhentsy i begletsy," *Vestnik iuga,* 1 September 1915.

87. Quoted in Kochakov, "Petrograd," p. 948.

88. Elsewhere she deployed this language to appeal for continued financial help from British aid donors to Russian and Polish support workers. Refugees served to cement international friendship and cooperation. Thurstan, *People,* pp. 24–25, 74–82.

89. *Zhizn' bezhentsev,* 7, October 1916, p. 1.

90. *Sputnik bezhentsa,* 2, 24–25 September 1915, p. 1.

91. "The refugee is not a tramp, is not an object of private or public charity, but is a citizen who bears a heavy burden for his country." *Bezhenets,* 6, 22 November 1915.

92. *Zhizn' bezhentsev,* 9, October 1916, p. 12. These sentiments were echoed by the town council of Velikie Luki, which opposed attempts to force refugees out of the town in the autumn of 1915: "Refugees are children of our motherland [*rodina*]." RGVIA f. 2032, op. 1, d. 282, ll. 33–37.

93. *Vestnik VOPB,* 40–41, 23–30 October 1916, p. 16.

94. The minutes of the Special Council for Refugees refer on one occasion to the need to preserve the health of refugee-"citizens" (*grazhdane*). See the comments made by A. I. Lykoshkin on 27 December 1916. RGIA f. 1322, op. 1, d. 13, l. 94ob.; *Komitet,* p. 13.

95. RGVIA f. 13273, op. 1, d. 32, ll. 28, 29. The entire file is filled with such petitions.

96. Zygmunt Bauman offers a rewarding discussion of this term in *Modernity and Ambivalence,* pp. 141–43.

97. RGIA f. 1322, op. 1, d. 16, l. 45, report dated 3 February 1916.

98. *Golos,* 173, 30 July 1916. Refugees from the Baltic were thought likely to be able to teach Russian peasants superior farming methods. But this proves the point. Refugees would bring wisdom from without; it was their very distinctiveness that allowed them to fulfill this role.

99. *BV,* 14983, 24 July 1915.

100. *TP,* 6, 1916, p. 12.

101. GAIaO f. 485, op. 1, d. 1179, l. 6; ibid., d. 1175, l. 43. Further evidence of poor conditions in central Asia, where refugees from Minsk, Grodno, Volynia, and Chelm vied with prisoners of war for living space in railway wagons, will be found in RGIA f. 1322, op. 1, d. 1, l. 40 and l. 260.

102. *Izvestiia Kostromskogo gubernskogo zemstva,* 10, September 1916, p. 21.

103. *Golos,* 250, 3 November 1916.

104. GAIaO f. 485, op. 1, d. 1181, l. 2, letter dated 22 August 1915.

105. *Golos,* 95, 27 April 1916.

106. LVVA f. 5963, op. 1, d. 2, l. 24. Zubchaninov discovered that this was not the first time that this doctor had sought to deter refugees from using the facilities of his ward.

107. The case concerned one Shanduro, who had been beaten up by a drunken policeman on the streets of the city. The policeman was subsequently found guilty of criminal assault. Having been discharged, he became liable for military service. See *Golos,* 48, 25 February 1916, and ibid., 54, 6 March 1916.

108. *Vestnik VOPB,* 1, December 1915, p. 13.

109. *Golos,* 73, 30 March 1916.

110. *Izvestiia VSG,* 20, December 1915, p. 181.

111. *Osobye soveshchaniia,* p. 47.

112. RGIA f. 1322, op. 1, d. 1, l. 27ob., Special Council, 3 October 1915. The availability of Russian citizenship is discussed in the context of resettling refugees from Galicia in Siberia. See *Izvestiia VZS,* 21, 15 August 1915, p. 74.

113. Skran, *Refugees,* p. 102.

114. *Izvestiia VSG,* 20, December 1915, p. 175. On the other hand, church authorities were willing to conduct marriage ceremonies between refugees with a minimum of fuss. *Iugobezhenets,* 16, 27 February 1916, p. 2.

115. RGIA f. 1322, op. 1, d. 1, l. 18ob., Special Council, 26 September 1915.

116. For an example from Orel, see *Izvestiia VSG,* 20, December 1915, p. 195.

117. On behalf of Severopomoshch', Nikol'skii asked several thousand refugees encamped in Roslavl' how they felt about their predicament. Two percent described themselves as "happy"; they presumably wished to ingratiate themselves with their interlocutor. The Tatiana Committee undertook a much more ambitious scheme in early 1917 (see below). But this was designed to create a public record of refugee experiences, not to encourage their systematic participation in relief. Siberian officials and relief workers decided to promote the resettlement of refugees in the countryside "only with the agreement of refugees themselves," but this hardly amounted to a fundamental change in attitude. *TP,* 6, 1916, pp. 15–16.

118. *Trudy vneocherednogo Pirogovskogo s"ezda,* p. 62.

119. *Izvestiia VSG,* 20, December 1915, p. 200 (Khar'kov); Gronsky and Astrov, *War and the Russian Government,* p. 237.

120. See the report of the governor of Akmolinsk in RGIA f. 1322, op. 1, d. 16, ll. 26–27.

121. M. Ganfman, "Zakonodatel'stvo," *Ezhegodnik gazety Rech'*, p. 497. This is one of the earliest published uses of the abstract noun *bezhenstvo*. It reappears in *Izvestiia VSG*, 20, December 1915, p. 192. The government eventually established an interdepartmental commission under the deputy minister of war, General Frolov, in order to discuss compensation terms for those whose property had been requisitioned or destroyed by military action. See RGIA f. 1322, op. 1, d. 13, l. 44, Special Council, 1 September 1916.

122. Neidgardt, speaking to the Special Council, 30 December 1916. Ibid., l. 90.

123. Nonetheless, some liberal-minded observers pointed out that there were many *vyselentsy* (Jews and Poles) who languished in Siberia without the right to move and with little material support. In mid-1916, the governor of Poltava decided that Galician *vyselentsy* should henceforth be regarded as "refugees," provided they were not POWs and not under police surveillance. *Ukrainskaia zhizn'*, 2, February 1916, pp. 101–103; ibid., 7–8, July–August 1916, p. 116.

124. *Komitet,* p. 457.

125. *TP,* 6, 1916, pp. 17–18.

126. RGIA f. 1322, op. 1, d. 1, l. 282, P. P. Meyer to Special Council, 19 March 1916. Similar ideas were mooted in Enisei province, according to *Ukrainskaia zhizn'*, 2, February 1916, pp. 101–103. Prince Urusov proposed that the farms of German and Austrian settlers be handed to refugees. *TP,* 4, 1916, p. 356.

127. Ibid., 8, 1916, p. 269.

128. F. I. Veinberg, Special Council, 17 October 1915. RGIA f. 1322, op. 1, d. 1, l. 33ob.

129. *Izvestiia VSG,* 20, December 1915, p. 194.

130. Ibid., 33–34, June 1916, pp. 297–300; *Irkutskie eparkhial'nye vedomosti,* 22, 15 November 1915, p. 799.

131. RGIA f. 1322, op. 1, d. 1, l. 287ob., Special Council, 26 March 1916, discussing a petition from the "Russian People's Council of Carpathian Rus'." However, Belorussian refugees who settled in central Asia found conditions extremely difficult. *TP,* 4, 1916, pp. 357–58.

132. Thurstan, *People,* p. 94.

133. *Simbirskie eparkhial'nye vedomosti,* 19, October 1916, pp. 502–503.

134. *Spisok tsirkuliarov,* pp. 51–52.

135. Thurstan, *People,* p. 135. For other reports of student activity, including entertainment put on for refugees, see *Golos,* 227, 6 October 1915; *Izvestiia VSG,* 20, December 1915, pp. 180–81 (Saratov).

136. *Komitet,* p. 243; *Studenty—bezhentsam,* 24 August 1915, containing poems and stories from students in Rostov and Nakhichevan, as well as a brief and rather unrevealing report about students' attitudes to the war.

137. *Gimnazisty—bezhentsam,* 8 November 1915, p. 1.

138. First mentioned at the committee meeting on 21 September 1916. RGIA f. 1276, op. 12, d. 1382, ll. 387–90. See also *TP,* 9, 1916, pp. 393–94; *Zinojums,* 51, 22 December 1916. The exhibition was scheduled to open in April, although it never actually took place.

139. *Izvestiia KTN,* 17, 1 February 1917, p. 10; *TP,* 10, 1916, p. 512, where this initiative was seen as a contribution to "the history of war in general as well as to a representation of refugee displacement [*peredvizhenie*], life, and labor."

140. *Armianskii vestnik,* 8, 19 February 1917, pp. 19–21.

141. *Zinojums,* 51, 22 December 1916; Olavs, *Latviesu beglu,* pp. 144–46. Nothing came of these elaborate plans: the timing of the exhibition was judged inappropriate by the Special

Council for Refugees when the proposal was raised at its meeting on 28 April 1917. RGIA f. 1322, op. 1, d. 13, l. 142ob. However, it appears that many items of refugee provenance were submitted from far afield. Typical items submitted by Latvian refugees included jewelry, dolls in national costume, embroidery, leather goods, and furniture.

142. "Sobranie materialov o bezhenskom dvizhenii," *Izvestiia KTN*, 15, 1 January 1917, pp. 10–11; *Otchet o deiatel'nosti osobogo otdela*, pp. 65–70. An analogous proposal had been made a year earlier by the southwestern office of the Union of Zemstvos, but nothing appears to have come of it. Urging that as much detailed information as possible be gathered about "refugeedom, as a social and economic phenomenon," the anonymous author pointed out that this would be of "enormous interest . . . what is not used immediately will be useful later on in the completion of a general historical picture of refugeedom by an expert, who will be given all the material that has been collected." *Izvestiia VZS*, 28, 1 December 1915, p. 143. The first indication of the Tatiana Committee's interest came in the form of a letter from Mme. Glukhovtsova, wife of a marshal of the nobility in Rogachevsk uezd, whose proposal was discussed at a meeting of the committee on 16 September 1916. RGIA f. 1276, op. 12, d. 1382, ll. 376–78.

143. *Izvestiia KTN*, 9, 1 October 1916, pp. 5–6; *TP*, 9, 1916, p. 394. Similar initiatives were taken independently by the Latvian Cultural Bureau in Moscow. *Beglu kalendars*, pp. 85–88.

144. Studies of charitable activity before the war confirm that no analogous initiatives— designed to explore the life history of the deprived and destitute—were framed. As one reformer wrote in 1885, "Suppose we meet a pitiful beggar child on the street. . . . We should stop, question him, go after him to his relatives, penetrate the reasons for his begging." Quoted in Lindenmeyr, *Poverty*, p. 206. But the aim was to understand the motives of the individual child, in order to dissuade him from begging, not to relate his experience to a broader social phenomenon. In an analogous wartime project, the Jewish ethnographer Solomon Rapoport appealed to Jews to "document their own lives" and experiences. Roskies, *Against the Apocalpyse*, p. 135.

145. E. Glukhovtsova, "Skazka zhizni," *Izvestiia KTN*, 18, 15 February 1917, pp. 21–28; Iakov Vol'rat, "Begstvo ot germantsev i skitaniia," ibid., 19, 15 April 1917, pp. 17–22; V. I. Pashchuk, "Iz Kholmshchiny v Krym: rasskaz bezhentsa-psalomshchika," ibid., 23, 15 July 1917, pp. 17–23; Bogdan Stepanets, "Iz rasskazov bezhentsev: zapisano v Rogacheve vo vremia massovogo dvizheniia bezhentsev v 1915," ibid., 25, 15 September 1917, pp. 13–16; N. Belova, "Rasskazy i soobshcheniia ochevidtsev i uchastnikov bezhenskogo dvizheniia: iz Liublinskoi gubernii v Vetlugu," ibid., 26, 15 October 1917, pp. 14–16. For brief extracts from refugees' correspondence, see Vera Slavenson, "Bezhenskoe: po povodu pisem bezhentsev," *Vestnik Evropy*, 51, no. 7, 1916, pp. 292–301.

146. *Izvestiia KTN*, 23, 15 July 1917, p. 24. The subcommittee was chaired by V. F. Solntsev, and included the MVD official V. I. Komarnitskii and Professor Platon Vasenko. A key influence was the distinguished historian Sergei Platonov, who insisted that refugees should be encouraged to speak in their own uninhibited voice. See his comments at the April conference of Tatiana Committee delegates, reported in ibid., 20, 15 May 1917, p. 8. Yet more was at stake than the collection and preservation of memoirs. Threatened with the dissolution of the Tatiana Committee after the February revolution, Neidgardt maintained that the accumulation of historical materials would allow future relief workers to learn practical lessons from the history of refugeedom in 1915–17. Ibid., p. 4.

147. Compare the remarks in a Jewish newspaper that Russia's Jewish refugees had

shown a "yearning to become people once again." *Evreiskaia zhizn'*, 2, 10 January 1916, p. 40.

148. *Gorizont*, 176, 7 August 1915, p. 1; Ionnisian, *Polozhenie bezhentsev v Aleksandropol'skom raione*, p. 7; Fedorov, "Bezhentsy v Sibiri," p. 254. Officials sometimes cautioned against this policy. See the remarks of Khvostov in February 1916, quoted in RGIA f. 1276, op. 12, d. 1408, l. 6.

149. *Bezhenets*, 3, 25 October 1915.

150. *UR*, 221, 12 August 1915, quoting N. L. Murav'ev, governor-general of Moscow.

151. "One only has to see the happy face of the refugee and the soldier, who have found their loved ones or their household belongings, in order to understand their joy at having what was lost restored to them." *Komitet*, p. 26.

152. *Severnyi bezhenets*, 12, 30 March 1916, p. 2; Shveder, *"Bezhentsy,"* p. 25.

5. REFUGEES AND GENDER

1. "Adult males constituted only 22 per cent of the total." Polner, *Russian Local Government*, p. 170.

2. The parliamentarian Efremov told his colleagues in August 1915 that, because so many refugees were very young or old men, "it is very welcome to have a woman's warm attention." *GDSO*, 10th sitting, col. 830. Around 15 percent of Armenian refugees were below the age of five. RGIA f. 1276, op. 19, d. 1223, l. 13. According to a survey of 806,000 refugees conducted in July 1916, the typical refugee family comprised 3.7 members. *Izvestiia VSG*, 34, July 1916, p. 223.

3. On women and the public sphere before the war, see Stites, *The Women's Liberation Movement*; Edmondson, *The Feminist Movement in Russia*; and Engelstein, *The Keys to Happiness*, pp. 280–98. On military nursing see Meyer, "The Impact of World War One," p. 220.

4. "Mother Russia" was often invoked as the inspiration for humanitarian action: "The Russian interior has taken the devastated borderlands to its heart in a maternal fashion." *Moskovskie vedomosti*, 234, 11 October 1915.

5. Engel, *Between the Fields and the City*.

6. Compare Loizos, *The Heart Grown Bitter*, pp. 176–81. The work of Rose Glickman and Christine Worobec is relevant here, in tracing the emergence of women's roles in the family and village economy and society before 1914. Worobec, "Victims or Actors?"; Glickman, "Women and the Peasant Commune."

7. As we saw in the previous chapter, eyewitnesses drew attention to the desperate behavior of some mothers who, unable to cope, abandoned or even murdered their children. For the behavior of "good" mothers—"the poor mother with the child in her arms"—see *Iugobezhenets*, 24, 16 May 1916, p. 1.

8. Russian generals behaved leniently toward female German settlers who could show that their husbands served in the Russian army. Nelipovich, "Rol' voennogo rukovodstva," p. 274.

9. In the words of one scholar, "That most masculine of enterprises, the Great War, the 'apocalypse of masculinism,' feminized its conscripts by taking away their sense of control." Elaine Showalter, *The Female Malady*, p. 173. The discourse of the "effeminate" and "powerless" Jew, unable to protect women from pogrom, is elaborated in Billie Melman, "Regeneration: Nation and the Construction of Gender in Peace and War—Palestine Jews, 1900–1918," in Melman, *Borderlines*, pp. 121–40.

10. Refugee women were occasionally allowed to be "shell-shocked": one young refugee engaged in conversation with a newspaper reporter, but panicked when she heard a loud noise that (she explained later) reminded her of an artillery barrage. *Bezhenets,* 3, 25 October 1915.

11. Shveder, "*Bezhentsy,*" pp. 4–7, 11, 24. Shveder was the author of several popular works on the natural world.

12. Vetlin, Sviashchennik, *Bezhentsy.* The story has a tragic end; brother and sister are both killed by German bullets, "and the last thought Vania had was that they had at last managed to get away from the enemy. They were saved."

13. Anon., *Kak i pochemu stali my ubiitsami,* p. 6. These issues figure prominently in Higonnet et al., *Behind the Lines;* Higonnet, "Not So Quiet"; Melman, *Borderlines.*

14. Thurstan, *People,* pp. 38, 59. Thurstan's presence in Russia was facilitated by the National Union of Women's Suffrage Societies.

15. *Izvestiia KTN,* 10, 15 October 1916, pp. 14–15.

16. *Zinojums,* 4, 28 January 1916, revealing that Latvian women "cannot and will not wash clothes at a hole in the ice, [yet] the Russian peasant expects his servants to work in his way."

17. *Komitet,* p. 421.

18. *Vestnik VOPB,* 47–48, 29 January 1917, p. 13.

19. *BV,* 15031, 17 August 1915; *Izvestiia KTN,* 6, 15 August 1916, p. 7. However, refugee women in Simbirsk refused to work as weavers unless they were given a loom for domestic use. They had no wish to work "in a common place." *Simbirskie eparkhial'nye vedomosti,* 3, January 1917, p. 44. Similar comments were made by and about Latvian women who "prefer to be independent." *Zinojums,* 29, 21 July 1916.

20. *BV,* 14985, 25 July 1915.

21. Cited in Khatisov, "Memoirs," p. 105; for a general discussion see Engel, "Not by Bread Alone."

22. *Izvestiia Moskovskoi gubernskoi zemskoi upravy,* 10–12, October–December 1915, pp. 63–64. This behavior would probably now be called a panic attack. Colin Murray Parkes, *Bereavement,* p. 50.

23. Ananov, *Sud'ba Armenii,* p. 21.

24. Osherovskii, *Tragediia,* pp. 6–7.

25. *Zhizn' bezhentsev,* 3, September 1916, p. 3; "Geroistvo bezhenki," *Vestnik iuga,* 6 September 1915.

26. Thurstan, *People,* pp. 66–68, 74–75. The NUWSS paid for a new maternity hospital to be built in Petrograd. For pre-1914 provision, see Ransel, *Mothers of Misery;* on postrevolutionary intervention, see Elizabeth Waters, "Teaching Mothercraft."

27. They needed "to be guarded from evil-intentioned attacks on their honor," in the words of one contemporary. "Pomoshch' bezhentsam," *TP,* 9, 1915, p. 364.

28. *Trudy vneocherednogo Pirogovskogo s"ezda,* p. 77.

29. Ibid. Conversely, tsarist officials believed before the war that "freedom from patriarchal authority" encouraged female prostitution. Engel, *Between the Fields,* p. 197.

30. *Iugobezhenets,* 4, 23, November 1915, p. 4. Virtually the same language was used in a guide issued on behalf of refugees in 1916, warning young women of the risks of being seduced by smooth-talking men. *Sputnik bezhentsa,* p. 17. Such means of recruitment were "relatively rare" before 1914, but they nevertheless formed part of the rhetoric of urban danger. See Engel, *Between the Fields,* p. 175, and Bernstein, *Sonia's Daughters,* pp. 292–95.

31. Senator O. Val'ter, speaking to the Special Council, 26 November 1915. RGIA f. 1322, op. 1, d. 1, ll. 61–63ob.

32. *BV,* 15011, 7 August 1915; *Rech',* 214, 6 August 1915.

33. Thurstan, *People,* p. 64. Contrast the remarks of St. Petersburg's sole female guardian of juveniles: "All their stories are so simple and at the same time so awful; but how to help them and what to do, I do not know." Quoted in Neuberger, *Hooliganism,* p. 205.

34. Ibid., p. 186, for the suggestion that juvenile prostitution before 1914 ranked lower than outrage about male offenses to public order. Blok's description is quoted in Dixon, "The Orthodox Church," p. 134.

35. "Commission to Meet the Spiritual Needs of Refugees." RGIA f. 1322, op. 1, d. 23, 1. 4. See also *TP,* 1, 1916, pp. 51–2 for Koni's remarks about the evacuation of "houses of ill repute" (*doma ternimosti*). Members of the commission included Koni and the leading Jewish spokesman, G. B. Sliozberg. Both men served on the Special Council for Refugees.

36. A Russian general appeared to support this view: Igel'strom to Evert, 4 July 1915. RGVIA f. 2020, op. 1, d. 131, ll. 131–34. For an exploration of motives given by prostitutes before 1914, see Engel, *Between the Fields,* pp. 185–89.

37. Thurstan, *People,* pp. 69–72. Some reformers also called for boys to be taught a trade, such as tailoring or carpentry, in order to deter them from street crime. Thurstan met a young man who advocated the wider dissemination of the "Boy Scout principle." See also Neuberger, *Hooliganism,* p. 72.

38. *Vestnik VOPB,* 3, 10 January 1916, p. 13. A Ukrainian refugee organization also complained that "despair and need" drove many women ("and children as young as seven or eight years of age") to prostitution. RGVIA f. 13273, op. 1, d. 27, l. 11.

39. Laura Engelstein detects the medical "profession's . . . greater eagerness to shoulder the corrective burden previously borne by the administrative arm of the state," as well as a continued espousal by some members of a doctrinal belief in the "benign effects of enlightenment and social action." *The Keys to Happiness,* pp. 283–84, 297.

40. "Drama bezhentsev," *Vestnik iuga,* 10 November 1915.

41. RGVIA f. 13273, op. 1, d. 12, l. 32, journal of Sobezh, 3 May 1917. The typescript of the meeting contains a curious slip. Ermolov was obviously male, but the note states that he asked for a girl to be placed *pod ee nadzorom,* literally "under her supervision."

42. "Iz 'chernoi knigi,'" pp. 283–85, 292–95. One story concerned a woman whose "reward" for having concealed Cossack soldiers from the Germans was to be raped and beaten by Cossack troops when they returned to her village. The editor of these documents drew attention to mass rape in Smorgon', Glubokoe, Vidsy, and Lemeshevichi, where "defenseless women, separated from their husbands and fathers, were at the mercy of a wild Cossack horde." Ibid., p. 294.

43. For the dramatic tale of rape in a Moscow suburb, see *Vestnik iuga,* 25 September 1915.

44. "Polozhenie turetskikh armianok," *Armiane i voina,* 7, September 1916, p. 105. There is some ambiguity about this comment; it is not clear if the author meant Turkish or Armenian men, or both. In any case he called for workhouses (*doma trudoliubiia*) to offer women sanctuary and work.

45. *Armianskii vestnik,* 35, 25 September 1915, p. 10.

46. Ibid., 6, 5 February 1917, p. 19; Osherovskii, *Tragediia,* p. 8. An analogy was drawn in the same article with German troops' sexual assault of French women on the western front, a subject discussed by Ruth Harris, "'The Child of the Barbarian.'"

47. *Armianskii vestnik,* 6, 5 February 1917, p. 18.

48. Osherovskii, *Tragediia,* p. 8.

49. RGIA f. 1322, op. 1, d. 23, l. 3. See also the positive assessment of refugee relief in Kiev, in Thurstan, *People,* p. 117.

50. *Mshak,* 92, 3 May 1915, p. 3; *Pailak,* 17, 12 March 1915, p. 2; Akopian, *Zapadnaia Armeniia,* p. 193.

51. Aristocratic women, especially in Moscow, acted as patrons of refugee relief. Violetta Thurstan, *People,* pp. 89–90, cites the work undertaken by Countess Bobrinskaia. The most exalted role, of course, belonged to Grand Duchess Tatiana, who was praised for attending and chairing sessions of the committee that bore her name. An eyewitness could not resist adding that Tatiana was "most winning with her vivacity and the mischievous sparkle in her eyes." A. Russian [*sic*], *Russian Court Memoirs,* p. 159.

52. In many instances the ladies' committees were subordinated to diocesan committees. See *Saratovskie eparkhial'nye vedomosti,* 1–2, 1–11 January 1916, pp. 26–30.

53. *Komitet,* p. 417.

54. *Ekaterinoslavskaia zemskaia gazeta,* 28 July 1915. For the ladies' committee in Ekaterinoslav, see ibid., 11 September 1915.

55. *Ekaterinburgskie eparkhial'nye vedomosti,* 50, 13 December 1915, p. 851.

56. *Komitet,* p. 260.

57. Quoted in *Mshak,* 4, 1915, p. 1. See also *Gorizont,* 180, 12 August 1915, p. 3.

58. Ibid., 5, 9 January 1915, p. 2.

59. *Simbirskie eparkhial'nye vedomosti,* 23, December 1915, p. 923.

60. "A woman," writing in *Zhenskoe delo,* 18, 15 September 1915, p. 2. The subsequent issue publicized the efforts of Moscow women to attend at railway stations and to serve hot meals. Ibid., 19, 1 October 1915, pp. 1–2. This brief report appears to have exhausted the journal's interest in refugee welfare.

61. *Iugobezhenets,* 6, 7 December 1915, p. 1.

62. *Vestnik VOPB,* 6, 8 February 1916, p. 5.

63. RGIA f. 1276, op. 12, d. 1382, ll. 57–62.

64. See the descriptions in *Izvestiia KTN,* 1, 29 May 1916, p. 1, and *Iugobezhenets,* 24, 10 May 1916. Refugees from Minsk and Galicia were presented to the royal family on their visit to Odessa. The lucky girl chosen to offer a gift of a cloth embroidered with "a little Russian [i.e., Ukrainian] pattern" was Sofia Stakhner. The task of presenting an icon was entrusted to a boy, Nikolai Shvets. Kazanskii, *Galitsko-russkie bezhentsy,* pp. 41–42.

65. Both quoted in *Izvestiia KTN,* 5, 1 August 1915, p. 11.

66. Ibid., 9, 1 October 1916, p. 8; ibid., 11, 1 November 1916, p. 12.

67. *Komitet,* p. 74.

68. Moore, *Formation of a Persecuting Society,* p. 101.

69. I have come across the names of A. I. Goremykina (wife of the prime minister) and Baroness Sofia Buxhoeveden, lady-in-waiting to Empress Alexandra. Both were doubtless figureheads. Certainly neither figures in any of the minutes of committee meetings, and the surviving personal file of Buxhoeveden contains but one brief memorandum relating to refugees in the care of the Tsarskoe selo office of the Tatiana Committee. GARF f. 742, op. 1, d. 14.

70. Alfred Meyer observes that *Zhenskoe delo* sought to "reassure the warrior in the field that the home front was well taken care of and that the domestic hearth he was protecting was in good shape," but that "by the end of 1916, if not before, such morale-building

letters had been replaced by letters in which women complained about their difficult lives, their loneliness, their tiredness, and their despair." Meyer, "The Impact of World War One," p. 224.

71. "It did not occur to me that in a study of politics the relative absence of women was in itself a challenging problem," writes Peter Loizos; he attempts to rectify this omission in *The Heart Grown Bitter*, from which the quotation is taken (p. 194).

72. See chapter 4 and Appendix 2.

73. "No one who has visited these districts can be unmoved by the nakedness of women and children," according to one account of refugees in the Armenian sanctuary at Etchmiadzin. *Ashkhatank*, 29, 1916, p. 4.

6. REFUGEES AND THE LABOR MARKET

1. This statement needs to be modified to take account of workers who were evacuated along with their factories. See Sidorov, *Ekonomicheskoe polozhenie*, pp. 213–28, and, for a firsthand account, Dune, *Notes of a Red Guard*.

2. One exception was a commission established in December 1915 by the Third Army, with the participation of the public organizations, Severopomoshch', and the Tatiana Committee. It resolved to assist refugees in finding work, "so that these impoverished householders can stand on their own feet and, in due course, having saved some money, once more become useful members of society and the state." RGVIA f. 2049, op. 1, d. 446, l. 12.

3. *Izvestiia VSG*, 20, December 1915, p. 168. The authorities in Khar'kov estimated that only one-quarter of refugees were capable of work (*trudosposobny*), the remainder being "the elderly, women, and children." The report noted that demand for agricultural workers, as well as for stonemasons and concrete mixers, was currently unsatisfied. Ibid., pp. 189, 191. The All-Russian Labor Exchange calculated that between 17 and 20 percent of all refugees were *trudosposobny*. Rumiantsev, *Rabochii klass*, p. 148. In Siberia, the proportion of refugees who were regarded as capable of work was put at no more than 10 percent (Krasnoiarsk) and 20 percent (Tomsk). See *TP*, 6, 1916, p. 22.

4. According to *Armianskii vestnik*, 9, 26 February 1917, p. 10, only 15,000 individuals out of a total estimated refugee population of 360,000 were considered to be capable of work.

5. Vort, "Promyshlennyi trud." See also Sidorov, *Ekonomicheskoe polozhenie Rossii*, pp. 55–94.

6. When the governor of Iaroslavl' province told local relief workers that able-bodied refugees "should in no circumstances be left idle," in view of the serious strains on public finance caused by the war, he was simply following directives from Petrograd, where it was agreed that refugees had an obligation to seek work rather than rely on government welfare. GAIaO f. 485, op. 1, d. 1175, ll. 89–90. See also *TP*, 5, 1916, p. 462.

7. *BV*, 15091, 16 August 1915. The unsigned article suggested that this would solve the problem of "Russian gold" that disappeared across the frontier with China. The issue is discussed more fully in Siegelbaum, "Another 'Yellow Peril.'"

8. Beskrovnyi et al., *Zhurnaly Osobogo soveshchaniia*, p. 129, session held on 15 July 1915.

9. Vort, "Promyshlennyi trud."

10. Fewer than a quarter of the 2.8 million refugees recorded on 1 July 1916 were adult males of working age, most of whom had little knowledge or experience of non-agricultural

work. Polner, *Russian Local Government,* p. 170; *Golos,* 231, 10 October 1915; ibid., 278, 5 December 1915; Slavenson, "Bezhenskoe," p. 293.

11. *BV,* 14977, 18 July 1915; ibid., 14983, 24 July 1915. On Latvians' qualities, see *Zinojums,* 14, 7 April 1916.

12. Ibid., 29, 21 July 1916, reporting that Latvian domestic servants in Omsk were paid between 10 and 12 rubles a month, with board and lodging. RGIA f. 1322, op. 1, d. 16, ll. 36, 85.

13. *Golos,* 278, 5 December 1915; *Izvestiia VSG,* 20, December 1915, pp. 177, 193; *Ekaterinburgskie eparkhial'nye vedomosti,* 37, 13 September 1915, p. 657; Thurstan, *People,* p. 135.

14. *Izvestiia KTN,* 6, 15 August 1916, p. 3. "Hearts, kidneys, stomachs, larynxes are coated in special enamel colors and are in no way inferior to foreign models."

15. *BV,* 15021, 12 August 1915.

16. RGVIA f. 13273, op. 1, d. 29. ll. 10–11ob.

17. Ibid., d. 79, l. 7. The employment office of Sobezh included several leading members of the "third element" in the VZS and VSG, such as N. S. Chetverikov, A. N. Sysin, M. M. Shchepkin, and S. B. Veselovskii.

18. *Izvestiia VSG,* 20, December 1915, pp. 167, 176–77; *TP,* 8, 1915, pp. 239, 244 for labor exchanges in Smolensk, Voronezh, and Zhitomir. For the Caucasus, see TsGAA f. 50, op. 1, d. 78, l. 8.

19. V. M., "Pomoshch' bezhentsam," *Izvestiia Moskovskoi gubernskoi zemskoi upravy,* 8–9, August–September 1915, pp. 19–22.

20. *Izvestiia VSG,* 19, November 1915, p. 34; Vort, "Promyshlennyi trud."

21. *TP,* 8, 1915, p. 240.

22. Vort, "Promyshlennyi trud."

23. Lindenmeyr, *Poverty,* pp. 174–89.

24. RGIA f. 1284, op. 194, d. 30–1917, l. 7; TsGAA, f. 50, op. 1, d. 78, l. 8. Organization of refugee labor was also seen as the key to overcoming shortages of manufactured goods and foodstuffs. The municipal artels (work associations) in Mariupol' were held up as examples of good practice, supplying consumers with much-needed items such as shoes, clothes, and crackers.

25. *Izvestiia VZS,* 32, 1 February 1916, pp. 194–95; ibid., 33, 15 February 1916, pp. 90–91. For an analogy between "refugeedom" and "spontaneous misfortunes" (i.e., unemployment) see A. Meier, "Obshchestvennye raboty i bezhentsy," *TP,* 1, 1916, pp. 64–68.

26. This example is taken from a letter written by Professor Grabskii, exiled chairman of the Polish National Democratic Party in L'vov, to the chief of the Kiev Military District. RGVIA f. 1759, op. 4, d. 1744, l. 40.

27. For background see Struve, *Food Supply,* pp. 297–303; *Ekonomicheskoe polozhenie Rossii,* vol. 3, pp. 33–71.

28. *Izvestiia VZS,* 33, 15 February 1916, p. 78.

29. RGIA f. 1322, op. 1, d. 34, ll. 1–5; ibid., l. 335ob., for a figure of 201,000 refugees in agriculture as of June 1916; Polner, *Russian Local Government,* p. 155. See chapter 3 for refugees' preference for settling in towns. By contrast, a Novgorod newspaper maintained that "many . . . farmers are bored with town life" and were eager to work as agricultural laborers. *Severnyi bezhenets,* 3, 26 January 1916, p. 1.

30. RGIA f. 1322, op. 1, d. 1, l. 25ob., Special Council, 3 October 1915. Two weeks later it was reported that 60,000 Polish refugees [sic] were on their way from Bobruisk to Kiev to help with the sugar crop. Ibid., l. 37ob.

31. Peasant farms engaged only 20,000 POWs, far fewer than the numbers on private farms. N. P. Oganovskii, "Polozhenie sel'skogo khoziaistva v 1916 godu," *Izvestiia VZS*, 51, 1916, p. 60; *Ekonomicheskoe polozhenie Rossii*, vol. 3, p. 443. Landowners' preference for cheap POW labor is described in *TP*, 6, 1916, p. 23.

32. *Kratkii obzor deiatel'nosti Pribaltiiskogo Latyshskogo komiteta*, p. 1.

33. *Vestnik Riazanskogo gubernskogo zemstva*, 4–5, April–May 1916, pp. 98–99. Latvian refugee organizations did nothing to question these assumptions; see chapter 7, where it is shown that Latvians' cultural and economic superiority was believed to distinguish them from the "backward" Russian peasantry. There is an interesting contrast with Hutu refugees in Tanzania, who frequently identified themselves as good cultivators; "but when 'true cultivators' was a label affixed by the antagonistic other (Tutsi or Tanzanian), it had the effect of capturing the Hutu in castelike subordination, in *hutuness*, and of naturalizing their blockage from education and intellectual pursuits." Malkki, *Purity and Exile*, p. 134.

34. *UR*, 223, 14 August 1915. Needless to say, urban observers had a vested interest in finding as many arguments as they could to support the evacuation of refugees from Russia's "overcrowded" towns to the countryside. According to Sheila Fitzpatrick, village blacksmiths prospered during the 1920s and subsequently suffered persecution as "kulaks." Fitzpatrick, *Stalin's Peasants*, pp. 158–61.

35. *Simbirskie eparkhial'nye vedomosti*, 22, November 1916, p. 572.

36. Ibid., p. 573; ibid., 4, February 1917, pp. 67–70. Compare the attitude expressed by an elderly Greek refugee woman from Asia Minor whose family had settled in Piraeus: "Before we came here what were they? We opened their eyes. They didn't know how to eat or dress. They used to eat salt fish and wild vegetables. It was we who taught them everything." Hirschon, *Heirs of the Greek Catastrophe*, p. 31.

37. Homo Longus, "Dve kul'tury," *Bezhenets*, 7–8, 6 December 1915.

38. Anon., "My i latyshi," *Vestnik VOPB*, 30–31, 15–21 August 1916, pp. 11–12. The author was a peasant from Mariupol' uezd, Ekaterinoslav province.

39. In Pskov, for example, "what kind of work can women find in the countryside in winter . . . ? Russian farms are very small, and there is insufficient work even for family members. . . . Here is not Latvia, where there are jobs to do in every room, every house, every season." *Zinojums*, 4, 28 January 1916. Note that when refugees asked for loans to enable them to acquire an inventory to work land they had rented, the government turned them down; the Special Council took the view that refugees were supposed to work as agricultural laborers, not as farmers. RGIA f. 1322, op. 1, d. 1, l. 281, Special Council, 19 March 1916.

40. RGIA f. 1284, op. 194, d. 43–1916, ll. 10–13. This did not stop the municipal authorities in Moscow from creating "colonies" for juveniles between 13 and 15 years of age, who were to be sent to work on peasant farms and large estates. *TP*, 6, 1916, p. 51.

41. *Izvestiia VSG*, 20, December 1915, p. 168.

42. For the voluntary organizations' support for migration, see *Izvestiia VZS*, 33, 15 February 1916, pp. 96–97; their frustration at refugees' reluctance to move to villages is evident in *Izvestiia VSG*, 33–34, June 1916, p. 299.

43. In January 1916, the Special Council established a commission under the chairmanship of Senator A. I. Lykoshkin to plan the utilization of refugee labor, which subsequently rejected the use of compulsory measures to allocate refugees to jobs. RGIA f. 1322, op. 1, d. 1, ll. 168–70.

44. Ibid., d. 34, ll. 3–4; GAIaO f. 485, op. 1, d. 1175, ll. 89–90, reporting a proposal from the Special Council on 12 March 1916. This had been discussed by the Special Council, where it was argued that welfare allowances should not be set so generously that refugees

were encouraged to abandon the search for work. RGIA f. 1322, op. 1, d. 1, ll. 3, 8. See also S. B. Veselovskii, "Ob usloviiakh pomoshchi trudosposobnym bezhentsam," *Izvestiia VZS,* 33, 15 February 1916, pp. 83–99. Veselovskii trained as a historian, joined the history faculty at MGU, and published widely in the Soviet period on sixteenth-century Russia. His views on the negative consequences of compulsion were echoed by fellow members of Sobezh's employment office. RGVIA f. 13273, op. 1, d. 79, l. 7.

45. RGIA f. 1322, op. 1, d. 1, ll. 187–92, Special Council, 28 January 1916; *Izvestiia VZS,* 33, 15 February 1916, p. 78.

46. RGIA f. 1322, op. 1, d. 1, l. 189. For similar measures in Tomsk, see *Izvestiia VSG,* 20, December 1915, pp. 184–85.

47. Ibid., 33–34, June 1916, pp. 299–300, pointing out that the Union of Towns would step in to fill any gap left by the withdrawal of official relief payments. On the double punishment of refugees, see *TP,* 6, 1916, p. 23.

48. Ibid., d. 34, ll. 1–5; A. B., "Sel'sko-khoziaistvennye druzhiny," *Zhizn' bezhentsev,* 7, October 1916, p. 7. In Vitebsk, a total of 12 gangs were made up of around 50 workers (plus women and children), each with 50 plows, 100 horses, and 50 carts.

49. *TP,* 5, 1916, p. 464.

50. Letter addressed to the Special Council for State Defense, 6 July 1915, cited in Maevskii, *Ekonomika russkoi promyshlennosti,* p. 322.

51. RGIA f. 1322, op. 1, d. 1, l. 336, Special Council, 21 June 1916.

52. Another 246 were craftsmen, *remeslenniki,* and 209 were construction workers. Details from Rumiantsev, *Rabochii klass,* p. 148.

53. Spustek, *Polacy w Piotrogrodzie,* p. 217. Polish refugees worked in the big engineering factories in the capital, such as Putilov and Novyi Lessner.

54. *TP,* 10, 1916, p. 512.

55. V. Z., "Bezhentsy po selam Alatyrskogo uezda," *Simbirskie eparkhial'nye vedomosti,* 19, October 1916, pp. 500–503. In this article, an unnamed priest reported on a visit to several villages in Simbirsk.

56. *Gorizont,* 193, 28 August 1915, p. 3.

57. Letter from A. I. Guchkov to A. A. Polivanov, 17 September 1915. RGVIA f. 369, op. 1, d. 31, ll. 178–80. Two thousand were juveniles, and 6,000 were women workers from the surrounding localities. Guchkov, chairman of the Central War Industries Committee, stated that the region's metallurgical firms needed an additional 30,000 workers.

58. Kir'ianov, *Rabochie Iuga Rossii,* p. 41.

59. Memorandum from Moscow War Industry Committee to the Special Council for State Defense, 6 July 1915, noting that many refugees did not know the Russian language, and doubting the commitment of refugees, who, generally speaking, wished to go "home." RGVIA f. 369, op. 1, d. 96, ll. 215–16.

60. Rumiantsev, *Rabochii klass,* pp. 148–49. Nikols'kii, "Bezhentsy," p. 46, mentions an (unnamed) enterprise in Smolensk whose manager recruited as many able-bodied refugees as he could and provided them with living quarters.

61. *Izvestiia VZS,* 32, 1 February 1916, p. 195. See also the comments of Shchepkin at the first session of the Special Council. RGIA f. 1322, op. 1, d. 1, l. 3, and Dagaev, "Bezhentsy v Sibiri," p. 22.

62. Polner, *Russian Local Government,* p. 170. See also Keep, *The Russian Revolution,* p. 32: "The refugees who arrived from the combat zone were usually destitute and demoralized; they could hardly be expected to work with a will."

63. GAIaO f. 485, op. 1, d. 1177, l. 3. Similar remarks about the "psychological condition" of refugees and its impact on their ability to work were made by a subcommittee of the Special Council for Refugees. RGIA f. 1322, op. 1, d. 34, l. 4. In Nikolas Rose's words, "The psyche of the citizen was discovered as a new continent for psychological knowledge and for the deployment of the professional skills of the technician of subjectivity." See Rose, *Governing the Soul,* p. 32.

64. *Izvestiia VZS,* 33, 15 February 1916, p. 85.

65. Thurstan, *People,* p. 6. On the other hand, some relief workers believed that work would serve to lighten the refugees' mood. *Iugobezhenets,* 5, 30 November 1915, p. 1.

66. *Izvestiia VZS,* 33, 15 February 1916, p. 85.

67. *Vestnik VOPB,* 19, 22 May 1916, p. 14.

68. *Izvestiia VSG,* 20, December 1915, p. 178.

69. Ibid., 33–34, June 1916, p. 297.

70. RGVIA f. 13273, op. 1, d. 62, ll. 13–14.

71. See the remarks of *Golos Kavkaza,* quoted in *Vestnik VOPB,* 28–29, 31 July–7 August 1916, p. 15: "It is delightful to live on state allowances, doing very little; one only had to be recognized as an 'unhappy' Caucasian refugee to be allowed to refuse all offers of work." The author went on to say that refugees should be compelled to work for their keep.

72. *Bezhenets,* 3, 25 October 1915.

73. S. V. G., "Slova i tsifry," *Zhizn' bezhentsev,* 2, September 1916, p. 3. Similar comments were made in *Vestnik VOPB,* 44, 25 December 1916, pp. 6–7, where the author hoped that the forthcoming congress of the Tatiana Committee would finally allow this slander to be laid to rest.

74. *Golos,* 235, 15 October 1915; 115, 21 May 1916. Two-fifths of all refugees were under the age of 15. Of the remainder, only a quarter were registered at the local labor office as unable to find work. One-third had family responsibilities. The others were sick or elderly.

75. *Izvestiia VZS,* 33, 15 February 1916, pp. 87–88. In November 1915, the Union of Zemstvos asked its local labor bureaus to ascertain the reasons for refugees' refusal to work: "The shock to their morale and the exhaustion . . . their unwillingness to part from family members . . . the unsuitability of the work that has been offered." Ibid., 28, 1 December 1915, p. 84.

76. RGVIA f. 13273, op. 1, d. 79, l. 7.

77. *Izvestiia VZS,* 28, 5 February 1916; GAIaO f. 485, op. 1, d. 1177, l. 13, journal of the Provincial Commission on Refugee Relief, 3 October and 24 November 1915.

78. *BV,* 14983, 24 July 1915.

79. *Vestnik Riazanskogo gubernskogo zemstva,* 1, January 1916, p. 76.

80. *Dekrety sovetskoi vlasti,* vol. 6, pp. 122–23.

81. Veselovskii, "Ob usloviiakh," p. 86.

82. Ibid. A similar attitude was reported by Zubchaninov to the Special Council for Refugees. RGIA f. 1322, op. 1, d. 1, l. 37ob.

83. There is another instance in *TP,* 6, 1916, p. 22, where the Siberian newspaper *Sibir'* reported refugees as saying, "The state drove us here; let the state support and feed us." An identical comment appeared in a letter from General Brylin to the commander of the southwestern front, 1 September 1916. RGVIA f. 2005, op. 1, d. 43, l. 47ob.

84. Some Jewish refugees tried to settle on farms in the southern province of Tauride, but gave up on account of physical exhaustion, not because of local hostility. *Evreiskaia zhizn',* 7, 16 August 1915, p. 24.

85. Cherniavsky, *Prologue,* pp. 59, 61. 65–66. Krivoshein went on to argue that, although competition in the towns would be healthy for the national economy, "the village was another matter entirely. Not only must one not allow Jews there, one must also fight illegal penetration in every way."

86. There were inevitably "difficulties." Jewish businessmen from leather factories in the Baltic region found that officials denied them the right to follow their evacuated workforce and settle in the Russian interior. "Komu eto nuzhno?" *Bezhenets,* 7 8, 6 December 1915.

87. Brutskus, "Gde ustroit nashikh bezhentsakh?" p. 11. Brutskus anticipated that they would find work in the central industrial region, although not, of course, in Moscow. On the "ruined" Jewish artisan, see *The Jews in the Eastern War Zone,* p. 111.

88. RGIA f. 1284, op. 194, d. 43–1916, ll. 10–13. Similar remarks were made about Galicians in Rostov. RGVIA f. 2005, op. 1, d. 43, l. 47ob.

89. RGIA f. 1322, op. 1, d. 1, l. 42ob., Special Council, 24 October 1915. The spokesman for the Ministry of Finances argued that the refugee intelligentsia should rely instead on national and professional societies.

90. *Izvestiia VZS,* 33, 15 February 1916, p. 85; Vort, "Promsyhlennyi trud," for a rehearsal of the dilemmas facing professional people.

91. *BV,* 14989, 27 July 1915. For a tribute to Tolstoi from the medical profession, see *Trudy vneocherednego Pirogovskogo s"ezda,* p. 79. See also Tolstoi, *Dnevnik 1906–1916,* pp. 654–55, 668, 672.

92. *TP,* 8, 1915, p. 240.

93. *Iugobezhenets,* 34, 13 August 1916, p. 1. Oprysk at the time was languishing in a village in Ekaterinoslav.

94. RGIA f. 1322, op. 1, d. 1, l. 332ob., Special Council, 21 June 1916.

95. See the remarks of M. M. Shchepkin to the Special Council, 10 September 1915, Ibid., l. 3. Shchepkin argued subsequently that refugees should be paid an adequate allowance, rather than a meager sum that would "encourage" (that is, compel) them to enter the labor market. Ibid., l. 8, 14 September 1915.

96. Note also in this connection the comment of the MVD official A. I. Tyshkevich, to the effect that "the refugee who receives a job essentially ceases to be a refugee." Ibid., l. 7ob.

97. *Simbirskie eparkhial'nye vedomosti,* 4, February 1917, p. 70.

7. REFUGEES AND THE CONSTRUCTION OF "NATIONAL" IDENTITY

1. RGIA f. 1322, op. 1, d. 16, l. 26, citing the governor of Akmolinsk province; *GDSO,* 10th sitting, 14 August, cols. 808–10; Knox, *With the Russian Army,* vol. 1, p. 322.

2. *Sputnik bezhentsa,* 6, 3–4 October 1915, p. 3, describing Nizhnii Novgorod.

3. I borrow this apposite phrase from Wright, *The Village That Died,* p. 41. On the lack of prewar mass national sentiment see Weeks, *Nation and State,* p. 125.

4. A group of refugees (probably from Galicia) refused to be settled in Tauride province, where "the population is sparse and consists largely of Germans and Tatars," who were thought likely to give them a hostile reception. *Izvestiia VZS,* 27, 15 November 1915, p. 63.

5. V. Vodovodov, quoted in *Armianskii vestnik,* 18, 29 May 1916, p. 4; ibid., 6, 5 February 1917, p. 18. Tbilisi had long been home to Armenians, who constituted two-fifths of its population in 1897 and who dominated the city's commercial affairs. Presumably Vodovodov was alarmed at the prospect of plebeian in-migration.

6. As one Latvian newspaper put it, "The reason why even cultivated Russians take Latvians for Germans is their very scanty knowledge about the 'small peoples' of Russia. All strange Europeans are 'chuzhaki' [foreigners] or 'nemtsy' ["Germans"] so far as they are concerned." *Lidums,* 170, 27 June 1915.

7. *Zinojums,* 14, 7 April 1916.

8. *Lidums,* 296, 1915; Anon., "Investigation of Our Settlements," *Dzimtenes Atbalss,* 5, 1917.

9. Homo Longus, "Toska po rodine," *Bezhenets,* 5, 8 November 1915.

10. See the remarks about the Jewish Relief Committee in Petrograd, reported in *BV,* 15009, 6 August 1915, as well as the debate in the Special Council, 26 November 1915. RGIA f. 1322, op. 1, d. 1, l. 64. Not all municipal authorities supported the formation of national organizations: officials in Vitebsk were notoriously hostile.

11. *BV,* 15001, 3 August 1915.

12. *Golos,* 232, 12 October 1915.

13. *TP,* 10, 1915, p. 468; ibid., 1, 1916, p. 59; *Kratkii otchet deiatel'nosti Pribaltiiskogo Latyshskogo komiteta,* pp. 120–40.

14. *Izvestiia VSG,* 20, December 1915, p. 189; *TP,* 10, 1915, p. 470; *Mshak,* 196, 3 September 1916, p. 3; *Ashkhatank,* 74, 1917, p. 3.

15. *Izvestiia VZS,* 34, 1 March 1916, pp. 98–101. The law of 1 July 1914 permitted private schools to offer instruction in the vernacular.

16. The Jewish school in Rezhitsa was staffed by "two old, sick Melamed Jews, who get in one another's way, shout at one another, and have to cope with thirty skinny, half-starved boys. The teachers often abandon their lessons, warm themselves by the stove, leave the children to their own devices, take a pinch of snuff, and complain to one another about the infirmities of old age, about the cost of living and the miserliness of the [Jewish] committee." Ibid., 35–36, 15 March–1 April 1916, pp. 179. The Tatiana Committee also encouraged non-Russian cultural and educational activity by establishing a "Literary Fund," specifically to support refugee writers whose first language was other than Russian. *Rech',* 244, 5 September 1915; *TP,* 8, 1915, p. 235.

17. RGIA f. 1322, op. 1, d. 36, ll. 15–36ob.; *Vestnik Riazanskogo gubernskogo zemstva,* 1, January 1916, pp. 71–80. In Petrograd, the Union of Towns planned to establish a "children's colony" in the countryside, "for the children of poor refugees, regardless of nationality." *TP,* 6, 1916, p. 50.

18. *Izvestiia VSG,* 20, December 1915, pp. 167, 187; for Novgorod, see *Komitet,* p. 274. Practice in Vladimir is described in ibid., p. 747, and in *Vladimirskie eparkhial'nye vedomosti,* 37, 12 September 1915, pp. 746–47.

19. RGIA f. 1322, op. 1, d. 1, l. 63ob.; Z. Mindlin, "Pervye itogi poseleniia evreev vo vnutrennikh guberniiakh," *Evreiskaia nedelia,* 27, 1915, p. 15.

20. *Komitet,* p. 92.

21. Paustovsky, *Slow Approach,* p. 236. "In Moscow one can hear Polish spoken at every step," reported *Bezhenets,* 2, 18 October 1915.

22. *Izvestiia VZS,* 33, 15 February 1916, p. 89.

23. RGIA f. 1276, op. 17, d. 479, l. 21; ibid., f. 1284, op. 194, d. 26–1917, l. 9.

24. Ibid., f. 1322, op. 1, d. 1, ll. 290–290ob., Special Council, 30th sitting, 26 March 1916. See also *UR,* 230, 21 August 1915, where they are urged to cooperate with public organizations, the Tatiana Committee, and the government plenipotentiaries. By late 1916, a

progressive newspaper urged Russians to form such committees "on broad democratic foundations," including representatives from local cooperatives. *Zhizn' bezhentsev,* 10, November 1916, pp. 1–2.

25. Oganovskii, *Vragi li russkomu narodu evrei?;* Paléologue, *La Russie des Tsars,* vol. 1, pp. 335–36.

26. M. Aleinikov, "Cherta rasshiraetsia," *Evreiskaia zhizn',* 8, 23 August 1915, pp. 1–4, arguing for full equality for Russia's Jews and drawing an analogy between Jews and American "Negroes." The history of Russian Jewry during the war is placed in a broader context by Frankel, "The Paradoxical Politics of Marginality."

27. Mindlin, "Pervye itogi"; Kirzhnits, "Bezhenstvo," p. 177; "Iz 'chernoi knigi,'" pp. 242–43; Averbakh, *Zakonodatel'nye akty,* vol. 2, p. 776.

28. M. Mysh', "K voprosu o rasshirenii cherty evreiskoi osedlosti," *Vestnik grazhdanskogo prava,* 6, 1915, pp.137–49. Jews were legally allowed to stay in Petrograd for a maximum of seven days, unless an extension was granted by the police. In May 1916 all Jews were ordered to leave the city, and Jewish orphanages and hostels were closed, leaving only a handful of craftsmen behind. *Evreiskaia zhizn',* 30, 24 July 1916, pp. 33–34. For the ban on Jewish settlement in the Caucasus see *Bezhenets,* 4, 1 November 1915, reporting a decision made by the viceroy, who cited "local conditions."

29. Around 95 percent of Jewish refugees who left the Pale resided in towns, compared to 86 percent of Jews who remained in the Pale. *Otchet Tsentral'nogo evreiskogo komiteta,* p. 55. See also Rogger, *Jewish Policies,* p. 169, and Löwe, *The Tsar and the Jews,* pp. 325–31.

30. Brutskus, "Gde ustroit nashikh bezhentsev?" p. 10.

31. *Izvestiia KTN,* 13, 1 December 1916, p. 19; *Otchet Tsentral'nogo evreiskogo komiteta,* p. 55.

32. Brutskus, "Gde ustroit nashikh bezhentsakh?" pp. 13–15. Brutskus was not only an economist with a growing reputation, but also a member of the "special section" of the Tatiana Committee that dealt with the registration of missing refugees.

33. *Evreiskaia zhizn',* 10–11, 6 September 1915, pp. 27–30. The quotation is from a speech by the Moscow Jewish dignitary Motylev.

34. Löwe, *The Tsar and the Jews,* p. 377; Rogger, *Jewish Policies,* p. 105.

35. "Soveshchanie gubernatorov v 1916g.," *Krasnyi arkhiv,* 33, 1929, pp. 145–69. For the May Laws see Weeks, *Nation and State,* pp. 118–19. They did not apply to Russian Poland.

36. Sliozberg, *Dela minuvshikh dnei,* vol. 3, pp. 335–42; *Evreiskaia zhizn',* 5, 2 August 1915, pp. 20–22.

37. Cherniavsky, *Prologue,* pp. 61, 70, 85. In his memoirs, Sliozberg denies that he and his colleagues made any threats or promises about the supply of credit to the Russian government.

38. Mysh', "K voprosu o rasshirenii cherty evreiskoi osedlosti"; Rogger, *Jewish Policies,* p. 105.

39. Thurstan, *People,* pp. 150, 153.

40. This figure is taken from *Otchet Tsentral'nogo evreiskogo komiteta,* p. 13. It represented one-third of the total funds available to the Central Jewish Committee for Refugee Relief. See Nichols, *The Uneasy Alliance,* pp. 33–34.

41. The phrase belongs to Yasmine Ergas, "Growing Up Banished: A Reading of Anne Frank and Etty Hillesum," in Higonnet et al., *Behind the Lines,* p. 92.

42. Gran, Brutskus, and the leading Cadet, Maksim Vinaver, joined the executive of

EKOPO in August 1916; Ibid., pp. 7–8, 43–44; and the entry for EKOPO in *Kratkaia evreiskaia entsiklopediia.*

43. S. Chernovich, "Problemy 'novoi cherty,'" *Evreiskaia zhizn'*, 15, 11 October 1915, pp. 10–12. Zionism remained at this stage a minority faith.

44. Ibid., p. 11. The author cited the charitable activities of Lithuanian Jews among Polish Jewish refugees.

45. Mindlin, "Pervye itogi," p. 24.

46. *Evreiskaia zhizn'*, 2, 10 January 1916, pp. 30–35, reporting on a congress of representatives engaged in refugee relief, held in Minsk between 22 and 25 December 1915.

47. *Otchet Tsentral'nogo evreiskogo komiteta,* pp. 43–44; Mindlin, "Pervye itogi," pp. 24–25; Zipperstein, "The Politics of Relief," p. 32. The levy imposed on Russia's Jewish population is described in *Evreiskaia zhizn'*, 5, 2 August 1915, p. 35. The revenue from this source did not amount to much more than 3 million rubles, compared to a receipt of 10 million from overseas and 17 million from central government.

48. *Otchet Tsentral'nogo evreiskogo komiteta,* p. 45.

49. *Golos,* 247, 30 October 1916; ibid., 274, 2 December 1916; *Izvestiia VZS,* 21, 15 August 1915, p. 52.

50. Mindlin, "Pervye itogi," p. 14; Zipperstein, "The Politics of Relief," p. 24.

51. Mindlin, "Pervye itogi," p. 14. Mindlin came across similar actions in Ivanovo-Voznesensk.

52. Ibid., p. 15. Before the war, only 90 Jewish families lived in Tambov, with a total population of 53,000.

53. MVD to deputy commissioner for refugees, Riga, 9 April 1916. LVVA f. 5963, op. 1, d. 2, l. 15.

54. Chernovich, "Problemy," p. 11.

55. As early as 1836, a government publication referred to Armenians as "like the people of Moses . . . dispersed about the face of the earth, gathering wealth under the weight of their rulers, unable to enjoy their own land. This is the cause of the Armenian's lack of character: he has become a cosmopolitan. His fatherland becomes that land where he can with the greatest advantage and security and through the resourcefulness of his mind make for himself profit." Quoted in Suny, *Looking toward Ararat,* p. 39.

56. *Mshak,* 60, 22 March 1915, p. 5.

57. Akopian, *Zapadnaia Armeniia,* pp. 195–96. *Armianskii vestnik,* edited by I. T. Amirov, appeared weekly throughout 1916. *Armiane i voina* was edited by A. A. Inanov and published in Odessa; ten issues appeared during 1916. Scientific and archeological expeditions were also mounted in 1915 and 1916 to areas that had earlier been part of the Ottoman empire. Russian archaeologists made important discoveries about the ancient state of Urartu in the Lake Van region. In addition, foreign sympathizers mobilized public opinion abroad, with the result that donations began to be made to the cause of Armenian refugee relief. The Armenian communities in Britain, France, and the United States sent contributions to relieve the suffering of refugees. For an early example, see *Mshak,* 53, 12 March 1915, p. 3; Ionissian, *Polozhenie bezhentev v Aleksandropol'skom raione,* pp. 6–7. Pro-Armenian publications soon followed, including Emily Robinson, *Armenia and the Armenians,* the proceeds from which were destined for refugee relief. See also *Gorizont,* 219, 29 September 1915, p. 3; *Mshak,* 101, 10 May 1916, p. 3; ibid., 16, 24 January 1917, p. 3; Price, *War and Revolution,* p. 183, for the Lord Mayor's Fund for Armenians. One newspaper reported in 1917 that Americans sent 1.5 million rubles each month to support Armenian refugees. *Ashkhatank,* 58, 1917, p.

4. Other details in *Armiane i voina,* 4, June 1916; *Armianskii vestnik,* 9, 26 February 1917, p. 10; Hacobian, *Armenia and the War.*

58. Details in *Gorizont,* 9, 17 January 1915, p. 1; *Mshak,* 21, 31 January 1915, p. 3; ibid., 223, 10 October 1915, p. 1; ibid., 103, 12 May 1916, p. 3; *Pailak,* 2, 12 March 1915, p. 1; *Ashkhatank,* 63, 1916, p. 3; with a summary in TsGAA f. 50, op. 1, d. 185, l. 34. Other important agencies included the Armenian Agrarian Society, the Tbilisi Merchants' Committee, and the Elizabeth Fedorovna committees. *Izvestiia VSG,* 20, December 1915, p. 191. Visits made to the Caucasus by members of the central Tatiana Committee are detailed in *Otchet o deiatel'nosti osobogo otdela,* pp. 14–18. These efforts are summarized in Arutiunian, "Pervaia mirovaia voina," pp. 89–102.

59. TsGAA f. 50, op. 1, dd. 1, 33; RGVIA f. 2100, op. 1, d. 582, l. 44; *Gorizont,* 185, 19 August 1915, p. 3; ibid., 195, 30 August 1915, p. 3; ibid., 241, 27 October 1915, pp. 1–2; ibid., 5, 10 January 1916, p. 3; *Mshak,* 212, 27 September 1915, p. 3; *Ashkhatank,* 36, 1917, p. 3.

60. *Gorizont,* 175, 6 August 1915, p. 3, reporting an appeal by the Catholicos for government intervention. See also Ionnisian, *Polozhenie bezhentsev v Aleksandropol'skom raione,* p. 8; Kirakosian, *Zapadnaia Armeniia,* p. 421.

61. *Paikar,* 23, 5 January 1916, p. 2; *Ashkhatank,* 41, 1916, p. 3; A. Sarikiants, "Nashi bezhentsy i kolonii," *Armianskii vestnik,* 9, 26 February 1917, p. 10. In addition to Moscow and Petrograd, Sarikiants made an exception of Nakhichevan, the Armenian settlement near Rostov that was founded in 1780 and was home to 71,000 people by 1914. See *UR,* 213, 4 August 1915. Kirakosian, *Zapadnaia Armeniia,* p. 423, maintains that the Armenian bourgeoisie failed to act sufficiently quickly or generously, compared to the "multinational working class of Russia and the Transcaucasus."

62. *Armiane i voina,* 4, June 1916, p. 57. As early as January 1915, Armenians in the north Caucasus town of Armavir resolved that it was "unnecessary to approve the relocation of refugees to the north Caucasus or to Russia." *Mshak,* 3, 6 January 1915, p. 1. The Armenian intelligentsia affirmed its view in May 1916 that "orphaned refugees should under no circumstances be given up to private persons, but should be looked after only in the Armenian national organizations' own institutions." *Izvestiia VSG,* 34–34, June 1916, pp. 300–301.

63. *Ashkhatank,* 41, 1916, p. 3; *TP,* 2, 1916, p. 160. The criticisms by the editor of *Mshak* of the Armenian Central Committee in Tbilisi quickly led to the withdrawal of his invitation to attend its meetings. *Gorizont,* 19, 25 January 1915, p. 3.

64. Khatisov, or Khatisian, had been active in Transcaucasian politics since 1900, and first became mayor of Tbilisi in 1910. Having been a supporter of the Cadets, in 1917 he enlisted in the Dashnaktsutiun. Between August 1919 and May 1920, he was prime minister of independent Armenia. His memoirs, which appeared in the *Armenian Review,* are uninformative about his wartime career.

65. Suny, *Looking toward Ararat,* pp. 19–22. Painters such as M. Saroian, V. Surenian, F. Terlemezian, and E. Tatevosian activated the Armenian Artists' Society in Tbilisi and arranged several exhibitions to raise funds for refugee relief.

66. *Armiane i voina,* 1, March 1916, p. 15, quoting Papadzhanov; ibid., 2–3, April–May 1916, pp. 32–33; Akopian, *Zapadnaia Armeniia,* p. 195.

67. Quoted in Ananov, *Sud'ba Armenii,* p. 31; Somakian, *Empires in Conflict,* p. 78.

68. Hovannisian, *Armenia,* pp. 57, 62–63. In support of this policy, Armenian refugees who returned to their homes were not allowed to carry weapons, despite the risk (as General

Tamamshev pointed out in May 1916) of attacks from local Kurds. This rescinded a previous order issued in August 1915. RGVIA f. 2100, op. 1, d. 582, ll. 17, 44; ibid., d. 645, ll. 20–1, 44–ob. See also Somakian, *Empires in Conflict,* pp. 98, 107–10.

69. Prince Gadzhemukov to General Iudenich, 14 March 1917. RGVIA f. 2168, op. 1, d. 274, ll. 2–3. The author maintained that Armenian politicians' promises of tangible support to the Russian war effort had a hollow ring.

70. Grave, *Burzhuaziia,* pp. 89, 93, 96; other parts of the speech were reported in *Rech',* 72, 14 March 1916. See also Osherovskii, *Tragediia armian-bezhentsev,* p. 11.

71. "Obshchii obzor," *Izvestiia VSG,* 29–30, April 1916, pp. 211–18.

72. Hovannisian, *Armenia,* pp. 57, 64–67. The population of the region had fallen from 350,000 in 1910 to 15,000 by the beginning of 1916. There were only 11,000 Armenians left, compared to 185,000 six years earlier. Other groups had also been decimated. The Jewish community fell from 25,000 to 400, the Kurdish population from 72,000 to 3,000, and the Turkish community from 47,000 to just 85. *Armianskii vestnik,* 12–13, 24 April 1916, p. 34; *Armiane i voina,* 9, November 1916, p. 137.

73. Iudenich to Bishop Mesrop, 3 March 1916. RGVIA f. 2100, op. 1, d. 645, l. 1. General Tamamshev to Bolkhovitinov, Caucasian Army HQ, 17 June 1916. Ibid., ll. 44–ob.; Aganasian, "Ocherednye nuzhdy," pp. 243–49.

74. "Bezhentsy," *Armianskii vestnik,* 9, 3 April 1916, p. 10; *Rech',* 129, 12 May 1916; *Armianskii vestnik,* 12–13, 24 April 1916, pp. 35–36; ibid., 6, 5 February 1917, p. 18; ibid., 8, 19 February 1917, p. 21. For the responsibility of relief workers to ensure that orphans eventually reclaimed the property that belonged to their fathers, see *Armiane i voina,* 8, October 1916, p. 110.

75. N. Akhumov, "K s"ezdu armian," *Rech',* 127, 10 May 1916; ibid., 128, 11 May 1916; *Armiane i voina,* 2–3, April–May 1916, pp. 32–33; *Armianskii vestnik,* 17, 22 May 1916, pp. 21–22, emphasizing the all-party composition of the congress.

76. *Rech',* 128, 11 May 1916; ibid., 129, 12 May 1916. A second congress was scheduled for September 1916, in either Etchmidzian or Erevan, but military activity in the Caucasus prevented it from taking place. Eventually it convened in Petrograd in May 1917. *Armianskii vestnik,* 42, 13 November 1916, pp. 8–9; *TP,* 5, 1916, pp. 467–68; and *Rech',* 127, 10 May 1917.

77. Editorial, *Armianskii vestnik,* 32, 4 September 1915; A. A. [Agasian?], "Bezhentsy-armiane," *Armiane i voina,* 5, July 1916, p. 72. See also Hovannisian, *Armenia,* pp. 67–68, and Agaian, "Armianskie politicheskie partii."

78. Cohen, *Global Diasporas,* p. 27.

79. Davies, *God's Playground,* vol. 2, pp. 382–86. Germany's clandestine imperialist designs on Poland are outlined in Fischer, *Germany's Aims in the First World War,* pp. 236–44, 271–73. Fischer points out that the frontiers of the proposed Polish state were reserved for future determination.

80. Cherniavsky, *Prologue,* p. 123.

81. Wildman, *The End of the Russian Imperial Army,* p. 104; Beliakevich, "Iz istorii sozdanii pol'skikh natsional'nykh formirovanii."

82. Miliukov, *Political Memoirs,* pp. 17–18, 101–102. Dmowski had adopted a similar position during 1905. See Weeks, *Nation and State,* p. 116. Lednicki was an active member of Polish religious, cultural, and charitable societies in Moscow. His career details will be found in *Polski slownik biograficzny* (Wroclaw, 1971).

83. GARF f. 5115, op. 3, d. 220, l. 21; Davies, "The Poles in Great Britain."

84. GARF f. 5115, op. 3, d. 220, l. 6.

85. RGIA f. 1322, op. 1, d. 13, l. 42; *TP,* 6, 1916, pp. 46–47.

86. GARF f. 3333, op. 1a, d. 68, ll. 8, 27. In one case, a Russian officer had extorted money from a Polish refugee, who petitioned the confederation from Turgai oblast in Siberia. But the Polish confederation was unable to secure any redress.

87. *BV,* 14987, 26 July 1915; Swietoslawska-Zolkiewska, "Dzialalnosc"; Spustek, *Polacy w Piotrogrodzie,* pp. 228–38.

88. *TP,* 10, 1915, p. 469. The effort was repeated the following year. Ibid., 9, 1916, p. 396; see also *Izvestiia KTN,* 11, 1 November 1916, p. 23, and *Zhizn' bezhentsev,* 10, November 1916, p. 1. The Polish committee envisaged a monthly levy of 30 kopecks per person.

89. GARF f. 5115, op. 3, d. 220, l. 15; *Bezhenets,* 2, 18 October 1915; *Vestnik VOPB,* 47–48, 29 January 1917, p. 13.

90. Ibid., 51–52, 26 February 1917, pp. 5–6.

91. Grabski to Sobezh, July 1916. RGVIA f. 13273, op. 1, d. 39, ll. 43–46.

92. *UR,* 227, 18 August 1915. The refugees were described as "brat"ia-vyselentsy," that is, compatriots who had been forced out of Poland. On resistance to settlement in Siberia, see *TP,* 5, 1916, p. 463. On other occasions, Polish leaders referred to their compatriots as *izgnanniki,* "the banished ones." RGVIA f. 13273, op. 1, d. 39, ll. 8–12. See also the Duma debate on 14 August 1915. *GDSO,* 10th sitting, cols. 800–801, 808–10.

93. GARF f. 5115, op. 3, d. 11, l. 13; ibid., d. 220, ll6–17; RGVIA f. 13273, op. 1, d. 39, ll. 3, 8–12, for objections by the Polish Citizens' Committee to the dispersal of family members. The Khar'kov branch of the Tatiana Committee drew attention to refugees from the Privislinskii krai [sic] who "have begun to find salvation in the heart of Russia." *Komitet,* p. 451.

94. RGIA f. 1322, op. 1, d. 1, l. 46ob., Special Council, 11 November 1915.

95. *TP,* 6, 1916, p. 21. Life in Siberia was adjudged contrary to Polish culture and "unique way of life" (*samobytnost'*).

96. In August 1915, Janis Zalitis complained about the indifference of part of the Latvian intelligentsia to the national struggle. *BV,* 15059, 31 August 1915.

97. Cakste had been elected to the First Duma, but he lost his right to participate in future parliamentary business after he signed the Vyborg Manifesto in protest at its dissolution. Other members of the LCWC included J. Zalitis, J. Goldmanis, and K. Bachmanis. For its history, see *Kratkii obzor deiatel'nosti Pribaltiiskogo Latyshshkogo komiteta,* and Bachmanis, *Latvju tauta beglu gaitas.*

98. *BV,* 14995, 30 July 1915; *Izvestiia VSG,* 33–34, June 1916, p. 302; *Trudy vneo-cherednogo Pirogovskogo s"ezda,* p. 84.

99. RGIA f. 1322, op. 1, d. 1, ll. 6ob., 44; ibid., d. 13, ll. 44ob.–45. By October 1916, more than 200 Latvian organizations operated across Russia. *Beglu kalendars,* pp. 108–17.

100. RGIA f. 1322, op. 1, d. 13, l. 45. The LCWC's activities were publicized in the newspaper *Zinojums.* Refugee almanacs, published in Latvian in an edition of 30,000 copies, went on sale in bookshops, priced at 20 kopecks. On Latvian theater, see A. Berzins, "Musu teatrs beglu gada," *Beglu kalendars,* pp. 73–82.

101. Bachmanis, *Latvju tauta beglu gaitas,* pp. 200–10; *TP,* 1, 1916, p. 60; ibid., 3, 1916, p. 265; ibid., 5, 1916, p. 463.

102. *Lidums,* 70, 1915. The report in question concerned Tobol'sk. However, in the same issue a correspondent from Arkhangel'sk stated that Latvian settlers had "lost nothing of their

culture and language; furthermore, they have taught their neighbors (Russians, Tatars, Bashkirs) to cultivate land and to arrange it on the Baltic pattern. We know of some Russians who have learned Latvian." Great importance was attached to the role of teachers in eastern Siberia in preserving Latvian culture. Ibid., 88, 1915.

103. *Dzimtenes Atbalss,* 18–19, 1916. See also Anon., "Latvia and Latvian Settlements," ibid., 102, 1916.

104. Jekabs Ligotnu, "Latvian Culture in Siberia," *Dzimtenes Atbalss,* 46, 1916. Other writers argued that "Latvia means people not only from Kurzeme, Vidzeme, and Latgale, but also from settlements wherever they may be—Brazil, Shanghai, Krasnoiarsk, Novgorod, Ufa, or Eniseisk." Ibid., 192, 1916.

105. Quoted in *BV,* 15059, 31 August 1915.

106. The first prime minister of Latvia was Karlis Ulmanis, leader of the Latvian Peasant Union, established in April 1917; another leading member, Zigfrids Meierovics, became foreign minister.

107. *Lidums,* 209, 5 August 1915.

108. *BV,* 14977, 18 July 1915; ibid.,14987, 26 July 1915; ibid., 14995, 30 July 1915, quoting Janis Zalitis. For Latvians' perception of themselves as solid, adaptable, and dependable, see *Zinojums,* 14, 7 April 1916.

109. Wildman, *The End of the Russian Imperial Army,* p. 104; Burdzhalov, *Vtoraia russkaia revoliutsiia,* pp. 260–61, for radical politics in Nizhnii Novgorod, Khar'kov, Tver', and Vitebsk.

110. Strazhas, *Deutsche Ostpolitik;* Fischer, *Germany's Aims,* pp. 273–79.

111. Page, *Formation,* pp. 29–32. In November 1916, the German High Command gave permission for organized political activity by Lithuanian patriots. Previously, the German authorities had limited their activities, arresting the social democrat Augustinas Janulaitis, subsequently foreign minister in the first Lithuanian government. Strazhas, *Deutsche Ostpolitik,* pp. 90–93.

112. M. Ycas, *Pirmasis nepriklausomos,* pp. 35–37; *Kratkii obzor deiatel'nosti Litovskogo obshchestva,* p. 1. The committee initially confined its activities to the town of Vilna. Its members were Catholics and nationalists to a man. Biographical details of many of these figures will be found in *Lietuviu enciklopedija* (Boston,1956). Some of them later formed part of the German-sponsored Lithuanian assembly, the Taryba. An active Jewish relief committee in Vilna established Yiddish and Hebrew primary schools and a renowned Jewish high school. Mendelsohn, *Zionism in Poland,* p. 77.

113. *Rech',* 233, 25 August 1915.

114. Congress complaints were reported in *TP,* 1, 1916, p. 59. Other details from Strazhas, *Deutsche Ostpolitik,* pp. 81–83. The Lithuanians also disapproved of the decision to channel funds to the Polish Citizens' Committee in Warsaw, in order to assist refugees in Suwalki, even though the bulk of its inhabitants were Lithuanian. *Kratkii obzor deiatel'nosti Litovskogo obshchestva,* p. 7.

115. *TP,* 3, 1916, p. 265.

116. "Soveshchanie litovtsev-tekhnikov," *Vestnik VOPB,* 11, 13 March 1916, pp. 12–13.

117. Quoted in *Rech',* 233, 25 August 1915. The phrase "moral degradation" appears in Ycas, *Pirmasis nepriklausomos,* p. 38.

118. Ibid., p. 42. Working-class sympathizers pointed to the "bourgeois" composition of the Lithuanian committee. They advised that funds should be sent instead to workers'

sickness-benefit societies. *Kova,* 2, 8 January 1915. (I owe this reference to Jimmy White.) Strazhas, *Deutsche Ostpolitik,* pp. 71–73. Swiss-based Lithuanians also rallied to the cause. Viscont, *La Lituanie,* pp. 132–33.

119. RGIA f. 1322, op. 1, d. 1, ll. 66, 69, 70, with comments by Plehve and by A. N. Neverov, former governor of Akmolinsk, and later assistant minister of agriculture. Whether this suspicion also applied to Lithuanian Catholic refugees is not clear.

120. Ycas, *Pirmasis nepriklausomos,* p. 38.

121. *TP,* 10, 1916, p. 508.

122. This term appears in *Komitet,* p. 13. Elsewhere the Tatiana Committee observed that "the war against the Germans is not conducted by Libau or Yalta, by Kars oblast or Kaluga province, but by indivisible Russia [*vsia nerazdel'naia Rossiia*]." GARF f. 651, op. 1, d. 39, l. 56.

123. *Sputnik bezhentsa,* 4, 29–30 September 1915, p. 1.

124. M. Titov, "Otkliki na grozu i buriu voiny," *Ekaterinburgskie eparkhial'nye vedomosti,* 37, 13 September 1915, pp. 655–57. The importance of an attachment to the Orthodox faith emerges in the comments made about a concert of religious songs that a group of refugees from Chelm province gave to an audience in Irkutsk. The reporter spoke of their "profound devotion" to a 300-year-old tradition of song (the *Bogoglasnik*), which he explained in terms of the "unhappy union" between Orthodoxy and Catholicism in parts of Galicia and Russian Poland. The simple and devout songs reminded Russians that their real link was with Rus', and not with the Catholic church. *Irkutskie eparkhial'nye vedomosti,* 7, 1 April 1916, pp. 254–56.

125. *Samarskie eparkhial'nye vedomosti,* 23, 1 December 1915, p. 841; Jahn, *Patriotic Culture.*

126. Neutatz, *Die "deutsche Frage,"* p. 405.

127. *Vestnik VOPB,* 18, 15 May 1916, p. 10.

128. *GDSO,* 5th sitting, 3 August 1915, cols. 360–61, 434–36. See also Striegnitz, "Der Weltkrieg," pp. 134–39. Around 50,000 Volga Germans served in the tsarist army during the First World War.

129. RGIA f. 1284, op. 194, d. 22–1915, l. 3; *Ukrainskaia zhizn',* 4–5, April–May 1916, p. 127. There is some evidence to suggest that refugees were pressured into taking over the land belonging to German colonists. Nelipovich, "Rol' voennogo rukovodstva," p. 275. Hostility to these settlers appears to have been widespread in the Russian army. See Wildman, *The End of the Russian Imperial Army,* pp. 92–93, 113, citing a soldier's letter in 1916: "Are we to blame that the government acquired enemies by letting in German colonists?"

130. *Zhizn' bezhentsev,* 10, November 1916, p. 1.

131. *Golos,* 237, 17 October 1915.

132. *Rech',* 68, 10 March 1916.

133. See the remarks in *Vestnik VOPB,* 16–17, 1–8 May 1916, pp. 10–11, reporting on an Old Believer settlement in Ufa, where refugees found it hard to find jobs unless they were prepared to work for a pittance. Old Believers were accused of driving refugees out of their apartments.

134. Not that this process always worked in one direction. The Tatiana Committee praised a Muslim divine in Ufa who understood and respected the religious beliefs of Russian refugees and allowed them to celebrate Orthodox services in the garden he maintained in his "very simple home, in a purely Tatar village." *Izvestiia KTN,* 6, 15 August 1915, p. 12.

135. See the remarks in RGIA f. 525, op. 225/2747, d. 463, ll. 4–5.

136. He took special steps to ensure that the dietary needs of Russians were respected at Christmas. *Ekaterinburgskie eparkhial'nye vedomosti,* 1, 3 January 1916, pp. 11–12; ibid., 3, 17 January 1916, p. 61.

137. *Golos Rossii,* 5, 3 April 1916.

138. *Sputnik bezhentsa,* 3, 26–28 September 1915, p. 1. N. E. Markov was an extreme reactionary who sat in the third and fourth dumas.

139. This and a letter from refugees in Rostov were published in *Vestnik VOPB,* 8–9, 21–28 February 1916, p. 13.

140. Gr. Ian-Luk, "Bezhentsy," *Ufimskie eparkhial'nye vedomosti,* 7, 1 April 1916, p. 244. One of the fifty-eight relief agencies operating in Petrograd in May 1916 called itself the "Council of the Society for National Education, in Memory of P. A. Stolypin." *Spisok organizatsii,* p. 88.

141. The council was dominated by conservative parliamentarians and landowners, including senators N. P. Zuev, G. G. Chaplinskii, and S. P. Beletskii; Duma deputies G. G. Zamyslovskii and N. P. Markov; and Lt.-Gen. M. M. Borodkin. RGIA f. 525, op. 225/2747, d. 463, ll. 6–8, 13; *Vestnik VOPB,* 1, December 1915, pp. 7–8.

142. *TP,* 9, 1915, p. 361; the committee's statutes were published in *Vestnik VOPB,* 5, 31 January 1916, pp. 3–5.

143. By March 1916 the society boasted 40 schools, 59 children's homes, 17 hostels for the elderly, 7 feeding points, 7 labor exchanges, 27 workshops, 4 warehouses, and 105 reading rooms. Details in RGIA f. 525, op. 225/2747, d. 463, ll. 4–5; also *TP,* 2, 1916, pp. 156–57. For the Samara branch, see *Samarskie eparkhial'nye vedomosti,* 23, 1 December 1915, pp. 839–41.

144. *Izvestiia KTN,* no. 6, 15 August 1916, reporting the contents of a telegram sent by the MVD to the governor of Tambov province, who was asked to rectify this state of affairs.

145. Malkki, *Purity and Exile,* p. 155.

146. *Sputnik bezhentsa,* 3, 26–28 September 1915, p. 1.

147. Weeks, *Nation and State,* p. 123.

148. RGIA f. 1322, op. 1, d. 1, l. 33, 10th sitting of the Special Council, 16 October 1915 (report from Duma deputy D. I. Chikhachev); see also *Vestnik VOPB,* 15, 24 April 1916, pp. 11–12. Details of its activities have not survived in the records I have consulted.

149. A conference of refugee welfare organizations held in Moscow in April 1917 resolved to give priority to the formation of cadres of Belorussian teachers, "taking account of the lack of an intelligentsia among the poorly educated Belorussian peasantry." RGVIA f. 13273, op. 1, d. 64, l. 74.

150. The council was formed in 1900, in order to propagate pro-Russian sympathies among the Ukrainian peasantry in Galicia. Ibid., f. 2005, op. 1, d. 43, ll. 47–111ob.

151. Ibid., d. 44, ll. 1–14. In the autumn of 1916 General Brusilov ordered an investigation, which found that the leading figure in the council, V. F. Dudykevich, had embezzled the committee's funds, and planned to sow discord between a pro-Moscow group, on the one hand, and the "radical Ukrainians" on the other, in the interests of undermining the latter. The writer Korolenko labeled Dudykevich a local version of Bobrinskii, the aggressive Ukrainophobe whom we met earlier as governor of L'vov. *Ukrainskaia zhizn',* 10–11, October–November 1916, pp. 115–16, 139–41. Nonetheless, Dudykevich's organization survived at least until October 1917.

152. "Galichane v Rostove," *Ukrainskaia zhizn',* 11–12, December 1915, pp. 138–50.

153. RGVIA f. 13273, op. 1, d. 27, ll. 10–11.

154. *Ukrainskaia zhizn'*, 11–12, December 1915, p. 133. The unnamed author complained about the lack of support from the public organizations.

155. *Sputnik bezhentsa*, 4, 29–30 September 1915, p. 1; ibid., 7, 6–7 October 1915, p. 1. "Russia is the watchword of eastern Europe," according to an editorial in ibid., 6, 3–5 October 1915, p. 1. The editor granted that the "Little Russian" language might be taught in tsarist schools, but he resolutely opposed all forms of "separatist" activity.

156. "Bezhat' ili ne bezhat'?" *Ukrainskaia zhizn'*, 10, October 1915, pp. 84–85.

157. Kazanskii, *Galitsko-russkie bezhentsy*, p. 8.

158. Ibid., pp. 22–33.

159. G. Sofinskii, "Bezhentsy v Balashovskom uezde," *Saratovskie eparkhial'nye vedomosti*, 22, 1 August 1916, pp. 852–53; Smirnov-Kutacheskii, "Bezhentsy-galichane," p. 131.

160. Weeks, *Nation and State*, p. 65.

161. Smirnov-Kutacheskii, "Bezhentsy-galichane," pp. 134–35.

162. Mariia Ancharova, "Galichane v Rostove," *Rech'*, 114, 27 April 1916; Ancharova was unable to convince her skeptical informant that Russia recognized freedom of religion. See also Ivan Rudnytsky, "The Fourth Universal and Its Ideological Antecedents," in Hunczak, *The Ukraine*, pp. 203–204.

163. Hovannisian, *Armenia*, p. 89. V. I. Frolov, the chairman of the Baku Committee to Aid Refugees, spoke of his work as a small contribution to "smoothing the sharp edges of the national question in the Caucasus." Ionnisian, *Polozhenie bezhentsev v Aleksandropol'skom raione*, p. 4. At least one contemporary source speaks of persistent "national jealousies" as a factor hampering the relief effort. *Izvestiia VSG*, 29–30, April 1916, pp. 211–18.

164. Editorial, *Armiane i voina*, 1, March 1916, p. 1.

165. The journal *Work Relief* paid tribute to the cooperation between the labor exchanges operated by various national committees. *TP*, 10, 1915, p. 472. At the same time, we should not forget that contemporaries drew attention to jealousies that were fueled by rumors of the differential financial support given to national communities.

166. Calhoun, *Critical Social Theory*, pp. 255–56.

167. Consider the exhibition planned for the spring of 1917 on "Russia and Her Devastated Borderlands": "The greater the quantity of material collected for the exhibition, the better it will be for refugees from each national minority, because the level of their development and their labor will be clearly demonstrated. Members of the broad educated public will better understand the suffering and tribulations of the given ethnic group [*narodnost'*]." *Izvestiia KTN*, 13, 1 December 1916, pp. 10–11.

168. See Calhoun, *Critical Social Theory*, pp. 256–59, for an emphasis on the individual's relation to the nation, the corresponding emergence of a "categorical identity," as opposed to a relational identity, and the importance that attaches to "identity-forming collective discourse" within a transformed political public sphere.

8. REVOLUTION AND REFUGEEDOM

1. Prince G. E. L'vov, a casualty of the events in summer 1915, now led the first provisional government. Yet L'vov did not command universal admiration among Russia's liberal elite; Paul Miliukov, who served as his foreign minister, described him as a "twit" (*shliapa*). Cited in Katkov, *February 1917*, p. 498.

2. "As the war comes to an end, we know well that the so-called refugee question will become even more prominent and acute." *Zhizn' bezhentsev*, 1, September 1916, p. 1.

3. Ibid., 10, November 1916, pp. 1–2; A. N., "Medlit' prestupno," ibid., pp. 8–9.

4. The number of refugees had also swelled toward the end of 1916, in the aftermath of the abortive Rumanian campaign. Beliaev to Lodyzhenskii, 22 November 1916. RGVIA f. 2005, op. 1, d. 43, l. 28.

5. *Sputnik bezhentsa,* p. 41.

6. The Polish Duma deputy F. I. Loshkeit pointed to the plight of impoverished Catholic clergy, who had received no payment for services rendered to their displaced flock. RGIA f. 1322, op. 1, d. 13, ll. 63–65, Special Council, 3 December 1916.

7. *Mshak,* 277, 13 December 1916, p. 3.

8. RGIA f. 1322, op. 1, d. 13, l. 63.

9. Viceroy of the Caucasus, 15 December 1915. TsGAA f. 50, op. 1, d. 120, l. 90; *Mshak,* 282, 18 December 1916, p. 3, for complaints that Poles and Latvians were relatively protected from these cuts. Cuts in central government spending forced the closure of organized welfare activity in several towns, including Smolensk, the nearby town of Orsha, and distant Omsk. *Zhizn' bezhentsev,* 7, October 1916, p. 1.

10. *TP,* 4, 1916, p. 354.

11. Stavka had few kind words to say about Zubchaninov's organization. An eyewitness in Mogilev, pointing to the millions of rubles spent by Severopomoshch', reported that it was nicknamed "Severonemoshch'" ("Northern Impotence") and "Sebepomoshch'" ("Help Yourself"). Lemke, *250 Dnei,* p. 281; RGVIA f. 2049, op. 1, d. 447, ll. 5, 6–7, 29–29ob., 33–34, 45–46.

12. *TP,* 1, 1917, p. 48. Overhead costs represented 4.7 percent and 1.8 percent respectively of total turnover. In Zubchaninov's case, this was higher than the Tatiana Committee.

13. Iugobezhenets was now responsible for just two provinces, Volynia and Podol'ia. Zubchaninov retained authority in twelve provinces, including five in the interior of European Russia, which Khvostov proposed to hand over to local authorities. A warning of the consequences of closing the offices of Severopomoshch' was carried in *Zhizn' bezhentsev,* 7, October 1916, p. 1.

14. RGIA f. 1276, op. 12, d. 1427, ll. 10–11ob., memorandum dated 12 December 1916. An article in *Vestnik VOPB,* 2, 3 January 1916, pp. 4–6, noted that "local people in the vicinity of the front suffer the same kind of deprivations as refugees."

15. Since reduced to seven. Urusov revealed in his letter of resignation that he had worked without salary, thereby "donating" some 14,000 rubles to the war effort. In a curt reply, Stürmer scarcely acknowledged the role Urusov had played. RGIA f. 1276, op. 12, d. 1424, ll. 1–4.

16. *Iugobezhenets,* 36, 8 September 1916, p. 1.

17. In a report in *TP,* 8, 1916, pp. 270–71, Zubchaninov is quoted as saying that some of his responsibilities had already been transferred to local authorities. Evgenii Nikol'skii, for example, handed his over to the Union of Zemstvos. He emigrated in February 1918, but his wife died four days before their departure from Moscow for Vladivostok, and he "was left completely alone." Nikol'skii, "Bezhentsy," p. 99.

18. RGIA f. 1322, op. 1, d. 13, l. 87, Special Council, 27/30 December 1916. See also the remarks on this renewed manifestation of *stikhiinost'* in *Izvestiia VSG,* 33–34, June 1916, pp. 292–94. Jews were to be prevented from making the return journey, since they were "unsuitable" for productive economic activity.

19. Lemke, *250 dnei,* p. 606.

20. *TP,* 3, 1916, p. 264.

21. *Izvestiia VSG,* 33–34, June 1916, p. 295.

22. M. M. Gran, "Deiatel'nost' otdela pomoshchi bezhentsam Petrogradskogo oblastnogo komiteta," ibid., 33, June 1916, pp. 57–67.

23. *Izvestiia KTN,* 5, 1 August 1916, p. 3; T. K., "K vozvrashcheniiu bezhentsev," *Vestnik VOPB,* 26–27, 17–24 July 1916, pp. 7–9.

24. As early as November 1915, Bishop Anastasii told the Special Council that the return of refugees was likely to be even more intractable a problem than the original displacement. "Pomoshch' bezhentsam," *TP,* 10, 1915, p. 463.

25. "Itogi goda," *Zhizn' bezhentsev,* 4, September 1916, pp. 8–9.

26. Special Council, 15 September and 3 December 1916. RGIA f. 1322, op. 1, d. 13, ll. 60, 70–70ob.; *TP,* 8, 1916, p. 271.

27. The new chairman, B. A. Engel'gardt, insisted that the Special Council should be cautious in allocating public funds, adding that although its "duty is to aid refugees, such help should not be regarded as a form of charity." Special Council, 18 March 1917. RGIA f. 1322, op. 1, d. 13, ll. 100ob. In June 1917 he asked the government for additional funds in order to mitigate the "threatening position of refugees." GARF f. 3333, op. 2, d. 1a, ll. 2–11.

28. RGIA f. 1322, op. 1, d. 1, l. 101.

29. Ibid., d. 13, ll. 103–103ob.; *Izvestiia KTN,* 20, 15 May 1917, p. 4.

30. RGIA f. 1322, op. 1, d. 13, ll. 106–107ob., Special Council, 20 March 1917. The committee launched its own quiet campaign in the pages of its house journal, publishing letters from grateful recipients of assistance. *Izvestiia KTN,* 19, 15 April 1917, pp. 6–7; *Vestnik VOPB,* 49–50, 12 February 1917, p. 9; *Obzor o deiatel'nosti osobogo otdela,* pp. 42–47.

31. The proposal was opposed by V. G. Averin (Khar'kov), who threatened to leave the congress forthwith; he was supported by delegates from Kaluga and Pskov. However, the proposal had the backing of Neidgardt himself, as well as delegates from Kovno and Voronezh, and it was duly accepted. *Trudy Vtorogo Vserossiiskogo s"ezda,* pp. 80–87.

32. The congress lasted from 7 through 10 April. Those attending included N. N. Nadezhin from Sobezh; I. K. Gudz (Tula), representing the Union of Zemstvos; I. I. Zhukov (Kaluga) from the Union of Towns; K. O. Bachmanis, representing the Central Latvian Committee; E. I. Peshkova from children's welfare organizations; V. A. Obolenskii, from the Petrograd Union of Towns, and A. A. Isaev from the Petrograd Oblast Union of Towns. The historians S. B. Veselovskii and V. I. Giliarovskii also took part. Invitations were sent to Neidgardt, chairman of the Tatiana Committee, and Engelgardt, chairman of the Special Council, but neither took up the offer to attend. RGVIA f. 13273, op. 1, d. 64, ll. 1, 12–13.

33. RGIA f. 1322, op. 1, d. 1, ll. 337–44; see also the brief report in *Izvestiia VSG,* 44, 1917, p. 183. The congress voted to dissolve the Tatiana Committee and to transfer its local business to municipal and zemstvo refugee committees.

34. RGVIA f. 13273, op. 1, d. 64, l. 16.

35. RGIA f. 1322, op. 1, d. 1, l. 337.

36. In accordance with the emphasis on citizenship, refugees were to be enfranchised and allowed to vote for the proposed constituent assembly, on the basis of their original place of residence. Special efforts were also to be made to establish whether some refugee children could be repatriated, "for the sake of preventing a complete severance from their native land." RGVIA f. 13273, op. 1, d. 64, ll. 59–65, 74.

37. RGIA f. 1322, op. 1, d. 13, l. 113ob.

38. GARF f. 3333, op. 2, d. 1a, ll. 15–18. Kornilov was also opposed to compulsory deportations.

39. Zemgor Refugee Section, memorandum to Stavka, 11 September 1917. RGVIA f. 2005, op. 1, d. 44, ll. 39–ob. See also RGVIA f. 13273, op. 1, d. 16, ll. 153–58.

40. *Mshak,* 11, 18 January 1917, p. 3.

41. Gosudarstvennyi arkhiv Voronezhskoi oblasti f. 104, op. 1, d. 82, l. 6, memorandum dated 21 October 1917. I am grateful to Vladimir Zakharov for making a copy of this document available to me.

42. V. A. Bulgakov reporting to the Special Council, 28 April 1917. RGIA f. 1322, op. 1, d. 1, l. 143. The crisis in public finances led the provisional government to cut the budget для for refugee relief in the summer of 1917, prompting the Special Council to protest at the abdication of its responsibility toward refugees who had been led to believe that their economic position would not deteriorate further. Ibid., l. 155, Special Council, 13 July 1917.

43. The displaced Germans (*vyselentsy*) "are in a completely different situation from refugees who were forced to flee from the sudden attack by enemy troops." Ibid., l. 143ob.

44. Ibid., ll. 143, 166.

45. RGVIA f. 2005, op. 1, d. 28, ll. 323–ob., 335; ibid., f. 1759, op. 4, d. 1816, ll. 64–65, 98–ob., for petitions asking for the right to return home. There were obvious difficulties facing German settlers who wished to return to their farms: apart from a shortage of transport, "their colonies . . . may have been taken over by refugees," according to officers on the southwestern front. Ibid., f. 2005, op. 1, d. 28, ll. 322–ob., 31 August 1917; see also Fleischauer, "The Ethnic Germans in the Russian Revolution."

46. Rogger, *Jewish Policies,* pp. 349–50.

47. In Khar'kov, Latvian refugees announced that "war as a means of conquest is unacceptable to us, but in view of the fact that part of Latvia is in the hands of the enemy we must support Russia in its war until peace is finally concluded." *Dzimtenes Atbalss,* 31, 22 April 1917. For a patriotic statement by Riga's municipal duma, pointedly—and timidly— submitted on behalf of the "Pribaltiiskii krai" ("Baltic region") to the leaders of "our dear homeland, great Russia," see LVVA f. 2736, op. 1, d. 40, l. 10, 4 March 1917.

48. *Dzimtenes Atbalss,* 21, 15 March 1917; ibid., 24, 25 March 1917; ibid., 28, 12 April 1917, reporting meetings in Helsingfors, Khar'kov, Kazan', and Novgorod. See also Germanis, "Die Autonomie," p. 22, and Burdzhalov, *Vtoraia russkaia revoliutsiia,* pp. 262, 265. A meeting of 48 public organizations in Riga on 8 March 1917 launched the task of political and administrative restructuring and resolved that all government employees must know Latvian.

49. *Dzimtenes Atbalss,* 26, 5 April 1917; ibid., 51, 5 July 1917. The refugees' newspaper asserted that Latvia comprised the following districts: Vidzeme, Kurzeme (minus seven *pagast*s [i.e., volosts] in the southwest, and the district of Palanga), Jaunroze *pagast* in the district of Verava, Latgale (including Daugavpils, Rezekne, and Ludza in Vitebsk province), and Akniza and "some other territory" in Lithuania; "the southern border of Latvia in Latgale has to be decided on the basis of a census and/or referendum." Ibid., 21, 15 March 1917. Latgale was the predominantly Catholic region that formed part of the province of Vitebsk, having been ceded to Russia during the first partition of Poland.

50. The Latvian social democratic newspaper *Cina* appealed to the inhabitants to stay in Riga, but many leading social democrats were instructed to leave the city. Liberal activists such as Ulmanis and Valters (the future minister of the interior) remained behind. Germanis, "Die Autonomie," pp. 44, 47.

51. Such a council had already been advocated by delegates who attended a meeting of Latvian organizations in Moscow in March; Goldmanis and Zalitis were criticized at a con-

gress of Latvian riflemen (27–29 March) for their procrastination. *Dzimtenes Atbalss,* 21, 15 March 1917.

52. Klive, *Briva Latvija,* pp. 217–37. Klive chaired the meeting of the LPNC. The declaration was penned by the Latvian writer Karlis Skalbe.

53. Ibid.; Silde, *Latvijas Vesture,* pp. 207–11.

54. Ligotnu, *Latvijas Valsts Dibinasana,* pp. 402–26. A supporter in Khar'kov asked hopefully "for a list of projects in order to seek donations from Latvian millionaires in Khar'kov."

55. The main refugee newspaper "consoled itself that Latvian workers at this historic time do not yield to class interests, but take part with other refugees in the debates on autonomy for Latvia." *Dzimtenes Atbalss,* 51, 5 July 1917.

56. Suny, "Nationalism and Class," p. 237; Germanis, "Die Autonomie," pp. 64–65. The Latvian constitution of November 1918 gave all refugees the right to return. It also respected the rights of non-Latvian minorities, giving proportional representation to minority groups and providing for elementary education in the mother tongue. But the nationality law of 1921 allegedly "excluded from citizenship large numbers of Jews who were obliged to leave the country at the beginning of the war, and who are now unable to return because they had not been registered." Mair, *The Protection of Minorities,* p. 114.

57. I draw here on brief summaries of *Proletarine revoliucija Lietuvoje* and Bronius Vaitkevicius, *Socialistine revoliucija Lietuvoje,* kindly prepared by Dr. J. D. White.

58. Rauch, *The Baltic States,* pp. 40–41; Senn, *Emergence,* pp. 25–27.

59. The full text of the First Universal is translated in Hunczak, *The Ukraine,* pp. 382–85. Full independence was not declared until 25 January 1918, with the promulgation of the Fourth Universal.

60. Allen, *The Ukraine,* p. 276.

61. Ibid., p. 280. See also Guthier, "The Popular Basis of Ukrainian Nationalism."

62. Allen, *The Ukraine,* pp. 283–87.

63. *Protokoly, postanovleniia i materialy,* pp. 16, 50, 63–64. In January 1919 the Bolsheviks recognized the new Soviet republic of Belorussia.

64. Grand Duke Nicholas was recalled to Petrograd, and administrative responsibility for the region was assumed by Khatisian, the Georgian Menshevik Noe Zhordania, and D. Popov, on behalf of the Army of the Caucasus. The provisional government moved to establish a "Special Transcaucasian Committee" (Ozakom), which governed the occupied Ottoman territories as well as the Russian Caucasus. No places were found on Ozakom for the Dashnaks, who promptly complained that it was unrepresentative of the Armenian people. See Hovannisian, *Armenia,* pp. 70, 75–80; Suny, *Looking toward Ararat,* pp. 120–21.

65. These refugees could prove their right to reclaim their farms only if they retained title deeds to the property. However, Ianushkevich had ordered these to be seized in 1916, as part of the tsarist strategy of encouraging Russian colonization. Ananov, *Sud'ba Armenii,* p. 24.

66. N. Akhumov, "K s"ezdu armian," *Rech',* 127, 10 May 1917, expresses disappointment that Armenian refugees and local relief workers were unable to attend.

67. Hovannisian, *Armenia,* pp. 63, 78–80.

68. Ibid., p. 97.

69. Suny, *Looking toward Ararat,* pp. 125–29; Hovannisian, *Armenia,* chapters 7, 8, and 9.

70. Suny, *Looking toward Ararat,* p. 137. See also the remarks of Armenian politicians

in late 1917, summarized by one scholar as the view that "the struggle for physical self-preservation hampered the development of national consciousness and unity." Hovannisian, *Armenia,* p. 89.

71. Dunsdorfs, "Bevölkerungs- und Wirtschaftsprobleme," pp. 326–27.

72. Ycas, *Pirmasis nepriklausomos,* p. 38, for the view that the committee "prepared the people for future action and created the foundations for a future cultural and political edifice. . . . It unearthed the buried name of Lithuania and forced even non-Lithuanians to recognize that we ourselves were the masters of our country." Ycas had become deputy chairman of the Tatiana Committee in March 1917. *Izvestiia KTN,* 20, 15 May 1917, p. 16.

73. By early 1917, around 500 Armenians were employed by the Armenian Central Welfare Committee. Arutiunian, "Pervaia mirovaia voina," p. 90.

74. Petition dated 1 May 1919. GARF f. 3333, op. 1a, d. 102, l. 86.

75. Skultans, *The Testimony of Lives,* p. 6.

76. *Bezhenskaia pravda,* 1, 29 October 1917, p. 6. This newspaper described itself as a "herald of the new life and specific ideals and aspirations of refugees." Significantly, only one issue ever appeared.

77. Ibid., p. 9.

78. Ibid., pp. 9–11. There were signs at the congress that the Bolsheviks supported the refugees' union in the face of hostility from the provisional government, but the party did this for tactical reasons.

79. Chebaevskii, "K istorii," pp. 68–69.

80. Tsentroplenbezh met several times each week. The minutes of early meetings can be consulted in GARF f. 333, op. 2, d. 14. The first three meetings were chaired by Gillerson, about whom nothing is known; Unshlikht took over at the end of April. Karl Radek also attended occasionally. Iosif Unshlikht was a founding member of the pro-Bolshevik Social Democratic Party of the Kingdom of Poland and of Lithuania (SDKPiL). Jailed by the tsarist authorities in 1913, he subsequently became a member of the executive of the Petrograd Soviet and a prominent figure in the Petrograd Military Revolutionary Committee. A member of the NKVD collegium from mid-November 1917, he held office with Tsentroplenbezh until the end of 1918. Thereafter he spent several months on party and military duties in Lithuania and Belorussia. By the early 1920s—his career unhindered by his contribution to the cause of the "left Communists" in 1918—Unshlikht had risen to become vice-president of Feliks Dzerzhinskii's OGPU. In short, he is one of the most unpleasant people to figure in this book. Korzhikhina, *Sovetskoe gosudarstvo,* p. 98; Leggett, *The Cheka,* pp. 271–73. The appointment of Unshlikht's successor, Tikhmenev, was announced in *Izvestiia TsKPB,* 21, April 1919.

81. *Dekrety sovetskoi vlasti,* vol. 2, pp. 165–67, 462–63, decrees dated 27 April and 21 June 1918. In June 1918, on the eve of the outbreak of the Russian civil war, Sovnarkom subordinated the national committee of the Red Cross, as well as the Union of Towns and the Union of Zemstvos, to Tsentroplenbezh. In August the children's homes administered by Sobezh were taken over by the Commissariat for Social Security. RGVIA f. 13273, op. 1, d. 14, l. 73. The collegium published a weekly paper, *Izvestiia tsentral'noi kollegii o plennykh i bezhentsakh,* Moscow, 1918–19. The first issue appeared on 2 June 1918, the last in April 1919. In May 1919, the collegium was subordinated to the Commissariat for Internal Affairs (NKVD), rather than coming under the immediate authority of Sovnarkom. *Dekrety sovetskoi vlasti,* vol. 5, pp. 231–32.

82. GARF f. 3333, op. 8, d. 62, ll. 2–3. Many of its employees had worked previously for the Red Cross, as statisticians, translators, and the like. Few of those named in the personnel files had careers with the public organizations. Ibid., op. 2, d. 285.

83. "Soobshchenie v pechat' po delu reevakuatsii bezhentsev," 21 April 1918. Ibid., d. 322, l. 2.

84. Ibid., op. 8, d. 62, l. 3.

85. Possessions that were forbidden included gold, silver (to the value of 1 ruble and above), notes to a value of more than 1,000 rubles (sick and disabled persons were entitled to take up to 2,000 rubles), precious stones and jewelry ("to the extent that the amount exceeds normal personal needs"), firearms, cameras, binoculars, furs and hides, printed material and photographs that might damage the military and economic interests of the republic, and foodstuffs (more than one pud, including more than half a pud of grain). Ibid., ll. 13–18, 80–81. The decree was published in *Plennyi i bezhenets* (Saratov), 1, 1–15 November 1918, p. 1. Formal permits to leave Soviet-held territory could be issued only by provincial and uezd boards, and not by Soviets acting in collusion with the German army. GARF f. 3333, op. 2, d. 14, l. 17.

86. Ibid., d. 322, ll. 10–ob., 30 May 1918.

87. "Otchet po voprosu o vozmozhnykh formakh reevakuatsii bezhentsev," Minsk, 26 May 1918. Ibid., ll. 83–91.

88. This figure presumably refers to the twelve months since the October revolution. *Izvestiia TsKPB*, 18, 7 November 1918, pp. 4, 11. Around 375,000 refugees left Soviet Russian territory between May and August inclusive. GARF f. 3333, op. 8, d. 62, l. 3. "Refugees" entitled to assistance had to belong to one of the following categories: those who had "settled"; those who had started on their journey home; those who had been stopped en route, in order to work in the rear; and those who had been stopped in the vicinity of the front. Sovnarkom instructions, 28 January 1919. Ibid., ll. 98–ob.

89. Ibid., op. 1a, d. 102, l. 159.

90. Ibid., op. 2, d. 322, l. 4; d. 76, ll. 4–6.

91. *Izvestiia TsKPB*, 17, 3 November 1918, pp. 2–3. The anonymous author played into the hands of the German officials when he wrote of his hopes that the day would soon dawn when the frontier was open, allowing a "new Germany" to extend a welcome to "fraternal fighters for freedom."

92. "We have before us an example not of the re-evacuation of refugees but of a gigantic labor exchange where refugees are treated like cattle [*zhivoi tovar*]." Ibid.; also ibid., 13, 15 September 1918, pp. 5–6; ibid., 20, 23 December 1918, pp. 11–13.

93. Their legal status as citizens of Poland, Latvia, etc. was resolved only in 1920. In the meantime, unless they had expressed a wish to the contrary, they were deemed to have accepted by default the offer of Russian citizenship made on 13 July. *Prikaz* dated 14 August 1918, GARF f. 3333, op. 8, d. 8, ll. 1, 2, 57; *Dekrety sovetskoi vlasti,* vol. 3, pp. 103–104, decree dated 27 July 1918.

94. Yuri Felshtinsky, "Legal Foundations," p. 338.

95. Narkomnats had already established national subcommissariats. For example, the Polish commissariat contacted the Union of Zemstvos in March 1918, in order to determine the size of the Polish refugee population on Russian territory and to prepare for their repatriation. Lescinski to VZS, 6 March 1918. RGVIA f. 13273, op. 1, d. 39, l. 48.

96. *Izvestiia TsKPB*, 9, 11 August 1918, pp. 1–2. As late as June 1918, the Union of Towns still operated feeding stations at border crossing points.

97. As argued by the legal department (*pravovoi otdel*), n.d. GARF f. 3333, op. 8, d. 62, l. 105.

98. Belorussian People's Commissariat to Tsentroplenbezh, Saratov, 17 March 1919. Ibid., op. 7, d. 64, ll. 45–ob.

99. *Izvestiia TsKPB,* 3, 23 June 1918, pp. 5–6; GARF f. 3333, op. 2, d. 332, ll. 83–91, for the desperate situation in Orsha in May and June.

100. Ibid., d. 76, ll. 4–6.

101. Ibid., d. 332, ll. 83–91; ibid., d. 76, ll. 11–13. *Prilozhenie k Izvestiiam TsKPB,* 1, 18 August 1918, p. 6 (V. Balitskii); *Izvestiia TsKPB,* 10, 18 August, 1918, p. 1; A. Mokievskii, "Sovetskaia vlast' v dele pomoshchi plennym i bezhentsam Iaroslavskoi gubernii," ibid., 20, 23 December 1918, pp. 11–13. Refugees in Kursk were reported to be reluctant to admit to infectious disease, lest they become separated from their loved ones—just as they had behaved, understandably, in 1915. GARF f. 3333, op. 2, d. 76, ll. 31–38.

102. That is, the refugees would be entitled to a share in the land only once the land norms of local people had been satisfied. See Figes, *Peasant Russia, Civil War,* pp. 138–44.

103. Okninskii's comments are quoted in ibid., p. 142.

104. As reported by Belorussian refugees in Penza, *Protokoly, postanovleniia i materialy,* p. 21.

105. Keep, *The Russian Revolution,* pp. 406–407, expresses the plausible view that "the determining factors seem to have been the strength of the claimant's connection with the community and the plentifulness of land available."

106. *Plennyi i bezhenets,* 3–4, 16–30 November 1918, pp. 55–56; GARF f. 3333, op. 7, d. 64, l. 78.

107. *Plennyi i bezhenets,* 9–10, 1–15 February 1919, p. 6.

108. GARF f. 3333, op. 1a, d. 102, ll. 7, 40. Tsentroplenbezh replied that the border with Grodno was closed, and that it had no resources of its own to assist refugees in Zaraisk.

109. *Plennyi i bezhenets,* 3–4, 16–30 November 1918, pp. 56–57. S. M. Mazlakh, chair of the provincial board in Saratov, maintained that many refugees had been taught by the old regime to become parasites. Now there was a desperate need to put them to work, in order to improve the prospects for the spring sowing campaign. Zika, "Domoi!" *Plennyi i bezhenets,* 9–10, 1–15 February 1919, pp. 7–11, did not beat around the bush, telling refugees that they should give up any idea of returning home before the summer at the very earliest. Those who refused to work forfeited the right to food and other forms of material assistance. "TP," n.d., GARF f. 3333, op. 8, d. 62, l. 102.

110. As in Saratov in the spring of 1919. Ibid., op. 7, d. 64, l. 81.

111. Ibid., op. 2, d. 332, ll. 1–3.

112. Ibid., op. 7, d. 1, ll. 28–29ob.; *Plennyi i bezhenets,* 3–4, 16–30 November 1918, p. 56. Stories of rotten potatoes are recounted in *Protokoly, postanovleniia i materialy,* p. 21.

113. GARF f. 3333, op. 1a, d. 102, l. 18; ibid., op. 7, d. 64, ll. 12–13.

114. Ibid.

115. Ibid., op. 1a, d. 102, l. 21; ibid., op. 7, d. 64, ll. 12–13.

116. *Izvestiia TsKPB,* 18, 7 November 1918, p. 4.

117. *Plennyi i bezhenets,* 1, 1–15 November 1918, p. 5, *prikaz* dated 29 October.

118. Zika, "Neskol'ko slov bezhentsam," *Plennyi i bezhenets,* 1, 1–15 November 1918, p. 17.

119. "Ko vsei bezhenskoi bednote v RSFSR," *Izvestiia TsKPB,* 18, 7 November 1918, p. 4. The author argued that solidarity should have been strengthened by the fact that the

wealthiest refugees had already found a warm welcome among the reactionary governments of Germany, Austria, and Ukraine. In a different vein, another writer found it perfectly understandable that less well-off refugees should wish to "cease playing the role of nomads, far from enjoying the sympathy of the settled population," and to return "home." *Plennyi i bezhenets,* 1, 1–15 November 1918, p. 6.

120. Skran, *Refugees,* pp. 32–40.

121. Ibid., p. 82. For further detail, see Simpson, *The Refugee Problem,* pp. 181–85.

122. Skran, *Refugees,* pp. 82–83.

123. Under the terms of the treaty with Latvia (12 May 1920), the Soviet state undertook to repatriate a minimum of 2,000 refugees and prisoners per week. GARF f. 3333, op. 2, d. 166, ll. 3–6. An agreement with Poland on the exchange of "internees, prisoners, hostages, and refugees" was reached in Riga in November 1920. Ibid, d. 136, l. 102.

124. Fisher, *The Famine in Soviet Russia,* p. 29.

125. A distinction was drawn between refugees and *optanty,* i.e., those who had already opted for non-Soviet citizenship. GARF f. 3333, op. 7, d. 7, ll. 1–2ob. In August 1921, the ARA found near Sebezh "crawling freight trains of gaunt refugees, ill-clad, hungry and sick, crammed together like animals." Fisher, *Famine,* p. 71.

126. Quoted in Skran, *Refugees,* p. 103.

127. Ibid., p. 105.

128. Ibid., p. 122, registering also the extreme difficulties faced by refugees during the depression of the 1930s. Some European politicians revealed their own warped sense of refugee identity: the bigoted British Under-Secretary of State for Foreign Affairs, Cecil Harmsworth, condemned as "an intolerable nuisance" the thousands of myriad "Cossacks, Kalmucks, priests, generals, judges and ladies" who sought the protection of the British government. Ibid., p. 149. For an astringent overview of the consequences of war, see Arendt, *Origins of Totalitarianism,* pp. 269–302.

129. GARF f. 3333, op. 1a, d. 102, contains many such petitions from "forgotten" refugees. Others took the view that the agency was "petty and unimportant." Ibid., op. 2, d. 332, ll. 10–11.

130. Petition from refugees in Kursk, 10 January 1919. Ibid., op. 7, d. 1, l. 11. See also the letter from a "peasant refugee" in Kursk, dated 23 March 1919. Ibid., ll. 44–45.

131. *Protokoly, postanovleniia i materialy,* pp. 63–64.

132. These departments were established in May 1916 by the Armenian congress. *Armianskii vestnik,* 18, 29 May 1916.

9. CONCLUSION

1. The category of *raznochintsy* ("people of various ranks") underwent a series of transformations between 1700 and 1900. Its very plasticity represents a contrast with the immutable category of the refugee. Wirtschafter, *Social Identity in Imperial Russia,* pp. 63–71.

2. *Zhizn' bezhentsev,* 4, September 1916, pp. 8–9. Other references to "nomadic life" include Sysin, "Sanitarnoe sostoianie Rossii," pp. 49–50. In an unusual formulation, an Armenian newspaper commented that "the majority of refugees [in the Caucasus] belong to the farming estate [*soslovie zemlevladel'tsev*]." *Gorizont,* 27, 5 February 1917, p. 1.

3. RGIA f. 1322, op. 1, d. 1, l. 60ob. (A. F. Koni). Refugee relief workers commonly drew attention to aspects of loss: "Refugees now have nothing, and they are far from the family graves on which they might have been able to pour out their grief." Quoted in *Viatskie*

eparkhial'nye vedomosti, 35, 27 August 1915, p. 1072. For other emphatic comments about dispossession and degradation, see the editorial in *Severnyi bezhenets,* 12, 30 March 1916, p. 2, and "Itogi goda," *Zhizn' bezhentsev,* 4, September 1916, pp. 8–9. Brutskus, "Gde ustroit nashikh bezhentsev?" p. 11, speaks of the hope that Jewish refugees might be reunited with their household possessions. Downward social mobility thus effaced the distinction drawn by some observers between "refugees" who, by virtue of wealth, had been able to leave their homes voluntarily, and those who were forced to leave.

4. In September 1916, the Special Council debated temporary rules to provide loans for refugees, in order to allow them to establish household economic units, for purposes of "consumption" rather than profit. RGIA f. 1322, op. 1, d. 13, ll. 43–43ob., Special Council, 1 September 1916.

5. Diane Koenker, "Urbanization and Deurbanization in the Russian Revolution and Civil War," in Koenker et al., *Party, State, and Society in the Russian Civil War,* pp. 81–104; Daniel R. Brower, "'The City in Danger': The Civil War and the Russian Urban Population," in ibid., pp. 58–80.

6. Brower, "The City," p. 65; Lewin, *The Making of the Soviet System,* p. 212.

7. Fitzpatrick, "Ascribing Class"; McAuley, *Bread and Justice,* pp. 397–403; Orlovsky, "The Antibureaucratic Campaigns of the 1920s," p. 299.

8. It is striking that when the Bolshevik press wanted to draw attention to the wartime "dilution" of the working class by non-working-class elements, it referred to them as "refugees." Kochakov, "Petrograd," p. 948.

9. *Vestnik VOPB,* 1, December 1915, p. 2.

10. Or, in contrast, to reflect on the opportunities that refugeedom created for the economic development of underpopulated space, particularly Siberia, where the settlement of refugees figured in one account as a means of ensuring the region's "economic, cultural and civic progress." Dagaev, "Bezhentsy v Sibiri," *TP,* 6, 1916, p. 28.

11. Compare the frequent expressions of alarm about the "excesses" committed by Russia's "itinerant element" (*brodiachii element*), as in RGIA f. 1322, op. 1, d. 1, l. 2 (Shcherbatov). In another formulation, Galician refugees were likened to a "horde." *Russkaia mysl',* 9, 1915, p. 130.

12. Siberia was sometimes portrayed as an exception. Dagaev wrote that "from the 1860s refugees [sic] have poured into Siberia, seeking sanctuary from land hunger and harvest failure in their homeland." *TP,* 6, 1916, p. 28. See also Bassin, "Russia between Europe and Asia."

13. Quoted in *Bezhentsy i vyselentsy,* p. 50; see also Slavenson, "Bezhenskoe," pp. 295–96.

14. *Izvestiia VSG,* 20, December 1915, p. 190 (Khar'kov); A. M-r [sic], "Pomoshch' bezhentsam," *TP,* 8, 1915, p. 230.

15. Shchepkin, *Bezhentsy,* p. 2.

16. *Armianskii vestnik,* 9, 26 February 1917, p. 10.

17. *Izvestiia VSG,* 20, December 1915, pp. 182, 192, 194 (Smolensk, Viatka, and Orenburg); the term *naplyv* is found frequently, as in *Gorizont,* 18, 24 January 1915, p. 1; *Izvestiia VZS,* 21, 15 August 1915, p. 52; *TP,* 1, 1916, p. 64; and *Komitet,* p. 453. The "deluge of refugees inundating all of Russia" appears in RGVIA f. 13273, op. 1, d. 37, ll. 13–14, and *Komitet,* p. 13; the "human torrent" (*zhivoi potok*) figures in RGIA f. 1276, op. 19, d. 1148, l. 2. The "avalanche" image appears in *Sputnik bezhentsa,* 1, 22–23 September 1915, p. 1. For the analogy between refugeedom and "earthquake," see RGIA f. 1322, op. 1, l. 1, l. 2

(Zubchaninov). The description of refugees as "lava" appears in *UR*, 209, 31 July 1915. For refugees as locusts, see Nikol'skii, "Bezhentsy," p. 48. "Threatening images of invasions and floods" are noted by Brower, *The Russian City*, pp. 83–84, where they were linked in particular to Jewish in-migration.

18. Malkki, *Purity and Exile*, pp. 15–16. A far-reaching discussion of societal fears of "flooding," derived in the first instance from the experience of the German Freikorps after the First World War, is provided by Theweleit, *Male Fantasies*, pp. 229–56.

19. See Toine van Teeffelen, "Metaphors and the Middle East: Crisis Discourse on Gaza," in Pieterse and Parekh, *The Decolonization of Imagination*, pp. 113–25.

20. Mindlin, "Pervye itogi," p. 16, referring to the inhabitants of Murashkino, Tambov province.

21. To be sure, many Jewish refugees wished to return home, because "the graves of our forefathers and our creative labors link us to these places." But others looked instead to Siberia as a land of new opportunity. See Brutskus, "Gde ustroit nashikh bezhentsev?" pp. 11, 14–15.

22. Wolff, *Inventing Eastern Europe*, pp. 369–70; Eley, "Remapping the Nation," p. 221; Kulischer, *Europe*, pp. 171–73.

23. But not uniformly so. Not only did the provinces closest to the front in 1914–17 have some of the lowest rates of temporary out-migration (Volynia, Podol'ia, Minsk, Mogilev, and Vitebsk); so too did some of the provinces that received large numbers of refugees during the war—Ekaterinoslav, Samara, and Saratov. To the extent that villagers in these provinces were now exposed to refugees and prisoners of war, an exposure to outsiders here may have been much more of a cultural shock than it was for the rural population of the central industrial region and the northwest. The statistics are presented in Mints, *Trudovye resursy SSSR*, pp. 118–23.

24. This phrase is taken from Roper, *Oedipus and the Devil*, p. 154. I am aware that community is itself a problematic term, which entails a complex of mediated relationships that give rise to conflict and bitterness, as well as having the capacity to promote cooperation and the pooling of resources. But the ever-present anger and hostility are here manifested by insiders who possessed a common link with the land and who survived misfortune together. The suspicion and hostility that were directed against outsiders represented a different level of engagement. See the remarks of Sabean, *Power in the Blood*, p. 28.

25. Compare the decisive stance taken by the French Huguenot community of Le Chambon during the Second World War; three centuries of Protestantism and experience of religious persecution induced the villagers to take a deliberate decision, at great personal risk, to offer sanctuary to refugees from other parts of occupied Europe. The story is told in Hallie, *Lest Innocent Blood Be Shed*.

26. Calhoun, *Social Theory and the Politics of Identity*. For an emphasis on the discovery of self by means of dialogic exchange, see Taylor et al., *Multiculturalism*, pp. 32–37. In Lyndal Roper's view, "human behaviour is not solely determined by conscious consideration, and identity is not a secure possession but a piecemeal process of identifications and separations." Roper, *Oedipus*, p. 5.

27. For the privileges conferred by the Tatiana Committee on refugee students and teachers from L'vov, see Thurstan, *People*, p. 116. The situation in Kiev is described in *Izvestiia KTN*, 6, 15 August 1916, p. 7; RGIA f. 1322, op. 1, d. 1, ll. 60–62, Special Council, 26 November 1915; *Izvestiia VSG*, 20, December 1915, p. 180.

28. I have appropriated this phrase from Hall, *White, Male and Middle Class*, p. 213.

29. On shared narratives, see Margaret Somers and Gloria D. Gibson, "Reclaiming the Epistemological 'Other': Narrative and the Social Constitution of Identity," in Calhoun, *Social Theory,* pp. 37–99.

30. Laqueur, *Making Sex,* p. 19. I am thinking here of the assertion of innate national characteristics and the significance that contemporary patriots attached to different national-cultural practices. See also Ann Stoler, "'Mixed-Bloods' and the Cultural Politics of European Identity in Colonial Southeast Asia," in Pieterse and Parekh, *Decolonization,* p. 43: "The perceived danger of *métis* 'rootlessness'—of ambiguous cultural affinities and locations—may have expressed deeper political anxieties on the part of those who ruled. The fear of 'mixed-bloods' may not have been about their burden to the state as so often claimed, but about the empowerment that cultural hybridity conferred; about groups that straddled and disrupted cleanly marked social divides and whose diverse membership exposed the arbitrary logic by which the taxonomies of control were made."

31. Suny, *Looking toward Ararat,* pp. 4–5.

32. On the notion of hybridity and the "postmodern" condition, see Bhabha, *The Location of Culture.*

33. Yet it is also worth pointing out that some relief workers emphasized not national difference but human solidarity: "The idea of humanity, the belief in the fact that each person has the right to positive regard by others by virtue of the fact that he is a human being . . . whatever his nationality is not germane to the present matter" (i.e., of refugee relief). V. I. Frolov, quoted in Ionnisian, *Polozhenie bezhentsev v Aleksandropol'skom raione,* p. 4.

34. Eley, "Remapping," p. 211.

35. Writing of a farm laborer who had been evacuated from the Dorset village of Tyneham in 1943, Patrick Wright points out that his "map of Tyneham was not defined . . . in terms of birds, fauna, folklore and ancient field names. Instead, it was dominated by the rural class structure that had shaped every detail of life, and squeezed vast canyons of social distance into that tiny English valley." Wright, *The Village That Died,* p. 344.

36. Eley, "Remapping," p. 220.

37. In the aftermath of the collapse of the Soviet Union, researchers have found that most forced migrants reject the "refugee" label, because of its pejorative connotations. I detect less shame in the period covered by this book, largely—I suspect—because refugeedom in 1915–17 was not so closely bound up with massive territorial reconfigurations, as it was after 1991. In addition, it was then possible to link up with national relief organizations that accorded greater primacy to national affiliation than to any stigma of refugeedom. Pilkington, *Migration.* Compare the proud assertion of "refugeeness" (*prosphygiá*) among the Greek refugee community of Piraeus, described in Hirschon, *Heirs of the Greek Catastrophe.*

38. For a few examples among many, see A. Kovaleva's appeal for assistance: "I hope that this request from an unhappy and lonely refugee [*bezhenka*] will find a response." RGVIA f. 13273, op. 1, d. 32, l. 10; *Vestnik VOPB,* 4, 24 January 1916, p. 11 ("Ia, bezhenka Kolmskoi gubernii"; "Fedor Pandukii, bezhenets Grodnenskoi gubernii," etc.); ibid., 19, 22 May 1916, p. 14 ("Ia bezhenets . . . "); *Izvestiia KTN,* 19, 15 April 1917, pp. 6–7 (letter signed by "*Bezhenka* P. Iaskor"). Urusov's newspaper regularly published letters and small ads, in which refugees sometimes identified themselves as "peasant," sometimes as "refugee," and sometimes as "peasant-refugee" (*krest"ianka-bezhenka*). *Iugobezhenets,* 21, 10 April 1916, p. 4; see also *Vestnik VOPB,* 11, 13 March 1916, p. 16. In August 1916, another grateful recipient of assistance wrote, "I humbly thank you for your kindness in not abandoning us unhappy refugees." *Izvestiia KTN,* 5, 1 August 1916, p. 11. *Zhizn' bezhentsev,* 9, October 1916, p. 16,

published a letter that began "I, *bezhenka* Mariia Deptulo, am searching for my nine-year-old grandson Stefan." Slavenson, "Bezhenskoe," p. 295, drew attention to the widespread use by refugees of "the very word 'refugee,' an entirely new expression."

39. "We aren't Gypsies, but poor people." Shveder, *"Bezhentsy,"* pp. 18, 31. The voice denying the "gypsy" quality of refugeedom is that of an old man. Nevertheless, it was not easy to shake off old habits, and the tendency to characterize displacement in these terms continued after the war, as in Krueger, *Die Flüchtlinge,* pp. 51–52, where the author describes how German settlers "on the 10th July 1915 began their life as Gypsies."

40. V. Tkach, "Mysli bezhentsa," *Vestnik VOPB,* 40–41, 23–30 October 1916, p. 16.

41. Malkki, *Purity and Exile,* pp. 153–58.

42. RGVIA f. 13273, op. 1, d. 32, l. 28, letter to Sobezh dated 17 November 1915.

43. I am also conscious of the need to attend to the "individual voice in a field dominated by political decisions and administrative decrees that neutralize the concreteness of despair and death." Friedlander, "Trauma." Nor do I wish to overlook the impact of refugee displacement on the world-view of individuals who contributed to the relief effort. Konstantin Paustovsky is an interesting example of a young man whose experience of war—with its attendant excitements, its inculcation of personal responsibility, and its capacity to generate waste and loss—helped to underscore "the utter helplessness of the world to which I belonged, the utter lonely rootlessness of my unsettled [*sic*] life." Paustovsky found comfort in the world of the imagination. Paustovsky, *Slow Approach,* pp. 166, 175–76. Might we not at the same time allow some refugees the capacity for real or imaginary liberation that comes from travel, albeit a fettered rather than an unhindered perambulation?

44. Bettelheim, *The Informed Heart,* p. 35.

45. Fentriss and Wickham, *Social Memory.* For one such attempt, see Hirschon, *Heirs of the Greek Catastrophe,* pp. 15–17, who remarks on "the bridge of memory" that "recreated the meaningful past and provided them [refugees] with the guidelines for a coherent adjustment to a new way of life."

46. Connerton, *How Societies Remember,* p. 17.

47. Ibid., p. 37, for the "social spaces . . . which we occupy, which we frequently retrace with our steps, where we always have access, which at each moment we are capable of mentally reconstructing."

48. *Bezhenets,* 1, 4 October 1915, p. 1.

49. To take one example, refugees were deprived of access to village or town cemeteries where previous generations were buried. Instead, their passage from the borderlands to the Russian interior was marked by makeshift gravestones, whose significance may have been lost on those who came across them. *Severnyi bezhenets,* 17, 4 May 1916, p. 2; also the remarks by the Belorussian refugee Vasilevich in July 1918 ("the sorrowful path that refugees trod at the beginning of the war was strewn with crosses and graves"), reported in *Protokoly, postanovleniia i materialy,* p. 28.

50. Some refugees made music together, a collective endeavor that both reasserted dignity and provided a kind of bridge between past and present. The Rumanian composer Georges Enescu (1881–1955), who found himself in Petrograd in 1917, organized concerts in which refugee musicians took part.

51. One refugee expressed an aversion to joining others on the way eastward: "You lose your individuality in the mass, and you can't make your own independent decisions." *Zhizn' bezhentsev,* 7, October 1916, p. 6.

52. E. Vystavkina, "Ikh dushi," *Sputnik bezhentsa,* 1, 22–23 September 1915, p. 1.

53. Fussell, *The Great War,* pp. 79–80.

54. A leading Soviet figure referred to new mines and factories as "railway stations" and as one enormous "nomadic gypsy camp." Sergo Ordzhonikidze, quoted in Lewin, *The Making of the Soviet System,* p. 221. In her study of the 1930s, Sheila Fitzpatrick talks of "a substantial peasant-refugee population roaming the countryside." Fitzpatrick, *Stalin's Peasants,* p. 88.

55. See the petition from Ludwig Schive, 11 July 1915, inviting the authorities to investigate the members of his family. RGVIA f. 1759, op. 4, d. 1732, ll. 23–24.

56. For attempts to discipline refugees at the outset by prescribing rules of conduct, see *BV,* 14983, 24 July 1915, describing the hostel for refugees in Petrograd. Also relevant in this regard were the attempts to devise a "refugee exhibition" in the spring of 1917 (see above). Photographs were also, of course, a form of public display. An ironic reflection of the exhibitionary impulse was the decision to house refugees in buildings set aside in Ekaterinoslav for an agricultural show. A. K-sov, "Sredi bezhentsev: territoriia vystavki," *Ekaterinoslavskaia zemskaia gazeta,* 11 September 1915.

57. See chapter 2 for the dispute between the unions of towns and zemstvos, on the one hand, and the Tatiana Committee, on the other, regarding the collection of information about the number of refugees by a central agency. Compare Fussell, *The Great War,* pp. 184–87, for the rhetoric of the wartime form. The forms filled in by refugees left no room for personal messages. The theme of wartime surveillance is taken up in new and imaginative ways by Holquist, "'Information Is the Alpha and Omega of Our Work.'"

58. Several spokesmen felt, for example, that the cinema exerted a bad influence on Russia's impressionable youth. Spasskii, "Bor'ba," *Severnyi bezhenets,* 8, 2 March 1916, p. 1.

59. *TP,* 7, 1916, pp. 147–48. For the creation of colonies, designed to promote hard work, respect for property, and a dig-for-victory mentality, see RGIA f. 1276, op. 12, d. 1382, l. 253. Official and voluntary agencies created "colonies" for orphaned children, in an attempt to deter crime and instill appropriate patterns of behavior. The foundations of post-revolutionary practice were already established by 1915. Only in 1926 did the state decide to promote adoption as an alternative to socialized childcare. Goldman, *Women, the State and Revolution,* chapter 2.

60. The Tatiana Committee conceded the need to involve refugees in its work, but only after its future was called into doubt by the revolution of February 1917. For the naming of individual refugees (other than those who were named as part of the energetic effort to reunite families), see *Simbirskie eparkhial'nye vedomosti,* 23, December 1915, pp. 925–26, giving the names of two refugee girls from Grodno (Karpinskaia and Kucheiko) and six sextons (*psalomshchiki*). Such instances were very rare.

61. Harrell-Bond, *Imposing Aid,* chapter 7 and passim.

62. "Such ethical practices do not merely serve interests by way of legitimation or justification; they are in part productive of interests." Osborne, "Bureaucracy as a Vocation," p. 291. Contemporary reports often allude to coordinated action by local elites; in the industrial town of Ivanovo-Voznesensk, for example, the local Union of Towns organized a committee for refugee relief, including "the charitable society, the Polish committee, doctors, factory owners, and representatives of the intelligentsia." *Izvestiia VSG,* 20, December 1915, p. 193.

63. Werth, "Through the Prism of Prostitution," p. 13.

64. Foucault, "Governmentality," in Burchell et al., *The Foucault Effect,* p. 102. See also the discussion in Rose, *Governing the Soul,* p. 5. I cannot help but feel, however, that Rose's emphasis on the accumulation of knowledge about the subject in modern society effaces a

basic distinction between democratic and non-democratic societies. For a number of other reservations, see Engelstein, "Combined Underdevelopment," and ensuing discussion. Engelstein finds little to be gained from "applying" Foucault to a society in which the law was never allowed to shape the disciplining of the self. Crucially, however, she is dealing with the peacetime state; the First World War created a distinct set of difficulties for a state that sought to retain its police-administrative capacity.

65. "An Interview with Michel Foucault," in Rabinow, *The Foucault Reader*, pp. 381–90.

66. In Foucault's words, "My goal has not been to analyze the phenomena of power, nor to elaborate the foundations of such an analysis. My objective, instead, has been to create a history of the different modes by which, in our culture, human beings are made into subjects." Ibid., p. 7.

APPENDIX 1

1. Volkov, *Dinamika*, pp. 72–73; Polner, *Russian Local Government*, p. 166; Thurstan, *People*, p. 163.

2. *GDSO*, 25th sitting, 18 February 1916, col. 1843; Prokopovich, *Voina*, p. 111; *TP*, 7, 1916, pp. 132–34.

3. RGIA f. 1322, op. 1. d. 13, l. 91.

4. *Predvaritel'nye svedeniia*; Volkov, *Dinamika*, pp. 68–69.

5. Demosthenov, "Food Prices," p. 298.

6. Gran maintained that as many as 45 percent of Jewish refugees may have fallen into this category. Tsarist officialdom did not recognize as refugees those who were confined to a strip of territory 40 kilometers from the front, even though many civilians had been displaced but remained trapped within this zone. Gran, "Opyt izucheniia sanitarnykh posledstvii voiny." Levine, *The Russian Revolution*, p. 76, speaks of a figure "as high as 13 million" refugees and states that the total "was beyond doubt not less than ten million."

7. Volkov, *Dinamika*, p. 70. See also *Izvestiia KTN*, 5, 1 August 1916, pp. 3–4.

8. Volkov, *Dinamika*, pp. 71–72. This represented 4,889,000 from the western borderlands and 367,000 from the Caucasus.

9. Ibid., p. 72.

10. *Izvestiia TsKPB*, 18, 7 November 1918, p. 11.

11. *Izvestiia VSG*, 34, 1916, p. 224. A lower percentage for Volynia appears in *TP*, 9, 1916, p. 391.

12. *Izvestiia VSG*, 34, 1916, p. 223. These figures diverge somewhat from those cited in the minutes of the Special Council, 27/30 December 1916. RGIA f. 1322, op. 1, d. 13, l. 95ob.

13. *Obzor o deiatel'nosti osobogo otdela*, pp. 31–34.

14. Cited from Kursk state archive in an unpublished paper by A. N. Kurtsev, "Bezhenstvo," p. 12.

15. *TP*, 10, 1916, pp. 509, 511; ibid., 1, 1917, p. 53, noting 15,000 Rumanians from Dobrudja. See also RGIA f. 1276, op. 12, d. 1382, ll. 402–405. The Tatiana Committee in October 1916 pointed out that their presence made its work even more imperative.

16. *TP*, 1, 1917, p. 53; *Komitet*, p. 32.

17. Ibid., p. 264.

18. Polner, *Russian Local Government*, p. 170.

19. Kulischer, *Europe*, p. 32.

BIBLIOGRAPHY

Archives

Russian Federation

Gosudarstvennyi arkhiv rossiiskoi federatsii

 f. 651 Tatiana Nikolaevna Romanova

 f. 742 S. K. Buksgevden

 f. 3333 Tsentral'naia kollegiia po delam plennykh i bezhentsev 1915–1923

 f. 5115 Pol'skie organizatsii pomoshchi bezhentsam v gody pervoi mirovoi voiny

Rossiiskii gosudarstvennyi istoricheskii arkhiv

 f. 525 Kantseliariia imp. Aleksandry Fedorovny

 f. 796 Kantseliariia Sinoda

 f. 1276 Sovet Ministrov, 1905–1917

 f. 1284 Departament obshchikh del Ministerstva vnutrennykh del

 f. 1291 Zemskii otdel Ministerstva vnutrennykh del

 f. 1322 Osoboe soveshchanie po ustroistvu bezhentsev

Rossiiskii gosudarstvennyi voenno-istoricheskii arkhiv

 f. 369 Osoboe soveshchanie po oborone gosudarstva

 f. 1759 Shtab Kievskogo voennogo okruga

 f. 2003 Shtab verkhovnogo glavnokomanduiushchego (Stavka)

 f. 2005 Voenno-politicheskoe i grazhdanskoe upravlenie pri verkhovnom glavnoko-manduiushchem

 f. 2020 Kantseliariia glavnogo nachal'nika snabzhenii armii Severno-zapadnogo fronta

 f. 2032 Kantseliariia glavnogo nachal'nika snabzhenii armii Severnogo fronta

 f. 2042 Upravlenie inspektora zapasnykh i opolchenskikh chastei armii Severnogo fronta

 f. 2049 Kantseliariia glavnogo nachal'nika snabzhenii armii Zapadnogo fronta

 f. 2068 Kantseliariia glavnogo nachal'nika snabzhenii armii Iugo-zapadnogo fronta

 f. 2100 Shtab glavnokomanduiushchego voiskami Kavkazskogo fronta

 f. 2168 Shtab Kavkazskoi armii 1914–1918

 f. 2170 Upravlenie glavnogo nachal'nika snabzhenii Kavkazskoi armii

f. 13273   Otdel po ustroistvu bezhentsev Vserossiiskogo Zemskogo i Gorodskogo
             soiuzov

Gosudarstvennyi arkhiv Iaroslavskoi oblasti (Iaroslavl')

f. 73   Kantseliariia Iaroslavskogo gubernatora

f. 485   Iaroslavskaia gubernskaia zemskaia uprava

f. 509   Iaroslavskaia gorodskaia duma

Gosudarstvennyi arkhiv Voronezhskoi oblasti (Voronezh)

f. 104   Voronezhskii gubernskii ispolnitel'nyi komitet Vremennogo pravitel'stva

Armenia

Tsentral'nyi gosudarstvennyi arkhiv Armenii

f. 50   Erevanskaia komissiia "Bratskoi pomoshchi"

Latvia

Latvijas Valsts Vestures Arhivs (Latvian State Historical Archive, Riga)

f. 2736   Rigas Pilsetas Dome (Riga Municipal Duma)

f. 5626   Baltijas Latviesu Beglu Apgadasanas Komiteja (Latvian Refugees' Relief
             Committee)

f. 5963   Upravlenie tovarishchestva upolnomochennogo po ustroistvu bezhentsev

Other Unpublished Primary Sources

Hoover Institution of War, Revolution and Peace, Hoover Institution Archives
    Evgenii Aleksandrovich Nikol'skii, "Bezhentsy v velikuiu voinu 1914–1918gg.," manu-
    script, 1934, 100 pp., folder XX 575-10.V
RGIA Library

file 2415   "Materialy o plane evakuatsii goroda Kieva 1916g."

file 2416   "Materialy po voprosu ob evakuatsii uchrezhdenii i naseleniia v period per-
             voi mirovoi voiny"

file 2431   "Spisok pravitel'stvennykh uchrezhdenii i dolzhnostnykh lits evakuirovan-
             nykh po voennym obstoiatel'stvam iz raiona voennykh deistvii v drugie
             punkty."
Peter H. Liddle Collection, Brotherton Library, University of Leeds, England
    Violetta Thurstan papers

Reference Works

Bol'shaia sovetskaia entsiklopediia. 65 vols. Moscow: Izdatel'stvo sovetskogo entsiklopediia,
    1926–1947.
Dictionary of American Biography. Supplement 4 (1946–1950). New York: Charles Scribner's,
    1974.
Ezhegodnik gazety Rech' na 1915. Petrograd: Rech', 1915.
Kratkaia evreiskaia entsiklopediia. Jerusalem: Keter, 1976–.
Lietuviu enciklopedija. 36 vols. Boston: LEL, 1953–1969.

Polski slownik biograficzny. Wroclaw: PAN, 1971.

Rutman, R. E. *Rossiia v period pervoi mirovoi voiny i fevral'skoi burzhuazno-demokraticheskoi revoliutsii*. Leningrad: Biblioteka Akademii Nauk, 1975.

Wieczynski, J. L., ed. *Modern Encyclopedia of Russian and Soviet History*. 58 vols. Gulf Breeze, Fla.: Academic International Press, 1976–1994.

Journals

Armiane i voina (Odessa, monthly, 1916, no. 1, March–no. 11, February)

Armianskii vestnik: ezhenedel'nyi zhurnal obshchestvennoi i natsional'noi zhizni (Moscow, 1916, no. 1–no. 48)

Ekaterinburgskie eparkhial'nye vedomosti

Ekaterinoslavskie eparkhial'nye vedomosti

Evreiskaia nedelia (Moscow, 1915–1917)

Evreiskaia starina

Evreiskaia zhizn': obshchestvenno-politicheskaia i literaturnaia gazeta (Moscow, 1915–1917)

Ezhemesiachnyi zhurnal literatury, nauki i obshchestvennoi zhizni (Petrograd, 1914–1916)

Golos Rossii: ezhenedel'nyi obshchestvenno-politicheskii zhurnal

Irkutskie eparkhial'nye vedomosti

Izvestiia Glavnogo komiteta Vserossiiskogo Soiuza gorodov (nos. 1–44, 1914–1917)

Izvestiia Glavnogo komiteta Vserossiiskogo Zemskogo Soiuza (Moscow, nos. 1–66, 15 October 1914–1 July 1917)

Izvestiia Komiteta Ee Imperatorskogo Vysochestva Velikoi Kniazhny Tatiany Nikolaevny (Petrograd, biweekly, no. 1, 29 May 1916–no. 26, 15 October 1917; issue no. 19 appeared as *Izvestiia Tatianinskogo komiteta;* thereafter as *Izvestiia Vserossiiskogo komiteta dlia okazaniia pomoshchi postradavshim ot voennykh deistvii*)

Izvestiia Kostromskogo gubernskogo zemstva

Izvestiia Moskovskoi gubernskoi zemskoi upravy

Izvestiia Tsentral'noi kollegii o plennykh i bezhentsakh (Moscow, 1918–1919)

Latviesu beglu apgadasanas centralkomitejas zinojums

Letopis' voiny (Petrograd, 132 issues, 1914–1917)

Permskaia zemskaia nedelia

Plennyi i bezhenets (Saratov, no. 1–2, 1–15 November 1918–no. 9–10, 1–15 February 1919)

Promyshlennost' i torgovlia

Russkaia budushchnost': natsional'no-progressivnyi, obshchestvenno-politicheskii ezhenedel'nik (August 1915–February 1917)

Russkie zapiski (1914–1917)

Samarskie eparkhial'nye vedomosti

Saratovskie eparkhial'nye vedomosti

Simbirskie eparkhial'nye vedomosti

Sinii zhurnal

Tobol'skie eparkhial'nye vedomosti

Tomskie eparkhial'nye vedomosti

Trudovaia pomoshch': izvestiia popechitel'stvom o domakh trudoliubiia i rabotnikh domakh (1897–1917, monthly except July/August)

Tul'skie eparkhial'nye vedomosti

Tverskie eparkhial'nye vedomosti

Ufimskie eparkhial'nye vedomosti
Ukrainskaia zhizn': ezhemesiachnyi nauchno-literaturnyi i obshchestvenno-politicheskii zhurnal
   (Moscow, 1912–1917)
Vestnik grazhdanskogo prava
Vestnik trudovoi pomoshchi sredi evreev (Petrograd, 1915–1916)
Vestnik vospitaniia
Vestnik Vserossiiskogo obshchestva popecheniia o bezhentsakh (Petrograd, 1915–1917)
Viatskie eparkhial'nye vedomosti
Vladimirskie eparkhial'nye vedomosti
Zhenskoe delo (Moscow, 1910–1918)
Zhizn' bezhentsev: ezhenedel'nyi illiustrirovannyi zhurnal (Petrograd, 1916)
Zhurnal Ministerstva iustitsii

Newspapers

Ashkhatank ("Labor") (Erevan, 1916–1917)
Bezhenets (Moscow, 4 October–23 December 1915)
Bezhenets (Baku, 1915–1916)
Bezhenskaia pravda (organ Vserossiiskogo soiuza bezhentsev, one issue, 29 November 1917)
Birzhevye vedomosti (St. Petersburg, 1901–1916)
Den' (1914–1917)
Dzimtines Atbalss ("Echo of the Fatherland") (1915–1918)
Ekaterinoslavskaia zemskaia gazeta (1915–1916)
Gimnazisty—bezhentsam (Rostov, one issue, 8 November 1915)
Golos (Iaroslavl')
Gorizont ("Horizon") (Tbilisi, 1915–1917)
Iugobezhenets: gazeta organizatsii po ustroistvu bezhentsev iugo-zapadnogo fronta (Odessa, no. 1,
   1 November 1915–no. 36, 8 October 1916)
Iuzhnyi krai
Kova
Lidums ("The Clearing")
Moskovskie vedomosti
Mshak ("Laborer") (Tbilisi, 1915–1917)
Novoe vremia
Paikar ("The Struggle") (Tbilisi, 1916–1917)
Pailak ("Enlightenment") (Shushi, 1915–1917)
Rech'
Rodina
Russkaia mysl'
Russkoe slovo
Severnyi bezhenets (Novgorod, weekly; 34 issues, 12 January–31 August 1916)
Sputnik bezhentsa: kvartironanimatel'naia i trudiashchegosia spravochnaia gazeta (Moscow, nos.
   1–7, 1915)
Studenty—bezhentsam (one issue, 24 August 1915)
Utro Rossii
Vestnik iuga (daily, 1912–1916)
Vestnik Penzenskogo zemstva
Vestnik Riazanskogo gubernskogo zemstva

Official and Semi-official Publications

Averbakh, O. I. *Zakonodatel'nye akty, vyzvannye voinoiu 1914–1916gg.* 4 vols. Vilna/Petrograd, 1917.

Beglu kalendars 1917 gadam. Peterpils, 1916.

Bezhentsy i vyselentsy. Moscow, 1915.

Bezhentsy v Tomskoi gubernii: spisok semeistv bezhentsev i adresa ikh. Tomsk, 1916.

Gosudarstvennaia Duma. Stenograficheskie otchety. Fourth Duma, Session Four (1915–1916), Petrograd, 1915–1916.

Komitet Ee Imperatorskogo Vysochestva Velikoi Kniazhny Tatiany Nikolaevny po okazaniiu vremennoi pomoshchi postradavshim ot voennykh deistvii, 14 sentiabria 1914 g. po ianvaria 1916 g. 2 vols. Petrograd, 1916.

Kratkii obzor deiatel'nosti Litovskogo obshchestva po okazaniiu pomoshchi postradavshim ot voiny. Vilna: M. Kukhta, 1915.

Kratkii ocherk deiatel'nosti Vserossiiskogo Zemskogo Soiuza. Moscow, 1916.

Kratkii ocherk deiatel'nosti Zemskogo Soiuza, 12 marta po 9 dekabria 1916 g. Moscow, 1917.

Kratkii otchet deiatel'nosti Pribaltiiskogo Latyshskogo komiteta po okazaniiu pomoshchi postradavshim ot voiny. Riga: Miuller, 1915.

Ocherk deiatel'nosti Petrogradskoi oblastnoi organizatsii Vserossiiskogo soiuza gorodov za pervyi god voiny. Petrograd, 1916.

Osobye soveshchaniia i komitety voennogo vremeni. Petrograd, 1917.

Otchet o deiatel'nosti osobogo otdela komiteta Ee Imperatorskogo Velichestva Velikoi Kniazhny Tatiany Nikolaevny po registratsii bezhentsev v 1915g. Petrograd, 1916.

Otchet o deiatel'nosti osobogo otdela Tatianinskogo komiteta v 1916. Petrograd, 1917.

Otchet Tsentral'nogo evreiskogo komiteta pomoshchi zhertvam voiny, s nachala deiatel'nosti po 30 iiunia 1917g. Petrograd, 1918.

Predvaritel'nye svedeniia o chisle bezhentsev v imperii po dannym gubernatorov na 20 dekabria 1915g, Petrograd, 1916.

Protokoly, postanovleniia i materialy Vserossiiskogo s"ezda bezhentsev iz Belorussii v Moskve, 15–21 iiulia 1918g. Moscow, 1918.

Rossiia v mirovoi voine 1914–1918gg v tsifrakh. Moscow: Tsentral'noe statisticheskoe upravlenie, 1925.

Spisok organizatsii, vedaiushchikh dela pomoshchi bezhentsam na 1 maia 1916g. Vypusk 1. Moscow, 1916.

Spisok tsirkuliarov komiteta Ee Imperatorskogo Velichestva Velikoi Kniazhny Tatiany Nikolaevny s sentiabria 1914 po 1 ianvaria 1917g. Vypusk 1. Petrograd, 1917.

Sputnik bezhentsa: sobranie prakticheskikh svedenii i sovetov dlia bezhentsev. Petrograd, 1916.

Trudy vneocherednogo Pirogovskogo s"ezda, 14–18 aprelia 1916 goda. Moscow, 1917.

Trudy Vtorogo Vserossiiskogo s"ezda predstavitelei mestnykh otdelenii Vserossiiskogo komiteta pomoshchi postradavshim ot voiny (Tatianinskogo), 16–19 aprelia 1917g. Petrograd, 1917.

Dissertations and Other Unpublished Work

Arutiunian, A. A. "Pervaia mirovaia voina i armianskie bezhentsy, 1914–1917." Unpublished Candidate's dissertation, Erevan, 1989.

George, Mark. "The All-Russian Zemstvo Union and the All-Russian Union of Towns, 1914–1917: A Political Study." Unpublished Ph.D. dissertation, University of London, 1986.

Gleason, William. "The All-Russian Union of Towns and the All-Russian Union of Zemstvos in World War One, 1914–1917." Unpublished Ph.D. dissertation, Indiana University, 1972.

Kurtsev, A. N. "Bezhenstvo." Unpublished paper presented to the conference "Russia during the First World War," European University, St. Petersburg, June 1998.

Published Works

A. Russian [sic]. *Russian Court Memoirs, 1914–1916.* London, 1917.

Agaian, Ts. P. "Armianskie politicheskie partii i pervaia mirovaia voina." In A. L. Sidorov, ed., *Pervaia mirovaia voina,* pp. 335–46. Moscow: Nauka, 1968.

Akopian, S. M. *Zapadnaia Armeniia v planakh imperialisticheskikh derzhav v period pervoi mirovoi voiny.* Erevan: Izd. Akademiia nauk Armianskoi SSR, 1967.

Allen, W. E. D. *The Ukraine: A History.* Cambridge: Cambridge University Press, 1940.

Ananov, N. I. *Sud'ba Armenii.* Moscow: Zadruga, 1918.

Anon. *Kak i pochemu stali my ubiitsami i grabiteliami.* Moscow, 1917.

Arendt, Hannah. *The Origins of Totalitarianism.* London: Allen and Unwin, 1951.

Bachmanis, Kristaps. *Latvju tauta beglu gaitas.* Riga, 1925.

Baedeker's Russia 1914. Reprint, London: G. Allen and Unwin, 1971.

Ball, Alan. *And Now My Soul Is Hardened: Abandoned Children in Soviet Russia, 1918–1930.* Berkeley: University of California Press, 1994.

Baron, Salo. *The Russian Jew under Tsars and Soviets.* Revised ed. New York: Schocken Books, 1987.

Barthes, Roland. *Mythologies.* London: Vintage Books, 1993.

Bassin, Mark. "Russia between Europe and Asia: The Ideological Construction of Geographic Space." *Slavic Review,* 50, 1991, pp. 1–17.

Bauman, Z. *Modernity and Ambivalence.* Cambridge: Polity Press, 1991.

Beliakevich, I. I. "Iz istorii sozdanii pol'skikh natsional'nykh formirovanii v sostave russkoi armii." In A. L. Sidorov, ed., *Pervaia mirovaia voina,* pp. 158–69. Moscow: Nauka, 1968.

Benthall, Jonathan. *Disasters, Relief and the Media.* London: I. B. Tauris, 1993.

Berger, John. *A Seventh Man.* London: Penguin, 1975.

Bernstein, Laurie. *Sonia's Daughters: Prostitutes and Their Regulation in Imperial Russia.* Berkeley: University of California Press, 1995.

Beskrovnyi, L. G. et al., eds. *Zhurnaly Osobogo soveshchaniia po oborone gosudarstva.* Moscow: Institut istorii SSSR, 1975.

Bettelheim, Bruno. *The Informed Heart.* Harmondsworth: Peregrine Books, 1986.

Bhabha, Homi K. *The Location of Culture.* London: Routledge, 1994.

Brower, Daniel. *The Russian City between Tradition and Modernity, 1850–1900.* Berkeley: University of California Press, 1990.

Buchanan, Sir George. *My Mission to Russia and Other Diplomatic Memories.* 2 vols. London: Cassell, 1923.

Burchell, Graham, et al., eds. *The Foucault Effect: Studies in Governmentality.* Hemel Hempstead: Harvester-Wheatsheaf, 1991.

Burdzhalov, E. N. *Vtoraia russkaia revoliutsiia: Moskva, front, periferiia.* Moscow: Nauka, 1971.

Calhoun, Craig. *Critical Social Theory.* Oxford: Blackwell, 1995.

Calhoun, Craig, ed. *Social Theory and the Politics of Identity.* Oxford: Blackwell, 1994.

Chambers, Iain. *Migrancy, Culture, Identity.* London: Routledge, 1994.

Chebaevskii, F. V. "K istorii organizatsii sovetskogo apparata." *Istoricheskii arkhiv,* 5, 1956, pp. 63–87.

Cherniavsky, Michael, ed. *Prologue to Revolution: Notes of A. N. Iakhontov on the Secret Meetings of the Council of Ministers, 1915.* Englewood Cliffs, N.J.: Prentice-Hall, 1967.

Clowes, Edith W., et al., eds. *Between Tsar and People: Educated Society and the Quest for Public Identity in Late Imperial Russia.* Princeton: Princeton University Press, 1991.

Cohen, Robin. *Global Diasporas.* London: UCL Press, 1997.

Connerton, Paul *How Societies Remember.* Cambridge: Cambridge University Press, 1989.

Corrsin, Stephen D. "Warsaw: Poles and Jews in a Conquered City." In Michael Hamm, ed., *The City in Late Imperial Russia,* pp. 123–51. Bloomington: Indiana University Press, 1986.

Dadrian, Vahakn N. *The History of the Armenian Genocide: Ethnic Conflict from the Balkans to Anatolia to the Caucasus.* Providence: Berghahn, 1995.

Davies, Norman. *God's Playground: A History of Poland.* 2 vols. Oxford: Clarendon Press, 1982.

Davies, Norman. "The Poles in Great Britain, 1914–1919." *Slavonic and East European Review,* 50, 1972, pp. 63–89.

Dekrety sovetskoi vlasti. 6 vols. Moscow: Gospolitizdat, 1959–1973.

Diakin, V. S. *Russkaia burzhuaziia i tsarizm v gody pervoi mirovoi voiny, 1914–1917.* Leningrad: Nauka, 1967.

Dixon, Simon. "The Orthodox Church and the Workers of St. Petersburg, 1880–1914." In Hugh McLeod, ed., *European Religion in the Age of Great Cities, 1830–1930,* pp. 119–41. London: Routledge, 1995.

"Dokumenty o presledovanii evreev." *Arkhiv russkoi revoliutsii,* 19, 1928, pp. 245–84.

Doroschenko, Dmytro. *Die Ukraine und Deutschland.* Munich: Ukrainische Freie Universität, 1994.

Douglas, Mary. *Purity and Danger: An Analysis of Concepts of Pollution and Taboo.* Harmondsworth: Penguin, 1970.

Drampian, R. G. *Martiros Sergeevich Sar'ian.* Moscow: Iskusstvo, 1964.

Dune, Eduard. *Notes of a Red Guard.* Champaign-Urbana: University of Illinois Press, 1993.

Dunsdorfs, Edgars. "Bevölkerungs- und Wirtschaftsprobleme bei der Staatsgründung Lettlands." In J. von Hehn et al., eds., *Von den baltischen Provinzen zu den baltischen Staaten: Beiträge zur Entstehungsgeschichte der Republiken Estland und Lettland 1917–1918,* pp. 315–29. Marburg: J. G. Herder-Institut, 1971.

E. P., Sviashchennik. *Bezhenstvo i bezhentsy.* Odessa: Tipografiia Odesskogo voennogo okruga, 1916.

Edmondson, Linda H. *The Feminist Movement in Russia, 1900–1917.* Stanford: Stanford University Press, 1987.

Ekonomicheskoe polozhenie Rossii nakanune Velikoi Oktiabr'skoi sotsialisticheskoi revoliutsii. 3 vols. Leningrad: Nauka, 1957–1967.

Eksteins, Modris. *Rites of Spring: The Great War and the Birth of the Modern Age.* Ealing: Black Swan Press, 1990.

Eley, Geoff. "Remapping the Nation: War, Revolutionary Upheaval and State Formation in Eastern Europe, 1914–1923." In Peter Potichnyj and Howard Aster, eds., *Ukrainian-Jewish Relations in Historical Perspective,* pp. 205–46. Edmonton: Canadian Institute of Ukrainian Studies, 1988.

Engel, Barbara A. *Between the Fields and the City: Women, Work, and Family in Russia, 1861–1914.* Cambridge: Cambridge University Press, 1994.

Engel, Barbara A. "Not by Bread Alone: Subsistence Riots in Russia during World War One." *Journal of Modern History,* 69, 1997, pp. 696–721.

Engelstein, Laura. "Combined Underdevelopment: Discipline and the Law in Imperial and Soviet Russia." *American Historical Review,* 98, 1993, pp. 338–53.

Engelstein, Laura. *The Keys to Happiness: Sex and the Search for Modernity in Fin-de-Siècle Russia.* Ithaca: Cornell University Press, 1992.

Felshtinsky, Yuri. "The Legal Foundations of the Immigration and Emigration Policy of the USSR, 1917–1927." *Soviet Studies,* 34, 1982, pp. 327–48.

Fentriss, James, and Chris Wickham. *Social Memory.* Oxford: Blackwell, 1992.

Ferris, Elizabeth G. *Beyond Borders: Refugees, Migrants, and Human Rights in the Post–Cold War Era.* Geneva: World Council of Churches, 1993.

Figes, Orlando. *Peasant Russia, Civil War: The Volga Countryside in Revolution, 1917–1921.* Oxford: Clarendon Press, 1989.

Fischer, Fritz. *Germany's Aims in the First World War.* New York: W. W. Norton, 1967.

Fisher, H. H. *The Famine in Soviet Russia, 1919–1923.* New York: Macmillan, 1927.

Fitzpatrick, Sheila. "Ascribing Class: The Construction of Social Identity in Soviet Russia." *Journal of Modern History,* 65, 1993, pp. 745–70.

Fitzpatrick, Sheila. *Stalin's Peasants: Resistance and Survival in the Russian Village after Collectivization.* New York: Oxford University Press, 1994.

Fleischauer, Ingeborg. "The Ethnic Germans in the Russian Revolution." In Edith R. Frankel et al., eds., *Revolution in Russia: Reassessments of 1917,* pp. 274–84. Cambridge: Cambridge University Press, 1992.

Florinsky, Michael. *The End of the Russian Empire.* New Haven: Yale University Press, 1931.

Frankel, Jonathan. "The Paradoxical Politics of Marginality: Thoughts on the Jewish Situation during the Years 1914–1921." *Studies in Contemporary Jewry,* 4, 1988, pp. 3–21.

Freeze, Gregory L. "The *Soslovie* (Estate) Paradigm and Russian Social History." *American Historical Review,* 91, 1986, pp. 11–36.

Friedlander, Saul. "Trauma, Transference, and 'Working Through.'" *History and Memory,* 4, 1992, 39–55.

Frierson, Cathy A. *Peasant Icons: Representations of Rural People in Late Nineteenth-Century Russia.* Oxford: Oxford University Press, 1993.

Fussell, Paul. *The Great War and Modern Memory.* New York: Oxford University Press, 1975.

Gaponenko, L. S. *Rabochii klass Rossii v 1917 godu.* Moscow: Nauka, 1970.

Gay, Peter. *The Cultivation of Hatred: The Bourgeois Experience, Victoria to Freud.* London: Harper Collins, 1994.

Gellner, Ernest. "The Coming of Nationalism and Its Interpretation: The Myths of Nation and Class." In Gopal Balakrishnan, ed., *Mapping the Nation,* pp. 98–145. London: Verso, 1996.

Germanis, Uldis. "Die Autonomie- und Unabhängigkeitsbestrebungen der Letten." In J. von Hehn et al., eds., *Von den baltischen Provinzen zu den baltischen Staaten: Beiträge zur Entstehungsgeschichte der Republiken Estland und Lettland 1917–1918,* pp. 1–68. Marburg: J. G. Herder-Institut, 1971.

Gleason, William. "The All-Russian Union of Zemstvos and World War One." In T. Emmons and W. Vucinich, eds., *The Zemstvo in Russia,* pp. 365–82. Cambridge: Cambridge University Press, 1982.

Glickman, Rose. "Women and the Peasant Commune." In R. Bartlett, ed., *Land Commune and Peasant Community in Russia,* pp. 321–38. London: Macmillan, 1990.

Goldman, Wendy. *Women, the State and Revolution: Soviet Family Policy and Social Life, 1917–1936.* Cambridge: Cambridge University Press, 1993.

Gourko, B. *Memories and Impressions of War and Revolution in Russia, 1914–1917.* London: John Murray, 1918.

Graf, Daniel W. "Military Rule behind the Russian Front, 1914–1917: The Political Ramifications." *Jahrbücher für Geschichte Osteuropas,* 22, 1974, pp. 390–411.

Graham, Stephen. *Russia in 1916.* London: Cassell, 1917.

Gran, M. M. "Opyt izucheniia sanitarnykh posledstvii voiny." In M. M. Gran et al., eds., *Trudy komissii po obsledovaniiu sanitarnykh posledstvii voiny,* vol. 1, pp. 7–46. Moscow: Narkomzdrav, 1923.

Grave, B. B., ed. *Burzhuaziia nakanune fevral'skoi revoliutsii.* Moscow-Leningrad: Gosudarstvennoe izdatel'stvo, 1927.

Gronsky, P. P., and N. I. Astrov. *The War and the Russian Government.* New Haven: Yale University Press, 1929.

Guthier, Steven L. "The Popular Basis of Ukrainian Nationalism in 1917." *Slavic Review,* 38, 1979, pp. 30–47.

Hacobian, A. P. *Armenia and the War.* London: Hodder and Stoughton, 1917.

Haimson, Leopold H. "The Problem of Social Identities in Early Twentieth-Century Russia." *Slavic Review,* 47, 1988, pp. 1–20.

Hall, Catherine. *White, Male and Middle Class: Explorations in Feminism and History.* Cambridge: Polity Press, 1992.

Hallie, Philip. *Lest Innocent Blood Be Shed: The Story of the Village of Le Chambon and How Goodness Happened There.* New York: Harper and Row, 1979.

Hamm, M. F. "Liberal Politics in Wartime Russia: An Analysis of the Progressive Bloc." *Slavic Review,* 33, 1974, pp. 453–68.

Harcave, Sidney, ed. *The Memoirs of Count Witte.* New York: M. E. Sharpe, 1990.

Harrell-Bond, Barbara. *Imposing Aid: Emergency Assistance to Refugees.* Oxford: Oxford University Press, 1986.

Harris, Ruth. "'The Child of the Barbarian': Rape, Race, and Nationalism in the First World War." *Past and Present,* 141, 1993, pp. 170–206.

Harvey, David. *The Condition of Postmodernity: An Enquiry into the Origins of Cultural Change.* Oxford: Blackwell, 1990.

Higonnet, Margaret. "Not So Quiet in No-Woman's-Land." In Miriam Cooke and Angela Woollacott, eds., *Gendering War Talk,* pp. 205–26. Princeton: Princeton University Press, 1993.

Higonnet, Margaret, et al., eds. *Behind the Lines: Gender and the Two World Wars.* New Haven: Yale University Press, 1987.

Hirschon, Renée. *Heirs of the Greek Catastrophe: The Social Life of Asia Minor Refugees in Piraeus.* Oxford: Clarendon Press, 1989.

Holquist, Peter. "'Information Is the Alpha and Omega of Our Work': Bolshevik Surveillance in Its Pan-European Context." *Journal of Modern History,* 69, 1997, pp. 415–50.

Hovannisian, Richard G. *Armenia on the Road to Independence, 1918.* Berkeley: University of California Press, 1967.

Hunczak, Taras, ed. *The Ukraine, 1917–1921: A Study in Revolution.* Cambridge, Mass.: Harvard University Press, 1977.

Hunt, Lynn, ed. *The New Cultural History.* Berkeley: University of California Press, 1989.

Hutchinson, John F. *Politics and Public Health in Revolutionary Russia, 1890–1918.* Baltimore: Johns Hopkins University Press, 1990.

Ionnisian, A. G. *Polozhenie bezhentsev v Aleksandropol'skom raione.* Baku: Bakinskii komitet pomoshchi bezhentsam, 1915.

Ishkhanian, B. *Narodnosti Kavkaza.* Petrograd: Knizhnyi magazin, 1917.

Iukhneva, N. V. *Etnicheskii sostav i etnosotsial'naia struktura naseleniia Peterburga, vtoraia polovina XIX–nachalo XX veka.* Leningrad: Nauka, 1984.

"Iz 'chernoi knigi' rossiiskogo evreistva: materialy dlia istorii voiny 1914–1915g." Edited by S. M. Dubnow. *Evreiskaia starina,* 9, 1918, pp. 195–296.

Jahn, Hubertus. *Patriotic Culture in Russia during World War I.* Ithaca: Cornell University Press, 1995.

The Jews in the Eastern War Zone. New York: American Jewish Committee, 1916.

Kaiser, Robert. *The Geography of Nationalism in Russia and USSR.* Princeton: Princeton University Press, 1994.

Karakasidou, Anastasia. *Fields of Wheat, Hills of Blood: Passages to Nationhood in Greek Macedonia.* Chicago: University of Chicago Press, 1997.

Katkov, George. *February 1917.* London: Fontana, 1967.

Kazanskii, P. E. *Galitsko-russkie bezhentsy v Odesse 1915–1916g.* Odessa: Tipografiia Eparkhial'nogo doma, 1916.

Kedourie, Elie. *England and the Middle East: The Destruction of the Ottoman Empire, 1914–1921.* London: Mansell, 1987.

Keep, John. *The Russian Revolution: A Study in Mass Mobilization.* London: Macmillan, 1976.

Kerblay, Basile. *Oeuvres choisies de A. V. Cajanov.* Vol. 2. Paris: Mouton, 1967.

Khatisov, A. "Memoirs of a Mayor." *Armenian Review,* 3, 1950, pp. 97–115.

Kirakosian, D. *Zapadnaia Armeniia v gody pervoi mirovoi voiny.* Erevan: Izdatel'stvo Erevanskogo universiteta, 1971.

Kir'ianov, I. Iu. *Rabochie Iuga Rossii 1914–fevral' 1917g.* Moscow: Nauka, 1971.

Kirzhnits, A. "Bezhenstvo." In *Bol'shaia sovetskaia entsiklopediia,* vol. 5, cols. 176–78. Moscow: Izdatel'stvo sovetskogo entsiklopediia, 1927.

Kirzhnits, A. "Bezhentsy i vyselentsy." In *Sibirskaia sovetskaia entsiklopediia,* vol. 1, cols. 262–63. Moscow: Sibirskoe kraevoe izdatel'stvo, 1929.

Klier, John D., and Shlomo Lambroza, eds. *Pogroms: Anti-Jewish Violence in Modern Russian History.* Cambridge: Cambridge University Press, 1992.

Klive, A. *Briva Latvija, Latvija Tapsana, Atminas, verojumi un atzinumi.* Riga: Gramatu draugs, 1969.

Knox, Alfred. *With the Russian Army, 1914–1921.* 2 vols. London: Hutchinson, 1921.

Kochakov, V. M. "Petrograd v gody pervoi mirovoi voiny." In *Ocherki istorii Leningrada,* vol. 3, pp. 932–1000. Leningrad: Akademiia nauk SSSR, 1956.

Koenker, D. P., et al., eds. *Party, State, and Society in the Russian Civil War: Explorations in Social History.* Bloomington: Indiana University Press, 1989.

Kohn, S. *The Cost of the War to Russia: The Vital Statistics of European Russia during the World War.* New Haven: Yale University Press, 1932.

Kondrat'ev, N. D. *Rynok khlebov i ego regulirovanie vo vremia voiny i revoliutsii.* 1922. Reprint, Moscow: Nauka, 1991.

Korzhikhina, T. P. *Sovetskoe gosudarstvo i ego uchrezhdeniia: noiabr' 1917g.–dekabr' 1991g.* Moscow: Rossiiskii gosudarstvennyi gumanitarnyi universitet, 1994.

Kovalevskii, G. T., et al., eds. *Ekonomika Belorussii v epokhu imperializma 1900–1917.* Minsk: Izdatel'stvo Akademii nauk BSSR, 1963.

Krueger, Alfred. *Die Flüchtlinge von Wolynien.* Plaven: G. Wolff, 1937.

Kulischer, E. M. *Europe on the Move: War and Population Changes, 1917–1947.* New York: Columbia University Press, 1948.

Kuper, Leo. *Genocide: Its Political Use in the Twentieth Century.* New Haven: Yale University Press, 1981.

Laqueur, Thomas. *Making Sex: Body and Gender from the Greeks to Freud.* Cambridge, Mass.: Harvard University Press, 1990.

Leggett, George. *The Cheka: Lenin's Political Police.* Oxford: Clarendon Press, 1981.

Lemke, M. K. *250 dnei v tsarskoi stavke.* Petrograd: Gosudarstvennoe izdatel'stvo, 1920.

Levene, Mark. "Frontiers of Genocide: Jews in the Eastern War Zones, 1914–1920 and 1941." In Panikos Panayi, ed., *Minorities in Wartime: National and Racial Groupings in Europe, North America, and Australia during the Two World Wars,* pp. 83–117. Oxford: Berg, 1993.

Levine, Isaac Don. *The Russian Revolution.* London: Bodley Head, 1917.

Lewin, Moshe. *The Making of the Soviet System: Essays in the History of Interwar Russia.* London: Methuen, 1985.

Lieven, Dominic. *Nicholas II: Emperor of All the Russias.* London: John Murray, 1993.

Ligotnu, Jekabs. *Latvijas Valsts Dibinasana.* Riga, 1926.

Lih, Lars. *Bread and Authority in Russia, 1914–1920.* Berkeley: University of California Press, 1990.

Lindeman, Karl. *Prekrashchenie zemlevladeniia i zemlepol'zovaniia poselian sobstvennikov.* Moscow: K. L. Men'shova, 1917.

Lindenmeyr, Adele. *Poverty Is Not a Vice: Charity, Society and the State in Imperial Russia.* Princeton: Princeton University Press, 1996.

Lobanov-Rostovsky, A. *The Grinding Mill: Reminiscences of War and Revolution in Russia, 1913–1920.* New York: Macmillan, 1935.

Loizos, Peter. *The Heart Grown Bitter: A Chronicle of Cypriot War Refugees.* Cambridge: Cambridge University Press, 1981.

Löwe, Hans-Dietrich. *The Tsar and the Jews: Reform, Reaction and Anti-Semitism in Imperial Russia, 1772–1917.* Chur: Harwood Academic, 1992.

Lubny-Gertsyk, L. I. *Dvizhenie naseleniia na territorii SSSR za vremia voiny i revoliutsii.* Moscow: Gosplan, 1926.

Macartney, C. A. "Refugees." In E. Seligman, ed., *Encyclopedia of the Social Sciences,* vol. 13, pp. 200–205. New York: Macmillan, 1935.

Maevskii, I. V. *Ekonomika russkoi promyshlennosti v gody pervoi mirovoi voiny.* Moscow: Gospolitizdat, 1957.

Mair, Lucy P. *The Protection of Minorities: The Working and Scope of the Minorities Treaties under the League of Nations.* London, 1928.

Malkki, Liisa. "National Geographic: The Rooting of Peoples and the Territorialization of National Identity among Scholars and Refugees." *Cultural Anthropology,* 7, 1992, pp. 24–44.

Malkki, Liisa. *Purity and Exile: Violence, Memory, and National Cosmology among Hutu Refugees in Tanzania.* Chicago: University of Chicago Press, 1995.

Marrus, Michael R. *The Unwanted: European Refugees in the Twentieth Century.* Oxford: Oxford University Press, 1985.

Mayer, Arno. *Why Did the Heavens Not Darken? The "Final Solution" in History.* London: Verso, 1990.

McAuley, Mary. *Bread and Justice: State and Society in Petrograd, 1917–1922.* Oxford: Clarendon Press, 1991.

McNeill, William H. *The Pursuit of Power: Technology, Armed Force, and Society since A.D. 1000.* Chicago: University of Chicago Press, 1982.

Melman, Billie, ed. *Borderlines: Genders and Identities in War and Peace, 1870–1930.* London: Routledge, 1998.

Melson, Robert. *Revolution and Genocide: On the Origins of the Armenian Genocide and the Holocaust.* Chicago: University of Chicago Press, 1992.

Mendelsohn, Ezra. *Zionism in Poland: The Formative Years, 1915–1926.* New Haven: Yale University Press, 1981.

Meyer, Alfred G. "The Impact of World War One on Russian Women's Lives." In Barbara E. Clements, Barbara A. Engel, and Christine D. Worobec, eds., *Russia's Women: Accommodation, Resistance, Transformation,* pp. 208–224. Berkeley: University of California Press, 1991.

Miliukov, Paul. *Political Memoirs, 1905–1917.* Ann Arbor: University of Michigan Press, 1967.

Mints, L. E. *Trudovye resursy SSSR.* Moscow: Nauka, 1975.

Moore, Robert I. *The Formation of a Persecuting Society: Power and Deviance in Western Europe, 950–1250.* Oxford: Blackwell, 1987.

Moskoff, William. *Hard Times: Impoverishment and Protest in the Perestroika Years—The USSR, 1985–1991.* New York: M. E. Sharpe, 1993.

Nelipovich, S. G. "Rol' voennogo rukovodstva Rossii v 'nemetskom voprose' v gody pervoi mirovoi voiny 1914–1917." In I. R. Pleve, ed., *Rossiiskie nemtsy: problemy istorii, iazyka i sovremennogo polozheniia,* pp. 262–83. Moscow: Voennaia byl', 1996.

Nelipovich, S. G. "V poiskakh 'vnutrennego vraga': deportatsionnaia politika Rossii 1914–1915." In *Pervaia mirovaia voina i uchastie v nei Rossii 1914–1918,* vol. 1, pp. 51–64. Moscow: Gotika, 1994.

Netesin, Iu., and Ia. Krastyn'. "Ekonomika Latvii v gody pervoi imperialisticheskoi voiny." In *Ocherki ekonomicheskoi istorii Latvii 1900–1917gg.,* pp. 268–322. Riga: Zinatne, 1968.

Netesin, Iu. N. *Promyshlennyi kapital Latvii, 1860–1917gg.* Riga: Zinatne, 1980.

Neuberger, Joan. *Hooliganism: Crime, Culture and Power in St. Petersburg, 1900–1914.* Berkeley: University of California Press, 1993.

Neutatz, Dietmar. *Die "deutsche Frage" im Schwarzmeergebiet und in Wolhynien: Politik, Wirtschaft, Mentalität und Alltag im Spannungsfeld von Nationalismus und Modernisierung, 1856–1914.* Stuttgart: F. Steiner, 1993.

Nichols, Bruce. *The Uneasy Alliance: Religion, Refugee Work and US Foreign Policy.* New York: Oxford University Press, 1988.

Nolde, Boris E. *Russia in the Economic War.* New Haven: Yale University Press, 1928.

Offer, Avner. *The First World War: An Agrarian Interpretation.* Oxford: Clarendon Press, 1989.

Oganovskii, N. P. *Vragi li russkomu narodu evrei?* Moscow: Zadruga, 1916.

Olavs, V. *Latviesu beglu apgadasanas centralkomiteja.* Riga, 1931.

Orlovsky, Daniel. "The Antibureaucratic Campaigns of the 1920s." In T. Taranovski, ed., *Reform in Modern Russian History: Progress or Cycle?* pp. 290–310. Cambridge: Woodrow Wilson Center and Cambridge University Press, 1995.

Osborne, Thomas. "Bureaucracy as a Vocation: Governmentality and Administration in Nineteenth-Century Britain." *Journal of Historical Sociology,* 7, 1994, pp. 289–313.

Osherovskii, L. Ia. *Tragediia armian-bezhentsev.* Piatigorsk: Armianskoe blagotvoritel'noe obshchestvo, 1915.

Paléologue, Maurice. *La Russie des Tsars pendant la grande guerre.* 3 vols. Paris: Plon-Nourrit, 1922.

Pares, Bernard. *The Fall of the Russian Monarchy.* London: Jonathan Cape, 1939.

Parkes, Colin Murray. *Bereavement: Studies of Grief in Adult Life.* Harmondsworth: Penguin, 1975.

Paustovsky, Konstanin. *Slow Approach of Thunder.* London: Harvill Press, 1965.

Pearson, Raymond. *The Russian Moderates and the Crisis of Tsarism, 1914–1917.* London: Macmillan, 1977.

Pieterse, Jan Nederveen, and Bikhu Parekh, eds. *The Decolonization of Imagination: Culture, Knowledge and Power.* London: Zed Books, 1995.

Pilkington, Hilary. *Migration, Displacement and Identity in Post-Soviet Russia.* London: Routledge, 1998.

Polner, Tikhon J. *Russian Local Government during the War and the Union of Zemstvos.* New Haven: Yale University Press, 1930.

Price, M. Philips. *War and Revolution in Asiatic Russia.* London: Allen and Unwin, 1918.

Prokopovich, S. N. *Voina i narodnoe khoziaistvo.* 2nd ed. Moscow: Sovet Vserossiiskikh kooperativnykh s"ezdov, 1918.

Proletarine reviliucija Lietuvoje, 1918–1919: revoliuciniu ivikiu Lietuvoje dalyviu atsiminimai. Vilnius, 1960.

Rabinow, Paul, ed. *The Foucault Reader.* Harmondsworth: Penguin, 1991.

Ransel, David. *Mothers of Misery: Child Abandonment in Russia.* Princeton: Princeton University Press, 1988.

Rauch, George von. *The Baltic States: The Years of Independence.* London: C. Hurst, 1974.

Rempel, David G. "The Expropriation of the German Colonists in South Russia during the Great War." *Journal of Modern History,* 4, 1932, pp. 49–67.

Rieber, Alfred J. *Merchants and Entrepreneurs in Imperial Russia.* Chapel Hill: University of North Carolina Press, 1982.

Riley, Denise. *"Am I That Name?" Feminism and the Category of "Women" in History.* London: Macmillan, 1988.

Robinson, Emily. *Armenia and the Armenians.* London, 1916.

Rogger, Hans. *Jewish Policies and Right-Wing Politics in Imperial Russia.* Basingstoke: Macmillan, 1986.

Roper, Lyndal. *Oedipus and the Devil: Witchcraft, Sexuality and Religion in Early Modern Europe.* London: Routledge, 1994.

Rose, Nikolas. *Governing the Soul: The Shaping of the Private Self.* London: Routledge, 1990.

Roskies, David G. *Against the Apocalypse: Responses to Catastrophe in Modern Jewish Culture.* Cambridge, Mass.: Harvard University Press, 1984.

Rumiantsev, E. D. *Rabochii klass Povolzh"ia v gody pervoi mirovoi voiny i fevral'skoi revoliutsii.* Kazan': Izdatel'stvo Kazanskogo universiteta, 1989.

Sabean, David. *Power in the Blood: Popular Culture and Village Discourse in Early Modern Germany.* Cambridge: Cambridge University Press, 1984.

Schama, Simon. *Citizens: A Chronicle of the French Revolution.* Harmondsworth: Penguin, 1989.

Schechtman, Joseph. *European Population Transfers, 1939–1945.* New York: Oxford University Press, 1946.

Schmidt, Christopher. "Über die Bezeichnung der Stände (*sostojanie-soslovie*) in Russland seit dem 18. Jahrhundert." *Jahrbücher für Geschichte Osteuropas,* 38, 1990, pp. 199–211.

Scott, Joan Wallach. *Gender and the Politics of History.* New York: Columbia University Press, 1988.

Senn, Alfred. *The Emergence of Modern Lithuania.* New York: Columbia University Press, 1959.

Shacknove, A. "Who Is a refugee?" *Ethics,* 95, 1985, pp. 274–84.

Shchepkin, M. M. *Bezhentsy i organizatsiia pomoshchi im v sviazi s rabotami Osobogo soveshchaniia.* Moscow: VSG, 1916.

Showalter, Elaine. *The Female Malady: Women, Madness and English Culture, 1830–1980.* London: Virago, 1987.

Shuval, Judith. "Refugees: Adjustment and Assimilation." In D. Sills, ed., *International Encyclopedia of the Social Sciences,* vol. 13, pp. 373–77. New York: Macmillan, 1968.

Shveder, Evgenii. *"Bezhentsy": rasskazy iz velikoi voiny.* Moscow: K. Zikhman, 1915.

Sidorov, A. L. *Ekonomicheskoe polozhenie Rossii v gody pervoi mirovoi voiny.* Moscow: Nauka, 1973.

Siegelbaum, L. H. "Another 'Yellow Peril': Chinese Migrants in the Russian Far East and the Russian Reaction before 1917." *Modern Asian Studies,* 12, 1978, pp. 307–29.

Silde, A. *Latvijas Vesture 1914–1940.* Stockholm: Daugava, 1976.

Simpson, Sir John Hope. *The Refugee Problem: Report of a Survey.* Oxford: Oxford University Press, 1939.

Skran, Claudene. *Refugees in Inter-war Europe: The Emergence of a Regime.* Oxford: Clarendon Press, 1995.

Skultans, Vieda. *The Testimony of Lives: Narrative and Memory in Post-Soviet Russia.* London: Routledge, 1998.

Sliozberg, G. B. *Dela minuvshikh dnei: zapiski russkogo evreia.* 3 vols. Paris, 1934.

Smith, S. A. "Writing the History of the Russian Revolution after the Fall of Communism." *Europe-Asia Studies,* 46, 1994, pp. 563–78.

Somakian, Manoug J. *Empires in Conflict: Armenia and the Great Powers, 1895–1920.* London: I. B. Tauris, 1995.

"Soveshchanie gubernatorov v 1916g." *Krasnyi arkhiv,* 33, 1929, pp. 145–69.

Spustek, I. *Polacy w Piotrogrodzie, 1914–1917.* Wroclaw: Panstwow Wydawnictwo Naukowe, 1966.

Starkov, P. S. "Pereselenie v Sibiri za vremia imperialisticheskoi voiny i revoliutsii 1914–1918." *Zhizn' Sibiri,* 7–8, 1926, pp. 29–37.

Stites, Richard. *The Women's Liberation Movement in Russia: Feminism, Nihilism, and Bolshevism, 1860–1930.* Princeton: Princeton University Press, 1978.

Stone, Norman. *The Eastern Front, 1914–1917.* London: Hodder and Stoughton, 1975.

Strazhas, A. *Deutsche Ostpolitik im ersten Weltkrieg: Der Fall Ober Ost 1915–1917.* Wiesbaden: Harrassowitz, 1993.

Striegnitz, Sonja. "Der Weltkrieg und die Wolgakolonisten." In Dittmar Dahlmann and R. Tuchtenhagen, eds., *Zwischen Reform und Revolution: Die Deutschen an der Wolga 1860–1917,* pp. 134–46. Essen: Klartext, 1994.

Struve, P. B., ed. *Food Supply in Russia during the World War.* New Haven: Yale University Press, 1930.

Suny, Ronald G. *Looking toward Ararat: Armenia in Modern History.* Bloomington: Indiana University Press, 1993.

Suny, Ronald G. "Nationalism and Class in the Russian Revolution: A Comparative Discussion." In Edith R. Frankel et al., eds., *Revolution in Russia: Reassessments of 1917*, pp. 219–46. Cambridge: Cambridge University Press, 1992.

Swietoslawska-Zolkiewska, Janina. "Dzialalnosc oswiatowa polskich organizacji w Moskowie, 1915–1918." *Przeglad Historyczno-Oswiatowy*, 32, 1989, pp. 383–405.

Sysin, A. N. "Sanitarnoe sostoianie Rossii v nastoiashchem i proshlom." *Sotsial'naia gigiena*, 1, 1922, pp. 63–94; 2, 1923, pp. 35–59.

Taylor, Charles, ed. *Multiculturalism: Examining the Politics of Recognition*. Princeton: Princeton University Press, 1994.

Thaden, E., ed. *Russification in the Baltic Provinces and Finland, 1855–1914*. Princeton: Princeton University Press, 1981.

Theweleit, Klaus. *Male Fantasies: Women, Floods, Bodies, History*. Cambridge: Polity Press, 1987.

Thurstan, Violetta. *The People Who Run: Being the Tragedy of the Refugee in Russia*. New York and London: G. P. Putnam's Sons, 1916.

Tolstoi, I. I. *Dnevnik 1906–1916*. St. Petersburg: Evropeiskii dom, 1997.

Tudorianu, N. L. *Ocherki rossiiskoi trudovoi emigratsii perioda imperializma*. Kishinev: Shtiintsa, 1986.

Tuitt, Patricia. *False Images: The Law's Construction of the Refugee*. London: Pluto Press, 1996.

Turton, David. "Conference Report, Addis Ababa, September 1992." *Disasters*, 17, 1993, pp. 263–66.

Vainshtein, A. L. *Narodnoe bogatstvo i narodnokhoziaistvennoe nakoplenie predrevoliutsionnoi Rossii*. Moscow: Gosstatizdat, 1960.

Vaitkevicius, Bronius. *Socialistine revoliucija Lietuvoje 1918–1919 metais*. Vilnius, 1967.

Vetlin, Sviashchennik. *Bezhentsy: rasskaz*. Tver': Tverskie eparkhial'nye vedomosti, 1916.

Viscont, Antoine. *La Lituanie et la guerre*. Geneva: Atar, 1917.

Volkov, E. Z. *Dinamika narodonaseleniia SSSR za vosem'desiat let*. Moscow: Gosudarstvennoe izdatel'stvo, 1930.

Waldron, Peter. "States of Emergency: Autocracy and Emergency Legislation, 1881–1917." *Revolutionary Russia*, 8, 1995, pp. 1–25.

Walker, Christopher J. *Armenia: The Survival of a Nation*. London: Croom Helm, 1980.

Waters, Elizabeth. "Teaching Mothercraft in Post-Revolutionary Russia." *Australian Journal of Slavonic and East European Studies*, 1, 1987, pp. 29–56.

Weeks, Theodore. *Nation and State in Late Imperial Russia: Nationalism and Russification in the Western Provinces, 1863–1914*. DeKalb, Ill.: Northern Illinois University Press, 1996.

Werth, Paul. "Through the Prism of Prostitution: State, Society and Power." *Social History*, 19, 1994, pp. 1–16.

Wharton, Edith. *Certain People*. London: D. Appleton, 1930.

Wildman, Allan. *The End of the Russian Imperial Army: The Old Army and the Soldiers' Revolt, March–April 1917*. Princeton: Princeton University Press, 1980.

Winter, Jay. *Sites of Memory, Sites of Mourning: The Great War in European Cultural History*. Cambridge: Cambridge University Press, 1995.

Wirtschafter, E. K. "Problematics of Status Definition in Imperial Russia: The *Raznocincy*." *Jahrbücher für Geschichte Osteuropas*, 40, 1992, pp. 319–39.

Wirtschafter, Elise Kimerling. *Social Identity in Imperial Russia*. De Kalb: Northern Illinois University Press, 1997.

Wolf, Lucien. *The Legal Sufferings of the Jews in Russia.* London: Fisher Unwin, 1912.

Wolff, Larry. *Inventing Eastern Europe: The Map of Civilization on the Mind of the Enlightenment.* Stanford: Stanford University Press, 1994.

Woodward, Llewellyn. *Great Britain and the War of 1914–1918.* London: Methuen, 1967.

Worobec, Christine. "Victims or Actors? Russian Peasant Women and Patriarchy." In E. Kingston-Mann and T. Mixter, eds., *Peasant Economy, Culture, and Politics of European Russia,* pp. 177–206. Princeton: Princeton University Press, 1991.

Wright, Patrick. *The Village That Died for England: The Strange Story of Tyneham.* London: Cape, 1995.

Ycas, M. *Pirmasis nepriklausomos Lietuvos desimtmetis.* London, 1955.

Young, Iris. "Together in Difference: Transforming the Logic of Group Political Conflict." In Will Kymlicka, ed., *The Rights of Minority Cultures,* pp. 155–76. Oxford: Oxford University Press, 1995.

Zipperstein, Steven J. "The Politics of Relief: The Transformation of Russian Jewish Communal Life during the First World War." *Studies in Contemporary Jewry,* 4, 1988, pp. 22–40.

Zolberg, A. R., et al. *Escape from Violence: Conflict and the Refugee Crisis in the Developing World.* New York: Oxford University Press, 1989.

INDEX

Index

Index

PETER GATRELL is Professor of Economic History and Head of Department at the University of Manchester. He is author of *The Tsarist Economy, 1850–1917* and *Government, Industry, and Rearmament in Russia, 1900–1914*. He has also contributed to the *Critical Companion to the Russian Revolution, 1914–1921* and *Russia's Great Reforms, 1855–1881*. Currently he is working on a history of Russia's home front during World War I. He is also interested in the economic, social, and cultural impact of industrialization in Europe between the years 1750 and 1930.